Christmas 2004

An Illustrated History of the Treaty of Waitangi

An Illustrated History of the
Treaty of Waitangi

Claudia Orange

BRIDGET WILLIAMS BOOKS

First published in New Zealand in 2004
by Bridget Williams Books Ltd,
P O Box 5482, Wellington, New Zealand

Text © Claudia Orange, 2004
Illustrations © Copyright-holders listed

This book is copyright. Apart from fair dealing for the purpose of private study, research, criticism, or review, as permitted under the Copyright Act, no part may be reproduced by any process without prior permission of the publishers.

National Library of New Zealand Cataloguing-in-Publication Data
Orange, Claudia.
An illustrated history of the Treaty of Waitangi / Claudia Orange.
Previous ed.: Allen & Unwin, 1990.
Includes bibliographical references and index.
ISBN 1-877242-16-0
1. Treaty of Waitangi (1840) 2. Maori (New Zealand people)—Land tenure—History. 3. Maori (New Zealand people)—Government relations—History. 4. New Zealand—History. I. Title.
993—dc 22

ISBN 1-877242-16-0

Cover design: Eyework Design, Wellington
Frontispiece: Part of the original Treaty signed at Waitangi in 1840, Archives New Zealand/Te Rua Mahara o te Kawanatanga, 1A 9/9
Editing: Bridget Williams, Alison Carew
Picture research: Tom Rennie, Clare Taylor, Claire Ongley
Internal design and typesetting by Afineline, Wellington
Printed by Astra Print, Wellington

Contents

Preface		1
Chapter One:	An Independent Land – New Zealand to 1840	2
Chapter Two:	The Treaty of Waitangi – 1840	22
Chapter Three:	A Matter of Mana – 1840 to 1870	46
Chapter Four:	Colonial Power and Maori Rights – 1870 to 1900	78
Chapter Five:	Into the Twentieth Century – 1900 to 1975	108
Chapter Six:	New Departures – 1975 to 1987	142
Chapter Seven:	The Roller-coaster Years – 1987 to 1990	176
Chapter Eight:	A Decade of Claims – the 1990s	206
Chapter Nine:	Into the Twenty-first Century	244

Appendix One: Texts of the Treaty of Waitangi	280
Appendix Two: Treaty Signatories	283
Appendix Three: Iwi Locations, 2001	317
Appendix Four: Maori Land, 1860–1939	318
Appendix Five: Waitangi Tribunal Timeline	320
A Note on Text, Illustrations and Sources	325
Bibliography	328
Index	336

Preface

Over the last thirty years, the Treaty of Waitangi has had a profound impact on life, history and politics in New Zealand. Research for this book spans those decades, beginning as work for a doctorate and continuing in 2004, as the foreshore and seabed legislation is debated. The thesis was published as *The Treaty of Waitangi* in 1987, and two shorter books followed.

Shifts in perspective over the last two decades have led to this new publication. Covering two hundred years from the first contacts between the British Crown and the Maori people to the present day, it is an account of the interweaving of events and institutions, of groups and individuals, that have shaped the country's present position on the Treaty.

An Illustrated History of the Treaty of Waitangi is intended as an independent study, one that argues no particular case but records a complex history. As any commentator approaches the present, the story inevitably becomes more opaque, the issues more densely tangled – and this is especially so for the historian, used to the longer view. This book is, then, a short history and a snapshot taken at a particular moment. I hope that it may be useful to those who seek to understand the issues that confront New Zealand today.

Many institutions and individuals – Maori and Pakeha – have provided generous assistance. They are too many to name, but I am especially grateful to the following: the staff of the Waitangi Tribunal, the Office of Treaty Settlements, the Crown Forestry Rental Trust, the National Library, the Alexander Turnbull Library, Archives New Zealand, Te Puni Kokiri, the Ministry for Culture and Heritage and the Museum of New Zealand Te Papa Tongarewa.

Illustrations came from a range of sources. Collections held by museums and libraries (especially the Alexander Turnbull Library), and by print media such as the *Dominion Post* and *Mana*, have made a significant contribution to this book. The role of individual photographers in creating a visual record of contemporary events cannot be underestimated.

The work of many researchers and writers has informed my research over the years. Participants in recent events have been ready with interviews or information. Readers have generously made suggestions, through to the last moment. My thanks goes to them all. The selection of information and the opinions in this book are, however, my own.

Bridget Williams has been my publisher since 1987; her absolute commitment and that of the BWB team made the project possible. Rod Orange provided invaluable encouragement and a patient ear throughout.

To all those who have given so much to this book, my heartfelt thanks.

Claudia Orange
Wellington, September 2004

CHAPTER ONE

An Independent Land — New Zealand to 1840

The history of the Treaty of Waitangi begins in 1769, the year in which the British explorer James Cook first visited the country that Europeans called New Zealand. Cook found a land of independent tribes who thought of themselves as tangata maori – the ordinary people, the people of the land. For them, the arrival of Cook's ships on their three exploratory voyages meant the beginning of new relationships, both within the country and with the world beyond.

Maori quickly established a barter trade with the newcomers. Cook's vessels needed food and water; Maori saw the value of household items such as scissors, mirrors and nails (which were used for carving). Each side had to come to terms with the other to get what it wanted. Both tried force, but both found that more could be gained by negotiation. It was the start of a promising relationship.

Trade expands

In 1788, the British government established a convict colony in New South Wales, and Sydney soon became the staging post for those wanting to exploit New Zealand's resources – seals, whales, timber and flax. From around 1800, sealing gangs from Sydney and Hobart were to be found around the coast in the far south, while British and American sperm-whalers visited the northern harbours to refresh and refit. From the mid 1820s, commercial activity turned to timber, flax, shore-whaling, shipbuilding and general trading. Europeans depended on Maori for provisions, services and access to resources; in return, Maori sought European goods.

Most Europeans who came to New Zealand at this time stayed only briefly, but a few traders made more or less permanent bases. These trader-settlers were a varied lot – the adventurers who frequented most frontier societies, a sprinkling of escaped convicts, and some Pakeha-Maori (Europeans who had 'gone native'). There were also several missionaries and their families: the Anglican Church Missionary Society (CMS) established its first station in the Bay of Islands in 1814, the Wesleyan Missionary Society (WMS) at Whangaroa in 1823. Both expanded north and south in the 1830s. But there were not many European residents before 1840; by one estimate, they numbered only five to six hundred in the South Island and fourteen hundred in the North Island in the 1830s, although there might be thousands of visitors each year.

The European impact was considerable, however, especially in coastal areas. Over time it brought changes to the Maori way of life throughout the country. At first, Maori sought things (such as nails, fish-hooks, metal tools or guns) that were substitutes for traditional items; by the 1830s, they were interested in new and different goods (blankets and calico, clothing of all kinds, tomahawks and clasp knives, pipes and tobacco). Since these were things that only Europeans could supply, Maori had a keen interest in the new relationship.

In the growing trade with the outside world, Maori provided not only provisions and labour for European business ventures but also land for traders to use as bases. The traders could only function by establishing a workable accord with local Maori, which they often cemented by

[previous page] *Maori fishing in Queen Charlotte Sound*, by Sydney Parkinson. Europe learnt of Maori skills from the detailed records of Cook, and those of the artists and scientists on his expeditions.
BY PERMISSION OF THE BRITISH LIBRARY, ADD23920 F.44

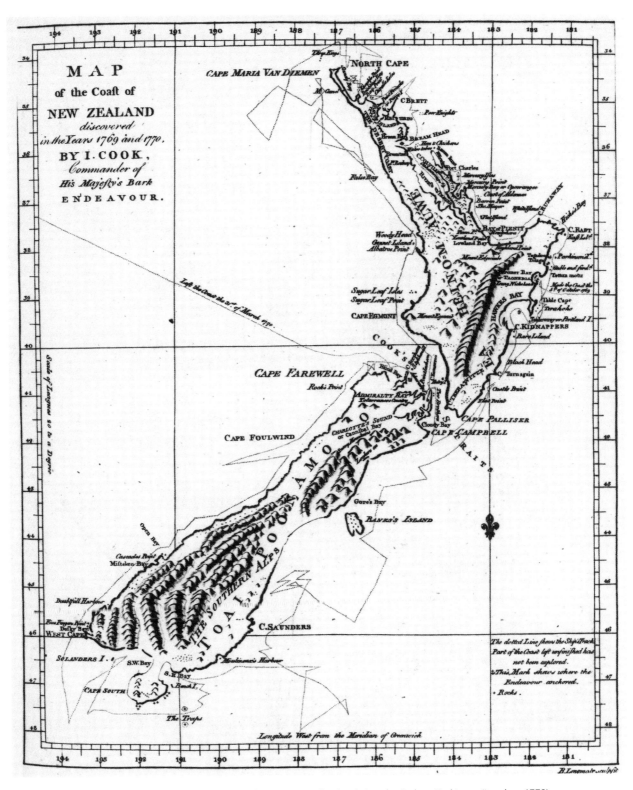

Map of New Zealand, an engraving from *A Journal of a Voyage to the South Seas* by Sydney Parkinson (London, 1773). The place names endowed by Cook left a lasting mark, a cultural overlay on the detailed naming of the land by Maori.

ALEXANDER TURNBULL LIBRARY, PUBL-0037-25

CHAPTER ONE: AN INDEPENDENT LAND

Knives, miscellaneous 400	Striped ticking material 100 *arshins*
Knives, garden size 20	Tumblers 120
Saws, one-man 10	Wire, copper 100 lbs
Saws, cross 10	Wire, iron 80 lbs
Chisels 30	Horn combs 250
Gimlets 125	Needles, various 5000
Rasps and files 100	Rings 250
Axes 100	Garnets 5 strings
Scissors 50	Beads, little and large 20 strings
Flints, 300	Wax candles 1000
Small bells, whistles 185	Mirrors, various 1000
Fringes, various shades 60 *arshins*	Red flannelette 218 *arshins*

These items were typical of the goods traded to Maori by visiting Europeans, in return for produce and services. The list is from the expedition led by F. Bellingshausen, which visited New Zealand in 1820.

SOURCE: FRANK DEBENHAM (ED.), *THE VOYAGE OF CAPTAIN BELLINGSHAUSEN TO THE ANTARCTIC SEAS, 1819–1821*, LONDON, 1945, VOL.I, P.13

relationships with women of the tribe. There were advantages for both sides and, in the years of early contact, Maori were the dominant partner; but it was a finely tuned balance, which gradually shifted to favour non-Maori, especially in areas where Maori began to depend on trade with Europeans. By the 1830s, many tribes were actively engaged in this trade, cultivating and preparing flax, producing crops such as potatoes, vegetables and fruit, and rearing pigs. Trade was moving from barter towards a cash economy.

Towards European settlement

The arrival of the Europeans brought change not only to life in Maori communities but also to the patterns of warfare. Intertribal fighting had always been a feature of Maori society, as issues of mana, revenge or territory were negotiated or settled. But the struggles grew fiercer as tribes acquired guns and as competition for raw materials and labour increased. From about 1814, northern Maori were using trade to arm themselves with muskets, powder and shot. This turned into an arms race and, by 1830, all tribes were equipped with European weapons.

From 1820 to 1835, the 'musket wars' led to a major redistribution of the Maori population, as some tribes fled attacks and others fought their way into new territory. Ngati Toa, for example, started in the Kawhia area and ended up north of Wellington, on a coastal strip that they shared with Ngati Raukawa who had made a long journey down from Maungatautari. The Maori population dropped sharply over this period, partly as a result of the wars (although European diseases, evident from the time of Cook's visits, probably took more lives). By the

The mission station at Rangihoua, on the northern shoreline of the Bay of Islands, dominated by the Maori settlement on the adjacent headland. Established in 1814–15, this was the first CMS mission in New Zealand. The painting dates from about 1821.
REX NAN KIVELL COLLECTION; BY PERMISSION OF NATIONAL LIBRARY OF AUSTRALIA

1830s, many Maori were tired of fighting and possibly conscious of changes at hand; they began turning to the missionaries as peacemakers, healers and teachers. The mission stations were also a great source of information about new skills and different ways of living.

Christian beliefs and practices, often adapted, spread rapidly. They were carried initially by Maori teachers (frequently liberated slaves), who took with them the new skill of literacy. In the 1830s, the missionaries translated religious texts and sections of the Bible, and printed thousands of copies. While historians debate the nature and degree of Maori conversion, there is no doubt that by 1840 Christian beliefs and teachings were widely known within Maori communities.

By the mid 1830s, trader-settlers were dotted sparsely around the New Zealand coast but the hinterland remained largely untouched. European commerce had focused on exploiting natural resources, not on obtaining or developing land. A few missionaries and traders had

CHAPTER ONE: AN INDEPENDENT LAND

Thoms's whaling station at Porirua. By the late 1830s, there were about thirty stations around the coastline of the South Island and the lower part of the North Island. They were often sizeable settlements, with Maori working alongside Europeans on the boats and processing the whales. ENGRAVING BY H. MELVILLE AFTER S. C. BREES, c. 1844; ALEXANDER TURNBULL LIBRARY, PUBL-0020-05-3

purchased land, but the acreage was seldom extensive. In the late 1830s, as Europeans increasingly looked to New Zealand as a place for permanent settlement, land speculators in Sydney began 'buying up' vast areas of Maori land at a faster pace. Most of the purchases were of dubious legality, and few were taken up. But this heralded a significant shift: the reliance established between European and Maori in the early years of contact was starting to break down, and the great European drive to wrest land from Maori had begun.

The Maori people and the British Crown

The colonial governors of New South Wales had always taken a special interest in New Zealand, and they were keen to maintain good relations with Maori in order to promote trade. Governor Philip King sent gifts – iron tools, fruit tree seedlings and livestock – to Te Pahi, a leading chief who controlled a good anchorage in the Bay of Islands. Te Pahi reciprocated with a stone mere (weapon) and beautifully woven cloaks when he and several of his sons visited

In the 1830s, Kororareka (Russell) was a busy port of call for Sydney traders and British, French, American and colonial whalers. Tribes from a wide surrounding area traded provisions and services in exchange for European goods.
ENGRAVING BY W. READ, AFTER J.S. POLACK, 1838; ALEXANDER TURNBULL LIBRARY, A-032-026

New South Wales in 1805–6, staying at Government House for nearly three months. King was impressed by Te Pahi's ability and shrewdness, and their relationship convinced him that Maori and British people could work together.

King, like other governors, was concerned about the predicament of Maori who were taken on as crew by visiting ships. Usually willing at first, they were often ill-treated and unpaid, then left stranded somewhere with no means of redress. In the early nineteenth century, several New South Wales governors attempted to curb this mistreatment on ships operating out of Sydney, but failed because New Zealand was independent territory, outside the limits of British authority. In 1817, 1823 and 1827, the British Parliament passed laws to make British subjects answerable for misdeeds committed outside British settlements or on the high seas. The laws proved impossible to enforce, but they did recognise New Zealand as independent territory.

The New South Wales chaplain, Samuel Marsden, had also been taking a special interest in Maori visitors. He shrewdly perceived that trade would lead to Maori dependence on

The chiefs Waikato and Hongi Hika with the missionary Thomas Kendall in England, 1820. Kendall began putting the Maori language into written form. Up until 1840, the missionaries printed almost all the reading material available in Maori. OIL PAINTING BY JAMES BARRY, 1820; ALEXANDER TURNBULL LIBRARY, G-608

Europeans and open the way to Christianity. He had a high opinion of the Maori people:

> The natives of New Zealand are far advanced in Civilization, and apparently prepared for receiving the Knowledge of Christianity more than any Savage nations I have seen. Their Habits of Industry are very strong: and their thirst for Knowledge great, they only want the means … The more I see of these People, the more I am pleased with, and astonished at their moral Ideas, and Characters. They appear like a superior Race of men.

Marsden invited chiefs and their sons to visit him at his Parramatta home, where they learnt agricultural techniques and trade skills. Maori leaders often met the Governor, and they expected this personal relationship with the Crown's representative to continue. Marsden promoted the belief that the British Crown had a paternal interest in Maori welfare, and also drew attention to the legislative efforts to curb the ill-treatment of Maori seamen on British ships. Some Maori wanted to visit the King himself, as Hongi Hika and Waikato did in 1820, meeting King George IV.

[1] Te Pahi, a senior chief from the northern Bay of Islands, was the first influential Maori leader to visit New South Wales. In 1805–6, he spent three months in Sydney; on his return to New Zealand, he took tools, seeds and livestock.
ENGRAVING, 1827, BY W. ARCHIBALD FROM A DRAWING BY G. P. R. HARRIS; ALEXANDER TURNBULL LIBRARY, A-092-007

[2] Te Rauparaha in 1842. By 1840, Europeans regarded Te Rauparaha as the most powerful chief in the Kapiti region. In the 1820s, he had migrated with his people from Kawhia to the Kapiti coast in one of several large migrations from the Waikato and Taranaki districts. WATERCOLOUR BY J.A. GILFILLAN, 1842; ALEXANDER TURNBULL LIBRARY, A-114-023

Marsden planned New Zealand's first mission station, set up by the CMS at Rangihoua in the Bay of Islands in 1814. It was not a success. But from Henry Williams's arrival at Paihia in 1823, the missions gradually gained some self-sufficiency. In the 1830s, their work was rewarded with many conversions and a widespread eagerness for literacy among Maori. Marsden, a frequent visitor to New Zealand, and the CMS missionaries encouraged the Maori people to believe that the British monarch had a special interest in protecting them from other foreign nations. In 1831, thirteen northern chiefs, afraid of a possible French invasion, petitioned King William IV for protection. Europeans, however, were looking for protection against threats from within New Zealand: Sydney traders complained that their business was sometimes risky because of fighting among the rival groups they traded with. But no chief had authority over the whole country, or even large parts of it, and there was no other authority or form of government to which the traders could appeal.

In 1830, Marsden and Governor Ralph Darling of New South Wales became concerned about the growing trade in preserved Maori heads. East Coast tribes were deliberately giving

[1] James Busby in 1832. British Resident from 1833, Busby told his superiors in New South Wales that: 'As far as has been ascertained every acre of land in this country is appropriated among the different tribes; and every individual in the tribe has a distinct interest in the property; although his possession may not always be separately defined.' His letters frequently recorded his powerlessness and lack of authority.
OIL PAINTING BY R. READ, SYDNEY, 1832; PRIVATE OWNER, COPY FROM ALEXANDER TURNBULL LIBRARY, NON-ATL-P-0065

[2] William Hobson, Lieutenant Governor in 1840. After his 1837 visit to New Zealand, Hobson wrote to his wife, Eliza, that he thought British intervention was necessary to keep other nations out, to protect settlers and to restrain their violence. He painted an accurate picture of the Maori population declining rapidly through European diseases, and observed that there was a great deal of British labour and capital invested in the country.
OIL PAINTING BY JAMES INGRAM MCDONALD, 1913; ALEXANDER TURNBULL LIBRARY, G-826-1

offence to their old enemies in the north by selling preserved Nga Puhi heads to European visitors. These heads, still recognisable to the victims' relatives, were often carried back into Nga Puhi territory. Marsden and Darling were afraid that these grisly transactions were putting the trading relationship between European and Maori at risk.

In the same year, one particular incident made the control of Europeans in New Zealand an urgent priority. The British captain and crew of the *Elizabeth* entered into a deal with the Ngati Toa chief, Te Rauparaha. In return for a cargo of flax, they took him and his war party from Kapiti to the South Island in order to wreak vengeance on unsuspecting Ngai Tahu at Akaroa. Many were killed, including the great southern chief Te Maiharanui, who was slowly tortured to death.

Long encouraged to believe that Britain would assist them if needed, Maori launched an appeal. Two Maori emissaries travelled to Sydney to lodge a protest with the Governor about the behaviour of the British captain and crew. But the culprits avoided punishment: while officials and lawyers argued about legal uncertainties regarding New South Wales jurisdiction over British subjects in New Zealand, the ship's captain jumped bail. Marsden, with some exaggeration, told Darling that the Maori people were looking for British protection from this kind of outrage. The *Elizabeth* affair had set a dangerous precedent for further European involvement in tribal warfare, and threatened British trade in New Zealand.

Appalled by the whole business, Governor Darling recommended to the Colonial Office in London that a British Resident be appointed in New Zealand. At much the same time, the British government was receiving other appeals from merchants, missionaries and individuals, also citing the *Elizabeth* affair. They, too, were seeking British intervention in New Zealand for a variety of reasons – commercial, humanitarian, legal, political and strategic – which reflected their different interests.

In 1832, the Colonial Office decided to appoint James Busby as British Resident. According to official records, the protection of the trading partnership – important by now to both British subjects and Maori – was the key factor in this decision.

A Declaration of Independence

In May 1833, James Busby arrived in the Bay of Islands, where there was a small European settlement. The Busby family made their home at Waitangi. As Resident, Busby was to operate under orders from the Governor of New South Wales and be paid from that colony's funds. His main duties were to protect 'well-disposed' traders and settlers, to prevent 'outrages' on the Maori and to apprehend escaped convicts. However, he had no means of enforcing his authority, for neither the British government nor the New South Wales Governor was willing to provide him with adequate funds or with military, naval or police support. He had no power to make arrests or to take sworn evidence. At best, he could act as a mediator in matters affecting British subjects, and as a kind of race relations conciliator (kaiwhakarite) between Maori and non-Maori. Europeans living in the Bay of Islands were initially optimistic about the protection of their interests, but they soon became exasperated by the powerlessness of the Resident's position. Repeatedly, they petitioned for more effective official support, and in 1838 set up a citizens' vigilante association to protect themselves – very often from each other.

If Europeans had expectations of Busby, so too did Maori, who sought his mediation in disputes, with little result. However, Busby took steps that Maori would later view as historically significant – actions that recognised the country's independence. Instructed by Governor Richard Bourke of New South Wales to introduce 'a settled form of government' among Maori, Busby was convinced that only the exercise of a 'collective' Maori sovereignty would put an end to intertribal warfare. His first opportunity came when the need for a national flag emerged. From 1829, ships built in New Zealand had sailed without a register. Beyond New Zealand waters, the ships – unregistered and with no acknowledged national flag – could be seized and their cargo impounded. (This had happened in 1830 to one ship in Sydney, to the chagrin of the Hokianga chiefs on board.)

Busby organised a great gathering at Waitangi on 20 March 1834, at which he invited twenty-five northern chiefs to choose a national flag. Three flags sent from Sydney were displayed on

HE WAKAPUTANGA O TE RANGATIRATANGA O
NU TIRENE.

1. KO MATOU, ko nga tino Rangatira o nga iwi o NU TIRENE i raro mai o Haurake, kua oti nei te huihui i Waitangi, i Tokirau, i te ra 28 o Oketopa, 1835. Ka wakaputa i te Rangatiratanga o to matou wenua; a ka meatia ka wakaputaia e matou he Wenua Rangatira, kia huaina, "KO TE WAKAMINENGA O NGA HAPU O NU TIRENE."

2. Ko te Kingitanga, ko te mana i te wenua o te wakaminenga o Nu Tirene, ka meatia nei kei nga tino Rangatira anake i to matou huihuinga; a ka mea hoki, e kore e tukua e matou te wakarite ture ki te tahi hunga ke atu, me te tahi Kawanatanga hoki kia meatia i te wenua o te wakaminenga o Nu Tirene, ko nga tangata anake e meatia nei e matou, e wakarite ana ki te ritenga o o matou ture e meatia nei e matou i to matou huihuinga.

3. Ko matou, ko nga tino Rangatira, ka mea nei, kia huihui ki te runanga ki Waitangi a te Ngauru i tenei tau i tenei tau, ki te wakarite ture, kia tika ai te wakawakanga, kia mau pu te rongo, kia mutu ai te he, kia tika te hokohoko. A ka mea hoki ki nga tau iwi o runga, kia wakarerea te wawai, kia mahara ai ki te wakaoranga o to matou wenua, a kia uru ratou ki te wakaminenga o Nu Tirene.

4. Ka mea matou, kia tuhituhia he pukapuka, ki te ritenga o tenei o to matou wakaputanga nei, ki te Kingi o Ingarani, hei kawe atu i to matou aroha; nana hoki i wakaae ki te Kara mo matou. A no te mea ka atawai matou, ka tiaki i nga Pakeha e noho nei i uta, e rere mai ana ki te hokohoko, koia ka mea ai matou ki te Kingi kia waiho hei Matua ki a matou i to matou tamarikitanga, kei wakakahoretia to matou Rangatiratanga.

Kua wakaaetia katoatia e matou i tenei ra i te 28 o Oketopa 1835, ki te aroaro o te Rehirenete o te Kingi o Ingarani.

Ko PAERATA, no te Patu Koraha.	Ko TAREHA, no nga te Rehia.
Ko URUROA, no te Taha Wai.	Ko KAWITI, no nga te Hine.
Ko HARE HONGI.	Ko PUMUKA, no te Roroa.
Ko HEMI KEPA TUPE, no te Uripotete.	Ko KEKEAO, no nga te Matakeri.
Ko WAREPOAKA, no te Hikutu.	Ko TE KAMARA, no nga te Kawa.
Ko TITORE, no nga te Nanenane.	Ko POMARE, no te Wanau Pane.
Ko MOKA, no te Patu Heka.	Ko WIWIA, no te Kapo Tahi.
Ko WARERAHI.	Ko TE TAO, no te Kai Mata.
Ko REWA.	Ko MARUPO, no te Wanau Rongo.
Ko WAI, no Ngaitewake.	Ko KOPIRI, no te Uritanewa.
Ko REWETI ATUA HAERE, no nga te Tau Tahi.	Ko WARAU, no nga te Tokawero.
Ko AWA.	Ko NGERE, no te Urikapana.
Ko WIREMU IETI TAUNUI, no te Wiu.	Ko MOETARA, no nga te Korokoro.
Ko TENANA, no nga te Kuta.	Ko HIAMOE, no te Uru o Ngongo.
Ko PI, no te Mahurehure.	Ko PUKUTUTU, no te Uri o te Hawato.
Ko KAUA, no te Herepaka.	

Ko ERUERA PARE, te Kai Tuhituhi.

Ko matou, ko nga Rangatira, ahakoa kihai i tae ki te huihuinga nei, i te nuinga o te Waipuke, i te aha ranei, ka wakaae katoa ki te wakaputanga Rangatiratanga o Nu Tirene, a ka uru ki roto ki te wakaminenga.

Ko NENE.	Ko PANAKAREAO.
Ko HUHU.	Ko KIWIKIWI.
Ko TONA.	Ko TE TIRARAU.

He mea ta i te Perehi o nga Mihanere o te Hahi o Ingarani, i Paihia.

He W[h]akaputanga o te Rangatiratanga o Nu Tirene: A Declaration of the Independence of New Zealand. This is an 1836 printing made on the Anglican mission press at Paihia. The original Declaration was written in longhand and contained chiefs' signatures and moko. Hobson was anxious to secure agreement to the Treaty of Waitangi from all who had signed the Declaration. ALEXANDER TURNBULL LIBRARY, W21

A Declaration of the Independence of New Zealand (English text)

1. We, the hereditary chiefs and heads of the tribes of the Northern parts of New Zealand, being assembled at Waitangi, in the Bay of Islands, on this 28th day of October, 1835, declare the Independence of our country, which is hereby constituted and declared to be an Independent State, under the designation of The United Tribes of New Zealand.

2. All sovereign power and authority within the territories of the United Tribes of New Zealand is hereby declared to reside entirely and exclusively in the hereditary chiefs and heads of tribes in their collective capacity, who also declare that they will not permit any legislative authority separate from themselves in their collective capacity to exist, nor any function of government to be exercised within the said territories, unless by persons appointed by them, and acting under the authority of laws regularly enacted by them in Congress assembled.

3. The hereditary chiefs and heads of tribes agree to meet in Congress at Waitangi in the autumn of each year, for the purpose of framing laws for the dispensation of justice, the preservation of peace and good order, and the regulation of trade; and they cordially invite the Southern tribes to lay aside their private animosities and to consult the safety and welfare of our common country, by joining the Confederation of the United Tribes.

4. They also agree to send a copy of this Declaration to His Majesty the King of England, to thank him for his acknowledgement of their flag; and in return for the friendship and protection they have shown, and are prepared to show, to such of his subjects as have settled in their country, or resorted to its shores for the purposes of trade, they entreat that he will continue to be the parent of their infant State, and that he will become its Protector from all attempts upon its independence.

Agreed to unanimously on this 28th day of October, 1835, in the presence of His Britannic Majesty's Resident.

[Here follow the signatures or marks of thirty-five Hereditary chiefs or Heads of tribes, which form a fair representation of the tribes of New Zealand from the North Cape to the latitude of the River Thames.]

English witnesses
(Signed) Henry Williams, Missionary, C.M.S.
  George Clarke, C.M.S.
  James C. Clendon, Merchant.
  Gilbert Mair, Merchant.

I certify that the above is a correct copy of the Declaration of the Chiefs, according to the translation of Missionaries who have resided ten years and upwards in the country; and it is transmitted to His Most Gracious Majesty the King of England, at the unanimous request of the chiefs.

(Signed) JAMES BUSBY,
  British Resident at New Zealand.

The English text of the Declaration of Independence. The word used for 'independence' in the original was 'rangatiratanga' (which would be used in the Treaty of Waitangi to translate 'possession'). The words 'all sovereign power and authority' were rendered as 'ko te Kingitanga, ko te mana i te w[h]enua'. The signatures indicate that thirty-four chiefs signed, with an additional signature from the kaituhituhi, or scribe.

SOURCE: *FACSIMILES OF THE DECLARATION OF INDEPENDENCE AND THE TREATY OF WAITANGI*, WELLINGTON, 1877, REPRINTED 1976

short poles and voted on; the winning flag was hoisted with the British flag alongside it, cheered by the crowd (which included some fifty Europeans) and honoured by a twenty-one-gun salute. A plan to have chiefs provide registration for locally built ships was shelved, and instead Busby supplied such ships with a 'certificate of registration' in the name of the independent tribes of New Zealand. Gazetted in Sydney, the flag was flown by ships and recognised by the British Admiralty. The flag was also flown on shore in the 1830s, at least in the Bay of Islands.

Busby's hopes that a government of confederated chiefs might evolve from the Waitangi meeting came to nothing. But the news that a Frenchman, Baron Charles de Thierry, was planning to set up his own independent state at Hokianga presented another opportunity. On 28 October 1835, Busby called a second meeting at Waitangi; there he persuaded thirty-four northern chiefs to sign the Declaration of the Independence of New Zealand. Under the title of the 'United Tribes of New Zealand', the chiefs asked King William IV 'to be the parent of their infant State … its Protector from all attempts upon its independence'. The British government received the Declaration, duly recognised the country's independence, and agreed to extend Crown protection. Chiefs from further south were invited to join the Confederation of United Tribes, and an annual congress at Waitangi was proposed. But, although Busby went on collecting signatures until September 1839, continuing intertribal competition and war prevented the congress ever taking place.

Plans for colonisation

In 1837, Governor Richard Bourke of New South Wales sent a naval captain, William Hobson, to the Bay of Islands to investigate fighting among Maori, which was thought to be a threat to trade as well as to lives. Bourke asked both Hobson and Busby to write reports on the situation in New Zealand. Knowing Britain's reluctance to become too involved, Hobson suggested that the Crown might take over several sites for settlements, along the lines of the early British 'trading factories' in India. A treaty would first have to be made with local Maori leaders, but the rest of the country would remain in Maori control. Busby, who had earlier dismissed the factory concept, suggested a protectorate over the whole country with the Crown administering affairs in trust for all inhabitants. The protectorate would be established gradually, with the assistance of chiefs, who would continue to lead their people and deal with Europeans, but under the guidance of British officials, who in many ways would be the real rulers of the country – or so Busby argued.

The two reports, with letters and petitions from traders to back them up, arrived at the Colonial Office in London in December 1837. They painted a sad (although somewhat exaggerated) picture of a country troubled by Maori fighting, crimes committed by British subjects, and disagreements between Maori and Pakeha over, for example, theft, trade deals and European-owned livestock straying onto Maori cultivations. As Resident, Busby could not solve these problems because he had no force to back him. And he had no means of stopping the activities of the land speculators who, in the late 1830s, were active in pressing Maori to sell land.

[1] The New Zealand national flag (1834) was white with a red St George's cross and, in the upper left corner, a blue field with a red cross and four white stars. The present flag of the Maori Women's Welfare League is very similar.
ALEXANDER TURNBULL LIBRARY, F22494½

[2] The flag flying at the Bay of Islands.
WATERCOLOUR BY EDWARD MARKHAM;
ALEXANDER TURNBULL LIBRARY, MS-1550-120

Around the same time, London officials were looking at the plans of a group formed in 1837 as the New Zealand Association and transformed in 1838 into the New Zealand Company. Its aim was to establish a New Zealand colony on the systematic principles of Edward Gibbon Wakefield. The scheme depended on the company acquiring cheap land in New Zealand that would then be sold at a high price to make a profit for shareholders and to fund colonisation. The company hoped for official approval, but did not want undue interference in carrying out its plans.

Officials at the Colonial Office were opposed to this scheme and to New Zealand colonisation generally, fearing that Maori would resist settlement on any large scale. They were also afraid that violence might erupt as groups of settlers tried to live permanently alongside Maori. The British record of dealings with native peoples in British settlements had been the

CHAPTER ONE: AN INDEPENDENT LAND   17

subject of a parliamentary committee report in 1837: ill-treatment and disease were shown to be common, both leading to the near-extinction of indigenous peoples. The British government did not want this new expansion of empire to have a detrimental impact on Maori – if indeed it decided to intervene in New Zealand. For intervention was also costly. It was with reluctance that the Colonial Office finally resolved to act on the New Zealand situation.

As the New Zealand Company became aware of the British government's position and the likely consequence in New Zealand, it moved fast. In May 1839, the company's ship *Tory* sailed from Britain with a group on board who were to buy land for settlement at Port Nicholson (Wellington) and elsewhere. In September that year, the company despatched the first of several shiploads of emigrants, with no assurance that land had actually been purchased.

Questions of sovereignty

The British government had made a decision about New Zealand before the *Tory* departed, but its pace was deliberate. Early in 1839, Hobson (then back in England) had been appointed Consul to an independent New Zealand. At the same time, he had discussions with the Colonial Office about setting up a British colony there – and, by implication, claiming sovereignty over the country. Officials spent the next eight months debating this issue.

They considered the international angle. Aware that large French and American whaling fleets were working in waters around New Zealand and using its harbours, they expected those nations to be resentful if Britain ended the country's independence. British authorities also knew of plans for a French settlement (which was established at Akaroa in 1840). In October 1838, the trader James Clendon was appointed American consul at the Bay of Islands.

British officials sought legal opinions on the international status of New Zealand. They did not view the country as a fully fledged nation-state, as it lacked the attributes by which such matters were officially measured (such as a recognisable authority or central government). Yet Britain had recognised New Zealand's independence – through the flag, the Declaration of Independence, and several pieces of legislation designed to curb the ill-treatment of Maori on the high seas. The Colonial Office decided that this sovereign independence should be formally transferred to Britain peacefully, and if possible by means of an agreement or treaty with Maori.

But how could they get Maori to agree? Officials were not sure if Maori leaders would understand what was meant if they were asked to cede sovereignty by signing a treaty. Officials were not always clear about what they expected themselves. Would Maori leaders think that possession of land was the same as sovereignty? For example, would Maori consider that they had lost all authority over any land purchased by Europeans? Uncertain of their ground, the officials proceeded with caution.

For a while, officials talked about asking Maori leaders for a cession – an entire surrender – of power and authority over certain areas only, which would be established as a Crown colony, with Maori rights to the rest of the country guaranteed and the national flag respected. But, after his 1837 visit, Hobson had formed the opinion (which he kept to himself) that Britain should try to get sovereignty over the whole country.

The New Zealand Company ships *Tory* and *Cuba* meeting in Cook Strait. The *Tory* left England in May 1839 and made a record time of ninety-six days to New Zealand. Four other emigrant ships were close behind.
PENCIL SKETCH BY CHARLES HEAPHY, 1840; ALEXANDER TURNBULL LIBRARY, MS-1550-120

When Hobson finally sailed for New Zealand in August 1839, he was given authority to make a treaty with Maori leaders to secure sovereignty over all or part of the country that Maori wished to cede. His instructions from Lord Normanby, the Secretary of State for Colonies, were to get the 'free and intelligent consent' of chiefs and to deal with them 'openly'. Normanby also explained, apologetically, why Britain had decided to make a colony in New Zealand — not because of the small settler population of only two thousand people, but to establish authority over the thousands of expected emigrants and to protect the rights and welfare of the Maori people. The instructions briefly outlined the business of setting up a colony. This included funding the administration of the colony from revenue raised largely by buying land from Maori and selling it at a profit.

These instructions reveal a significant shift in Colonial Office thinking. The early plans for a British colony envisaged a Maori New Zealand in which settlers would somehow be accommodated. By the time Hobson got his final instructions in August 1839, however, the plan was for a settler New Zealand in which the Maori people would have a special 'protected' position. The shift reflected a fatalistic acceptance that the tide of British colonisation could not be held back forever. The change of stance did not bode well for Maori. The protection of Maori alongside settler interests was an attempt to reconcile what had previously been seen as irreconcilable.

CHAPTER ONE: AN INDEPENDENT LAND

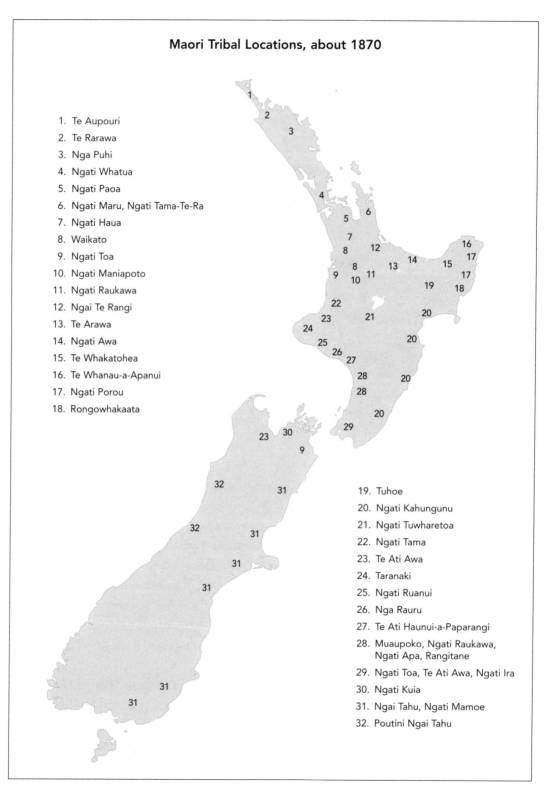

Maori tribal locations, about 1870. Major tribes only are indicated. Some locations reflect movements between 1800 and 1850. More recent locations, identified in the 2001 Census, are shown in Appendix Three.

SOURCE: THE OXFORD HISTORY OF NEW ZEALAND, ED. W. H. OLIVER WITH B.R. WILLIAMS, WELLINGTON, 1981; THE MAP IS DERIVED LARGELY FROM AJHR, 1870, D-23

On his way to New Zealand, Hobson stopped off in Sydney to change ships. There he conferred with Governor George Gipps, who was concerned about claims made by leading Sydney settlers and businessmen that they had bought extensive land tracts in New Zealand, taking in most of the South Island and parts of the North Island's eastern and northern coastlines. In anticipation of British sovereignty, Gipps adopted pre-emptive measures, swearing in Hobson as Lieutenant Governor of any territory he might acquire, and extending New South Wales jurisdiction to cover New Zealand. (Hobson reported initially to Gipps as well as to London until New Zealand became a fully fledged British colony in May 1841, with Hobson as Governor.) Another proclamation declared that title to land would be valid only if derived from the Crown, or confirmed by Crown-appointed commissioners; further private purchases were null and void. On 30 January, the day after he arrived in the Bay of Islands, Hobson would proclaim these restrictions to a public meeting, mainly of Pakeha (as Europeans were often called), at Kororareka.

With a small, ill-assorted group of officials to form the nucleus of a civil service, Hobson sailed for New Zealand in the *Herald* on 18 January 1840.

authority over the whole or any part of those islands — Her Majesty therefore
evil consequences which must result from the absence of the necessary Laws
herself to empower and to authorize me William Hobson a Captain in
Zealand as may be or hereafter shall be ceded to Her Majesty to invite
Articles and Conditions.

Article the

The Chiefs of the Confederation of the United Tribes of New Zealand and the
cede to Her Majesty the Queen of England absolutely and without reservation
Individual Chiefs respectively exercise or possess, or may be supposed to ex

Article the

Her Majesty the Queen of England confirms and guarantees to the Chiefs
thereof the full exclusive and undisturbed possession of their Lands and
individually possess so long as it is their wish and desire to retain the Sa
Chiefs yield to Her Majesty the exclusive right of Preemption over such la
agreed upon between the respective Proprietors and persons appointed by H

Article the

In consideration thereof Her Majesty the Queen of England extends to the Na
and Privileges of British Subjects.

Now therefore We the Chiefs of the Confederation of the United Tribes of New
and Independent Chiefs of New Zealand claiming authority over the Tribes and
to understand the Provisions of the foregoing Treaty, accept and enter into
attached our Signatures or marks at the places and the dates respectively
Done at Waitangi this sixth day of February in the year of our Lord on

CHAPTER TWO

The Treaty of Waitangi
— 1840

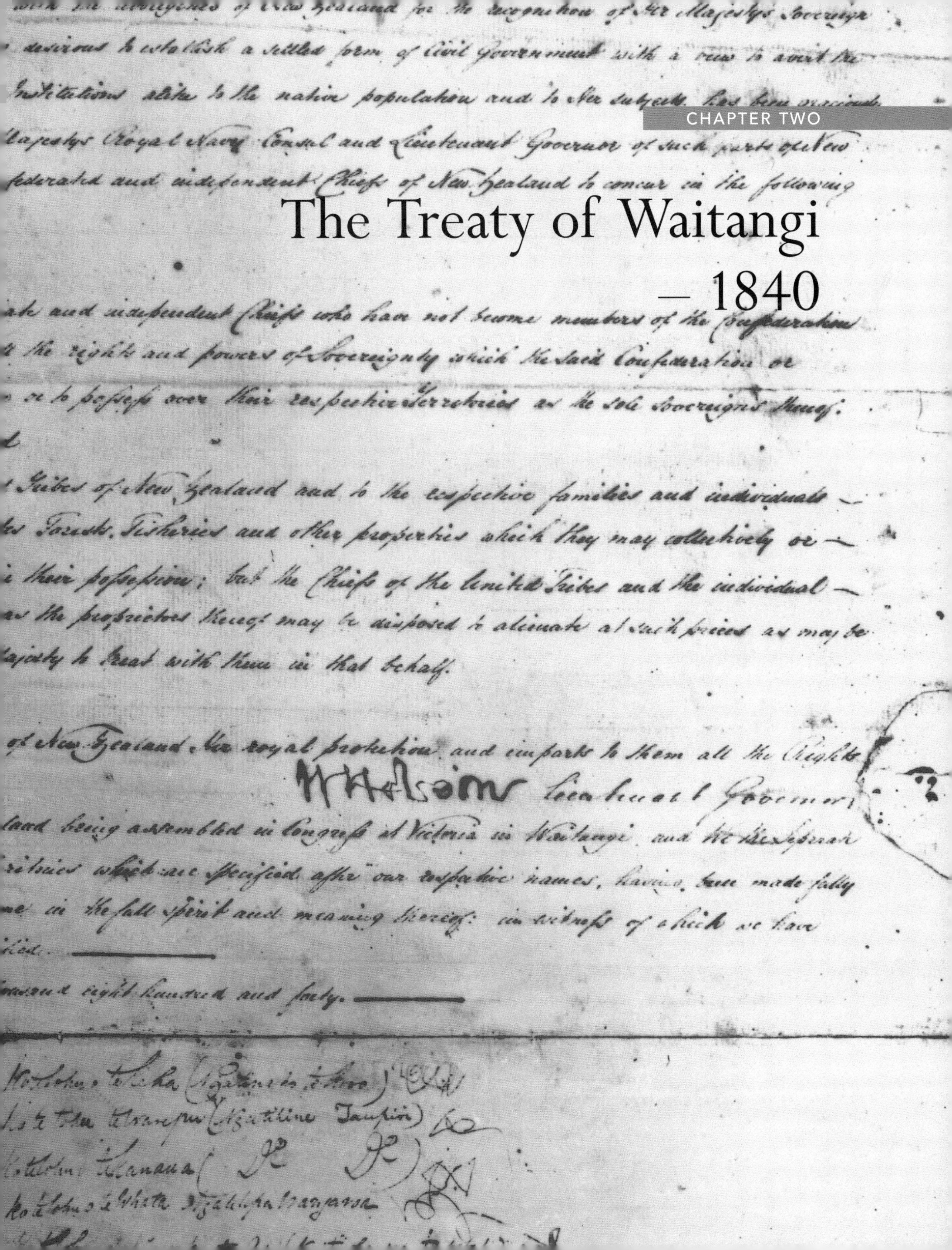

The *Herald* dropped anchor off Kororareka on Wednesday, 29 January 1840. Busby hurried on board to welcome Hobson and offered to organise a meeting of chiefs at the Residency (his Waitangi home) on 5 February. The following morning invitations went out to Confederation chiefs, and later to a few others.

Over the next few days, Hobson worked on the wording of the treaty he had been instructed to make with Maori. The task was difficult because he had no legal training and the Colonial Office had not provided him with a draft. He knew well enough, however, what the British government required: a cession of sovereignty, absolute control over all land transactions, and authority to impose law and order on both Maori and non-Maori. Several local missionaries gave advice and, with the help of his secretary, James Freeman, and George Cooper, Collector of Customs, he wrote a rough draft of a treaty, consisting of three articles.

Busby felt the document was inadequate and offered to redraft it. In this text, which Hobson received on 3 February, Busby had added an important promise to the second article: that Britain would confirm and guarantee Maori possession of their lands, their forests and their fisheries and other properties, for as long as they wished to retain them. Without that promise, Busby was sure no Maori would sign.

The first and second articles of the treaty incorporated the points that Britain wanted to secure: that the chiefs would give up 'sovereignty' (that is, the right to exercise power and authority); and that Britain would take complete control of all transactions in land, both its purchase from Maori and its sale to settlers. The third article offered the Maori people 'protection' and 'all the rights and privileges of British subjects'; benefits were implied (equal treatment in matters of law and order, for example), but there were also requirements (such as loyalty to the Crown).

Hobson then asked Henry Williams, a senior CMS missionary, to translate the treaty into Maori, which he did with the help of his twenty-one-year-old son Edward on the evening of 4 February. Although they were comfortable using the Maori language, they were not experienced translators; indeed, there were few people with such skills at the time. Henry's brother William might have been a better choice, had he been there. Henry Williams was aware of some of the problems, as he later explained: 'In this translation it was necessary to avoid all expressions of the English for which there was no expressive term in the Maori, preserving entire the spirit and tenor of the treaty.'

Whatever he intended, the result was not an exact translation of the English text. From the evidence available, we cannot be certain of Williams's motives. Hobson had been told to keep his official instructions private (they were published late in 1840), and it cannot be assumed that he explained them clearly to Williams. The missionaries had been asked by their superiors to support Hobson's negotiations, however, and this was probably what Williams was doing. What we do know is that the wording in the Maori translation was vague and ambiguous on crucial points. Williams may have deliberately chosen terms that obscured the transfer of sovereignty in order to secure Maori agreement, believing (as did most missionaries by this

[previous page] Detail from a copy of the Treaty in English, signed at Waikato Heads and Manukau Harbour.
ARCHIVES NEW ZEALAND/TE RUA MAHARA O TE KAWANATANGA, WELLINGTON OFFICE, IA 9/9

No te 30 o nga ra o Hanuere, 1840.

E taku hoa aroha,

Tenei ano taku ki a koe; na, tenei ano tetahi kaipuke manawa kua u mai nei, me tetahi Rangatira ano kei runga, no te Kuini o Ingarani ia, hei Kawana hoki mo tatou. Na, e mea ana ia, kia huihuia katoatia mai nga Rangatira o te Wakaminenga o Nu Tireni, a te Wenerei i tenei wiki tapu e haere ake nei, kia kitekite ratou i a ia. Koia ahau ka mea atu nei ki a koe, e hoa, kia haere mai koe ki konei ki Waitangi, ki taku kainga ano, ki tenei huihuinga. He Rangatira hoki koe no taua Waka-minenga tahi. Heoi ano, ka mutu taku,

Naku,

Na tou hoa aroha,

Na te PUHIPI.

---

30 January 1840

My dear friend,

I make contact with you again. A war ship has arrived with a chief on board sent by the Queen of England to be a Governor for us both. Now he suggests that all the chiefs of the Confederation of New Zealand, on Wednesday of this holy week coming, should gather together to meet him. So I ask you my friend to come to this meeting here at Waitangi, at my home. You are a chief of that Confederation.

And so, to conclude,
From your dear friend,
Busby.

The invitation to the Waitangi treaty meeting sent by James Busby to Tamati Waka Nene, 30 January 1840, with a translation. AUCKLAND MUSEUM/TAMAKI PAENGA HIRA, C21.784

[1] Henry Williams in old age, about 1865. He was known to Maori as Te Wiremu – and as 'Karu wha' ('Four-eyes') because of his spectacles. The explanations of the Treaty given by Williams were crucial to Maori understanding, or lack of it. Many Maori were literate in te reo by 1840 but not in English; in any case, few would have had a chance to read the Treaty in either language before signing. C. ATHOL WILLIAMS COLLECTION, ALEXANDER TURNBULL LIBRARY, F52461½

[2] Tamati Waka Nene, painted by Gottfried Lindauer in about 1871. Nene was closely associated with the Wesleyan missionaries in the Hokianga in the 1830s and had become a Christian. PARTRIDGE COLLECTION, AUCKLAND ART GALLERY/TOI O TAMAKI

[3] William Colenso had wanted an opportunity to speak at Waitangi on the morning the Treaty was signed. Many chiefs had only just arrived, and had missed the many discussions and explanations. Colenso was worried that Maori were placing too much trust on missionary advice to sign. They needed to understand fully the agreement they were making in the Treaty.
COLLECTION OF HAWKE'S BAY CULTURAL TRUST – HAWKE'S BAY MUSEUM, NAPIER

time) that Maori welfare would best be served under British sovereignty; or he may simply have done the best he could under the circumstances.

Making this translation was no simple task, for the Maori language did not have the words to render precisely every concept in the draft. In the first article, for example, Williams selected 'kawanatanga' for the English term 'sovereignty'. Kawanatanga (from 'kawana', an adaptation of 'governor') literally means 'governance' or 'governorship'; it does not convey the many facets of sovereign power and authority. To translate 'possession' in the second article, Williams used 'rangatiratanga', a word that suggested the chiefs would retain rather more chiefly authority and power than was likely in a British colony – or intended in New Zealand. It seems, too, that the exclusive right of the Crown in land transactions was not clearly conveyed to Maori.

Hone Heke and Eruera Maihi Patuone. After the signing on 6 February, Patuone presented Hobson with a greenstone mere (weapon) for Queen Victoria. He had known Hobson from the latter's 1837 visit, and the two men dined together on the *Herald*, where (it is recorded) the officers danced a quadrille to the tune of two fiddlers until dark. LITHOGRAPH AFTER AN ORIGINAL BY GEORGE FRENCH ANGAS; ALEXANDER TURNBULL LIBRARY, PUBL-0014-01

The debate: Wednesday, 5 February

Letters, reports and diaries left by officials and missionaries provide a good record of the events of 5 and 6 February. From early on the 5th, Maori groups began to arrive. The waters of the Bay of Islands came alive with canoes converging from all directions, each with thirty or more paddlers keeping time to the stroke. Settlers' boats joined the stream, and the ships anchored offshore had all their flags flying. Summer showers had cleared and the day was brilliantly fine; cicadas shrilled noisily. Outside the Residency grounds, stalls were set up to sell refreshments – pork, cold roasts, pies, baskets of bread, and stout, ale, brandy and rum. Special provisions were ready for Maori guests – half a ton of flour, five tons of potatoes, thirty pigs and other goods.

On the lawn in front of the Residency, the officers of the *Herald* had erected an enormous marquee; 120 to 150 feet (35 to 45 metres) in length, it was made of ships' sails and decorated with flags. A sergeant and three troopers of the New South Wales mounted police, who had arrived on the *Herald*, paraded in their scarlet uniforms. Hundreds of Maori sat in their tribal groups, smoking and talking. Some had come long distances and carried guns. Little parties of

Europeans strolled up and down – officers from the *Herald*, missionaries, traders, sailors. The crowd buzzed with excitement in the gala atmosphere.

At about 9 a.m., Hobson in full uniform stepped ashore on Waitangi beach. Accompanied by the captain of the *Herald*, Joseph Nias, he walked up the hill to the Residency. There, with Busby and Henry Williams, he looked over the translated treaty. With no knowledge of Maori, Hobson could not tell if the translation was accurate and had to rely on Busby and Williams, who made a few slight changes and were satisfied. Hobson then formally greeted local Europeans as they filed through the Residency.

Late in the morning, the official party moved in procession from the house to the marquee. On a raised platform at one end, Hobson sat down at a table covered with the Union Jack; others took up positions wherever they could. The tent filled rapidly, with over two hundred Maori taking up the main space. William Colenso, the printer at the nearby Paihia mission station, wrote an account of the scene:

> In front of the platform, in the foreground, were the principal Native chiefs of several tribes, some clothed with dogskin mats made of alternate longitudinal stripes of black and white hair; others habited in splendid-looking new woollen cloaks of foreign manufacture, of crimson, blue, brown, and plaid, and, indeed, of every shade of striking colour ... while some were dressed in plain European and some in common Native dresses ... here and there a ... taiaha, a chief's staff of rank, was seen erected, adorned with the long flowing white hair of the tails of the New Zealand dog and crimson cloth and red feathers.

Felton Mathew, Hobson's Acting Surveyor-General, commented that the women among the chiefs had 'their ears adorned with white feathers or the entire wing of a bird'. Bright sunlight picked out the vivid colours of the flags, and Mathew wrote that he would never forget the scene to the day he died.

A hush fell as Hobson began to speak. First he addressed the few dozen Europeans who were standing against the walls of the marquee, briefly explaining what he was about to do. Then he turned to the assembled Maori to talk about the treaty. He spoke in English with Henry Williams translating into Maori, while Colenso recorded his words and the debate that followed. Hobson said that the British people were free to go wherever they chose, and that the Queen was always ready to protect them. Because of her concern for the welfare of both Maori and European, he had been sent as Governor; but since the country was outside the Queen's dominion he lacked the authority needed to control British subjects. 'Her Majesty the Queen asks you to sign this Treaty,' he said, 'and so give Her that power which shall enable Her to restrain them.' He continued: 'I give you time to consider the proposal I now offer you. What I wish you to do is expressly for your own good as you will soon see by the Treaty. You yourselves have often asked the King to extend his protection [to you]. Her Majesty now offers that protection in this Treaty.'

Hobson concluded by reading the text of the treaty in English. Then Williams read the Maori translation; he said later that he had told the chiefs to listen carefully. He explained each part to them and warned them not to be in a hurry. He assured them that the missionaries

Sarah Mathew's September 1840 sketch of Te Tii marae, Waitangi, with Kororareka in the background. The chiefs camped at Te Tii for the February Treaty meeting, which took place at Busby's house, further up the rise to the left.
AUCKLAND CITY LIBRARIES, A12003

'fully approved of the treaty, that it was an act of love towards them on the part of the Queen [Victoria], who desired to secure to them their property, rights, and privileges'. Hinting at French interest in New Zealand, he said that the treaty was like 'a fortress for them against any foreign power which might desire to take possession of their country'.

For over five hours, through the heat of the day, chiefs spoke for and against the proposal. These were men from the northern tribes, mainly from the Bay of Islands and its hinterland. Their main concerns were about their authority, their land and trade dealings. Colenso took rough notes of the debate, translating Maori speeches as he did so. The following account is based on his notes.

> Rewa said: 'The Maori people don't want a governor! We aren't European. It's true that we've sold some of our lands. But this country is still ours! We chiefs govern this land of our ancestors.' Kawiti and others echoed his comments.
>
> 'Governor,' said Hakiro, striding up and down, 'some might tell you to stay here, but I say this is not the place for you. We are not your people. We are free. We don't need you and we don't want you.'

CHAPTER TWO: THE TREATY OF WAITANGI   29

Tareha joined in: 'We chiefs are the rulers and we won't be ruled over. If we were all to have a rank equal to you that might be acceptable. But if we are going to be subordinate to you, then I say get back to your ship and sail away.'

Many objected strongly to the land purchases that Europeans, especially the missionaries, had made. Hobson promised that all lands unjustly purchased would be returned to their Maori owners. 'That's good,' said Moka. 'That's as it should be. But we'll see what happens. Who will really listen to you? Who's going to obey you? The lands won't be returned.'

Uneasy about this attack on the missionaries, Williams explained to the Europeans present that all land sales before 1840 were going to be investigated. Hobson had already announced this at a large meeting of Europeans held at Kororareka on 30 January.

Whai asked: 'What will you do about trade dealings, and the cheating, lying and stealing of the whites?' He complained about Pakeha middlemen who bought up Maori produce cheaply to sell at inflated prices; he also touched on another matter that deeply angered the Maori people: 'Yesterday I was cursed by a white man. Is that the way things are going to be?'

Hobson sensed that the feeling of the meeting was running against him. Only a few chiefs had welcomed him. Rawiri Taiwhanga, one of the first Christian converts, was one. 'It's a good thing that you have come to be a governor for us,' he said. 'If you stay we will have peace.' Hone Heke was another. 'Governor,' he said, 'you should stay with us and be like a father. If you go away then the French or the rum sellers will take us Maori over. How can we know what the future will bring? If you stay we can be "all as one" with you and the missionaries.'

Then the Hokianga chief, Tamati Waka Nene, rose and turned towards the chiefs. 'I'm going to speak first to you. Some of you tell Hobson to go. But that's not going to solve our difficulties. We have already sold so much of our land here in the north. We have no way of controlling the Europeans who have settled on it. I'm amazed to hear you telling him to go! Why didn't you tell the traders and grog-sellers to go years ago? There are too many Europeans here now and there are children that unite both our races.' He looked at Hobson. 'Don't be too concerned with what these others are saying. We need you as a friend, a judge, a peacemaker and as governor. You must preserve our customs, and never permit our lands to be taken from us.' Eruera Maihi Patuone, his brother, agreed.

But Te Kemara leapt up and cried: 'No! Go back to your own land. It would be all right if we were going to be equal in rank and power, but if you are going to be above us, I say no. Will we end up like this?' and he crossed his wrists as if handcuffed. Suddenly he seized Hobson's hand, shaking it over and over, and roaring out in English: 'How d'ye do, eh, Governor? How d'ye do, eh, Mister Governor?'

Everyone – Maori and Pakeha – was convulsed with laughter, and Hobson decided that it was a good time to adjourn the meeting. They would meet again on Friday, 7 February.

That evening, Maori groups camped on the flat land near the mouth of the Waitangi River. Talk centred on the treaty. As Williams recalled:

A detail of the original Treaty signed at Waitangi and elsewhere in the north (see frontispiece).
ARCHIVES NEW ZEALAND/TE RUA MAHARA O TE KAWANATANGA, WELLINGTON OFFICE, IA 9/9

> There was considerable excitement amongst the people, greatly increased by … ill-disposed Europeans, stating to the chiefs … that their country was gone, and they now were only taurekareka [slaves]. Many came to us to speak upon this new state of affairs. We gave them but one version, explaining clause by clause, showing the advantage to them of being taken under the fostering care of the British Government, by which act they would become one people with the English, in the suppression of wars, and of every lawless act; under one Sovereign, and one Law, human and divine.

There is no record of what was said in the discussions later that night, but by the next morning most of the chiefs were keen to get the treaty signed immediately. Food was running short, and some had already left for home. Among the missionaries, there was concern that the chiefs would leave without signing. William Colenso suspected that someone had recalled the saying, 'Strike the iron while it is hot.' Another meeting with Hobson was hastily proposed for later that day.

The signing: Thursday, 6 February

The change of plan caught Hobson by surprise. Summoned ashore late in the morning of the 6th, he arrived in plain clothes, having snatched up his plumed hat. Several hundred Maori were waiting for him in the marquee and more stood around outside. Only Busby and a few other Europeans had turned up, among them the Catholic Bishop Pompallier. Hobson,

A view of the all-day feast given by Hobson on 13 February, the day after the Treaty signing at Hokianga. Held at Horeke, a well-established timber-milling site about 2 kilometres from Mangungu, the celebration began with a haka by fifteen hundred men, which the official party watched from boats anchored offshore. Then about three thousand people ate pork, potatoes, rice and sugar. Blankets and tobacco were given to chiefs. The Horeke guns fired a salute, answered by a volley from those of a local trader, G. F. Russell. INK SKETCH BY RICHARD TAYLOR; ALEXANDER TURNBULL LIBRARY, E-296-Q-169-3

nervous and uneasy, more than once expressed concern that the meeting could not be considered a 'regular public meeting' since the proper notice had not been given. He would not allow discussion, but would be prepared to take signatures.

On the table lay a tidily written treaty in Maori, copied overnight on to parchment by one of the missionaries, Richard Taylor. Henry Williams read it out once more. But before anyone could sign, Bishop Pompallier asked Hobson for a public assurance that religion in New Zealand would not be interfered with, that 'free toleration' would be allowed in 'matters of faith'. Hobson agreed. So the CMS missionary had to translate into Maori that 'all creeds alike' would receive Hobson's protection. Outraged at this concession to the Roman Catholics, Williams made a calculated attempt to get around the issue. He read out a carefully written statement: 'The Governor says the several faiths [beliefs] of England, of the Wesleyans, of Rome, and also the Maori custom, shall be alike protected by him.' The last item, Maori ritenga, was inserted at Colenso's suggestion to act as a 'correlative' to the one on Rome. The English missionaries hoped that the Catholic faith would suffer by association with ritenga (what Busby termed 'heathen practices'), which they had explicitly attacked as decadent and aimed to eliminate from Maori society. This assurance, not written into the treaty, is sometimes referred to as its fourth article.

KO **WIKITORIA**, te Kuini o Ingarani, i tana mahara atawai ki nga Rangatira me nga Hapu o Nu Tirani, i tana hiahia hoki kia tohungia ki a ratou o ratou rangatiratanga, me to ratou wenua, a kia mau tonu hoki te Rongo ki a ratou me te ata noho hoki, kua wakaaro ia he mea tika kia tukua mai tetahi Rangatira hei kai wakarite ki nga tangata maori o Nu Tirani. Kia wakaaetia e nga Rangatira maori te Kawanatanga o te Kuini, ki nga wahi katoa o te wenua nei me nga motu. Na te mea hoki he tokomaha ke nga tangata o tona iwi kua noho ki tenei wenua, a e haere mai nei.

Na, ko te Kuini e hiahia ana kia wakaritea te Kawanatanga, kia kaua ai nga kino o puta mai ki te tangata maori ki te pakeha e noho ture kore ana.

Na, kua pai te Kuini kia tukua a hau, a WIREMU HOPIHONA, he Kapitana i te Roiara Nawi, hei Kawana mo nga wahi katoa o Nu Tirani, e tukua aianei amua atu ki te Kuini; e mea atu ana ia ki nga Rangatira o te Wakaminenga o nga Hapu o Nu Tirani, me era Rangatira atu, enei ture ka korerotia nei.

Ko te tuatahi,
Ko nga Rangatira o te Wakaminenga, me nga Rangatira katoa hoki, kihai i uru ki taua Wakaminenga, ka tuku rawa atu ki te Kuini o Ingarani ake tonu atu te Kawanatanga katoa o o ratou wenua.

Ko te tuarua,
Ko te Kuini o Ingarani ka wakarite ka wakaae ki nga Rangatira, ki nga Hapu, ki nga tangata katoa o Nu Tirani, te tino Rangatiratanga o o ratou wenua o ratou kainga me o ratou taonga katoa. Otiia ko nga Rangatira o te Wakaminenga, me nga Rangatira katoa atu, ka tuku ki te Kuini te hokonga o era wahi wenua e pai ai te tangata nona te wenua, ki te ritenga o te utu e wakaritea ai e ratou ko te kai hoko e meatia nei e te Kuini hei kai hoko mona.

Ko te tuatoru,
Hei wakaritenga mai hoki tenei mo te wakaaetanga ki te Kawanatanga o te Kuini. Ka tiakina e te Kuini o Ingarani nga tangata maori katoa o Nu Tirani. Ka tukua ki a ratou nga tikanga katoa, rite tahi ki ana mea ki nga tangata o Ingarani.

(SIGNED,)

WILLIAM HOBSON, Consul & Lieutenant-Governor.

Na, ko matou, ko nga Rangatira o te Wakaminenga o nga Hapu o Nu Tirani, ka huihui nei ki Waitangi. Ko matou hoki ko nga Rangatira o Nu Tirani, ka kite nei i te ritenga o enei kupu, ka tangohia, ka wakaaetia katoatia e matou. Koia ka tohungia ai o matou ingoa o matou tohu.

Ka meatia tenei ki Waitangi, i te ono o nga ra o Pepuere, i te tau kotahi mano, ewaru rau, ewa tekau, o to tatou Ariki.

PAIHIA: Printed at the Press of the Church Missionary Society.

Hobson had two hundred copies of the Treaty in Maori printed on 17 February. The same day, Pomare II signed and, over the next months, signatures were collected in the Bay of Islands – among them, those of the great chiefs Kawiti and Tirarau.

ARCHIVES NEW ZEALAND/TE RUA MAHARA O TE KAWANATANGA, WELLINGTON OFFICE, IA 9/9

Pompallier then left the meeting – possibly to distance himself from the political act about to occur – and chiefs were invited to come forward and sign. Just as Heke was about to sign, Colenso asked Hobson if he thought that the chiefs really understood the treaty. 'If the Native chiefs do not know the contents of this treaty it is no fault of mine,' replied Hobson. 'I have done all that I could … They have heard the treaty read by Mr. Williams.' Colenso agreed, but pointed out that it had not been explained adequately; he was afraid that Maori would later hold the missionaries accountable, whereas their agreement needed to be 'their own act and deed'. Impatiently, Hobson brushed his protest aside, saying: 'I think that the people under your care will be peaceable enough: I'm sure you will endeavour to make them so.'

The signing went ahead. Busby called each chief by name from a list. It was probably Williams who told Hobson to try a few words in Maori. When each chief had signed, Hobson shook his hand and said: 'He iwi tahi tatou' ('We are [now] one people'). Williams must have known that the words would have a special meaning for the chiefs, especially those who were Christian: Maori and British would be linked, as subjects of the Queen and as followers of Christ. That afternoon, over forty Maori leaders put their names or their moko on the treaty parchment, affirming the agreement soon known as the Treaty of Waitangi. As the signing was drawing to an end, one chief gave a signal for three thundering cheers, which closed the meeting. Colenso was left to distribute gifts – two blankets and some tobacco – to each person who had signed.

Pleased with the outcome of the meeting, Hobson immediately reported to his superiors in London: 'I assured them [the Maori] in the most fervent manner that they might rely implicitly on the good faith of Her Majesty's Government.' By his account, he had secured the agreement of forty-six 'head chiefs', twenty-six of whom had earlier signed the Declaration of Independence. That, he wrote, 'must be deemed a full and clear recognition of the sovereign rights of Her Majesty over the northern parts of this island'.

He had been lucky. The following day – the date originally set for the signing – there was torrential rain and no one could leave the *Herald*. On Saturday 8 February, the ship ran up all her flags and fired a twenty-one-gun salute. According to Colenso, there was also a 'great display' at Kororareka 'in honour of the new British colony of New Zealand'. This statement was somewhat premature, since there had been no proclamation of sovereignty. Moreover, Maori agreement was still confined mainly to chiefs in the Bay of Islands. But, as the official record tells it, Hobson was optimistic about obtaining Maori signatures to the Treaty elsewhere.

The Hokianga signing

On 10 February, Hobson set out to gather more signatures. He went first to Waimate in the north, where several chiefs signed, and then on to the Hokianga. Leaders from both places had been at Waitangi and some had already signed. On 12 February, at the Wesleyan mission station at Mangungu on the Hokianga Harbour, up to a thousand Maori gathered; among them were chiefs used to negotiating business contracts with Europeans and some who had experience of the British colonies in Australia. Hobson's intentions were well known, and it was immediately

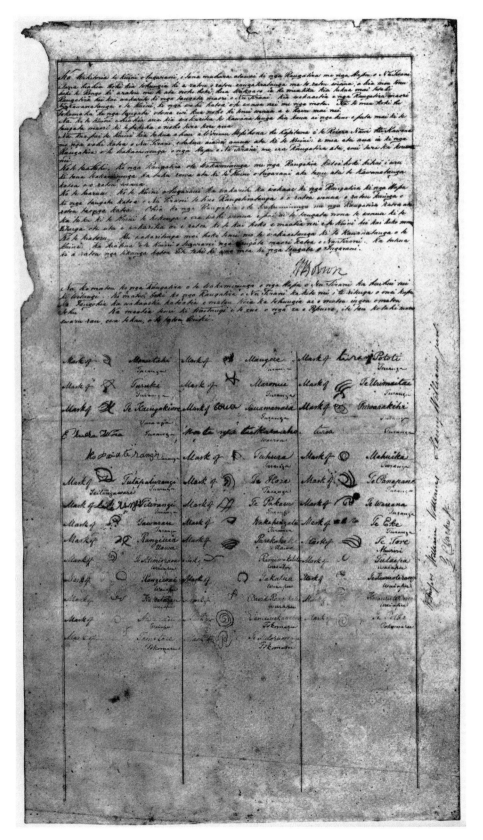

William Williams secured agreement from East Coast Maori on this copy of the Treaty.

ARCHIVES NEW ZEALAND/TE RUA MAHARA O TE KAWANATANGA, WELLINGTON OFFICE, IA 9/9

CHAPTER TWO: THE TREATY OF WAITANGI

The signing of the Treaty at the entrance to the Tamaki River – probably at Karaka Bay, now part of Auckland. Chiefs from the Waitemata-Hauraki area signed on 4 March and 9 July. WATERCOLOUR BY W. JORDAN; AUCKLAND MUSEUM/TAMAKI PAENGA HIRA, PD75

obvious that they had been widely discussed. The debates are summarised here from the notes taken by the missionary, Richard Taylor, and the Police Magistrate, Willoughby Shortland.

'We are glad to see the Governor,' said Te Taonui, 'but let him be a governor for the Pakeha. We'll be our own governor. How do the Pakeha behave to the blacks of Port Jackson? They treat them like dogs: a Pakeha kills a pig – the black comes to the door and eats the refuse.' Te Taonui knew; he had visited Sydney, and taken the name 'Makoare' after Governor Macquarie of New South Wales. Chiefs at Waitangi had also mentioned the British treatment of Aborigines.

Chiefs told Hobson that they were suspicious of British motives for making a treaty. 'We think you are going to deceive us,' said Mohi [Tawhai?]. 'The Pakeha tell us so. Where does the Governor get his authority? Is it from the Queen? Well, let him come. Let him stop all the lands falling into Pakeha hands. I want everyone to hear that. It's only right to say what we think.'

'We are not willing to give up our land,' Te Taonui said. 'The land is like a parent to us. We obtain all things from it. The land is our chieftainship. We will not give it up.' Other chiefs spoke about trade, both its benefits and its problems. Many, however, felt it was pointless to dwell on the past; Hobson was needed to give order and direction to the future.

After eight hours of debate, chiefs started signing; they began at around six in the evening and continued until midnight. John Hobbs, a local Wesleyan missionary who acted as interpreter, believed that the promises given by Hobson were crucial in securing Maori agreement. He had translated Hobson's 'repeated assurances … that the Queen did not want the land, but merely the sovereignty, that … her officers … might be able more effectually to govern her subjects … and punish those of them who might be guilty of crime'. Hobbs also told Maori that the land would 'never be forcibly taken', and gave Hobson's *most solemn assurance* that the Queen's government would always act with 'truth and justice'.

These explanations shaped Maori understanding of the Treaty, with one chief referring to it as a 'very sacred' deed that he must take care of. In this context, the Treaty was probably seen as a pledge, similar to a religious commitment or covenant, entered into by the two parties – the Maori chiefs and the British Crown. This understanding was evident in Maori debates on the Treaty in later years.

Although Hobson succeeded in obtaining sixty or more signatures at Hokianga, the visit was not without incident. Two major chiefs refused to sign, and one returned a gift of money. Another brought back his gift of blankets with a letter signed by fifty of his tribe; he wanted his name removed from the Treaty. Hobson refused, and irritably dismissed these incidents. He claimed that the Hokianga signing put the cession of sovereignty over the north 'beyond dispute'. A feast for three thousand Maori was held the next day to mark the event.

Extending the Treaty

Returning to the Bay of Islands, Hobson attended to business. On 17 February, two hundred copies of the Treaty in Maori were printed at Paihia. Four days later, Hobson sailed south in his search for more signatures. He stopped first at the Waitemata Harbour, and spent some days exploring the area in search of land suitable for European settlement. Suddenly he suffered a stroke, which paralysed his right side and impaired his speech. Henry Williams, who had left the ship to go to the mission station of Maraetai, succeeded in organising a meeting near the mouth of the Tamaki River, at which some sixteen chiefs from the western side of the Hauraki Gulf signed. But plans to continue south were dropped. The *Herald* sailed back to the Bay of Islands with the ailing Hobson, who made a gradual recovery at the Waimate mission station.

Willoughby Shortland (who was soon to be Colonial Secretary) now took over the task of organising further signings. Several copies of the Treaty in Maori were written out. Some were sent to missionaries stationed on the east and west coasts of the upper North Island, who were asked to call Treaty meetings. Others were taken on more lengthy journeys by (among others) Henry Williams, a trader named James Fedarb, and two army men, W. C. Symonds and Thomas Bunbury (who went as far as Stewart Island). Over a period of six months, nine or more copies of the Treaty would circulate around the country.

Some of the negotiators were not experienced in Maori ways. Bunbury, for example, became impatient at the lengthy discussions and refused to let a woman sign; he then failed to get the signatures of her companions (men possibly of lesser rank). But the missionaries

Rangi Topeora, painted here by Gottfried Lindauer, signed the Treaty at Kapiti in May 1840. The missionaries involved in Treaty negotiations allowed a number of women to sign – including Kahe Te Rau-o-te-rangi at Wellington, Rere-o-maki at Wanganui, Ana Hamu at Waitangi, and Ereonora at Kaitaia.
PARTRIDGE COLLECTION, AUCKLAND ART GALLERY/TOI O TAMAKI

who took part often knew the tribes well and understood many of their customs; they could be highly influential negotiators in Maori affairs, and allowed women to sign the Treaty. Henry Williams, for example, had two women sign his copy of the Treaty in the Cook Strait region; he later told Hobson that other women had complained about not being allowed to play a more prominent part, especially when the other party to the Treaty was a woman – Queen Victoria.

One woman of rank who signed was Ereonora, the wife of Nopera Panakareao. Nopera had prepared carefully for the meeting at Kaitaia, which was held at the end of April. He questioned missionaries and officials about the wording of the Treaty, especially the word 'sovereignty' or 'kawanatanga'. At the meeting he explained it to his people in this way: 'The shadow of the land goes to the Queen, but the substance remains with us.' ('Ko te atakau o te whenua i riro i a te Kuini. Ko te tinana o te whenua i waiho ki nga Maori.') 'We now have a man at the helm,' he said. 'Before, everyone wanted to steer. First one said, "Let me steer!" and then another, "Let me steer!" But we never went straight. Now we have a steersman.' A year later, Nopera had come to the conclusion that the substance of the land had gone.

The proclamation of British sovereignty

Meanwhile, the first New Zealand Company settlers had arrived, disembarking at Port Nicholson in January 1840. In March they had set up a form of government which, they claimed, derived its legality from authority granted by local chiefs. The flag of an independent New Zealand, made on the company's ship *Tory*, flew above the settlement.

Hearing of these moves, Hobson reasoned that the settlers were assuming powers of government that were the prerogative of the Crown. On 21 May, he proclaimed sovereignty over the whole of the country: over the North Island on the basis of cession by chiefs who had signed the Treaty of Waitangi, and over the South Island and Stewart Island on the basis that Cook had 'discovered' them. At this stage, Hobson held only the Treaty copy first signed at Waitangi and the one signed at Waikato Heads and Manukau Harbour. As for the South Island, he doubted that its 'uncivilized' Maori were capable of signing a treaty.

Unaware of Hobson's actions, Bunbury also proclaimed sovereignty: on 5 June at Stewart Island, by right of Cook's discovery, and on 17 June at Cloudy Bay, by right of cession of the South Island by several 'independent' chiefs (presumably, this meant that they were not part of the Confederation of United Tribes). The Colonial Office approved Hobson's proclamations, which were published in the *London Gazette* on 2 October 1840. Treaty meetings had continued after the proclamations; on 3 September, the last signature was put on a copy of the Treaty, somewhere near Kawhia. Over five hundred chiefs, among them up to twelve women of rank, had signed at about fifty meetings.

Hobson had kept British officials informed throughout the signing process and had sent them copies of the Treaty. In October, he despatched a final report, together with 'certified' copies of the Treaty in Maori and in English. He said nothing about any variations between the two texts, although it had already become apparent some months earlier (in April) that there were differences in meaning, and therefore in Maori understanding. Hobson was surely aware of this.

The differences that affected the meaning, particularly in the first two articles, were important:

ARTICLE 1

By the Treaty in *English*, Maori leaders gave the Queen 'all the rights and powers of sovereignty' over their territories.

By the Treaty in *Maori*, they gave the Queen 'te kawanatanga katoa' – the complete governance or government over their lands.

ARTICLE 2

By the Treaty in *English*, Maori leaders and people, collectively and individually, were confirmed in and guaranteed 'exclusive and undisturbed possession of their lands and estates, forests, fisheries, and other properties'.

By the Treaty in *Maori*, they were confirmed and guaranteed 'te tino rangatiratanga' – the unqualified exercise of their chieftainship – over their lands, villages, and all their treasures.

ARTICLE 3

The Treaty in *English* extended to Maori the Queen's protection and all the rights and privileges of British subjects. The *Maori* text conveyed this with reasonable accuracy.

The differences between the two texts were crucial to Maori understanding – or lack of it. Only thirty-nine chiefs signed a copy of the Treaty in English; most signed a copy in the Maori

Locations of Treaty Signings

	Location	Date	Signatures
1	**Waitangi**		**240 total**
1a	Waitangi	6 February	43
1b	Waimate	10 February	6
1c	Hokianga	12 February	64
1a	Waitangi [?]	17 February	1
	Paihia [?]	13 [?] May	4
	Russell	5 August	3
	Bay of Islands	6 February–August	34
1d	Waitemata	4 March	17
1e	Kaitaia	28 April	61
1d	Tamaki	9 July	7
2	**Manukau-Kawhia**		**13 total**
2a	Manukau	20 March	3
2b	Kawhia	28 April	1
		21 May	3
		25 May	1
		15 June	3
		27 August	1
		3 September	1
3	**Waikato-Manukau**		**39 total**
3a	Waikato Heads	March [April?]	32
3b	Manukau	26 April	7
4	**Printed Sheet**		**5 total**
4	Waikato Heads?	no date	
5	**Tauranga**		**21 total**
5	Tauranga	10 April–23 May	
6	**Bay of Plenty (Fedarb)**		**26 total**
6a	Opotiki	27 & 28 May	7
6b	Torere	11 June	2
		14 June	1
6c	Te Kaha	14 June	4
6d	Whakatane	16 June	12

	Location	Date	Signatures
7	**Herald-Bunbury**		**27 total**
7a	Coromandel	4 May	4
7b	Mercury Is.	7 May	2
7c	Akaroa	30 May	2
7d	Ruapuke	10 June	3
7e	Otago	13 June	2
7f	Cloudy Bay	17 June	9
7g	Mana (off-shore)	19 June	2
7h	Hawke's Bay	24 June	3
8	**Henry Williams**		**132 total**
8a	Port Nicholson	29 April	34
8b	Queen Charlotte	4 May	14
	Sound	5 May	13
8c	Rangitoto Island	11 May	13
8d	Kapiti	14 May	4
8e	Waikanae	16 May	20
8f	Otaki	19 May	8
	Tawhirihoe	21 May	3
8g	Manawatu	26 May	7
8h	Wanganui	23 May	10
		31 May	4
8i	Motungarara	4 June	2
9	**East Coast**		**41 total**
9a	Turanga (Gisborne)	5 May and later	25
9b	Uawa (Tolaga Bay)	16/17 May	2
9c	Waiapu		
	(Whakawhitira)	25 May	7
	(Rangitukia)	1 June	3
9d	Tokomaru	9 June	4

SOURCE: THIS INFORMATION IS DERIVED SUBSTANTIALLY FROM *FACSIMILES OF THE DECLARATION OF INDEPENDENCE AND THE TREATY OF WAITANGI*, WELLINGTON, 1877; REPRINTED 1976

Fedarb's Bill of 1 July 1840

Date	Place	Item	Amount
28 May	Opotiki	8 lbs tobacco at 3s	£1 4s 0d
		12 pipes at ½d	6d
15 June	Te Kaha	5 fancy pipes at 2s 6d	12s 6d
		½ lb tobacco	1s 6d
16 June	Torere	2 fancy pipes at 2s 6d	5s 0d
		½ lb tobacco	1s 6d
17 June	Whakatane	11 fancy pipes	£1 17s 6d
		4 ditto boxes	8s 0d
		3 looking glasses	4s 6d
		5 lbs tobacco	15s 0d
		4 rows beads	2s 0d
		1 slate	2s 0d
			£5 14s 0d

The trader James Fedarb was asked by Tauranga missionaries to get chiefs' agreement in that region. He lodged this bill for gifts given in the negotiations. SOURCE: FREEMAN TO COLENSO, 1 JULY 1840, COLENSO PAPERS, MS COL. 1833-63, IV, ALEXANDER TURNBULL LIBRARY

language that did not convey the meaning of the English text. Only some would have been able to read the Treaty in Maori, even if they had been given the chance. Explanations at Treaty meetings might have helped, given that discussion was essential to Maori in the customary building of relationships; but the records show that negotiators avoided commenting on differences in meaning. Their mission was to convince chiefs to sign, so their explanations skirted the complexities of sovereignty (as recognised under international law) to present an idealised picture of the workings of British sovereignty within New Zealand.

Thus the differences between the English and Maori texts laid the basis for different British (and later colonial) and Maori understandings of the Treaty of Waitangi, and for a debate over interpretation that has continued from 1840 to the present.

No unanimous Maori agreement

In his October 1840 report to the Colonial Office, Hobson also enclosed a list of Treaty signatories. Although he knew that a number of leading chiefs had not signed, he did not mention this fact. Te Wherowhero of Waikato had refused to sign, although he was probably asked twice. Symonds, who had taken the Treaty to him, said that Te Wherowhero was

[opposite page] Locations of Treaty signings. Archives New Zealand, Wellington, holds the nine Treaty sheets listed. In 1877, they were first published in *Facsimiles of the Declaration of Independence and the Treaty of Waitangi*. The names attributed to the sheets here are not part of any official record. See also Treaty signatories identified in Appendix Two.

CHAPTER TWO: THE TREATY OF WAITANGI 41

The chiefs in this lithograph from the 1840s are, from left, Mananui Te Heuheu and his brother Iwikau of Ngati Tuwharetoa, and Apihai Te Kawau of Ngati Whatua and his nephew, probably Paora Tuhaere. Mananui refused to sign and objected to Iwikau's signing. Apihai Te Kawau signed at Manukau Harbour. LITHOGRAPH AFTER GEORGE FRENCH ANGAS; ALEXANDER TURNBULL LIBRARY, PUBL-0014-56

offended because he had heard about the celebrations at Waitangi and found the Manukau signing feeble by comparison. The same was possibly true elsewhere; only in the north was Hobson able to provide the feast that was fitting on such an important occasion.

Other chiefs, such as Taraia Ngakuti Te Tumuhuia of Thames and Hori Kingi Tupaea of Tauranga, refused to sign because they wanted to retain full control over their affairs, and feared that this would be restricted by the Governor. Some chiefs were not given the chance to say yes or no to the Treaty. No Treaty meetings were held from Wanganui to Mokau, north of Taranaki, and most of the Hawke's Bay and Wairarapa chiefs were not invited to sign. On the Hawke's Bay coast, Bunbury had managed to find Te Hapuku, who signed with two other chiefs, but inland areas were left untouched.

Some tribal groups refused to sign altogether – among them, Te Arawa of Rotorua and Ngati Tuwharetoa of Taupo. Mananui Te Heuheu, the great Ngati Tuwharetoa chief, returned the blankets given to his younger brother Iwikau, who had signed in the Bay of Islands. Mananui saw no reason to put his mana under that of a mere woman – Queen Victoria.

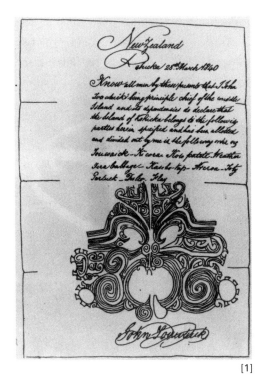 

[1] The full moko of the Ngai Tahu chief, Hone Tuhawaiki. Thomas Bunbury reported that Tuhawaiki 'came on board in the full dress staff uniform of a British aid-de-camp, with gold lace trousers, cocked hat and plume … accompanied by [his] orderly sergeant.' The chief, who spoke English, wanted to sign the Treaty immediately. He sought a guarantee that he and his people owned Ruapuke Island, and he wanted to register his 25-ton vessel. HOCKEN LIBRARY, UARE TAOKA O HAKENA, UNIVERSITY OF OTAGO, DUNEDIN, C/N 145. BY PERMISSION RENA FOWLER

[2] Wiremu Nera Te Awa-i-taia of Ngati Mahanga at Whaingaroa (Raglan). He signed the Treaty in March or April 1840 and later recalled that, like other chiefs, he had followed missionary advice. He said that chiefs were told that any nation other than Britain would have forcibly compelled the Maori people to give up possession of the country, whereas government by the British could be relied upon to be benevolent. ALEXANDER TURNBULL LIBRARY, F54121½

Almost everywhere, Maori leaders were extremely cautious about giving their agreement to the Treaty. Many objected strongly at Treaty meetings, but then signed anyway. Others signed willingly. Why, then, did so many sign? From what some of the chiefs said, at the time and later, we know that there were many different reasons.

A special relationship

Bunbury had stressed to Maori chiefs at Tauranga that the Treaty was just one more step in an ongoing relationship with the Crown – an argument that was probably used elsewhere. He acknowledged that the Maori had been recognised as an independent nation, but said that the 1835 'treaty' had been rendered 'abortive' by Maori fighting and lack of unity. The Queen now sought Maori agreement to a new treaty that would enable a regular government to be established to assist Maori more effectively and control the growing number of Europeans.

The relationship between Maori and the Crown dated back to the 1790s, when British naval ships first took timber for spars from the Coromandel. It had been extended by the two chiefs, Hongi Hika and Waikato, meeting King George IV in London, and by letters and appeals from Maori to the King in the early 1830s. Many chiefs expected that the Treaty would be the start of a new relationship with Britain, one that had a Christian basis. It would be a personalised relationship, with the Queen as the other party.

In this special relationship, the Treaty would also be akin to a covenant in the religious sense. This concept was familiar to newly literate Maori, who had been absorbing the ideas of *Te Kawenata Hou – The New Covenant*. By 1840, this Maori text of the New Testament had been printed, and widely circulated in sections. It was virtually the only Maori-language reading material available.

At Waitangi, Henry Williams had drawn on these teachings to encourage the notion that Maori and Pakeha could become one people in a temporal and spiritual sense. This understanding of the Treaty, involving strong elements of a covenant, masked the impersonal nature of the Crown as it would be embodied in a British colonial administration.

A balance of authority

To Maori signing the Treaty, its confirmation of rangatiratanga was undoubtedly crucial. 'Rangatiratanga' is a complex word for which there is no exact English equivalent ('possession' is the word in the English text). In 1840, it stood for Maori authority and autonomy – in effect, Maori sovereignty of a corporate kind. Maori no doubt thought that the mana of the land – the chiefs' authority over its resources and their allocation – would be retained; in fact, it would be increased by this agreement with the world's major naval power, which would defend the country against France or other nations. There was an expectation that the kawanatanga (sovereignty) of Article 1 would control troublesome Europeans, whereas the chiefs would look after their own people, their rangatiratanga secured in Article 2. There would have to be a sharing of authority in the country, but one that would boost chiefly mana and authority.

Land

The issue of land was usually foremost in influencing chiefs to sign – although they had different reasons. In some areas, the chiefs needed support against aggressive European land-buyers; in others, the chiefs were quite keen to sell land to the Governor. In the central North Island, which was largely unvisited by Pakeha, the Treaty was not seen as necessary to protect the land. Some tribes saw a new way of fighting old enemies: if they sold disputed land, they would no longer have to fight their rivals for it. And some obviously saw the Treaty as a way of furthering tribal interests – for example, a means of returning to lands from which they had been displaced. Wiremu Kingi Te Rangitake went to the Bay of Islands in 1840 to sound out the new government about his tribe returning to their Taranaki lands. This they later did.

Many chiefs hoped that the new agreement would bring peace to the country. Ngati Whatua leaders asked Hobson for his protection against their old enemies, Nga Puhi and Waikato, and offered him land on the Waitemata to build his capital. Hobson's insistence that all intertribal fighting should cease was not attractive to all tribes, however, and probably caused some to withhold their agreement.

Trade, settlement and change

There is no doubt that most of the tribes who accepted the Treaty hoped for a share in the benefits that would result. Settlers would bring more markets for produce, more goods to buy, and increased demand for Maori labour and services. These developments were already affecting Maori society, and increasing fast. An acceptance of change seems to have been a significant factor in Maori agreement to the Treaty. Acknowledging this, many chiefs expressed their belief that the clock could not be turned back and that new structures were needed. This awareness was more evident in areas of regular European contact, especially on the northern coasts, and less strong where contact was slight.

On the whole, however, the Treaty promised a good deal for Maori at the time. In their understanding of the Treaty, Article 2 confirmed chiefly power while Article 1 ceded a governance role to the Crown. Maori no doubt expected to be involved in some way in the government's management of public affairs. This was not, of course, defined in the treaty-making, and disillusion would set in rapidly as a weak administration began to exercise authority.

Missionary advice

In agreeing to the Treaty, Maori leaders believed above all that the missionaries' advice was wise and could be trusted: the Treaty would be good for the country and the people. The missionaries had been careful to explain the Treaty as the personal wish of the Queen; it was her 'act of love' and thus a sacred bond, since she was head of both the English church and the state.

But for Hobson, this religious understanding – if he grasped it at all – was just part of the business of getting Maori agreement to a transfer of sovereignty. Since 1837, he had been convinced that New Zealand was an ideal place to receive British settlers; Britain therefore needed the Treaty to reassure the Maori people and to get their cooperation before settlement began in earnest. After the northern signings, it is doubtful that Maori had any real freedom of choice in Treaty negotiations, since Hobson intended to assume sovereignty anyway. In 1840, the Treaty at least provided a basis for a working relationship. How that would evolve remained to be seen.

CHAPTER THREE

A Matter of Mana
— 1840 to 1870

Even while the Treaty was still being signed, Maori leaders in the north told Hobson that they were concerned about the future. Hobson tried to calm their fears, but by the end of 1840 some chiefs were convinced that their freedom was at risk. Government regulations would multiply, they said, and one governor would succeed another until the Maori people were 'ensnared'. Some regretted signing the Treaty. Government authority (kawanatanga) was already seen as a threat to chiefly authority (rangatiratanga) – although both were affirmed in the Treaty.

As a colonial administrative structure gradually evolved, their fears seemed justified. Initially, New Zealand was administered as a dependency of New South Wales, but by Royal Charter of November 1840 it became a Crown colony. As Governor, Hobson began to make laws and regulations for 'the peace, order and good government' of the country. He had a council of three senior officials and three appointees, but he ruled as an autocrat, answerable only to the Colonial Office in distant London. The small group of officials who had come with him from Sydney expanded as police and other officials were appointed; an army detachment arrived in April 1840.

For his dealings with the Maori people, Hobson followed Normanby's instructions and appointed a Chief Protector of Aborigines and several assistant protectors. They were intended to be impartial guardians of Maori welfare, but at the same time they were to act as government negotiators for the purchase of Maori land. George Clarke (senior), the first Protector, soon saw the conflict of interest inherent in these two functions.

Clarke could also see that kawanatanga and rangatiratanga would inevitably clash. And chiefly mana soon began to be undermined, by government regulations and laws that challenged the right of chiefs to run their own affairs. Late in 1841, for example, Hobson issued a regulation forbidding the felling of kauri. This angered the Hokianga chief Tamati Waka Nene, who had supported the Treaty. A few months later, a youth called Maketu was put on trial and hanged for the murder of a Pakeha woman, her child, her servant and a second child in her care, the granddaughter of Bay of Islands chief Rewa. It was the first real test of whether Maori would accept the British style of justice: northern chiefs cooperated rather than face the likely inter-tribal hostility.

While Maori might seek government arbitration in disputes between Maori and Pakeha, the government role was often resented when the differences were between Maori and Maori. Despite signs that many chiefs were ready to accept a level of British governance, there were definite limits. In particular, Maori were reluctant to submit to British law when they were not confident that the government could protect them if customary methods were abandoned. Maintaining chiefly authority was essential if tribes were to be kept under control, and chiefs were not prepared to relinquish more power than they considered essential. Their authority, however, was threatened by the presence and actions of increasing numbers of British settlers.

[previous page] A group of Maori take protest action in an effort to halt the survey of the road that was built by Governor Grey from Auckland towards the Waikato between 1861 and 1863. URQUHART ALBUM, ALEXANDER TURNBULL LIBRARY, C9071

Auckland in 1853. Hobson set up his capital here in 1841. In a decade, Auckland grew into a busy town that relied heavily on Maori trade. As Attorney-General William Swainson wrote: 'From a distance of nearly a hundred miles, the natives supply the markets of Auckland with the produce of their industry; brought partly by land carriage, partly by small coasting craft, and partly by canoes. In the course of the year 1852, one thousand seven hundred and ninety-two canoes entered the harbour of Auckland, bringing to market by this means alone two hundred tons of potatoes, fourteen hundred baskets of onions, seventeen hundred baskets of maize, twelve hundred baskets of peaches, twelve hundred tons of firewood, forty-five tons of fish, and thirteen hundred pigs; besides flax, poultry, vegetables ... '
LITHOGRAPH BY PATRICK JOSEPH HOGAN, 1853; ALEXANDER TURNBULL LIBRARY, A-004-005

Settlers

Auckland, Wellington and Nelson grew more rapidly than Maori had expected. Settlers were soon pressing the Governor for a say in the running of their affairs. The Colonial Office had anticipated this, but considered that giving power to settlers too soon was risky. The first governors – Hobson (who died in September 1842), Robert FitzRoy (1843–45) and George Grey (1845–53) – shared the Colonial Office's view that the safety of settlers and maintaining good relationships with Maori depended on showing respect for the Treaty. All three governors repeated its guarantees frequently on public occasions.

Nonetheless, the British government realised that some measure of settler self-government could not be withheld for too long, and in 1846 the British Parliament enacted a constitution for New Zealand. The right to vote was given to males with a property qualification who were literate in English. This decision effectively excluded Maori, many of whom were literate, but only in Maori. At that time, there were only thirteen thousand settlers living alongside a Maori population of around a hundred thousand. Governor Grey, knowing that such a system would result in war, succeeded in having the constitution suspended for five years. He also rejected as unworkable the Colonial Office's proposal to recognise, on a temporary basis, native districts in which Maori custom would be upheld by formally appointed chiefs, backed by the colonial law courts. Instead, he set up a system of resident magistrates to enforce British law.

Grey thus avoided any real negotiation with Maori over the key questions of political representation and a sharing of power, as well as the many thorny issues relating to land and law. The colonial administration continued to introduce laws and regulations for New Zealand through the 1840s, and expanded its role in areas such as the control of settlements, commerce and shipping. These were all matters affecting Maori communities, yet in 1846 Grey abolished the Protectorate, the government's main channel of liaison and communication with Maori. Instead, he established special relationships with certain chiefs, favouring them with gifts and other attentions. He also appointed land purchase officers, one of the first being Donald McLean, a former Protector.

Land

From 1840, Maori gradually became aware that they were no longer free to dispose of their lands as they chose. Under the terms of the Treaty, they could sell land only to the government. If they wanted to sell land and the government did not want to buy it, the land could not be sold to anyone else. If the government agreed to buy the land, officials could set a low price, and then on-sell the land to settlers at a much higher price. Maori communities naturally resented these restrictions, and some lodged appeals to the government.

Maori also found it strange that land could be resold from one settler to another. Before 1840, land had been sold to secure the occupation of a Pakeha who would be useful to the tribe; now, under the laws of the new government, selling to a Pakeha meant that Maori had permanently disposed of the land and all rights over it. Some Maori asserted continuing rights to land that had been sold; others began to raise questions about the ownership of metals and stones, and of other resources (plants, animals, birds and water) associated with land in which they had an interest.

During the Waitangi discussions about the Treaty, Hobson and Henry Williams had both promised that all pre-1840 land sales would be investigated. The land claims commissioners had begun their work during Hobson's governorship, bringing great agitation to both Maori and settlers. European and Maori evidence had to be given to justify a settler's claim to a piece of land. Where the sale was fair and the buyer was occupying the land, Maori and settler were usually satisfied. But the investigations often made Maori uneasy, for they revealed how much land had been sold. They also stirred up debate among settlers about Britain's recognition of Maori independence before 1840. If Maori were free to sell their land before 1840, settlers

50   AN ILLUSTRATED HISTORY OF THE TREATY OF WAITANGI

A very early photograph of another new town – Wellington in about 1858, looking towards Te Aro from Mulgrave Street. Wellington became the colony's capital in 1865. ALEXANDER TURNBULL LIBRARY, E-296-q-170

asked, why should the government now raise doubts about such sales? And why, where a sale was judged to be fair, should the Land Claims Commission limit it nonetheless to a maximum of 2,560 acres (1,037 hectares)? The Treaty was denounced by some settlers as a fraud.

Maori, too, wondered whose interests were being protected – their own or the government's? Maori dissatisfaction was fuelled by the government's decision that acreage above the 2,560-acre limit would go to the Crown. The promises given in the Treaty negotiations that 'all lands unjustly held' would be returned to Maori seemed to have been contravened. However, where speculative purchases were not upheld, the land and the purchase price (or goods) reverted to the Maori owners. But the 'surplus lands' issue would continue to rankle, and would be investigated by a government commission in 1947–48.

Some of the large land purchases, such as the 20 million acres (8 million hectares) claimed by the New Zealand Company in Wellington and elsewhere, created serious conflict between settler and Maori. Wellington Maori fought hard to retain control of local pa and cultivations

Commissioner William Spain investigates land claims at New Plymouth in 1844. In this pencil sketch by Edwin Harris, the Commissioner sits at a table outside a building too small to hold the assembly of Maori and settlers. PUKE ARIKI COLLECTION, A74-441

in the face of settler efforts to remove them from the land. Some leaders became incensed as the company pushed aside their objections and surveyed places still occupied by Maori communities – such as Te Aro and Pipitea – where settlers began to take up land. One chief, Wi Tako, wrote numerous letters to officials and newspapers; his evidence before the Land Claims Commission presided over by William Spain helped to prove that the New Zealand Company had not clearly explained to local Maori the terms of its purchase of Wellington land. The government's agent, George Clarke (junior), was appalled by the intransigence of settlers, by the arrogance of the company's agent, William Wakefield, and by vicious settler attacks on the government. Company excesses were curbed, although in time the government itself moved Maori off the land with meagre compensation.

By the early 1840s, Maori had become more cautious about land sales. They often sought to retain coastal areas and swamplands for the associated resources. They were reluctant to sell large areas of land, wanting to remain close to Pakeha settlement and continue trading both goods and services. They were prepared to tolerate a good deal of settler provocation and make concessions to government; but in land matters there was a limit beyond which Maori

[1] Wi Tako Ngatata, a Te Ati Awa leader at Port Nicholson (Wellington). One newspaper quoted him as saying: 'I ask you pakehas what did the Queen tell you? Did she say to you "Go to New Zealand and fraudulently take away the land of the natives"? You say no. Then why do you encroach upon land that has not been fairly purchased?' ALEXANDER TURNBULL LIBRARY, F70077½

[2] Te Rangihaeata was at the forefront of resistance to settler land claims in Wellington and Marlborough.
WATERCOLOUR BY ISAAC COATES, c. 1840; TASMAN BAYS HERITAGE TRUST/NELSON PROVINCIAL MUSEUM/BETT COLLECTION AC321

[3] Te Ruki Kawiti, a signatory to the 1835 Declaration of Independence, was reluctant to sign the Treaty but was finally persuaded to do so in May 1840. PHOTOLITHOGRAPH AFTER A WATERCOLOUR BY J. J. MERRETT, 1845; ALEXANDER TURNBULL LIBRARY, 37353½

refused to be pushed. At Wairau in 1843, for example, Nelson settlers became impatient to survey land they claimed and would not wait for a proper government investigation, which local chiefs expected. In a violent confrontation, both settler and Maori lives were lost. Similar disputes occurred in several districts of the North Island throughout the 1840s.

Challenges to British sovereignty

The major challenge to British authority was launched in the north by Hone Heke and his ally Kawiti. The flagstaff at Kororareka (Russell) was cut down in July 1844. Heke, who was behind the attack, saw the signal staff as a tohu (sign) that New Zealand was passing into British hands. Other northern Maori were also disappointed that the Treaty had not brought the expected benefits. Shifting the seat of government from the Bay of Islands to Auckland in 1841 had drawn trade and settlers away from the north; land sales, overseas shipping and the demand for Maori goods and services had all declined; port duties (previously taken by Maori) had raised the cost of imported goods. When the government had the flagstaff re-erected, it was brought

CHAPTER THREE: A MATTER OF MANA

Officers of the 58th Regiment. Two companies arrived in New Zealand in March 1845 to fight in the northern war, and reinforcements followed. AUCKLAND MUSEUM/TAMAKI PAENGA HIRA, C3877

down three more times. Through 1845 and into 1846, Heke's challenge to British sovereignty developed into a major confrontation between Maori troops (led by Heke and Kawiti) and British troops with Maori allies (among them the Treaty supporter Waka Nene).

More than most Maori leaders, Heke and Kawiti seem to have understood that the shadow of 'sovereignty' over the land was as much a threat to their chieftainship as any outright seizing of the land. In letters to the Governor, Heke made one point clear: he wanted British authority removed. The fighting, which brought more British troops to the country, proved that Maori were formidable warriors and capable of inflicting humiliating defeats. Nonetheless, in 1846 Kawiti and Heke sought peace, and the government wisely decided not to re-erect the flagstaff.

The Treaty debated

The Wairau affair and the northern war raised issues that were hotly debated by Maori and Pakeha in New Zealand, and by many in Britain as well. The big question, and one that would be discussed for years to come, was this: what were the rights and obligations that Maori and the Crown could expect under the Treaty? How might these be expressed in the colonial administration, and later in a New Zealand government? How could the welfare of Maori and settlers – often with opposing interests – be reconciled?

Auckland,
Nov. 8th, 1847

Oh Madam,

We salute you, our love is great to you, we have not forgotten your words nor your kind thoughts to all the world. Oh, Madam! listen to our words, all the Chiefs of Waikato. Let your love be towards us, and be kind to us, as Christ also hath loved all. May God incline you to hold fast our words, and we to hold fast yours for ever. Oh Madam, listen! The report has come hither, that your Elders (councillors) think of taking the Maoris land without cause. Behold, the heart is sad, but we will not believe this report, because we heard from the first Governor that with ourselves lay the consideration for our lands, and the second Governor repeated the same, and this Governor also, all their speeches were the same, therefore, we write to you to love our people, write your thoughts to us, that peace may abide with the people of these islands.

From your friend,
Te Wherowhero

From Earl Grey to Governor Grey.
Downing Street,
May 3rd, 1848

Sir,

You will inform Te Wherowhero and the other chiefs of Te Waikato district who signed the letter to the Queen inclosed in your Despatch of Nov. 13th, 1847, No.117, that I have laid it before Her Majesty, who has commanded me to express the satisfaction with which she has received this loyal and dutiful address, and to assure them that there is not the slightest foundation for rumours to which they allude and it never was intended that the Treaty of Waitangi should be violated by dispossessing the tribes which are parties to it, of any portion of the land secured to them by the Treaty without their consent. On the contrary Her Majesty has always directed that the Treaty should be most scrupulously and religiously observed. I take this opportunity of referring you to a letter which I have recently addressed to the Wesleyan Missionary Committee in answer to a representation on their part, also enclosed, expressing fears of intended infractions of the Treaty of Waitangi. That letter contains a full exposition of my views, both respecting the Treaty itself and also some portions of the general question as to the ownership of land in New Zealand, about which misunderstandings had arisen. I wish to refer you particularly to the explanation which I have there given of the meaning intended to be conveyed by a passage of land instructions.

I have etc,
(signed) GREY

The northern war had just finished when rumours circulated that the Governor was about to seize unoccupied and uncultivated Maori land. Four hundred Auckland settlers petitioned for the Treaty's land guarantee to be respected, and the Waikato leader, Te Wherowhero, appealed to the Queen. This is the text of his letter and the official response.

SOURCE: TE WHEROWHERO AND OTHER CHIEFS TO THE QUEEN, 8 NOVEMBER 1847, IN GREY TO EARL GREY, 13 NOVEMBER 1847; EARL GREY TO GREY, 3 MAY 1848;
IN *BRITISH PARLIAMENTARY PAPERS: COLONIES NEW ZEALAND*, VOL.6, 1847–50, [1002], [899]

For the early administrators, whose task was by no means easy, there were more immediate concerns. Were all Maori to be under British law, including those who had not signed the Treaty? And to what extent could the government allow Maori custom to continue? The Colonial Office answered these questions in the mid 1840s by ruling that all Maori were under British sovereignty and law. Its officials also noted that, as set out in Hobson's instructions, many Maori customs could still be allowed (with the exception of cannibalism); some adjustment of British law, however, might be necessary. Governors in New Zealand were left to devise a practical plan, but proved reluctant to pass special laws for Maori. Cautious not to offend settler sensitivities, and concerned that separate laws could become entrenched, they sought alternative ways of handling these issues.

Other questions, especially about land, were raised by Maori. Was it fair that the government had a monopoly on the buying and selling of Maori land, with the profit going to the Crown and not to Maori? In the early 1840s, a financially strapped government could neither purchase all the land Maori offered for sale nor pay the higher prices that Maori were starting to ask. Irritated by the restriction on land transactions, some Maori felt cheated by the Treaty.

In March 1844, Governor FitzRoy waived government pre-emption in land sales: now individuals could buy direct from Maori, paying a government fee of 10s per acre. When initial sales amounted to only 600 acres (240 hectares), a second waiver in October reduced the fee to a penny an acre and 100,000 acres (45,000 hectares) changed hands. However, since income from land sales provided the government with essential funds, Governor Grey restored the Crown's pre-emptive right on his arrival in November 1845; this right, which extended throughout the country except in districts where the New Zealand Company acted in lieu of the Crown, was upheld until 1862. Grey also tightened government control over land by making it an offence for settlers to occupy or interfere with Maori land in any way, including by leasing. These moves were intended to curtail both settler and Maori excesses, but they also restricted the freedom of Maori to utilise their lands in the manner of their choice.

The opponents of the Treaty (of whom there were many, in both New Zealand and Britain) argued throughout the 1840s that it did not in fact guarantee Maori ownership of all land in New Zealand, especially land they were not occupying or cultivating. In 1844, a British parliamentary committee recommended that any 'unused' land should become the property of the Crown. At first the British government vehemently rejected this proposal; but it was included in dispatches to Governor Grey in 1846. Grey shelved the idea as too dangerous, and argued that it was also unnecessary because Maori could be persuaded to sell 'unused' land at a very low price. He then proceeded to buy the Wairarapa and most of the South Island, encouraging sales with promises of schools, hospitals and other benefits. The promises were mostly unfulfilled.

Thus, both Maori and settlers had major concerns about issues of land and sovereignty over these years. Most settlers knew something of the terms of the Treaty; the colony's newspapers occasionally printed the English text, and regularly debated its terms and the application of Treaty-based policies. In 1842, the Maori text of the Treaty was printed in the *Maori Messenger*, a newspaper produced by the government for Maori readers.

Hone Heke's pa at Ohaeawai. When British troops attacked Ohaeawai in July 1845 as part of the northern war, they were repulsed and suffered many casualties. A new pa defence system contributed to the Maori victory. This painting was by Cyprian Bridge, one of the senior British officers. WATERCOLOUR BY CYPRIAN BRIDGE, 1845; ALEXANDER TURNBULL LIBRARY, A-079-005

Throughout the 1840s, officials and missionaries soothed Maori fears by arguing that the Treaty was a compact between the Queen and the Maori people. During the northern war, Henry Williams printed four hundred copies of the Treaty in Maori, and spent many days explaining to Maori groups that, because the Treaty was 'a sacred compact', neither the Queen nor the Governor would allow any 'tinihanga' (tricky business). At all significant meetings, Governor Grey repeated the Treaty promises and said they would be kept. Despite such assurances, Maori were uneasy; but their fears seem to have been mollified by the conviction that they enjoyed a special relationship with Queen Victoria and with her governors. Grey, in particular, encouraged Maori to feel that they had a personal relationship with him as the Queen's representative; and some chiefs wrote to the Queen and sent gifts.

The Maori view of government as personal and approachable lasted into the 1860s, by which time responsibility for Maori policy and administration was passing from a 'benevolent' governor to a settler parliament. Maori leaders were ill-equipped to deal with the impersonal kind of government that began to develop in the 1850s.

Upsetting the balance

By 1850, the balance sheet of benefits and disadvantages brought by the British since 1840 might have appeared favourable to many Maori. Some tribes had profited from land sales. Many supplied settlements such as Auckland, New Plymouth and Wellington with produce, often grown in outlying districts and brought in by canoe or in Maori-owned coastal vessels. Maori were employed in public works and on private contracts. They built rush cottages for new immigrants, at rates that varied with the size of the dwelling. Money earned by Maori contributed to the welfare of both Maori and settler, as shops in towns such as Auckland relied on Maori trade.

At Otaki, in the Waikato and elsewhere, flourishing Maori communities had horses and livestock, ploughs, mills, and fields of wheat and other crops. Maori also took part in the social life of the colony. In Auckland, there were regattas, social gatherings at Government House, and celebrations for the Queen's birthday and the colony's anniversary day. Churches were established, and the government made some provision for schooling and hospitals. Not everyone could share in these benefits, however, especially those in more remote districts. And some Maori leaders were keenly aware of the shortfall between the Treaty's promises and the government's performance in matters affecting land, law and order.

Settler society grew rapidly in the 1850s. The governing bodies sought by settlers were established under the 1852 Constitution Act, which provided for six provincial councils and a national parliament (the General Assembly) with a nominated Upper House and an elected Lower House. The right to vote was given to all males over the age of twenty-one who had a freehold estate of a certain value. Since most Maori property was communally owned and not registered with a title derived from the Crown, only the few Maori men who held Crown grants qualified for the vote.

So when a new Governor, Thomas Gore Browne, arrived in 1855, he did not find the two races 'forming one people', as Grey's reports to the British government had led him to believe. Aware that Maori played no part in the country's government despite their essential role in the economy, he decided to retain responsibility for Maori affairs himself. This arrangement did not work well, because Maori and settler interests were inextricably mixed: decisions on legislation, regulations, and law and order applied to the population as a whole, and Parliament could assert its influence over Maori policy by restricting the financial allocations needed to implement policy.

Browne knew that many Maori communities were living outside effective government authority. Little was being done to help them deal with new laws and regulations, introduced by the provincial councils as well as by the General Assembly. At the same time, chiefly

[1] Tamati Ngapora, a chief noted for his caution and diplomacy, painted in 1882 by Gottfried Lindauer. In the 1840s, Ngapora asked Governor Grey for a law to strengthen chiefly authority so that it would benefit Maori and Pakeha. Grey ignored the request. PARTRIDGE COLLECTION, AUCKLAND ART GALLERY/TOI O TAMAKI

[2] J. C. Richmond, a Taranaki settler, spoke for some (though not all) settlers when he looked forward to the Treaty being overruled so that Maori claims to the extensive bushlands would no longer be able to 'damp the ardour and cramp the energies of the industrious white man'. Richmond was later Native Minister. ALEXANDER TURNBULL LIBRARY, F31822½

[3] George Grey in 1854. Arriving in 1845 at the age of thirty-three, Grey was a powerful figure in nineteenth-century New Zealand, as both Governor (1845–53, 1861–68) and Premier (1877–79). Although sympathetic to Maori, and interested in their culture, he was determined to bring them into a settler world. DRAWING BY GEORGE RICHMOND, 1854; AUCKLAND ART GALLERY/TOI O TAMAKI

authority was not getting the official support that many Maori had expected from the guarantee of rangatiratanga in the Treaty's second article. In short, neither the government nor Maori authority was meeting Maori needs in a period of rapid change. A number of chiefs expressed their disquiet and frustration at this state of affairs.

In the late 1850s, the General Assembly introduced measures to provide local self-government for Maori and to improve law and order; but funds were limited, and the moves were too little and too late. By that time, Maori were too suspicious of government intentions and had started to organise alternative solutions.

Towards the end of the 1850s, many Maori sensed that settler attitudes were changing. The Maori and European populations were now even at about sixty thousand each, and Pakeha numbers kept growing steadily. New colonists tended to look on the Treaty as an unavoidable nuisance, a hangover from the colony's early days, which would best be ignored but would have to be worked around or accepted – at least for a time.

Wiremu Tamihana Tarapipipi Te Waharoa and two children. In the 1840s, Te Waharoa built a model Christian village near Matamata with a church, clusters of houses for family groups, a large meeting house, a post office and a flour mill. The schoolhouse had boarding accommodation for a hundred students. There were orchards and fields of various crops. His confidence in achieving justice through lawful means was shaken by the Waikato confiscations. He petitioned the Queen in 1865 and the New Zealand Parliament in 1866, to no avail.
NICHOLL ALBUM VII, ALEXANDER TURNBULL LIBRARY, 46644½

Power and authority

While Grey was Governor, he pushed ahead with land purchases. Under his Chief Land Purchase Commissioner, Donald McLean, procedures were worked out for negotiating sales at tribal meetings. If a meeting agreed to a sale, the purchase deed would often be signed by many of the tribe. Grey and McLean worked hard to overcome Maori reluctance to sell, sometimes using intense pressure to persuade chiefs (as Grey did in the Wairarapa) and sometimes dealing with only a few owners (as McLean began to do in the early 1850s). During Grey's term, they succeeded in buying about 3 million acres (1.2 million hectares) in the North Island, and nearly 30 million acres (12 million hectares) in the South Island.

Government promises of schools, hospitals and generous land reserves often persuaded chiefs to accept ridiculously low purchase prices. But it was hard to hold the government to these promises. In the South Island, where land was bought for the Otago and Canterbury settlements, Maori leaders were disappointed by the lack of reserves or by their small size.

Appeals were made immediately to government officials. Matiaha Tiramorehu was one who wrote repeatedly, as he did in 1849: 'This is the commencement of our speaking (or complaining) to you … we shall never cease complaining to the white people who may hereafter come here.' He later appealed unsuccessfully to the Queen, and his complaints would form part of the Ngai Tahu claim against the Crown, settled in the 1990s.

As long as the government was buying land, settlers did not see the Treaty as too great a barrier to the colony's development. But when Maori owners refused to sell, it was a different matter. Although sales continued in the 1850s, tribal leaders began to realise that land negotiations were seriously threatening their authority; they started asking more searching questions about the relationship between power and authority as exercised by chiefs on the one hand and government on the other. The situation had changed rapidly since 1840, and the need to reconcile the old with the new challenged young Maori leaders to think of fresh solutions.

The idea of a Maori king was promoted by Tamehana Te Rauparaha and his cousin, Matene Te Whiwhi. In 1853, they travelled through central North Island districts, seeking agreement from tribes for the selection of a king – a leader who would protect their lands and give them unity. There was little Pakeha settlement in the central North Island, and the two men thought it should stay that way. Their idea of a veto on land sales caught on, and so too did the wish for a king. A great meeting in south Taranaki in 1854 decided that land sales should end, or at least be curtailed. In 1858, Te Wherowhero of Waikato was installed as the first Maori King.

The leaders of the King movement wanted to see Maori and Pakeha living in peace. Chiefs such as Wiremu Tamihana Te Waharoa of Ngati Haua at Matamata had thriving villages, busy with agriculture and trade. He believed that the Maori King and the British Queen could work together in something like a partnership, and that the Treaty had provided a place for both the mana of chieftainship and the mana of the Crown.

Officials thought differently, as did most settlers. The King stood for Maori independence, which was unacceptable to those who wanted the Waikato and central North Island opened up for settlement. But the officials were divided: some thought that colonisation and the Treaty were incompatible; others held to the belief that the Crown was morally bound to uphold the Treaty compact. Many – and finally most – Pakeha thought that a war to assert British sovereignty was inevitable. A land sale in Taranaki became the test case.

The Waitara purchase

In 1859, a Te Ati Awa chief named Teira offered to sell the Governor a piece of land at Waitara, north of New Plymouth. Other chiefs had an interest in the land, and normally the government would have negotiated with all parties before finalising the deal. But the government knew that some Te Ati Awa, including the senior chief, Wiremu Kingi, were totally opposed to the sale. By accepting Teira's offer, the government aimed to break the opposition – to force the sale against the wishes of an important chief.

The Governor and his advisers argued (wrongly) that Kingi was not an owner, but considered that more was at stake than land: the heart of the matter was sovereignty and the government's

[1] Mary Martin, wife of William Martin. Like many other settlers, she was opposed to war as a way of overcoming difficulties. In the 1850s, she travelled through the Waikato, later writing: 'Our path lay across a wide plain ... For miles we saw one great wheat field ... Carts were driven to and from the mill by their native owners; the women sat under the trees sewing flour bags ... and babies swarmed around ... We little dreamed that in ten years the peaceful industry of the whole district would cease and the land become a desert through our unhappy war.' L. HARPER COLLECTION, ALEXANDER TURNBULL LIBRARY, F100129½

[2] The Chief Justice, William Martin (sitting), with Bishop G. A. Selwyn, in about 1860. They were among a small group of Europeans who launched a campaign in defence of the Treaty principles. ALEXANDER TURNBULL LIBRARY, F37288½

authority to run the affairs of the country. Some argued also that Teira had a right, as a British subject, to sell his land if he chose to. But this was a new way of dealing with Maori land ownership, and was seen by some (Pakeha as well as Maori) as breaking the Treaty's guarantees regarding land. Taranaki settlers, by and large, saw the Waitara purchase simply as a test of the government's strength. Communal ownership and chiefly authority were now at risk, as the question of sovereignty and the government's rights became the cause for war.

The sale went ahead, and the deed of purchase was signed. In early 1860, when surveyors went to mark out the land, Kingi's people peacefully challenged them and disrupted their work. British troops were sent in to protect the surveyors, and for a year – from March 1860 to March 1861 – fighting utterly disrupted the lives of Maori and settlers in Taranaki.

Governor Thomas Gore Browne with his wife Harriet, two of their children, and a member of his staff. Harriet Browne defended her husband's actions over the Waitara purchase. RUCK ALBUMS, ALEXANDER TURNBULL LIBRARY, F152187½

William Martin was one of a small group of Pakeha who now launched a campaign to defend Treaty principles. Chief Justice from the early days of the colony, now retired, he wrote eloquently about the spirit of the Waitangi agreement:

> Here in New Zealand our nation has engaged in an enterprise most difficult, yet also most noble and worthy of England. We have undertaken to acquire these islands for the Crown and for our race, without violence and without fraud, and so that the native people, instead of being destroyed, should be protected and civilised. We have covenanted with these people, and assured them the full privileges of subjects of the Crown. To this undertaking the faith of the nation is pledged. By this means we secured a peaceable entrance for the Queen's authority into the country, and have in consequence gradually gained a firm hold upon it. The compact is binding irrevocably. We cannot repudiate it so long as we retain the benefit which we obtained by it.

Martin's book, *The Taranaki Question*, was intended for members of the British and New Zealand Parliaments as well as the public in both countries. But British sympathisers were too far off to have any real influence on New Zealand affairs, and Governor Browne and his ministers were committed to asserting sovereignty.

The Kohimarama Conference, 1860

Browne knew that he would be criticised, by both Pakeha and Maori, for his policy on the Waitara land purchase. He decided to rally as much Maori support as possible by holding a large gathering of chiefs at Mission Bay in Auckland — a meeting known since as the Kohimarama Conference. Never before had the government made such an effort to sound out Maori opinion, and the conference was the most representative Maori gathering ever held under its auspices. Up to two hundred chiefs from various North Island districts attended, and Te Matenga Taiaroa came from the South Island. Some of the chiefs had signed the Treaty in 1840; all were related to someone who had signed. The only leaders absent were from Taranaki, and some from Waikato.

The speeches and debates extended over three to four weeks. Donald McLean, the Native Secretary and Chief Land Purchase Commissioner, chaired the meeting and appears to have been responsible for translating speeches given in English into Maori. Great emphasis was placed on the humanitarian element in the Treaty. Governor Browne opened the conference by dwelling at length on the three articles, repeating the pledges made in 1840 by the Crown and by chiefs, and stressing that the Treaty was the first fruit of a new British policy towards indigenous races, one that invited them to unite with the colonists and 'become one people under one law'. In this, the Crown played a special role:

> It is your adoption by Her Majesty as her subjects which makes it impossible that the Maori people should be unjustly dispossessed of their lands or property. Every Maori is a member of the British Nation; he is protected by the same law as his English fellow subject; and it is because you are regarded by the Queen as a part of her own especial people that you have heard from the lips of each successive Governor the same words of peace and goodwill.

Browne claimed that Treaty promises had been faithfully observed by the Crown, and then warned the conference that the Maori people could forfeit the rights and privileges of British subjects through acts regarded as disloyal to the Queen or her representatives.

Some chiefs realised that the Governor was threatening to make Crown obligations under the Treaty conditional on Maori acceptance of government authority. During the conference, speakers began to express their fear that the government might use the King movement to justify abrogating the Treaty. It was obvious to most that the government was looking for an expression of loyalty to the Crown. Tamati Waka Nene noted that Maori had done better under the British and the Treaty than the Tahitians under the French. He urged chiefs to consider the situation carefully: 'I am not accepting the Pakeha for myself alone, but for the whole of us.' He reminded them that, though many were old enemies, 'we are able to meet together this day, under one roof', thanks to the Christianity brought by the British. He added: 'I know no Sovereign but the Queen.' Nene also noted the great changes in New Zealand over a few decades: 'My wife does not know how to weave garments … Let the Europeans weave garments for me.' Pointing to the European style of house construction, he added: 'Shall we again feed upon the roots of the wild convolvulus, fern root, and the pollen of the bulrush?' There was no answer from the assembly.

The site of the Kohimarama Conference, 1860 – the Melanesian mission buildings at Mission Bay, Auckland – photographed at the time by John Nicol Crombie. URQUHART ALBUM, ALEXANDER TURNBULL LIBRARY, F11974½

A record of the conference – its speeches and debate in English and Maori – was kept by a secretary, and each chief checked his speech for accuracy before it was printed. This document was widely distributed at the time, and a copy is held by Archives New Zealand. The speeches show that many of the chiefs had not known in 1840 what signing the Treaty would mean to their people. Only when British authority extended into their tribal area had they realised what the impact would be. 'It is true I received one blanket,' said a Te Ati Awa chief from Wellington. 'I did not understand what was meant by it; it was given to me without any explanation.' Other chiefs wondered if the Treaty was still in force when it had been broken by the spilling of blood – at Wairau, in the northern war and in Taranaki. Nga Puhi leaders, however, had a very definite understanding of the Treaty as a sacred covenant, unifying Maori with Maori, and Maori with Pakeha.

[1]　　　　　　　　　　　　　　　　　　　　[2]　　　　　　　　　　　　　　　　　　　　[3]

[1] Paora Tuhaere of Ngati Whatua complained that most tribes had not been represented at the 1840 meeting at Waitangi. 'But this [Kohimarama] conference is … the real treaty upon which the sovereignty of the Queen will hang because here are assembled chiefs from every quarter … to discuss questions and to seek out a path.' ALEXANDER TURNBULL LIBRARY, 73327½

[2] Tamehana Te Rauparaha (from Otaki) was presented to Queen Victoria during his visit to England in 1851–52. In the 1860s, he was a successful sheep farmer. WATERCOLOUR BY GEORGE FRENCH ANGAS, 1851; ALEXANDER TURNBULL LIBRARY, C-114-002

[3] Tawhiao, the Maori King from 1860 to his death in 1894, succeeded his father, Te Wherowhero. ALEXANDER TURNBULL LIBRARY, F50874½

At the end of the first week of the Kohimarama Conference, McLean moved into a detailed explanation of the Treaty. He stressed its protective character, and read again the Governor's opening address. Browne had emphasised the benefits of the Treaty by discussing the second and third articles before the first (in which sovereignty was ceded). Thus the transfer of power was played down and presented as 'nga tikanga me nga mana Kawanatanga katoa' ('the authority and all the powers of governance or government') – an expansion of the Maori text of the Treaty.

The explanation of the second article was important in that it spelt out (as the Maori text had not) that Maori rights to forests and fisheries, as well as lands, were guaranteed. These rights had been covered by the Treaty in English and were presumably explained at the 1840 meetings, because the Governor's words and the explanation at the 1860 conference were accepted by the chiefs without comment.

Tamehana Te Rauparaha and Matene Te Whiwhi were at the conference; these two early supporters of the King movement had now become cautious about its consequences. Tamehana told the chiefs that they should make their commitment to the Crown clear. At the final conference session, chiefs resolved that they were 'pledged to each other, to do nothing inconsistent with their declared recognition of the Queen's Sovereignty, and of the union of the two races'. And they promised to abstain from anything that might break this covenant that they had 'solemnly entered into'. This pledge became known as the Kohimarama Covenant;

along with the conference as a whole, it was as important to Maori understanding of the Treaty as the meetings of 1840. The covenant represented a new or renewed commitment to the Treaty as a sacred deed. Many northern chiefs had always seen it this way, but now this perception was shared by other chiefs from all over the country, including tribes who had not signed in 1840. It was an important ratification of the 1840 agreement.

Government mana and Maori mana

The Kohimarama Conference left Maori leaders with an assurance that Maori mana had been guaranteed. Governor Browne and Donald McLean had stressed this aspect of the Treaty in their explanations. But the government's move to call the conference was also a recognition of rangatiratanga, and the meeting gave the chiefs an opportunity to assert their leadership. Chiefs used it to express their dissatisfaction with the unequal participation of Maori in law and government. They petitioned the Governor to make the conference a permanent institution. The government agreed, and promised to reconvene the assembly in 1861. Parakaia of Ngati Raukawa expressed his pleasure at the prospect of greater participation: 'Now, perhaps, for the first time, shall I fully enter into the arrangements of the English Government, and now, perhaps, for the first time, will what I have to say be heard.'

But the conference did not fulfil the Governor's intentions. Browne failed to get support from the chiefs for his Waitara policy. Many chiefs were critical of the government's failure to investigate Waitara carefully; they thought the dispute should have been referred to mediation by appointed Maori leaders. Browne had also hoped that the chiefs would condemn the King movement. But, although they were willing to accept the Queen's authority in its protective sense, many chiefs were reluctant to admit that the authority of a chief like the Maori King could not sit alongside that of the Queen. After all, the concept of a shared authority or mana, which the Treaty seemed to allow, was applicable to all chiefs and not just to the King. If they condemned the King, they would be agreeing to a diminishing of the chiefly status guaranteed by the Treaty as they understood it.

By the first half of 1861, the government seemed to be drifting towards a showdown on the question of sovereignty. Some Waikato Maori had become involved in the Taranaki fighting. Te Wherowhero, the first King, had died in June 1860 and his son Tawhiao had succeeded him. The King movement looked as though it would last. Browne was even more determined that it should be crushed; the movement's very existence was interpreted by the government as a rejection of British sovereignty.

About this time, rumours were circulating through Maori communities that the Governor was bent on depriving Maori of their land and destroying chiefly authority. In March 1861, Browne wrote to the *Maori Messenger* denying this charge and quoting the second article of the Treaty. But in May he sent a proclamation to the Waikato tribes accusing them of violating the Treaty. He demanded 'submission without reserve, to the Queen's sovereignty and the authority of the law'.

Wiremu Tamihana wrote a thoughtful reply. The King's closest advisers, he said, had always understood that the Treaty provided a place for an independent Maori leadership in cooperation

Razor Back Hill on the military road south of Auckland, leading into the Waikato Basin, the heartland of the King movement. Between 1861 and 1863, Governor Grey had the road built as part of his strategy to break the power of the Kingitanga.
URQUHART ALBUM, ALEXANDER TURNBULL LIBRARY, F4643½

with the Queen's sovereignty or mana. Frederick Weld, the government minister responsible for Maori affairs, read the letter as a statement of 'Maori nationality' or independence. Like some others in government, he was sure that European supremacy had to be imposed on 'native races' by force.

Wars of sovereignty

War did come, despite the efforts of many Maori and Pakeha to avoid it. With the government and the King movement holding different views of sovereign rights, a meeting of minds was near impossible. Grey returned as Governor in November 1861 and tried to negotiate. But at the same time he had a military road built from Auckland into the Waikato. Maori were highly suspicious of his plans. The King movement tried, in January 1863, to get his agreement to their terms, based on the Treaty's guarantee of Maori mana over lands, forests and fisheries. The King's control in the Waikato was to be respected; the Governor's road-making ('cutting

A peaceful village near the Mangatawhiri River. The King movement regarded the Mangatawhiri as a boundary that government roadworks should not cross.
DRAWING BY JOSEPH SELLENY, c. 1858; HOCKEN LIBRARY, UARE TAOKA O HAKENA, UNIVERSITY OF OTAGO, DUNEDIN, NEG 00721

the land's backbone') was to stop at the Mangatawhiri River; and no armed steamers (then being built) were to be allowed up the Waikato River.

Grey was evasive, and for some months a paper war of articles and reports in newspapers kept Maori and settlers on tenterhooks. Violent incidents flared on the border south of Auckland, and the government ordered Maori to withdraw from their settlements adjacent to the town. Reluctantly, they did so. Then, in May 1863, war broke out again in Taranaki, when nine soldiers were ambushed and killed at Oakura. Militant factions of the King movement, including Rewi Maniapoto, were involved. Grey and the government decided to strike a blow at Waikato. On 12 July 1863, British troops crossed over the Mangatawhiri River and the wars began in earnest. A proclamation, issued too late to reach the Waikato, warned the King's supporters that those who 'rebelled' would have their lands confiscated.

The New Zealand wars developed into a series of engagements, steadily expanding through the central North Island. In 1863 and 1864, British troops pushed further up the Waikato than was justified by the Maori opposition. Early in 1864, a new operation was begun at Tauranga.

CHAPTER THREE: A MATTER OF MANA   69

Captain Westrupp's camp in Poverty Bay, 1865. Westrupp was one of the officers in charge of settler militia and kupapa troops during the campaigns of 1865 and 1868–71. RHODES ALBUM, ALEXANDER TURNBULL LIBRARY, F110532½

Another campaign was launched in south Taranaki at the end of 1864, designed to make Taranaki habitable for settlers and to punish the independent-minded Ngati Ruanui. At this point, fighting became more extreme on both sides. The spread of the Pai Marire movement through North Island districts made the battlefield more complex. Developed in south Taranaki in 1862 as an attempt at peaceful adjustment to change, Pai Marire took a more violent turn from 1864. War brought many forms of pressure to Maori groups.

The war changed in character from the mid 1860s. The set-piece battles of the Waikato front gave way to protracted guerrilla campaigns on the North Island's west and east coasts. New leaders – Te Kooti and Titokowaru – appeared later in the decade as the war dragged to an uncertain and untidy end. What had started as moves against Taranaki and Waikato finally affected almost all North Island districts, directly or indirectly (the South Island tribes were little involved).

From the outset, the struggle was an unequal one. The first government troops were

Washing day at a military camp in the Waikato. Within two years of the invasion of the Waikato by British troops, the landscape had changed dramatically. The densely populated and cultivated land was confiscated and military townships were established at Hamilton, Cambridge, Alexandra (Pirongia) and Kihikihi. Privates were allocated 50-acre sections, while commissioned officers received larger grants. RHODES ALBUM, ALEXANDER TURNBULL LIBRARY, F4135½

British Imperial regiments, which at their height numbered over eleven thousand. Military supplies were ample, and the settler population was ready with further support (for many, the war was a commercial boon). Early in the Waikato campaign, local settlers joined the fighting, and their ranks were swelled by volunteers recruited in Australia. These colonial forces gradually supplanted the British troops, which began to withdraw in 1865. Maori who fought on the Queen's side played an increasingly important part, taking the opportunity to settle old scores against traditional enemies, a factor that marked the last stages of the fighting with bitterness and desperation. Maori who resisted were ill equipped to effect a lasting victory; they were outnumbered in every major confrontation, and they maintained their lines of supply with difficulty.

Heni Te Kirikaramu (also known as Jane Foley) was one of a number of women who fought in the wars of the 1860s. She stands here with the red silk flag, named Aotearoa, which she made for a Ngati Paoa leader, Wi Koka, when fighting with Kingitanga forces in the Hunua range south of Auckland. She was in the battle of Gate Pa near Tauranga but later fought on the government side with Te Arawa troops.
MUSEUM OF NEW ZEALAND TE PAPA TONGAREWA, B10370

Confiscations

The war was also waged on the political front. Legislation passed by the General Assembly provided statutory powers to support the war of sovereignty. The New Zealand Settlements Act 1863 allowed for confiscation of Maori land as a punishment for the war. The Act did grievous damage to Maori–Pakeha relationships, for it left the Maori people with a deep sense of injustice. Lands were to be confiscated from those in 'rebellion' in any district of the colony whatsoever; settlers would be established on these lands in sufficient numbers to deter Maori from further resistance; whatever land remained would be sold to defray war costs. Confiscation dispossessed 'friendly' Maori (kupapa) along with the 'rebels'. Kupapa (unlike 'rebels') might be given compensation by a court of arbitration, but this proved a doubtful benefit.

By an official proclamation issued in December 1864, over 3 million acres (1.2 million hectares) were confiscated in the Waikato, Bay of Plenty and Taranaki. Although about half of

A group of prisoners, captured at Weraroa pa at Waitotara, Taranaki, on a prison hulk in Wellington Harbour. The Suppression of Rebellion Act 1863 sanctioned extreme colony-wide measures to deal with 'rebellion'. In 1865, the Indemnity Act gave absolution for the use of force against Maori, at a time when the distinction between crime and acts of war was not always clearly drawn. ALEXANDER TURNBULL LIBRARY, F103605½

this area was subsequently paid for or returned to Maori ownership, the confiscation was manifestly unjust. Waikato lost almost all their lands, while Ngati Maniapoto territory went untouched; Ngati Haua (Wiremu Tamihana's tribe) lost a section of their land, as did Ngai Te Rangi at Tauranga. These groups included both 'friendly' Maori and 'rebels'. The King and his followers, virtually homeless, retreated into Maniapoto lands where they would always be visitors. Confiscation came to be seen by most Maori as a violation of the Treaty, leaving a permanent legacy of bitterness.

In Taranaki, Maori homes, pa and cultivations were destroyed indiscriminately. The confiscation of the entire coastal strip of the region dispossessed large numbers of Maori and created a bitterness towards the government as lasting as that in the Waikato. Here, too, many Maori considered the moves a breach of the Treaty. By the latter part of the 1860s, even Maori not directly involved in confiscation agreed; many felt that such a serious attack on the Treaty had an impact on all tribes.

CHAPTER THREE: A MATTER OF MANA

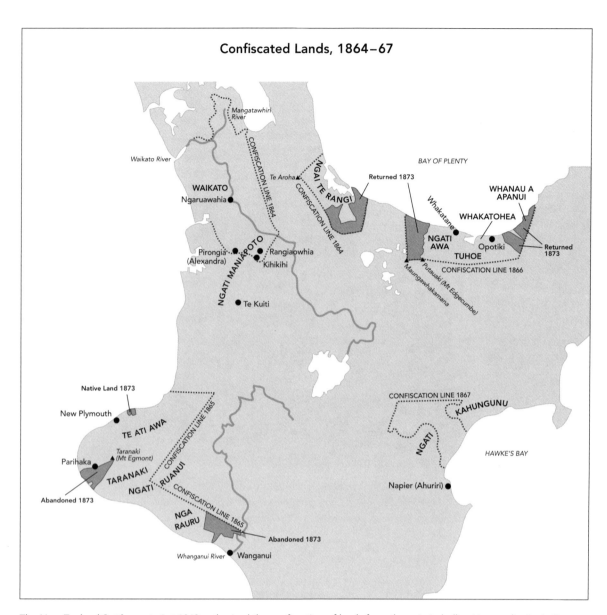

The New Zealand Settlements Act 1863 authorised the confiscation of lands from those in 'rebellion' in any district in New Zealand. This map shows the confiscation lines. Some of the land was later returned and some paid for. The following table shows the amount of land confiscated. The areas are in acres (1 acre = 0.4 hectares).

Locality	Area originally confiscated	Area purchased	Area returned	Area finally confiscated
Taranaki	1,275,000	557,000	256,000	462,000
Waikato	1,202,172	—	314,264	887,908
Tauranga	290,000	240,250	—	49,750
Opotiki	448,000	6,340	230,600	211,060
				1,610,718

In Poverty Bay, some 50,000 acres were confiscated.

SOURCES: THE MAP (BASED ON INFORMATION IN THE *APPENDIX TO THE JOURNALS OF THE LEGISLATIVE COUNCIL*, 1875) IS FROM JUDITH BINNEY, JUDITH BASSETT, AND ERIK OLSSEN, *THE PEOPLE AND THE LAND: TE TANGATA ME TE WHENUA*, WELLINGTON, 1990. THE FIGURES IN THE TABLE ARE DERIVED FROM 'THE ROYAL COMMISSION ON CONFISCATED LANDS', AJHR, 1928, G-7, PP.6–22, AND 'REPORT OF THE NATIVE LAND CLAIMS COMMISSION', AJHR, 1921–22, G-5, PP.14–20.

Mete Kingi of Wanganui, who attended the Kohimarama Conference, was the first Member for Western Maori in the House of Representatives, 1868–70. This photograph was taken in Christchurch by A. C. Barker in 1869. CANTERBURY MUSEUM, BARKER ALBUM 2, 420F

British withdrawal

As the war dragged on, many British troops and their officers came to the conclusion that they were simply fighting for land on behalf of the settlers, against an enemy they respected. Many settlers, too, were deeply disturbed that two peoples who had aimed to make a new nation together had ended up in violent conflict. New Zealand's resources were being stretched to the limit, and by the end of the decade there was a widespread yearning for peace.

The fighting was drawing to an untidy conclusion as the last British troops left towards the end of the 1860s; the British government determined to pour no more money into New Zealand. The colonial government, now fully responsible for the Maori people, was more prepared to state openly that Maori had signed away their control of the country in 1840. But it was sensitive to criticism from abroad of its policies and actions. Comments in the British Parliament and British press on the New Zealand government's treatment of Maori had often been hostile and scathing through the 1860s. *The Times* – at first guarded in its criticism – had increasingly questioned the actions of the settler government.

Also vocal was the humanitarian lobby that had been so active in the years before 1840, encouraging the Colonial Office to believe that settlement and the protection of Maori could be reconciled and made to work in New Zealand. In 1840, the same voices had promoted the idea of amalgamation, of the Maori inhabitants and British settlers eventually making 'one people' – a goal that survived even in the midst of war and outrage. The idealism persisted:

CHAPTER THREE: A MATTER OF MANA   75

A meeting at Mete Kingi's house, Wanganui, probably in the mid 1860s. The formality of the occasion is indicated by Mete Kingi (in the cloak) and the man speaking to him, probably Isaac Featherston, Superintendent of the Wellington Province.
ALEXANDER TURNBULL LIBRARY, G39-¹/₁

many thoughtful settlers recognised that significant groups of Maori had been allied to Pakeha throughout the war; many also understood the reasons for Maori resistance, and respected the Maori position. The dilemma, however, was how to get Maori to see what settlers regarded as the inevitable solution – a full acceptance by Maori of the Crown's sovereign rights, with all the benefits and responsibilities this entailed. The various shades of political opinion on Maori rights had come together on one point – if force failed, then the law must succeed in achieving the desired supremacy.

Finding a way to bring Maori into the General Assembly was considered essential; having a substantial section of the colony's population not directly represented was neither desirable nor wise. Maori were not acquiring property qualifications (individual title held under a Crown grant) fast enough to gain the franchise, and a stop-gap measure was needed. In 1867, legislation allowed for four Maori members to sit in the House of Representatives and gave the vote to all Maori men aged twenty-one years or over. (As voting was by declaration of preference to the returning officer, Maori were unable to cast their vote in secret.) With the majority of Maori voters in the North Island, the provision for Maori seats was generally accepted by the General Assembly: it counter-balanced provision made for gold miners in the South Island and was to end in 1872. It was extended, however, and Maori soon sat in the Legislative Council as well. In general, the Maori people were subject to the law administered by European magistrates and judges, and were entitled to sit on juries in certain circumstances. By the end of the 1860s, the policy of amalgamation was firmly established.

Some allowances were made for differences in the Maori situation, however. Special provision was introduced for Maori education, in the form of a native school system (finally discontinued in 1969) that would ultimately foster an entirely English speaking population; Maori children were soon able to enter the mainstream primary school system as well. The Native Department, established in the early 1860s, was allowed to continue, with Donald McLean as Native Minister from 1869 to the mid 1870s. McLean realised that the acceptance of British sovereignty was inevitably a slow process, and was prepared to adopt a gradualist approach in dealing with Maori issues.

It was some time before Maori leaders fully realised that responsibility for their affairs had been transferred from the British to the New Zealand government. That the Queen and her British Parliament had washed their hands of the Waitangi covenant was hard to believe – but they had.

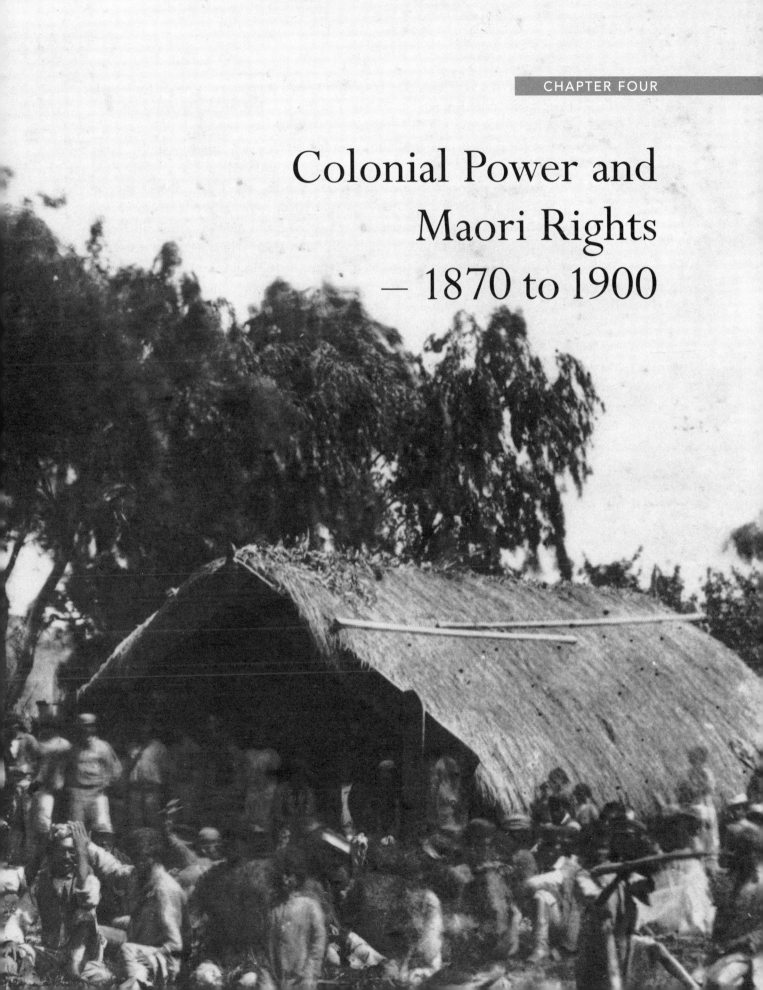

CHAPTER FOUR

Colonial Power and Maori Rights — 1870 to 1900

The wars finally ended around 1870. The government could claim a victory on the battlefield, albeit a narrow one. Politicians now spoke less of the Treaty's benefits to Maori and more of Maori obligations under it.

As a new colonial society emerged in a burst of immigration and development, the Treaty receded from settler consciousness. To immigrants with little knowledge of early New Zealand, the Waitangi agreement seemed largely irrelevant, a part of the country's history. The Maori population appeared to be declining steadily; there were likely to be few survivors. Yet the Treaty could not be completely ignored. The government still had to deal with Maori land, and sometimes with fisheries too. Occasionally, when Maori protest increased in the late 1870s and 1880s, the government was forced to discuss the 1840 agreement publicly. Official statements usually disparaged the Treaty, or talked of Maori commitments. It was a far cry from the ideals expressed at Waitangi.

For Maori, however, the Treaty became more relevant than ever after 1870, especially in the North Island as new areas were opened up for development. Government jurisdiction and Pakeha settlement began to touch the most remote Maori villages, providing Maori with common cause across tribes and partly overriding tribal differences. Whether or not iwi or hapu had signed the Treaty, the agreement increasingly became the basis for protest. Despite the fine words of governments, both British and colonial, Treaty promises had not been fulfilled. Disappointed and frustrated, many Maori forged a unity of purpose, looking to the Treaty for support in their conflicts with the government now that warfare had failed. Maori grievances, diverse and sometimes confused in their presentation, found kotahitanga (unity) in the Treaty.

The Native Land Court

In the years after the wars, the most serious attack on the vitality of Maori life came from the Native Land Court. The court had its origins in general dissatisfaction with the Crown land purchase system, in particular the pre-emptive right that was granted to the Crown by the Treaty. The need for a properly constituted tribunal to determine ownership of Maori land had been acknowledged for some years by the Colonial Office, by the New Zealand government, and by settlers who were impatient for direct dealing in Maori land. The concept also had supporters among Maori groups alarmed by the Waitara dispute and, in some instances, interested in handling their own land sales.

The Native Lands Act 1862 provided for a court comprising a panel of chiefs, presided over by a European magistrate. The court would determine the customary rights of ownership in an area of land, and issue a certificate of title in favour of the appropriate tribe, community or individuals. Once confirmed by the Governor, the certificate could be exchanged for a title granted by the Crown, whereupon customary title was extinguished. With the certificate of

[previous page] Donald McLean, Superintendent of Hawke's Bay, meeting with Maori to purchase Wairoa, 1865.
RHODES ALBUM, ALEXANDER TURNBULL LIBRARY, F110517½

Maori Population Trends, 1874–2001

Census Year	Maori Population	Total Population	Census Year	Maori Population	Total Population
1874	47,330	344,984	1956	137,151	2,174,062
1881	46,141	534,030	1966	201,159	2,676,919
1891	44,177	668,632	1976	270,035	3,129,383
1901	45,549	815,862	1986	405,309	3,307,084
1911	52,723	1,058,312	1991	434,847	3,373,926
1921	56,987	1,271,668	1996	523,371	3,618,300
1936	82,326	1,573,812	2001	526,281	3,737,277
1945	98,744	1,702,330			

SOURCE: FIGURES DERIVED FROM CENSUS RETURNS

title, owners were free to sell, lease or exchange their land interests to any person or persons. Sale could proceed directly from Maori to settler. (From 1894, the court's registration of the certificate led directly to a Crown grant.)

The 1862 Act was presented as a means of ascertaining and defining Treaty rights. As guaranteed by the Treaty's second article, ownership of land would be determined; as promised under the third article, Maori would have the same rights as other citizens. But in effect the Act's main purpose was to open up the North Island to settlement and development by speeding up settlers' access to land; politicians saw this as advantageous to Maori in that it would hasten their amalgamation, with all the benefits of civilisation that would bring.

The aspiration was genuine enough: by such means were Maori to be drawn into the mainstream of colonial life, enjoy the same rights and responsibilities as settlers, and flourish equally in a prosperous and progressive colony. It was assumed that Maori would initially establish the ownership of land as a tribe or hapu, with small pieces being cut out to sell in a gradual process. Few anticipated the extent to which Maori would use the Act to shed substantial blocks of land.

The Governor, in granting title, had the option of setting aside some of the land being sold as reserves for Maori; otherwise, the Act lacked safeguards against speculative purchasing and the total alienation of land. Prospective purchasers could now lease land and start dealing with owners prior to the award of title — at their own risk, but not illegally as under the Native Land Purchase Ordinance 1846. The 1862 Act laid the burden of costs — survey charges, court fees and other expenses related to hearings — largely on Maori.

War intervened, however, and the Act came into operation only in the Kaipara district and at Coromandel. It was initially regarded as an experiment, but in December 1864 the government moved to extend the Act's operations over the whole country. Since the 1862 Act had waived Crown pre-emption, the Native Land Purchase Department was no longer needed and was closed down; commissions to purchase land on behalf of the Crown were revoked.

More Native Lands Acts

The Native Land Court was now the main vehicle for converting Maori customary land into freehold land for purchase or lease by Europeans. A new Native Lands Act, passed in 1865, carried over most of the provisions of the 1862 Act. But it abandoned the panel of chiefs under a magistrate or judge, and set up a court on more formal lines akin to the Supreme Court; a judge now sat at each district hearing, assisted by one or two Maori assessors.

The 1865 Act brought in revolutionary changes. Evidence now had to be given formally in court; the opportunity for the chiefs, acting as a commission of inquiry, to seek out reliable local evidence and investigate the blocks informally was removed. Any Maori claiming a right in a land block could initiate a court investigation, and so force all members of a tribe to defend their own rights in the land. Certificate of title was seldom granted to a tribe or hapu as a whole. Normal practice was to vest title in ten chiefs (or fewer), who were supposed to be trustees for their tribe. In fact, they were able to sell their interest in the land and, if one chief died, his interest vested in the remaining titleholders. The land blocks often comprised hundreds of thousands of acres. The cost of taking claims to court, getting land surveyed and other expenses often got Maori leaders heavily into debt, and to repay loans they had to sell more land. Struggles between hapu were not uncommon, with some owners missing out altogether.

The 1865 Act effectively severed the threads of Crown protection; the way was now open for settlers to force Maori to relinquish their land. Legislators had ignored cautious counsels, and politicians justified the Act as encouraging 'amalgamation', equality of rights and the rapid 'Europeanisation' of land. It was described as 'the abandonment of the system of protectorate or dry-nursing', and as being in the best interests of Maori.

Yet the negative impact on Maori was soon visible. After the wars, about 1.6 million acres (650,000 hectares) of Maori land were taken through confiscation; the Native Lands Act 1865 and the work of the Native (later Maori) Land Court led to far more land being lost, and eventually affected all tribes. Subsequent amendments compounded the problems, and caused even tough politicians to reconsider their actions. Various remedies were suggested, but most did not find their way into legislation; where they did, they were often circumvented by presiding judges who disagreed with government officials.

The Native Land Act 1873 was an attempt to provide some protection for Maori. All owners of a block (often numbering hundreds) were now to be named in the certificate of title. This, in fact, led to the partitioning of large blocks into smaller holdings. From 1865, the court also had powers to decide succession: individual shares, on the death of their owners, were to pass to all natural heirs, unless a will specified otherwise. With each generation, the shares became smaller. The partitioning of large blocks, together with succession, caused land ownership to become fragmented and made it easier for blocks to be bought up. This situation persisted into the 1980s.

At best, the 1873 Act slowed down the alienation of land. But Parliament's primary aim was to establish a system of individual title in place of Maori communal title, and a succession of Acts in the 1880s added to the confusion created by the 1865 legislation. Under the Native Land Court, Maori customary land was converted into legal title as a preliminary to direct purchase either by the government or by individual settlers. Maori land holdings diminished steadily. Many aspects of the land alienation process came to be seen as breaches of the Treaty, and would be heard in claims brought before the Waitangi Tribunal in the late twentieth century.

A commission of inquiry

In 1891, a government commission of inquiry examined the administration of Maori land laws. Its report, submitted by W. L. Rees and James Carroll, condemned the Native Land Court's record over the preceding quarter-century:

> Numerous witnesses bear testimony to the gradual deterioration of the Native Land Court. It takes a longer time now to hear a case than formerly. Its fees and charges are greatly in excess of what they were. Its adjournments and postponements are more frequent and inconvenient. The applications for rehearings are greatly increased. It has gradually lost every characteristic of a Native Court, and has become entirely European – as Hone Peeti said, 'only the name remaining'. It has brought into existence a regular system of concocting false claims, by which the real owners are often driven out, and their land given to clever rogues of their own race. It no longer visits the land, nor guides and advises the Natives in friendly settlements. Its demand for excessive daily fees is so imperious that Natives not able to pay are refused a hearing, and thus in many cases the real owners are compelled to stand by and see their land given to strangers. Its decisions are never final. Even after years of occupation under a certificate, Crown grant, or transfer title, the occupier is liable to litigation, ejectment, and ruin owing to the numerous methods available for setting them at nought, or, at any rate, interfering with them through the ever varying conditions of the law.
>
> So complete has the confusion both in law and practice become that lawyers of high standing and extensive practice have testified on oath that if the Legislature had desired to create a state of confusion and anarchy in Native-land titles it could not have hoped to be more successful than it has been. Were it not that the facts are vouched upon the testimony of men whose character is above suspicion and whose knowledge is undoubted, it would be well-nigh impossible to believe that a state of such disorder could exist.

Between 1870 and 1892, government purchases of Maori land, financed at first under the Immigration and Public Works Act 1870, amounted to over 5 million acres (2 million hectares). By 1865, the entire South Island and Stewart Island had been purchased, apart from 175,000 acres (71,000 hectares) of reserves and land exempted from sale. But by 1892, Maori in the South Island had only a few reserves, and many were regarded as landless; in the North Island, the Maori people owned a little over a third of the land area, about 11 million acres (4.5 million hectares), of which a quarter was leased to Pakeha. Where restrictions were placed

A meeting to discuss land issues, held at Ahipara in the far north, in the late nineteenth century.
TAAFE COLLECTION, ALEXANDER TURNBULL LIBRARY, F26780½

on land sales, these proved no safeguard. Where reserves were made, they were not adequately protected. A long history of government maladministration and Maori grievance ensued, one that would not be seriously addressed until the 1990s.

By around 1900, another 3 million acres (1.2 million hectares) of Maori land had passed through the Native Land Court and been sold. Land loss continued until at least 1930. Numerous legislative Acts and two major commissions of inquiry did not halt the process. As Maori lands were reduced, Maori society increasingly suffered.

In order to settle their difficulties and grievances over land, Maori were encouraged, officially and privately, to make use of the law, a suggestion vigorously taken up in the 1870s. Some cases dragged on for years as they passed through either the Native Land Court or the main court system. Experience in the courts, however, demonstrated that the Treaty afforded Maori little protection. A landmark case in 1877 involved Wiremu Parata (a Ngati Toa and Te Ati Awa politician) and the Anglican Bishop of Wellington, Octavius Hadfield. Land had been given to the Church of England for educational purposes for Ngati Toa; efforts had been made

[1] James Prendergast, about 1886; Chief Justice of the Supreme Court, 1875–99. ALEXANDER TURNBULL LIBRARY, F79213½

[2] Wiremu Te Kakakura Parata, about 1876; farmer and Member of the House of Representatives, 1871–75.
ALEXANDER TURNBULL LIBRARY, F96331½

for some time to have this land returned to its former Maori owners because the terms of the original gift were not being fulfilled. Meanwhile, a Crown grant for the land had been issued to the church. The case was likely to call into question all similar religious, charitable and educational trusts in the colony, as the government knew. In deciding against Wi Parata, Chief Justice James Prendergast took the view that Maori were not sufficiently organised to have customs that the law could recognise; and that once a Crown grant had been issued, the courts were not going to test how accurately the Maori customary title had been investigated and extinguished. Prendergast's approach was influential; it set a precedent for a number of cases through the nineteenth and twentieth centuries.

Fisheries and food-gathering rights

Early European accounts emphasised the importance of fish and fishing in Maori life. In about 1840, William Colenso wrote: 'The seas around their coasts swarmed with excellent fish and crayfish ... Sometimes they would go in large canoes to the deep sea fishing, to some well known shoal or rock, 5 to 10 miles [8 to 16 kilometres] from the shore, and return with a quantity of large cod, snapper and other prime fish.' The catch was valuable to hapu both for

Fisheries were a major source of food for Maori, and fishing grounds were often jealously guarded. This pen and ink sketch of a Thames beach with fish strung up to dry was done by Charles Heaphy. AUCKLAND MUSEUM/TAMAKI PAENGA HIRA, PD56(85)1(9)

food and for trade. It was customary for tribes to share resources by exchanging fish for other delicacies. Edward Shortland, in his *Traditions and Superstitions of the New Zealanders*, published in 1856, noted:

> The inhabitants of the villages on the upper parts of the river Wanganui are celebrated parrot catchers … Every evening, the birds taken during the day are roasted over fires, and then potted in calabashes in their grease … Thus preserved, parrots and other birds are … sent as presents to parts of the country, where they are scarce; and in due time a return present of dried fish, or something else not to be obtained easily in an inland country, is received.

Certain fishing grounds were often used exclusively by particular hapu. Others could use them, but only with permission; sometimes, rights could be transferred. In the first two decades or more after 1840, the government gave some recognition to such customary rights, although there was no set policy. The Protector of Aborigines, for instance, had noted the significance of eel reserves. Such possessions were much prized, and rights of access or transfer of rights were often negotiated. In early land sales, Maori fishing rights were sometimes specifically acknowledged: George Clarke (junior) reserved fishing places in Wanganui during the settlement of the New Zealand Company purchase, and some were recognised in

In the 1880s, Ngai Te Rangi leader Hori Ngatai told the Governor of his concern about the lack of protection for his fishing rights in Tauranga Harbour. Fishing in the harbour had increased as Pakeha settlement spread, and people had encroached on areas that Ngatai customarily considered to be Ngai Te Rangi's. Recent legislation had also restricted Maori ability to claim such rights.
ALEXANDER TURNBULL LIBRARY, F111250½

the South Island. But verbal agreements were more usual and, with no written or legal guarantee, these were always vulnerable.

At that time, fish were abundant in New Zealand waters. However, tensions over access to fisheries developed as settlement expanded. From the 1850s, and to varying degrees around the country, the fishing and food-gathering rights confirmed by the Treaty were increasingly undermined or whittled away. In 1855, the resident magistrate at Kaipara, north of Auckland, wrote to Attorney-General William Swainson:

> On the West Coast between high and low water marks, there exists ... a bed of toheroa. This fishery is highly valued by the natives. At present, the value of the fishery as ... food has been discovered by the Europeans, and large quantities are carried [away] for the use of the workmen on the European stations.

Ngati Whatua, the local tribe, were asking for a rental to be paid for such use, but the Europeans were claiming that the land below high-water mark was the property of the Crown and for public use. Swainson was not too sure how to handle the complaint; it raised issues not only of Maori fishing rights but of foreshore rights too.

During the first decades of settlement, the foreshore was not automatically considered to be Crown property. The common law brought to New Zealand in 1840 recognised Maori customary rights to land and (in certain places) to the foreshore, which was seen by Maori as an extension of the land. Swainson's caution, however, indicates some general uncertainty about the matter. Historian Alan Ward notes in the *National Overview: Volume 1* (1997) that, with the establishment of the Native Land Court, customary rights to the foreshore were confirmed (or conceded), but only to specific foreshores rather than to the totality of the country's foreshores.

This was evident in a conflict between companies seeking gold-mining rights on the Thames foreshore and Maori owners of the adjacent land. Certain hapu of Ngati Maru had customary rights to fish the extensive mud-flats, which were famous flounder grounds. As one government agent observed, Maori fishing rights to mud-flats and offshore had not been seriously questioned before, although by this time government tended to assume that sale of the land meant that native title over adjacent foreshore was extinguished, unless specifically reserved. In the Thames case, Maori owned the adjoined land, and their rights to the foreshore had already been recognised by the Crown – first, in making gold-mining agreements and then in the Goldfields Act Amendment Act 1868.

The Crown, placed in an awkward position, passed the Shortland Beach Act 1869, which debarred private parties from purchasing or leasing the foreshore in question; compensation was paid to the Maori owners of adjoining land in the form of mining rights. The Shortland Beach Act related only to this piece of land, and the Crown might have moved to assert its prerogative to foreshore rights throughout the country, but did not do so. In 1870, however, Judge Fenton, in the Kauwaeranga judgement in the Native Land Court, expressed a concern that 'evil conseqences ... might ensue from judicially declaring the soil of the foreshore ... vested absolutely in the natives'. From then on, the court generally refrained from granting titles of this kind in the foreshore, although Ward notes that 'the question of whether it had the right or the power to do so still remained, as did the question of whether the foreshore was Maori customary land'. By the mid 1870s, however, there appears to be a firming up of government policy. With respect to foreshores, the Crown now relied on specific legislative provision, such as the Harbours Act 1878 (revised 1950); this stated that no part of the foreshore was to be granted or given away, other than with the authority of a special Act of Parliament.

Fishing rights were a different matter. The Crown drew a distinction between land (and water) rights and fishing rights, arguing that the latter did not involve ownership of land or land under the water. Maori fishing rights were increasingly confined to special (though seldom exclusive) usage rights in specific instances. This was allowed for in the Fish Protection Act 1877 and its later amendments and re-enactments. The Act dealt with salt- and fresh-water fisheries. Section 8 contained one of the very few references to the Treaty in nineteenth-century legislation:

> Nothing in this Act contained shall be deemed to repeal, alter, or affect any of the provisions of the Treaty of Waitangi, or to take away, annul, or abridge any of the rights of the aboriginal natives to any fishery secured to them thereunder.

(This section was to be re-enacted in section 88 (2) of the Fisheries Act 1983.) But in practice, it did not make Maori fishing rights secure under law. From time to time further enactments or provisions were made, but these offered small compensation for the extensive rights guaranteed in the Treaty's second article.

Other steps further diminished the recognition of Maori fishing rights. In 1903, the Coal Mines Amendment Act declared that the beds of navigable rivers belonged to the Crown. By 1910, the Crown was claiming that it had absolute ownership of lake beds as well (but this

A river board team, sent to open the bar of Lake Onoke. By opening the bar, settlers could reduce flooding; Maori needed to close it periodically in order to maintain their fishery. BURTON BROS. COLLECTION, ALEXANDER TURNBULL LIBRARY, F55757½

would be contested). Maori fishing and food-gathering rights were also being damaged by the introduction of foreign species – fish and birds that affected local species. Legislation introduced in the 1860s to protect the imported species and to control the taking of shellfish was strongly resented by Maori.

Protests over fishing rights

From the 1860s, however, Maori had begun to battle for fishing rights – offshore, and in foreshores, lakes, rivers and harbours. For example, Maori leaders and Pakeha officials drew the government's attention to the depletion of pipi beds in the Manukau Harbour and of oyster beds in the Bay of Islands. In 1869, James Mackay (a long-serving government officer in the Thames area) reported on Maori rights, as he saw them:

> The Natives occasionally exercise certain privileges or rights over tidal lands. They are not considered as the common property of all Natives in the Colony; but certain hapus or tribes have the right to fish over one mud flat and other Natives over another. Sometimes even this goes so far as to give certain rights out at sea. For instance, at Katikati Harbour, one tribe of Natives have a right to fish within the line of tide-rip; another tribe of Natives have the right to fish outside the tide-rip.

In 1877, Hori Kerei Taiaroa, Member of the House of Representatives for Southern Maori, wanted to know by what authority Europeans were 'plundering all the oysters and fish' from

Lake Onoke, with its opening into Palliser Bay, South Wairarapa, in the 1940s. ALEXANDER TURNBULL LIBRARY, F55753½

the Mangahoe Inlet in Otago and selling them in Dunedin. When John Ballance, then Minister of Native Affairs, visited Tauranga in 1885, the Ngai Te Rangi leader Hori Ngatai spoke plainly about the government's claim that the Crown owned the foreshore and seabed:

> Now, with regard to the land below high water mark immediately in front of where I live, I consider that that is part and parcel of my own land ... part of my own garden ... I am now speaking of the fishing-grounds inside the Tauranga Harbour. My mana over these places has never been taken away. I have always held authority over these fishing-places and preserved them; and no tribe is allowed to come here and fish without my consent being given. But now ... people [Europeans] ... are constantly here whenever they like to fish. I ask that our ... authority over these fishing-grounds may be upheld.

Sometimes a battle for fishing rights would go on for decades, as with the Wairarapa lakes dispute. The two lakes were a very important source of food for local Maori. Eels were caught in large numbers at the shingle bar that dammed the seaward end of the lower lake (Onoke), and dried eels were given away as gifts or exchanged with other tribes for preserved birds and shellfish. In 1853, the government purchased some land next to the lakeshore, and recognised Maori fishing rights in the area. But in the 1860s, local settlers pressured the government to open the shingle bar so that the lake would not flood the surrounding lands. Piripi Te Maari, a successful farmer in the area, was among those who appealed to the government to uphold the original agreement acknowledging Maori rights along the lakeshore. Settlers wanted the government to buy the lakes and quash Maori rights.

In 1886, Te Maari agreed to a compromise: the shingle bar would be opened for ten months of the year and closed only in February and March, at the height of the fishing season. The Ruamahanga River Board objected, and twice tried to force the bar open. Te Maari petitioned the government twice, secured a commission of inquiry (which was non-committal), took a case to the Court of Appeal (which dismissed it), threatened to go to the Privy Council and, in 1895, finally secured a government decision: the bar would be opened permanently and the Maori owners of the lakes would receive compensation for costs. The Crown gave the owners land in distant Mangakino – small recompense for decades of struggle and an unsatisfactory settlement.

Maori elsewhere faced similar difficulties, and these would continue into the twentieth century. In the South Island, in 1868, land was set aside to give access to fisheries – 212 acres (86 hectares) in Canterbury and 112 acres (45 hectares) in Otago. Yet the 1891 Commission on Middle Island Native Claims reported:

> The Natives at Waitaki … are very badly off for food-supplies … and, to make matters more trying for them, they cannot fish in the Waitaki for eels or whitebait, owing to that river being stocked with imported fish …
>
> The importance now of setting apart fishery easements for the Natives [at Lake Ellesmere] is much greater than heretofore, as they are gradually being deprived of all their former privileges in the settled parts of the country through the drainage of the land, as well as through all the rivers, lakes, and lagoons being stocked with imported fish.

In 1903, Tame Parata, the Member of the House of Representatives for Southern Maori, claimed that:

> … along the coast of Otago, and right up to Akaroa, there are a number of fishing-grounds that have been handed down to the Maoris by their ancestors, but have been overrun and made use of by everybody, including Europeans, in recent years. I do not object to the Europeans fishing at these places, but these reefs should be to some extent protected for the benefit of the Maoris; and there are other parts of the sea which are available for European fishermen to make use of.

Protests continued, as Maori leaders searched for ways to make their grievances heard by the government and by the public, but to no avail. Although fishing rights and foreshore rights overlapped in the Maori view, the Crown's distinction between the two persisted. By the early twentieth century, the Crown held that it had owned the foreshore since 1840, according to common law. The Crown continued to assert this, although aware that it was in a weak legal position.

Searching into the Treaty

Besides land and fisheries, there were many other reasons for the Maori people to look more closely at the Treaty of Waitangi in the years after the wars. The steady expansion of settlement,

CHAPTER FOUR: COLONIAL POWER AND MAORI RIGHTS 91

The deed for the sale of the Wairarapa lakes was signed at Papawai, Greytown, in 1896. The cheque is being handed over by Judge Butler, with James Carroll acting as mediator and Takarangi Mete Kingi as assessor. Among the Wairarapa leaders are Kingi Ngatuere, Te Whatahoro Jury, Eruha Piripi, Hamuera Tamahau Mahupuku, Wiremu Hutana Whakaka and Hoani Te Rangi-taka-i-waho. ALEXANDER TURNBULL LIBRARY, F7886A½

along with road-making, drainage and other public works, brought the most remote Maori communities under the control of local and central government. Maori with limited access to money felt penalised by rates demands and other levies. The Dog Tax Registration Act 1880, for example, was designed to reduce the numbers of Maori-owned dogs, which threatened sheep flocks; this tax was seen as infringing individual rights and drew strong protest.

By the 1870s, it was clear to many Maori that the Treaty offered very limited protection. The 1840 agreement had no power, for example, against the Public Works Acts of 1864 and 1876, which allowed land to be taken compulsorily for public development; nor was it helpful against subsequent legislation such as the Highway Boards Acts, the Railways Acts and a series of Drainage Acts. Officials were not blind to the effects on Maori; indeed, they openly acknowledged at times that the Crown was more likely to take Maori land for public works because it was easier to avoid paying compensation. Court decisions, various shady dealings and legislation were all playing a part in undermining the Treaty's guarantees.

Living in rough-hewn timber cottages like this, settlers began to clear the bush and break in the land. This family group is too well-dressed for everyday work; posing for a photograph was in itself an occasion, or perhaps an outing was planned. The photograph was taken in the Rangitikei district, probably in the 1870s.
HARDING DENTON COLLECTION, ALEXANDER TURNBULL LIBRARY, G307-1/1

Maori well-versed in Pakeha ways, such as Te Ati Awa leader Wi Tako Ngatata, drew the conclusion that Pakeha kept 'the body of the law' and gave Maori only 'the ghost of it'; others learnt the same lesson as experience of settlement broadened. In some cases, Maori rights were infringed by sheer official incompetence; in others, officials manipulated the administrative and judicial systems to Pakeha advantage. Sometimes, the executive and administrative arms of government were in conflict over Maori issues, to the detriment of Maori welfare. Even under Donald McLean (possibly the most sympathetic of Native Ministers after the wars), there was an ambivalence, a disconcerting compromise of Pakeha and Maori interests, that inevitably disadvantaged the Maori people.

Seeing that the Treaty was being interpreted in ways that restricted their autonomous rights, Maori leaders said that their mana was passing away or had already been lost — a conclusion they reached only after a great deal of soul-searching and debate. At a series of runanga (large gatherings) held in most North Island districts in the 1870s, Maori discussed ways of mending tribal ties damaged in the wars, of coming to terms with the Pakeha world, and of forcing the government to uphold the Treaty. Individual tribes had their own concerns, but all shared a common bond in the Treaty and in the relationship they understood it had established between

Eel weirs on the Whanganui River, 1924. Maori eel weirs and other fish traps on the river were 'indiscriminately … destroyed or done away with to provide a passage for river steamers. Any protest by the unfortunate people who owned the eel-weirs remained unheeded.' These findings from the Maori Land Court were reported by the 1950 Royal Commission on Claims Relating to the Whanganui River. MUSEUM OF NEW ZEALAND TE PAPA TONGAREWA, B161

Maori and the Crown. A variety of other matters, usually of local interest, also came to the attention of runanga; as a result, committees of a semi-permanent nature were maintained, giving the runanga some continuity of identity and purpose.

Repeated requests for government recognition of runanga and the committees met with no response; nor would the government reconvene the Kohimarama Conference, as some leaders requested. From the ongoing discussions, led by Ngati Whatua and Nga Puhi in particular, there eventually emerged a national body, the Kotahitanga of the Treaty of Waitangi, which linked several tribal groups. Three major meetings were held in Auckland in 1879, 1880 and 1881, and more were convened in the north from 1881 through to the 1890s. This activity was based in the north, where the Treaty had first been signed; the Waitangi agreement was central to the debates.

Ngati Maniapoto chiefs of the King Country, about 1884. Rewi Maniapoto, the great fighting chief, is standing at the left. After the wars of the 1860s, Tawhiao and his people withdrew behind the aukati, the confiscation line. The region under his jurisdiction – about 11,000 square kilometres – became known as the King Country. Europeans were warned to stay out.
BURTON BROS. COLLECTION, ALEXANDER TURNBULL LIBRARY, PA7-36-30

Meetings at Orakei

The first great meeting, convened by Paora Tuhaere of Ngati Whatua, was held at Orakei in March 1879. The gathering, which had official blessing, was attended by about three hundred chiefs and lasted nine days. For almost half that time, Tuhaere kept the discussion rigorously focused on the Treaty and its interpretation. The Treaty was read out, and so was the explanation that Governor Browne had given at the Kohimarama Conference of 1860. Tuhaere noted that, although the Treaty had been ratified on the Maori side (as had the 1860 conference), the Maori people were disillusioned with the trends of government policy, and felt that the Queen's protection – and therefore their mana – had passed away.

Chiefs attending the meeting were invited to comment on the Treaty and its effects. Speakers were reluctant to condemn the Treaty itself; instead, blame fell on the Native Land Court and the failure of the law to protect Maori interests. They were also willing to accept that Maori themselves had to take some responsibility for letting the land go. Benefits were weighed against disadvantages: the Treaty had enabled Maori to initiate cooperative, unified

A group at Pipiriki on the Whanganui River, in the 1880s. BURTON BROS., MUSEUM OF NEW ZEALAND TE PAPA TONGAREWA, C.010209

action that had not been possible before 1840; it was a covenant of peace and unity between tribes, and between Maori and Pakeha. But, as Tuhaere noted at some length, the Maori people were disillusioned with government policy, and felt that the Queen's protection had passed away. The chiefs referred confidently to Treaty clauses they considered had been violated; knowledge of the Treaty had grown as a result of the 1860 Kohimarama Conference and the experiences of the intervening years.

Like others, Tuhaere was puzzled by the erosion of fishing rights: 'They have been taken away, in spite of the words of this Treaty. I do not know how they went. They are not like lands or forests. You have to make an agreement before they can be handed over or taken.' The conference ended with resolutions asserting the mana of the Maori people 'over fishing grounds and deep water shark', 'over flounder and eel fisheries', and 'over sandbanks of pipi, rock oysters, mussels, paua, kina and scallops'.

Most speakers favoured adherence to the Treaty, partly because of allegiance given in 1840, and partly because of the real advantages they believed they had received as a people, especially the gifts of peace and protection. The British governance introduced by the Treaty had shielded them, they said, not only from foreign invasion but also from intertribal warfare.

Tuhaere had hoped that the Orakei parliament would influence government opinion, but its effect on official policy was minimal. From the meeting, however, came a new sense of

Orakei marae at the end of the nineteenth century. This land, which included Takaparawha (Bastion Point), was all that remained of Ngati Whatua's extensive lands. Apart from early sales, a headland was given to the Crown for defence purposes in 1859, and further land acquired in 1886. The whole block was partitioned in 1898 and the Crown moved to purchase most of it. Fierce protests over Ngati Whatua's land loss erupted at Bastion Point in the 1970s.
ALEXANDER TURNBULL LIBRARY: *AUCKLAND STAR* COLLECTION, 10806½; E-571-q-037-2

Parihaka in the 1870s was a model community, developed with modern amenities such as gas lighting (before it was installed in most towns). From 1869, the settlement became a focal point for Taranaki Maori, who were inspired by the teachings of Te Whiti and Tohu Kakahi. Adopting a policy of passive resistance, Te Whiti pressed for the return of confiscated lands and for Maori control of their own affairs. As land was surveyed, his people built fences across the roads that were being pushed through Maori cultivations. The fencers were arrested and jailed. ALEXANDER TURNBULL LIBRARY, F56542½

cohesion among Maori, and the Treaty stood as the symbol for a unity of purpose, bringing together many different aspirations. Tuhaere held further conferences at Orakei in March 1880 and March 1881. Those attending recalled that, in 1835, elders in the north had formed a confederation and had decided to hold annual runanga where chiefs would lay down laws for the country. Since the Treaty had recognised the Confederation of United Tribes and confirmed rangatiratanga (chieftainship), Maori leaders felt they were entitled to exercise their rights by holding conferences or parliaments. The concept of a Maori parliament was thereby given a hallmark of constitutional validity.

The Ngati Whatua conferences were particularly concerned about the government's handling of Te Whiti's passive resistance in Taranaki. There was also concern that the King movement had not been reconciled with the government. Both issues arose from the wars and land confiscations, which Maori saw as contravening the Treaty. Government retrenchment –

Parihaka was invaded by fifteen hundred volunteer troops in November 1881. Te Whiti, Tohu and another great Taranaki leader, Titokowaru, were charged with sedition. Te Whiti and Tohu were put on trial and jailed, first in New Plymouth and then (with a number of their followers) in the South Island. PARIHAKA ALBUM, ALEXANDER TURNBULL LIBRARY, F111053½

cuts in aid grants and in the paid services of chiefs as court assistants — added to the impression that the government was distancing itself from the Maori people. It was obvious, too, that the four Maori Members of the House of Representatives made little impact on parliamentary decisions; the government also ignored numerous appeals to increase their number so that Maori voters were more fairly represented. Noting that government policies were dividing the two races, the Ngati Whatua conferences resolved that the ideal of one people, officially expressed so often since 1840, should be brought to the government's attention once more.

Meetings at Waitangi

Nga Puhi had come to the same conclusion. In the 1870s, they began to draw government attention to the Treaty by focusing intertribal discussions on Waitangi. Meetings on Treaty-related matters were held on land known today as Te Tii marae, on the Paihia side of the Waitangi River mouth. This was where chiefs had retired on the night of 5 February 1840 to consider the Treaty before returning to Busby's lawn the next day to sign; and when the Governor visited the north in 1876, the main welcome was held at Te Tii.

The first of the Nga Puhi parliaments opened at Te Tii in March 1881, with over three thousand people attending. A meeting house, called Te Tiriti o Waitangi, had been specially built. A stone monument inscribed with the words of the Treaty in Maori had been placed in front of the house, where it still stands. The Union Jack flew over the grounds. The organisers included the Nga Puhi chief Aperahama Taonui, who had signed the Treaty, and sons of others who had signed. The discussion embraced Maori rights over foreshores, the return of confiscated lands, and the dog tax; but the main call of northern leaders was for a Maori parliament to weld the people into a united body to fight for Treaty rights. They wanted to be associated with the colonial government, but on Maori terms; they were not looking for separation.

William Rolleston, the Native Minister, attended. He was conciliatory but firm: there could be only one parliament; land confiscations were a 'fait accompli'; and the foreshores were for the use of all New Zealanders. To politicians such as Rolleston, a Maori population of around fifty thousand did not justify the formation of separate political bodies. At most, the government was prepared to accept the existence of runanga (especially when Maori support was needed), but would not encourage any Maori political organisation outside its control. With only half-hearted commitment, the government passed a Native Committees Act in 1883. This was a response to the longstanding request for the Maori committees operating in various districts throughout the country to have official recognition.

Maori had hoped that the Native Land Court would be supplanted by the committees, which would determine customary title to land. But the Native Committees Act simply authorised committees to advise the courts on customary title; the legislation fell far short of Maori requests for self-government, and even the limited opportunities it offered for local management by committees were deliberately frustrated by the government. Not surprisingly, Maori continued to press for greater control of their affairs. Nga Puhi established independent committees in the mid 1880s, and parliaments were held at Waitangi each year throughout the 1880s.

Petitions

In the 1880s, Maori turned to the colonial government, presenting hundreds of petitions to Parliament, many featuring the Treaty. Maori were using their rights as British subjects to petition and to claim justice, but the government and the courts found many reasons why these pleas could remain unheard, their requests unmet.

Determined to explore other avenues for influencing government policy, Maori leaders turned to Queen Victoria, with whom the Treaty had been made. She was the 'great mother' who had offered her protection in 1840. The idea of sending a Maori deputation to Britain had long been promoted by sympathetic Pakeha, and had been encouraged by the Aborigines Protection Society in Britain.

Two separate deputations took petitions to London: a group from Nga Puhi in 1882, and a Waikato party led by King Tawhiao in 1884. Both groups claimed to represent the interests of

Governor William Jervois holding a meeting with Waikato chiefs at Kawhia in 1884. The government wanted the King Country opened for settlement and Kawhia Harbour opened for shipping. At the time of the meeting, Tawhiao and his party were in Britain appealing against this sort of pressure being exerted on the Waikato people. ALEXANDER TURNBULL LIBRARY, 25749½

the Maori people as a whole, and both based their petitions on the Treaty. They were not successful, but the idea of securing redress for grievances sparked a tremendous amount of interest, contributing to a groundswell of agitation that was to lead many Maori towards organised, united political action.

The 1882 deputation was endorsed by several major chiefs connected with the Treaty of Waitangi movement, as it was called at the time. Led by Hirini Taiwhanga, who was fluent in English and experienced in government business, three petitioners travelled to London to ask the Queen to appoint a 'Royal English Commission' to investigate and rectify laws that contravened the Treaty. They also sought permission to establish a Maori parliament that would restrain the New Zealand government in its endeavours to set aside the Treaty.

The petition recounted at length Maori concerns about the confiscations, the Native Land Court, local body taxes, and the government's ill-treatment of Te Whiti. It listed legislative Acts and Ordinances that were said to be 'against the principles contained in the treaty', and outlined the history of Pakeha–Maori strife over land. The establishment of the King movement was described as a legitimate act to protect Maori lands in accordance with the Treaty's provisions.

[1] Maihi Paraone Kawiti was one of the main organisers of the meetings at Waitangi in the 1880s. The son of the chief Kawiti who had challenged British sovereignty in the 1840s, he had re-erected the flagstaff on the hill at Russell in 1858 with a group of warriors. ALEXANDER TURNBULL LIBRARY, 75214½

[2] Hirini Taiwhanga took a petition to England in 1882 with two other northern chiefs. He was the Member of the House of Representatives for Northern Maori, 1887–90. ALEXANDER TURNBULL LIBRARY, F35MM-00098

The petitioners were refused an audience with the Queen, and referred back to the New Zealand government. Supported in London by the Aborigines Protection Society and by a number of well-meaning British politicians, they departed with some hope that the trip had not been entirely in vain. It was a pattern that would be repeated by the next group of petitioners.

King Tawhiao's 1884 deputation expressed the same concerns as the Nga Puhi group and asked for a Maori parliament. They asked the Queen to 'confirm her words given in that treaty', and also pointed out that clause 71 of the 1852 Constitution could be interpreted as making provision for Maori custom and self-government. The Waikato document was a more coherent and fully fledged proposal for separate Maori self-government.

As in 1882, the British government blocked the group's approach to the Queen. Again, the Colonial Office consulted with the New Zealand government, and insisted that only that government could handle Maori matters. The failure of this second appeal was a bitter disappointment to the many tribes throughout New Zealand who had placed great hopes on the success of petitions to the British Crown. Maori leaders hoped that attitudes might change when the governments changed, as they did from time to time in both Britain and New Zealand.

Two further deputations went to England. In 1914, Te Rata Mahuta Potatau Te Wherowhero and a Waikato group were given an audience with King George V – on condition that grievances

The Maori mission to Britain in 1914. The King movement had established its own parliament, the Kauhanganui, in the 1890s. Here, the King's premier, Tupu Taingakawa, is seated; behind him are, from left, Mita Karaka, Te Rata Mahuta Potatau Te Wherowhero (who would become the fourth King) and Hori Tiro Paora.
AUCKLAND MUSEUM/TAMAKI PAENGA HIRA, B8278

were not discussed. This defeated the aim of the appeal, which was to seek justice, especially over the confiscation of Waikato land. In 1924, Tahupotiki Wiremu Ratana, the leader of a new Maori religious and political movement that based its rights on the Treaty, also took a petition to England, again without success.

The failure of these appeals was tangible proof of the extent to which officialdom could set the Treaty aside. And official attitudes were unlikely to change unless the colonial government took a different view or the Maori people could find an effective strategy to influence public opinion in favour of their rights. Maori protest and the search for change would continue nonetheless, and take on new shape over the following century.

CHAPTER FOUR: COLONIAL POWER AND MAORI RIGHTS   103

[1]

Kotahitanga parliaments

In the mid 1880s, plans were made for a Maori parliament at large meetings throughout the country, and especially at the Waitangi gatherings. Such a parliament would bring all tribes together in the spirit of kotahitanga – unity or oneness under the Treaty. Approaches were made to the King movement, which in the end opted to remain independent.

Tawhiao had failed to secure government agreement to requests akin to those set out in his petition to the Queen; these included an annual Maori council with existing committees under its jurisdiction. In the early 1890s, therefore, the King set up his own council, the Kauhanganui, comprising two houses of assembly. A constitution provided for a governmental structure with wide-ranging administrative functions. The Kauhanganui published its own newspaper, *Te Paki o Matariki*, featuring as part of its emblem the King's motto, 'Ko te mana motuhake' – a separate, independent authority. The King movement considered these moves to be reasonable, given its view of the Treaty as the basis for equality of rights between Maori and Pakeha. The Kauhanganui was the King's specific solution; others were seeking a different way.

Government actions in the 1880s appeared to offer Maori greater control over their affairs. More extensive consultation than usual accompanied moves to enact the Native Land Administration Act in 1886. Maori had hoped that the Act would restore the mana of the land by allowing for full Maori control, unencumbered by official restriction. But in its final form the Act failed to do this, although it did stop individuals dealing in tribal land. Longstanding Maori suspicion of the government made the new legislation a dead letter. The Act was repealed in 1888, and direct purchase restored.

[1, 2, 3] The Kotahitanga parliament met at various places in the North Island. These photographs were taken at a meeting at Pakirikiri, near Gisborne, in 1894. D. M. BEERE COLLECTION, ALEXANDER TURNBULL LIBRARY, G34259¼, G34257¼, G34255¼

CHAPTER FOUR: COLONIAL POWER AND MAORI RIGHTS   105

A gathering at Papawai pa, near Greytown, in 1896. Although the Kotahitanga parliaments did not meet at Papawai, many discussions relating to them took place there. The Premier, Richard Seddon, is standing to the left.
R. KEEDWELL COLLECTION, ALEXANDER TURNBULL LIBRARY, F170058½

This spate of legislation provided the impetus for the final formation of the Kotahitanga parliaments. Tuhaere of Orakei played an important role, chairing a decisive meeting at Waitangi in 1888 and injecting new vigour into the Maori desire for a unified body. Meetings in other centres moved towards full commitment, with a committee of chiefs elected to make representations to Parliament in Wellington. At the Waitangi meeting in March 1889, a pledge of union was drawn up for circulation to all tribes; those who signed committed themselves to Kotahitanga and recognised the mana of the Treaty, under which a Maori government would be set up.

Tuhaere held a second meeting at Orakei later the same month to consolidate the planning. With other leaders he stressed that the aim of the Kotahitanga movement was to unify the two races as one people, as the Treaty had intended, and to achieve unity of purpose among Maori – an urgent need, given the continuing exclusion of Maori from government. Their hope was that the government would ratify the Treaty on the basis of Maori understanding in 1840. It would prove a vain hope.

Meetings in the north in 1891 set up the first Kotahitanga parliament. It opened at Waitangi in April 1892, with a national parliament convening at Waipatu in Hawke's Bay in June. While

The Treaty of Waitangi meeting house at Te Tii marae, Waitangi, opened by the Prime Minister, William Massey, in 1922. The previous meeting house had collapsed in a gale in 1917. Several meeting houses had been built on the site, the first one in the late 1870s. To the left is a monument erected by northern leaders in 1881, and still standing. The words inscribed come from the Maori text of the Treaty. ALEXANDER TURNBULL LIBRARY, C9148

retaining the traditional runanga principle of consultation and deliberation, the Kotahitanga parliament also adopted more European procedures. There were electoral districts based on tribal boundaries, and the parliament itself had two houses – an upper house of fifty chiefs and a lower house of ninety-six younger men. Debate was to follow the pattern of the General Assembly. The business of the parliaments would be to sort out Maori needs and present them as effectively as possible to the Parliament in Wellington. The aim was not to supplant that Parliament but to supplement it.

An annual parliament was held in a different district each year, with the Maori members of the House of Representatives taking part in the sessions. But the government refused to give the Kotahitanga parliament official recognition, and simply ignored its advice and requests. Without any authority from the Crown, it was powerless. Although the parliament ceased to meet in 1902, the ideas and aims of Kotahitanga have continued.

While the Kotahitanga parliaments were being planned in 1890, New Zealand was celebrating its fiftieth anniversary as a British colony. People turned their minds back to the early years – not so much to the Treaty but to the arrival of the first settler ships in Wellington, and to the coming of Hobson on 29 January 1840 (which became the official anniversary day). The Treaty was clearly unimportant to Pakeha New Zealanders.

CHAPTER FOUR: COLONIAL POWER AND MAORI RIGHTS   107

CHAPTER FIVE

Into the Twentieth Century
— 1900 to 1975

For Maori people in the new century, the Treaty remained central in the struggle to gain rights from the government. They kept hoping that official attitudes to the Treaty might change: in time, new politicians and freshly elected governments might listen to Maori voices.

Sometimes they did. Taking office in 1890, the Liberal government initiated a commission of inquiry into the Maori land laws. This damned past practice, and led to some reforms in both the law relating to Maori land and its administration. In 1893, for example, provision was made to incorporate the multiple owners of the huge Mangatu block on the East Coast into a single legal entity; elected block management committees would be accountable to annual meetings of owners and to the Native Land Court. Historian Alan Ward comments: 'For the first time, an appropriate legal mechanism had been created to relate customary multiple ownership to the needs of modern economic management.' The Native Land Court Act 1894 adopted the principle of incorporation, which was widely used thereafter by tribes who had retained substantial areas of land. The Act also restored Crown pre-emption over most of the country, and gave the Native Land Court discretionary powers to sort out cases where some owners claimed to have been omitted from titles.

The same government, however, was committed to an active policy of purchasing land for settlement and was under constant pressure from the electorate to do so. In later claims to the Waitangi Tribunal, the government's land acquisition from Maori at this time featured alongside nineteenth-century injustices such as raupatu. In 1893, for example, Parliament authorised the Public Trustee to grant leases in perpetuity (at peppercorn rentals) over the West Coast Settlement Reserves created in Taranaki after the dispersal of the Parihaka community in 1882. In some circumstances, the land could even be sold. Some 300,000 acres (120,000 hectares) were affected.

To obtain land where transport links were being developed (for example, on the North Island main trunk railway), the Native Townships Act was passed in 1895. This Act provided for compulsory acquisition of land up to 500 acres (200 hectares). The title to this land was then held by the Crown in a complex arrangement, by which a fifth was left in trust for the Maori owners' use and occupation, and the rest rented out on their behalf. A new Native Townships Act in 1910, however, allowed for freeholding of town land; by 1920, the Crown had bought most of the subdivisions in towns set up under the Act, such as Otorohanga and Taumarunui, for lease or resale to settlers.

By means such as these, the drive to purchase land continued. It reached now into remote districts such as the Urewera, and areas like the King Country that had held out against land sales. When purchase abated at the turn of the century, it was due in part to protests expressed

[previous page] Some members of the New Zealand Pioneer Maori Battalion taking a break while working on the trenches near Gommecourt in France, July 1918. In the First World War, tribal and religious leaders such as Te Puea Herangi, Te Rata Mahuta and Rua Kenana urged neutrality on their followers. But other leaders – professional men and MPs such as Maui Pomare and Apirana Ngata – wanted Maori to go to the war to show they were as capable as Europeans. Several contingents of volunteer Maori Pioneers went before June 1917, when Maori became liable for conscription. At that stage, the fighting unit that became known as the Maori Battalion was formed. Some Waikato Maori were jailed for resisting conscription. ALEXANDER TURNBULL LIBRARY, G13414½

In the far north, Maori dug kauri gum to earn a living. Entire families were involved, with children absent from schooling for lengthy periods. Around 40 per cent of the far north's population were Maori, but by 1900 they eked out a living on less than 10 per cent of the land, most of it economically marginal. NORTHWOOD COLLECTION, ALEXANDER TURNBULL LIBRARY, G6280-½

by Maori in a variety of ways – through petitions to Parliament, a boycott of the Native Land Court in 1895, a petition from the Kotahitanga parliament to Queen Victoria in 1897 (her jubilee year), and the disruption of surveys in the Urewera. The crux of Maori protest was antagonism to the Native Land Court's practice and a plea for Maori organisations to retain authority over land.

A measure of self-government?

In 1900, Parliament passed two Acts that were meant to give some power to Maori in organising their own affairs: this was the Liberals' answer to demands for Treaty-based rights expressed by the Kotahitanga parliaments. The first, the Maori Councils Act, set up committees

A flax mill at Clevedon, south of Auckland, in the late nineteenth century. As this photograph suggests, the labour was usually Maori, the management Pakeha. Drawn into a money economy, Maori worked in a range of labouring occupations. A few were well off, and some shared the comfortable lifestyle of an emerging middle class; but the bulk of the population lived in poverty. Debts and the constant pressures to sell land were distracting and demoralising. AUCKLAND CITY LIBRARIES, A1342

of elders in Maori communities and gave them certain legal powers to deal with such matters as health and education. The health work was to be funded by donations, fees and government subsidies. The move was greeted enthusiastically, with a few exceptions, and committees were set up in most areas. Initially, their work proved most beneficial in improving hygiene and sanitation, but their powers were very limited and government funding was absurdly inadequate (it ceased altogether after 1909).

The second, the Maori Lands Administration Act, set up six (later seven) Maori land districts, each with a Maori land council partly appointed by the Native Minister and partly elected by Maori landowners. Most, but not all, council members were Maori. The councils largely dealt with land that had already passed through the Native Land Court; they could

Maori forestry workers in the central North Island in the 1920s. The part played by Maori workers in developing the region's extensive exotic forests is represented in a major Treaty claim in the early twenty-first century. The claim involves about a hundred separate claims, covering forests in the Taupo, Rotorua and Kaingaroa districts.
ARCHIVES NEW ZEALAND/TE RUA MAHARA O TE KAWANATANGA, WELLINGTON OFFICE, AAQA 6501, F152

determine whether land should be retained for owners' use or authorised for owners to lease. Land could also be vested voluntarily in the councils for leasing or management. By the end of 1905, only about 236,000 acres (95,000 hectares) had been vested in the councils, of which less than a quarter had been leased. Maori were evidently fearful of handing land over to official bodies, even those with a Maori majority.

The two Acts were promoted as measures of Maori self-government, but fell far short of that goal. The committees set up for health and education were woefully underfunded, and gradually became ineffectual. And Maori were clearly not keen to place land voluntarily in the hands of the Maori land councils. So in 1905 the Maori Land Settlement Act was introduced, enabling the Minister of Native Affairs to vest land compulsorily in Maori land boards for

These women on a west coast beach north of Auckland are gathering toheroa, a rich source of food. Plentiful in the nineteenth century, toheroa are now less available, and protective measures limit the numbers taken.
NORTHWOOD COLLECTION, ALEXANDER TURNBULL LIBRARY, G10576-½

leasing. The boards, which replaced the councils, had three appointed members (only one of them Maori) and powers to remove restrictions in the titles against direct leasing to settlers. The Act applied to land in the Northland and East Coast districts.

In the period 1900 to 1909, almost a million acres (400,000 hectares) of land were leased out with the consent of the councils or boards, mainly under the provisions of the 1905 Act. Thus, at the very time when Maori people were beginning to farm their land successfully, it became easier for Maori land to be brought into development by non-Maori. Settler pressure and government impatience to acquire Maori land and make it profitable could not be held back for long. Crown purchasing resumed in five land districts in 1905, and in Northland and the East Coast from 1908.

Meanwhile, a group of university-educated leaders was emerging for whom separatism had little attraction. Known collectively as the Young Maori Party, these men included Apirana Ngata (MP for Eastern Maori, 1905–43), Maui Pomare (MP for Western Maori, 1911–30) and Te Rangihiroa Peter Buck (MP for Northern Maori, 1909–14). The three were convinced that survival for Maori lay in shedding aspects of traditional life that held Maori back from engagement with the modern world. All were committed to working within the existing administrative and legislative framework. There was no questioning the rights assumed by

To our minds, what is now the paramount consideration ... is the encouragement and training of the Maoris to become industrious settlers. The statute-book may be searched in vain for any scheme deliberately aimed in this direction. The Legislature has always stopped short when it had outlined a scheme or method of acquiring Maori lands or rendering such available in different ways for European settlement. The necessity of assisting the Maori to settle his own lands was never properly recognised ... He was expected to do so, and to bear the burdens and responsibilities incident to the ownership of land. Because he has failed to fulfil expectations and to bear his proportion of local and general taxation he is not deemed worthy to own any land except the vague undefined area that should be reserved for his 'use and occupation.' But the causes that have conspired to the failure have not been investigated with a view to remedial measures. And where in spite of supreme difficulties the Maori has succeeded in making good use of his land the fact is not sufficiently recognised. The spectacle is presented to us of a people starving in the midst of plenty. If it is difficult for the European settler to acquire Maori land owing to complications of title it is more difficult for the individual Maori owner to acquire his own land, be he ever so ambitious and capable of using it. His energy is dissipated in the Land Courts in a protracted struggle, first, to establish his own right to it, and, secondly, to detach himself from the numerous other owners to whom he is genealogically bound in the title. And when he has succeeded he is handicapped by want of capital, by lack of training – he is under the ban as one of a spendthrift, easy-going, improvident people.

In dealing, therefore, with the lands now remaining to the Maori people we are of opinion that the settlement of the Maoris should be the first consideration. And it is because we recognise the impossibility of doing so on a comprehensive scale by the ordinary method of partition and individualisation that we recommend the intervention of a body, such as the Maori Land Board, to be armed with powers sufficiently elastic to meet the exigencies of the situation.

Part of the Stout-Ngata Commission's 'Report on Native Land Tenure', 1907. AJHR, 1907, G-1C, PP.14–15

government; the challenge was to make that power work for the good of their people. This was no easy task, as Ngata discovered when he failed to influence government over the cutting of Maori health grants in 1909.

The Native Land Act 1909

In 1907, Ngata was appointed with Robert Stout (Chief Justice and former Premier) to investigate Maori land issues. Their report predicted that Maori would become an impoverished and landless people unless government policy changed. The Native Land Act of 1909 adopted some of their suggestions; for example, £50,000 was set aside for Maori land development, but a similar amount was made available to buy Maori land. The Act consolidated some forty statutes affecting Maori land and set in place the foundations of policy for the next fifty years. All restrictions on title were removed, and the legal category of 'absolutely inalienable land'

[1] [2] [3]

[1] Maui Pomare, photographed as a student at Battle Creek College, Michigan, USA. A doctor, health reformer and politician, Pomare was a government Maori health officer from 1902 to 1910. He won the Western Maori seat in 1911, and held it for nearly twenty years, continuing to work for Maori health and welfare. ALEXANDER TURNBULL LIBRARY, F32138½

[2] Peter Buck, also known as Te Rangihiroa, trained as a doctor at Otago Medical School. In the early twentieth century, he campaigned with Maui Pomare to improve Maori health. Buck had a brief spell representing the Northern Maori electorate (1909–14) before moving into anthropology and museum work. RAMSDEN PAPERS, ALEXANDER TURNBULL LIBRARY, F37931½

[3] William Herries, Native Minister 1911–23, oversaw the drive for purchase of Maori land under William Massey's Reform government. GENERAL ASSEMBLY LIBRARY COLLECTION, ALEXANDER TURNBULL LIBRARY, F185-35MM-A

(papakainga) disappeared. These and other provisions in the Act facilitated the alienation of Maori land rather than slowing it.

One section of the 1909 Act allowed for Maori land to be taken for roads and railways, with no compensation. Minister of Native Affairs James Carroll (and possibly Ngata too) appears to have held the view that holding land in an undeveloped state was not beneficial to Maori. Both Carroll and Ngata preferred land to be leased rather than sold, but a number of pressures were working against them: the settlers' desire for freehold land, their resentment of Maori 'landlordism', and political pressure to make unproductive land profitable.

In 1911, the Reform government took office, with William Herries as Native Minister. It pushed ahead with purchase and leasing under the 1909 Act, and devised other means of securing Maori land. From 1913, membership of the Maori land boards changed, each board now comprising only the judge and registrar of the Native Land Court for that district. The shift eliminated Maori membership and eased the approvals required for land to be sold. Between 1911 and 1920, the Maori people lost half their remaining land; of the other half, some was leased to Pakeha and some was unsuitable for farming. In 1920, the Department of Maori Affairs estimated that only 19 acres (7.5 hectares) per head of farmable land remained

Maori working on a land development scheme in Hokianga, probably in the 1930s. With work opportunities extremely limited, the schemes had great promise of development and security, but they were not able to meet the needs of a growing population. WHINA COOPER COLLECTION

in Maori hands, and that the actual amount of land available varied considerably from one district to another.

Stemming this loss and making the remaining land productive was fraught with difficulties. Maori who wanted to farm faced real problems in securing loan money to develop their land. Maori land often did not have the legal title required by a loan agency. If the land did have a legal title, it might have hundreds of owners, who might not all agree on its use. Loan agencies were reluctant to lend in such cases. Incorporation was an option for those whose land was still intact, as on the East Coast, but most districts were not so well placed. Fragmentation of title, introduced through individualisation, succession and partition under the Native Land Act 1865, had created not only a multitude of owners in any block but also many absentee owners. Because these owners were often hard to identify or locate, and often had very small shares, the Crown and local bodies had authority to take land by notification through the Native Trustee, who in 1920 had replaced the Public Trustee as responsible for Maori land. This practice became common.

Payments for Unemployment Relief

Scale of Relief Payments Prior to 1936 (in pounds, shillings and pence)

	Pakeha			Maori
	Country Districts	Secondary Towns	Main Centres	
	£ s d	£ s d	£ s d	£ s d
Scheme 5				
Single man	12 0	14 0	17 6	9 6
Married man – without children	1 1 0	1 4 0	1 7 0	1 8 0
Married man – 1 child	1 5 0	1 8 0	1 11 0	1 2 0
Married man – 2 children	1 9 0	1 12 0	1 15 0	1 6 0
Married man – 3 children	1 13 0	1 16 0	1 19 0	1 10 0
Married man – 4 children	1 15 0	1 18 0	2 1 0	1 12 0
Married man – 5 children	1 17 0	2 0 0	2 3 0	1 14 0
Married man – 6 children	1 19 0	2 2 0	2 5 0	1 16 0
Married man – 7 or more children	2 1 0	2 4 0	2 7 0	1 18 0
Sustenance				
Single man	9 6	12 0	14 0	
Married man – without children	18 0	1 1 0	1 4 0	Maori
Married man – 1 child	1 2 0	1 5 0	1 8 0	were not
Married man – 2 children	1 6 0	1 9 0	1 12 0	eligible
Married man – 3 children	1 10 0	1 13 0	1 16 0	to receive
Married man – 4 children	1 12 0	1 15 0	1 18 0	sustenance
Married man – 5 children	1 14 0	1 17 0	2 0 0	
Married man – 6 children	1 16 0	1 19 0	2 2 0	
Married man – 7 or more children	1 18 0	2 1 0	2 4 0	

When Labour became the government in 1935, a system of relief payments was in operation that discriminated against the Maori people on the grounds that, since they did not live under the same conditions as Pakeha, they had fewer needs and consequently could be paid at a reduced rate. The above table gives the rates in force in December 1935. Scheme 5 was a system of rationed relief where workers were employed for only part of each week. Sustenance was paid to those who had no work at all.

Immediately Labour was in office, the government set about implementing a general increase in the relief rates to apply to both Pakeha and Maori. The Maori people were placed on the same scale as Pakeha from 1 June 1936. The resulting increases received by Maori ranged from 70 per cent to 121 per cent. An estimated 40 per cent of the Maori male workforce had been unemployed in 1933.

SOURCE: CLAUDIA ORANGE, 'A KIND OF EQUALITY: LABOUR AND THE MAORI PEOPLE 1935–1949', MA THESIS, UNIVERSITY OF AUCKLAND, 1977, PP.63, 64.

The Maori Battalion returns to a 'welcome home' hui and feast at Gisborne in 1919.
JAMES MCDONALD, MUSEUM OF NEW ZEALAND TE PAPA TONGAREWA, B.001153

Land development

The 1920s brought change. Gordon Coates was appointed Native Minister in 1921, and retained the portfolio when he succeeded William Massey as Prime Minister in 1925. A small farmer from the Kaipara district, Coates had Maori connections and was prepared to work with Ngata and Pomare. In 1926, the Maori land boards were authorised to advance money for land development, using the land as security even if the title was undecided. Ngata, as Native Minister in the 1928 United government and the 1931 Coalition, extended the land development schemes and the associated improvement of titles, as well as improving management of the schemes. He found ways of overcoming all sorts of handicaps, and by 1934 many thousands of acres were under development. When Labour won the 1935 election, more money was poured into the land schemes and by 1937 they were providing a living for about eighteen thousand Maori.

This expansion had some inherent difficulties, however. There was, in fact, little land suitable for farming left in Maori ownership. The land brought into development was too often of marginal quality. Development costs were a charge against the land and had to be recouped by the Native Department; this kept farmers on a tight budget. Problems with multiple ownership and with titles were circumvented by suspending owners' rights and by having nominated occupiers farm the land. But the rights of neither owners nor farmers were clarified: the former had no certainty about how or when the land might revert to their control; the latter had no security of tenure, and found the rigorous farm work and low income disheartening. Poor quality stock supplied by the Native Department and a lack of farm training did not help; nor did a certain lack of cultural sensitivity among departmental supervisors who acted as advisers.

The land schemes provided employment for many Maori, but by 1939 it was obvious that only limited numbers could be supported from farming and that other vocational training was needed. The Native Department nonetheless continued to view Maori as country people, based on the rural economy. The land schemes were, in the final analysis, of mixed benefit: they provided employment and established some economic farms, but many became heavily indebted and a number failed altogether.

Failure and success in the 1920s

In 1919, three Maori MPs sent a copy of the Treaty to the British government, whose puzzled acknowledgement noted that a copy was already on file. The MPs' action may have been prompted by the New Zealand government's record in not providing sufficient rehabilitation to Maori servicemen. As British subjects, Maori soldiers played their part in the First World War. When war ended, the government helped Pakeha soldiers to re-establish themselves in civilian life through trade training and farm schemes, but Maori soldiers considered the provision made for them inadequate.

At this time, too, Maori in several parts of the country were active in claiming Treaty rights. The Maori MPs had earlier asked the government to investigate a number of claims, but the request had been deferred because of the war. In 1920, however, a government commission reported on a petition submitted in 1909 by Tiemi Hipi and 916 Ngai Tahu, requesting an investigation into the Kemp purchase in the South Island. The purchase comprised most of present-day Canterbury and Otago, but Ngai Tahu claimed that they had sold only the coastal land, up to a line of foothills running from the Ashley River in the north to a line south of the Clutha River. The commission recommended the payment of a lump sum in compensation for the Crown's failure to fulfil its obligations (under the purchase agreement) to provide 'ample' or 'liberal' reserves. Ngai Tahu rejected the offer (but made a settlement later, in 1944).

In the Rotorua district, Maori had started legal action in the late nineteenth century to determine title to the Rotorua lakes, but it was only in the 1920s that the government was willing to negotiate. In 1922, an agreement was reached whereby the beds of Lake Rotorua

Two people fishing from a waka on Lake Rotoiti, about 1908. THOMAS PRINGLE, ALEXANDER TURNBULL LIBRARY, PA1-F-179-51-2

and thirteen other nearby lakes were vested in the Crown, along with the right to use their waters. In return, Te Arawa had certain fishing rights reserved to them and were paid compensation by way of an annuity of £6,000. This enabled them to set up the Arawa Trust Board to administer tribal interests and the compensation payments. In 1926, a similar agreement was reached with Ngati Tuwharetoa over their rights to Lake Taupo and adjoining streams; this was confirmed by legislation. Tuwharetoa received an annuity and a share of the revenue from fishing licences and camping fees; only they have the right to fish for freshwater crayfish, whitebait and certain other species in the lake. In 1946, Tuwharetoa were awarded further compensation. (In 1993, title to the bed of Lake Taupo and certain tributaries was vested in the tribe, to be managed jointly with the Department of Conservation. A similar model is proposed for twelve Rotorua lakes.)

Naturally, these moves created great interest in Maori communities. The Treaty became a major topic of debate on marae, and a flurry of publications discussed Treaty issues. For years, individuals and groups had tried, unsuccessfully, to have fishing rights of various kinds made secure. The two agreements on the lakes raised Maori hopes, not only about fishing rights but also about land and Maori authority in general. But the decisions on the lakes proved to be an

CHAPTER FIVE: INTO THE TWENTIETH CENTURY   121

[1] In 1912, Frederick Bennett, the first Maori Bishop in the Anglican Church, appealed for recognition of Te Arawa's rights to the Rotorua lakes. In 1922, negotiations with government led to recognition of certain fishing rights and a compensation payment. S. P. ANDREW COLLECTION, ALEXANDER TURNBULL LIBRARY, G18699-½

[2] Photographed here as a young woman, Te Puea Herangi led the Waikato revival in the twentieth century. She strove to rebuild the strength of the Kingitanga and to restore the well-being of communities damaged by the wars of the 1860s, confiscation and disease. In the 1920s, a new marae, Turangawaewae, was built at Ngaruawahia through hard work and fund-raising concerts. In the 1930s, Te Puea aimed to provide an economic base for her iwi communities on land development schemes established on small pockets of land at Waiuku and Onewhero. WILLIAM A. PRICE COLLECTION, ALEXANDER TURNBULL LIBRARY, G1920½

exception in government policy, not the rule. In 1929, Te Puea Herangi and other Waikato Maori petitioned unsuccessfully for the return of fishing rights in the Waikato River. This was just one of many petitions relating to lakes, rivers, lagoons, harbours and foreshores that were forwarded to government from the 1860s to the 1980s; in the same period, a number of legal cases relating to fishery rights were heard.

But the 1920s seemed to herald a new departure for land issues – not only land development but also land rights. The Sim Commission was appointed in 1926 to consider the 1860s confiscations in Taranaki, Waikato, Tauranga and Bay of Plenty; the government's aim was to diminish the sense of grievance felt by Maori about confiscation. The commission's terms of reference, however, were narrowly defined: the commission was not to consider any argument that Maori who repudiated British sovereignty could claim the benefits of the Treaty, nor the rights and wrongs of confiscation itself. Judge William Sim and his colleagues were to assess only whether the *extent* of confiscation had been justified in the circumstances, and to suggest a level of compensation, based on 1860s values, for any injustice in the *process* of confiscation. The commission reported that many of the confiscations had been excessive (in the case of

Taranaki, for example, they had simply not been justified), and that the attack and looting of Parihaka warranted redress. It recommended compensation payments for all areas affected, except Tauranga and the Bay of Plenty.

The Sim Report raised Maori hopes, but Maori MPs and tribal groups were not pleased with the compensation proposed. Neither the report nor the government's response was calculated to remove a sense of grievance. In subsequent moves, both the government and Maori seem to have treated the suggested levels of compensation as interim solutions. Further action was delayed as governments changed and as events in the 1930s and 1940s – Depression and war – intervened. Nonetheless, the wrong done by confiscation and the need for redress had been recognised; later, that recognition would be used as leverage to get further government action.

New political parties and Maori aspirations

Attention was also drawn to the Treaty by the Ratana movement, a growing political force in the 1920s. Tahupotiki Wiremu Ratana had emerged in 1918 as a faith-healer with remarkable powers. He believed he had a twofold mission: to transcend tribal divisions by uniting Maori under one God, and to improve Maori welfare. Attracting a wide range of followers, Ratana formed a political party to concentrate on current social problems and past grievances. The party's objective was to have the Treaty incorporated in legislation, an aim often referred to as 'ratification'; as part of the law of the land, the 1840 agreement would have to be recognised by the government and the courts.

The strength of Ratana's support was evident when his son Tokouru stood for Western Maori in the 1922 election, and nearly unseated the long-established MP Maui Pomare. With his party remaining for the meantime outside Parliament, Ratana tried other avenues. He took a petition to Britain, basing the Maori right of appeal to the monarch on the Treaty and seeking a royal commission to look into grievances. Like its predecessors, the petition was referred back to the New Zealand government. At the 1925 election, Ratana turned his efforts to winning the four Maori seats with his candidates.

Labour was also fighting to win these seats, and, in 1925, adopted the Treaty as part of its platform. If it became the government, Labour promised to set up a royal commission to investigate land claims 'arising out of and subsequent to the Treaty of Waitangi'; it would also set up a Maori council to provide the degree of autonomy so long sought by Maori leaders. The influence of Ratana was obvious: Labour leaders had visited the Ratana settlement, and the Labour supporter Rangi Mawhete acted as an intermediary between Labour and Ratana. By the 1931 election, both Labour and Ratana recognised that cooperation was desirable: Labour needed Maori backing; Ratana had that backing but again failed to win any seats in the 1928 and 1931 elections. Their policies were similar, both espousing the cause of the 'ordinary man', and both committed to implementing the Treaty.

When the first Ratana politician, Eruera Tirikatene, entered Parliament in 1932, Ratana and Labour took the first steps towards a formal alliance. Confirmed in 1935 when Labour

CHAPTER FIVE: INTO THE TWENTIETH CENTURY **123**

Tahupotiki Wiremu Ratana (centre), the founder of the Ratana Church, on the occasion of his birthday, 25 January 1933. With Ratana are men who were all to become MPs. Left (seated), H. T. Ratana; right (seated), E. T. Tirikatene; left (standing), P. K. Paikea; right (standing), T. Omana. In 1918, Ratana believed he had a special mission to unite the Maori people. He built a temple at the Ratana settlement, near Wanganui, and within a few years his church had more than twenty thousand members. The movement became politically active in the 1920s.
WILLIAM HALL-RAINE, MUSEUM OF NEW ZEALAND TE PAPA TONGAREWA, B13002

became the government, the alliance would last for nearly half a century. It ensured that the Treaty became more prominent on the central political stage than ever before: from the 1943 election, all four Maori seats were held by Ratana members, each candidate pledged to promote the Treaty. That pledge, together with the Ratana Party's continuing success at elections, ensured that agitation on the Treaty would not only continue but would do so at national level in that most public of forums, the country's Parliament. Ratana politicians worked hard to implement Labour's promises on the Treaty, for a long time with little result; but they kept alive the goal of building the Treaty into the law. Before that was achieved, however, public interest in the Treaty had been stimulated by an unexpected development.

Waitangi – the 'national memorial'

In May 1932, James Busby's residence at Waitangi, along with over 2,000 acres (800 hectares) of land, was gifted to the nation by the Governor General. Lord Bledisloe and his wife also launched an appeal to develop the property as a 'national memorial'. More than any other single factor, their actions led to renewed Pakeha interest in the Treaty and the events of 1840. The development of the site encouraged Maori interest too. Maori members of the Waitangi National Trust Board proposed ways to commemorate the gift. Nga Puhi decided to build a whare runanga beside the former Residency (now known as the Treaty House); the idea was adopted by other tribes and became a national project. The Maori building, standing beside the European house, was intended to symbolise the relationship established at Waitangi in 1840 and confirmed by Hobson's words: 'He iwi tahi tatou' ('We are [now] one people'). It was decided to lay the foundation stone of the whare runanga during a great hui that would celebrate the ninety-fourth anniversary of the Treaty's signing.

The gathering, hosted by Nga Puhi in early February 1934, centred on Te Tii marae at Waitangi. The event drew many Pakeha and a massive tribal representation of some ten thousand people from throughout New Zealand. Among the guests was the Maori King from Waikato, Koroki, whose attendance was seen as a gesture of friendship towards the government. It was exactly one hundred years since Britain acknowledged New Zealand's independence: a replica of the flag chosen in 1834 (known as the flag of the United Tribes of New Zealand) was flown at Waitangi alongside the Union Jack, although this was not noted in the published record of the 1934 events.

A second ceremony was held at the Treaty House, where a flagpole had been erected on the approximate spot where the Treaty had been signed. The pattern set at this official ceremony was to endure over the years — a government vessel anchored in the bay, the Union Jack unfurled, and officials expressing aspirations of nationhood and partnership. In 1934, these aspirations were contained in prayers composed by Bledisloe: that God 'grant that the sacred compact then made in these waters may be faithfully and honourably kept for all time to come', and that the union of the two races as one nation might be achieved through Christianity. Bledisloe maintained his interest in the property and was keen to publicise its history. He hoped that a nationwide consciousness would develop out of what was primarily, for Pakeha at least, an Auckland and Northland concern.

The 1934 events were regarded as a successful beginning. But the government probably did not grasp the level of difference between Maori and Pakeha perceptions of these joint ceremonies. For Maori, the celebrations were not merely an anniversary of the Treaty signing; they marked the centenary of Britain's acknowledgement of Maori independence in 1834, when the flag of an independent New Zealand was adopted. In so doing, they indicated that the Treaty was also an acknowledgement of Maori sovereignty (albeit of an undefined kind).

By contrast, the Governor General and the government were aiming to establish the Treaty as the foundation of the country's nationhood in which two races had joined together, with the Maori benefiting from the agreement. That there was conflict between these two views of

An early meeting of the Waitangi National Trust Board, held in front of the Treaty House, which had been James Busby's residence. The house, in disrepair when gifted to the nation by the Governor General in 1932, underwent extensive renovations. Further work was carried out in the late 1980s. A. JONES COLLECTION, ALEXANDER TURNBULL LIBRARY, F79960½

the past was already evident from the history of Maori protest. Setting up a national memorial was, in this context, likely to make the Waitangi property a focus for challenge as well as celebration in years to come.

The 1940 centennial

The centennial of 1940 created more interest among the general public than the 1934 celebrations had done. A major exhibition in Wellington was planned, and a series of historical publications commissioned. Research unearthed much early, half-forgotten history, generating newspaper articles and increasing public awareness of the country's origins. Newly minted currency of the mid 1930s included the Treaty signing on one coin; Thomas Bracken's poem, *God of Nations*, was adopted as the national anthem. Amid these stirrings of nationhood, the

In 1934, a great hui was held at Waitangi to celebrate the gift of the property where the Treaty was signed. The Treaty House stands across the bridge among the trees. In the foreground is Te Tii marae, prepared to host thousands of guests, as it often still does on Waitangi Day. ALEXANDER TURNBULL LIBRARY, F90801½

decision to hold a major centennial function at Waitangi gave the Treaty a central position in the public consciousness (in marked contrast to the anniversary of 1890).

As part of the celebrations, the Treaty documents and other relevant papers were temporarily held at Waitangi. This was the first time they had been treated as significant. In 1841, the set of signed Treaty sheets had been almost destroyed by fire; George Elliott, a government records clerk, rescued them from an iron box before the weatherboard cottage in Official Bay, Auckland, that had served as government offices went up in flames. The Treaty documents then disappeared from sight until 1865, when William Baker of the Native Department, at the request of Parliament, worked on them and produced a rather erroneous list of signatories. In 1869, Parliament again requested the documents for new translations to be undertaken, and facsimiles of the several Treaty sheets were made before they were put in storage in 1877. In 1911, Dr Thomas Hocken found the Treaty papers in Wellington's Government Buildings during a search for historical documents; by this time, several of the sheets had been damaged around the edges by water and two had been nibbled by rats. Restored and mounted, the sheets were kept in special boxes from then on. When they were sent to Waitangi in 1940, it was the first time they had been shown in public.

The Labour government was determined that the gathering at Waitangi in 1940 would be a great demonstration of national pride and unity. The outbreak of the Second World War in 1939 served to heighten that commitment. The celebrations appeared to be a success. Over ten thousand people attended, including many from different tribes and a group from the newly formed Maori Battalion. An impressive re-enactment of the Treaty signing was staged, and the speakers (among them the Governor General, Lord Galway) rose to the occasion with expressions of national unity. Newspapers published full-page features hailing Waitangi as 'the cradle of the nation' and the Treaty as the 'Magna Carta' or 'foundation of nationhood'. Such phrases, like the style of the celebrations themselves, would become entrenched through repetition at Waitangi ceremonies over the years.

The Maori people, however, did not support the ceremonies in 1940 as they had in 1934. The Depression had hit hard in their communities, with proportionately more Maori unemployed than Pakeha. The Labour government allocated more funding for the Native Affairs Department after 1935, especially for the land development schemes begun by Ngata, and it started to address the appalling situation in Maori housing. But despite Labour's goodwill, many Maori felt there was an insensitivity to Maori matters in government circles. They were also disappointed in Labour's failure to honour promises relating to Treaty grievances: many tribes (especially in Waikato and Taranaki) still felt sore that the injustices of the nineteenth century had not been settled, despite the recommendations of the 1928 Sim Report.

Waikato refused to attend the ceremony, although they had a hand in building the 100-foot (30-metre) waka that was launched at Waitangi. Others, like Ngai Tahu in the South Island, reminded the government that they were still waiting for settlement of claims that had been officially recognised since the 1850s; a final settlement would have been fitting in the centennial year, and they were disappointed. So, too, was Hoani Te Heuheu of Ngati Tuwharetoa, who had hoped for a favourable decision from the Privy Council on an appeal case involving Treaty rights. This followed his unsuccessful attempt, in a 1939 case brought against the Aotea District Maori Land Court, to establish that a statutory charge over ancestral tribal land was contrary to the Treaty.

Ngata used the occasion of the 1940 centenary to comment in Parliament that the substance of the land had gone to the Queen through the Treaty, leaving Maori only the shadow – the conclusion that the Kaitaia chief, Nopera Panakareao, had come to, after first telling his people in 1840 that only the shadow was passing away. The Native Minister, Frank Langstone, refuted the allegation, chiding Maori for their lack of gratitude and claiming that no other country in the world had such a good record – a claim that would often be repeated by government, and as often challenged by Maori. At the Waitangi function itself, Ngata asked the government to settle grievances so that Maori could 'close their eyes to the past'. Ngata and other leaders were also critical of the Petroleum Act 1937, which nationalised this resource without reference to

[1] The 30-metre long waka *Ngatokimatawhaorua* was launched at the 1940 Waitangi celebrations, and there was a re-enactment of the Treaty signing. Speakers made much of the unity of Maori and Pakeha. ALEXANDER TURNBULL LIBRARY, F2871 MNZ 1/4

[2] The Governor General, Lord Galway, inspecting Maori returned servicemen from the First World War at Waitangi celebrations, 1940. Eruera Tirikatene, MP for Southern Maori, is accompanying him. ALEXANDER TURNBULL LIBRARY, C9149

Apirana Ngata's farm and home, 'Waiomatatini', in the Waiapu valley on the East Coast.
JAMES MCDONALD, MUSEUM OF NEW ZEALAND TE PAPA TONGAREWA, B.010509

compensation for property rights where Maori were involved (an issue that emerged again in the twenty-first century). The Labour government, led by Peter Fraser from 1940, was not indifferent to Maori grievances and had begun to revisit the Sim Report's recommendations. But war postponed any resolution.

The Second World War and after

At the outbreak of war in 1939, the government decided not to enforce conscription for Maori. In the First World War, tribes who had suffered confiscation in the nineteenth century refused at first to volunteer and then resisted conscription. Arrests had been made in the Waikato, the only area where conscription was enforced. The Labour government, aware of a lingering sense of bitterness, sought a different approach this time.

So, in 1941, the Maori War Effort Organisation was established. Its main purpose was to encourage voluntary enlistment, but it also stimulated civilian support for the war effort and gave assistance with manpower. Under the leadership of the MP for Northern Maori, Paraire Paikea, a national network of Maori tribal committees was set up. Although the organisation

Apirana Ngata leading members of the Maori Battalion in a haka in front of the whare runanga, built on the Waitangi Treaty House grounds for the 1940 celebrations to signify the partnership of the two races. Ngata (MP for Eastern Maori 1905–43, Native Minister 1909–12 and 1928–34) wielded great influence among Maori. In 1922, he wrote an explanation of the Treaty, presumably in an attempt to get Maori to accept the government's understanding of rights of sovereignty and chiefly authority.
MAKING NEW ZEALAND COLLECTION, ALEXANDER TURNBULL LIBRARY, F2746½ MNZ

maintained close liaison with the government and the army, it gave Maori a degree of autonomy they had long sought, and increased their participation in the mainstream of New Zealand society. Tribal committees across the country recruited Maori soldiers, supplied 'manpower' for essential jobs, and raised funds for war work. The Maori Battalion fought with distinction in some of the hardest battles of the war, and suffered heavy casualties.

By the end of the war, a total of about seventeen thousand Maori had enlisted; recruitment was most successful on the East Coast, in Northland and in the Bay of Plenty. As in the First World War, Waikato leaders were reluctant for their people to enlist, but by 1942 a thousand had done so. This time, the government made better provision for Maori rehabilitation, although there would be problems in implementing it effectively.

New Zealand Labour Party records labelled this photograph 'A typical Maori dwelling'. The 1936 Census indicated that about 40 per cent of all Maori dwellings consisted of one or two rooms, with an average of five occupants; over four thousand dwellings were huts or whare. Housing surveys from 1937 revealed that around 36 per cent of Maori housing was not fit for habitation. The Labour government started to provide housing, mostly associated with the land development farms. But action was slow, and politicians and officials were reluctant to admit how bad the situation was. ALEXANDER TURNBULL LIBRARY, F37893½

Maori hoped that their efforts would lead, in peacetime, to more control of their own affairs and to a greater participation in government decision-making; but they were disappointed. With the passage of the Maori Social and Economic Advancement Act 1945, the tribal committees were brought under the Department of Native Affairs. Although the legislation enabled committees to develop marae facilities and associated activities, it did not help Maori participate in the mainstream economy. The department took on responsibility for Maori welfare in addition to the land schemes and the Native Land Court, and appointed its own welfare officers. The energies in Maori communities, released during the war years, were not harnessed for post-war development, as Peter Fraser had hoped.

In 1947, the first Maori head of the department was appointed, and it was renamed the Department of Maori Affairs. While these were important gestures, they were not the answer to Maori requests for a genuine sharing of power and autonomy, as a Treaty right. When the New Zealand Maori Council emerged from the district tribal committees in 1962, it provided a voice at national level; but over the years, Maori would tend to see the council as too closely allied with government authority.

Serious health problems among Maori were confirmed by surveys in the 1930s. Government measures included child care and regular checks; this visit from a district health officer and nurse took place on the Northland gumfields. NORTHWOOD COLLECTION, ALEXANDER TURNBULL LIBRARY, 6308-1/1

Labour's record

When Labour lost the 1949 election, it could claim to have moved at last on some issues of concern to Maori. Some long standing claims had been settled: in 1944, a compensation payment of £5,000 a year was confirmed to the Taranaki Maori Trust Board, followed in 1946 by a compensation payment of £6,000 a year to Waikato. In addition, Ngai Tahu had been awarded a payment of £10,000 a year for thirty years in settlement of their claims. In each case, however, the level of compensation was reluctantly accepted as the only option available. It was not an effective way of handling grievance, and Maori dissatisfaction laid the ground for later claims to the Waitangi Tribunal. Labour was clearly keen to keep its electoral support among Maori, and in its last term (1946–49) appointed several commissions of inquiry, most notably the Myers Commission to investigate claims relating to surplus lands.

Labour could also argue, with some accuracy, that across the whole socio-economic spectrum it had assisted the Maori people greatly. This was in part through policies aimed at giving all New Zealanders a decent standard of living. Health and welfare were priorities, but

Dobson Paikea, MP for Northern Maori, greets the Prime Minister, Peter Fraser, at the 1949 opening of the Maori Community Centre in Fanshawe Street, Auckland. This centre was a forerunner of urban marae. Maori began their migration to join the urban workforce during the Second World War. ALEXANDER TURNBULL LIBRARY, 16776¼

Labour had also made special efforts for Maori in housing and education. However, there was a legacy of neglect, and sometimes the remedies brought their own problems. Decisions on the provision of new housing, for example, were made on the basis of a Maori family's ability to repay a loan, at a time when most Maori had difficulty finding money for a deposit on a home or section. In the 1930s, stop-gap measures were adopted as the Native Affairs Department was overwhelmed with applications, and when the war began a solution to the Maori housing problem was deferred indefinitely.

Education policy was based on low expectations of Maori capacity. District high schools on the East Coast, where the student population was predominantly Maori, were created from re-classified native primary schools; they provided only two years of secondary education, specialising in home-making and technical courses. Maori urgently needed education that offered a much wider range of skills, as well as access to affordable rental housing in urban areas where many now lived. Trade and other training courses were developed only late in the 1940s. Pouring money into land development, as Labour did from the late 1930s, took care of only some in the Maori population. For the rest, the Labour government had little specific to offer.

The Maori Women's Welfare League was established as a pan-tribal organisation in 1952, with Whina Cooper as the first president. Maori women throughout the country worked to improve Maori welfare, and the league became an effective lobby group with annual conferences. The 1953 conference, at the Wellington Town Hall, is shown here.
T. RANSFIELD, ARCHIVES NEW ZEALAND/TE RUA MAHARA O TE KAWANATANGA, WELLINGTON OFFICE [ALEXANDER TURNBULL LIBRARY, F40544½ (AAQT 6401, A31013)]

In the final reckoning, Labour did not measure up to its promise of 'equality with racial individuality'. Like governments before and since, it would not advance Maori interests at the expense of electoral support. One casualty was the petition presented to Parliament by the Labour-Ratana MP Eruera Tirikatene, asking that the Treaty promises be incorporated in legislation; instead, the government decided in 1945 to print the Treaty and hang copies of it in every school and Maori meeting house in the country, 'as a sacred re-affirmation' of the 1840 agreement.

Through the 1950s and beyond, governments failed to meet Maori requests or needs in a manner that Maori believed would assist them. The 1951 Census revealed a Maori population of 115,676, of whom 57 per cent were aged twenty years or under (compared with 34.8 per cent of Pakeha), and with a higher birth rate than Pakeha. Education policies were still stressing the need to make Maori children into 'good farmers and good farmers' wives', when Census figures showed that Maori were moving to the towns and cities at an increasing rate. The greater part of the Maori workforce was employed in low-paid, unskilled work, which made Maori vulnerable to economic downturn. In the 1950s and 1960s, therefore, an increasingly urbanised Maori community was supporting larger numbers of dependants and facing the new challenges of city life. Maori birth rates started to drop only in the latter part of the 1960s.

As Maori moved to the towns and cities, they also began to establish urban marae, sometimes on a pan-tribal basis. These provided the opportunity for wide-ranging discussions and a new focus in political awareness. The long-standing battles over Treaty rights would continue; protest would become more intense, and some of it would centre on a new date in the national calendar, Waitangi Day.

Waitangi Day

In 1960, the second Labour government responded to the repeated requests of its Maori policy committee and fulfilled a 1957 election promise by bringing in the Waitangi Day Act: 6 February became a 'national day of thanksgiving, in commemoration of the signing' of the Treaty. Any region could substitute Waitangi Day for a holiday it already observed; but the legislation did not allow for a national holiday, as the Maori MPs had wished, and the Act caused barely a ripple on the nation's waters. Waitangi Day remained largely a northern affair.

Yet public interest was slowly growing. During the Second World War, the army had used the Waitangi property and restricted public access, but the Waitangi National Trust Board continued to work hard to promote the site. From 1948, an annual government grant augmented admission fees and other fundraising efforts, and from 1950 a government department shared responsibility for the property's maintenance and development. From brief ceremonies at Waitangi on 6 February, the scope of the event began to expand. The navy had replaced the flagpole in 1946–47, and established the tradition of holding an annual ceremony at Waitangi with a naval vessel anchored offshore. The Governor General and senior government representatives began to attend each year. Royal visitors regularly had Waitangi on their itineraries. Speeches stressed the legendary good relations between Maori and Pakeha, and drew attention to the ideal of 'one people'; but speechmakers seemed ignorant of resentments among Maori and the reality of life in Maori communities. The annual ceremonies were to become a forum for Maori criticism of the shortfall between government promise and practice; a new wave of Maori protest was about to begin.

Rising protest

In 1960, some Maori leaders joined the opposition to an All Black rugby tour of South Africa that excluded Maori players – an issue not handled well by either Labour or the incoming National government late in the year. It was one of the first signs that Maori might use more organised protest to highlight government inadequacies in what was now called 'race relations'.

136   AN ILLUSTRATED HISTORY OF THE TREATY OF WAITANGI

The flagpole at Waitangi. For years, the New Zealand navy has ensured that it was kept in good condition. The flagpole usually flies three flags – the New Zealand flag, the Union Jack, and the flag of the United Tribes of New Zealand (from 1834). In recent years, the flagpole has become a focus for protest action. ALEXANDER TURNBULL LIBRARY, C8864

Many Maori saw good cause for protest in the 1950s and 1960s. The National Party was in power for all but three of those twenty years. Despite some government assistance in areas of basic human need such as housing and education, a gap remained between promises and actions. There were also serious concerns about legislation, in particular the Maori Affairs Act 1953. Aimed at economic rationalisation and use of Maori land, this was nonetheless seen by some Maori as a discriminatory measure that disregarded ownership rights as well as traditional Maori values. An amendment in 1967 extended the compulsory acquisition of 'uneconomic interests' (introduced in the 1953 Act) and compulsory measures for the 'improvement' of Maori land (not applied to non-Maori land).

Such legislation, with its element of compulsion and the likelihood that more Maori land would be alienated, was bound to evoke protest. (Maori ownership rights would be reasserted by legislation passed in 1974.) Other legislation in the National period – the Maori Trustee Act 1953, the Town and Country Planning Act 1953, and the Counties Amendment Act 1961 – was also seen as contravening the Treaty. Tensions increased, and Maori were no longer prepared to remain silent. Their protests had a familiar ring: loss of land, denial of rangatiratanga, the right of Maori to control their own affairs. Many sensed a strong assimilative urge in Pakeha society – a new variation on the old theme of 'one people'. The Hunn Report on the Department of Maori Affairs (1960) crystallised Maori fears by assuming the ultimate demise of any separate Maori identity. Hunn considered it likely that intermarriage would create one people – all Pakeha, but some more brown than others. His definition of integration allowed Maori a part in the nation's identity, but his critics tended to overlook this.

It is usually forgotten that the Hunn Report carried clear statistical pointers about the need to boost Maori development, and for government commitment to that goal. Significant moves were made in housing and in education, but the bulk of the Maori population struggled to make ends meet. Thus the downturns in the economy over the last three decades of the century hit hardest at Maori, most of whom were still at the lower end of the socio-economic scale.

Through the 1960s and 1970s, Pakeha and Maori interest in Waitangi and the Treaty grew. The focus was, as ever, different. Pakeha saw the Treaty as part of a new exploration of the country's history. With the arrival of television in the 1960s, the annual Waitangi Day celebrations were broadcast to the nation. Waitangi Day ceased to be simply a northern affair, and began to attract national attention. Koro Dewes, a Maori academic and elder, accurately observed the drift of national sentiment: 'There is no doubt that many New Zealanders are beginning to search for something to believe in which will credibly express their nationalism, and so the Treaty of Waitangi is becoming recognised as a symbol of our nationhood.' But Dewes, reflecting the opinion of an articulate section of Maori society, urged the Pakeha majority 'who have a veto on whether things are done or not' to follow up words with actions, to make the Treaty a 'true symbol, with real meaning, and not just spurious sentimentalism'.

Dewes recommended that Waitangi Day be made a full national holiday – a step the Labour-Ratana MPs had been lobbying for – and perhaps the focus of a week-long festival of the arts, education and sport. The plea for a national holiday had its Pakeha supporters too. The New Zealand Founders' Society (established in the 1940s to promote pride in the country's early European settlement) wanted an all-New Zealand national day on 6 February, a date already observed by New Zealand's diplomatic posts overseas. Maori efforts to secure a national holiday, however, were part of a long-standing struggle to have the Treaty made enforceable in law. Official recognition of the date was seen as a first step towards more comprehensive legislation. In the New Zealand Day Act 1973, the Labour government responded by making 6 February a public holiday; it was a popular decision, although a change of name to New Zealand Day was reversed by the Waitangi Day Act 1976. People, it seemed, liked to remember Waitangi. (The 1976 Act also added the Maori text of the Treaty to the English text that had been included in the schedule to the 1973 Act.)

Maori leaders speak out

Meanwhile, national organisations such as the Maori Council and the Maori Women's Welfare League (established in 1952) were making submissions to the government, sometimes on request, about the Maori situation in relation to the Treaty. These documents were often in themselves a challenge to government. Henare Ngata, son of Apirana Ngata, concluded one report in 1971 by telling the National government that those who approached the Treaty in a

In 1960, South Africa refused to accept Maori players in a touring All Black rugby team. A rising tide of protest against South Africa's apartheid system brought both Maori and Pakeha onto the streets. MARTI FRIEDLANDER/BBC

CHAPTER FIVE: INTO THE TWENTIETH CENTURY 139

In the 1970s, the third Labour government tried to encourage pride in nationhood by creating new traditions. At the Waitangi ceremony in 1973, Norman Kirk invited a young Maori boy to walk with him to the rostrum for the Prime Minister's speech. NEW ZEALAND HERALD

positive frame of mind and were prepared to regard it as an obligation of honour would find it well capable of implementation. He was one of many with such convictions. But it was still mainly Maori who saw the need for laws to give effect to Treaty promises.

Yet Pakeha were beginning to search more critically into their history, and into the Treaty and its effects. Academic research gave new insights into the Maori point of view and, most importantly, made known the differences between the Maori and English texts of the Treaty. By the early 1970s, some historians had come to the conclusion that previous research had tended to over-emphasise the humanitarian concern in the original Treaty negotiations, and to under-estimate the impact of British and settler interests. This information gradually seeped into public consciousness, and produced a growing circle of Pakeha who sympathised with, and sometimes supported, Maori protest. But their numbers were few. For most Pakeha, information about the Treaty and aspects of New Zealand history that had grievously affected Maori was something new and often hard to accept.

In the 1970s, international change made itself felt within New Zealand – in particular, the post-war decolonisation of Africa, Asia and the Pacific; the growth of the civil rights movement in the United States; and the activities of the United Nations and its agencies, especially those dealing with indigenous peoples and human rights. Maori watched with interest the assertiveness of non-European groups emerging in the newly independent countries. The rapid success of some groups in establishing the right to self-determination contrasted sharply with Maori experience.

Maori also observed other minority groups struggling with government structures. Indigenous peoples in Canada and the United States were wringing concessions from their respective governments. By contrast, the Treaty of Waitangi seemed to have no teeth. Several legal cases in the latter part of the nineteenth and early twentieth centuries had shown that, unless the Treaty was incorporated in legislation, it would not be recognised in courts of law. This situation was about to change.

CHAPTER SIX

New Departures
— 1975 to 1987

The Treaty of Waitangi Act 1975

A new phase in the Treaty's history began with the passing of the Treaty of Waitangi Act in October 1975. Few appreciated just how significant the event was. For forty years, Labour-Ratana MPs had been committed to this goal, and it was exactly fifty years since the Labour Party had first recognised the Treaty in a policy statement. It was a triumph for Matiu Rata, MP for Northern Maori, who had taken the initiative in pushing the legislation through.

Rata had two aims: to educate the public about the Treaty and to establish a process for settling grievances. When he promoted the New Zealand Day Act 1973, he hoped New Zealanders would use the national holiday on 6 February both to celebrate the partnership initiated by the 1840 Treaty and to learn more about it. His second aim was to secure a tribunal to hear claims concerning Treaty breaches. The Treaty of Waitangi Act 1975 would provide for this.

The Act established the Waitangi Tribunal as a permanent commission of inquiry into claims by Maori against the Crown – that is, 'where any Maori claims that he or any group of Maoris of which he is a member is or is likely to be prejudicially affected' by legislation, regulations, Crown policy or practice, or any act done or omitted by or for the Crown. If the Tribunal considered that Maori interests were, or could be, prejudicially affected, it could make recommendations on the appropriate course of Crown action. The Tribunal consisted of a chairman (the Chief Judge of the Maori Land Court) and two appointees, one on the recommendation of the Minister of Justice and the other – a Maori – on the recommendation of the Minister of Maori Affairs.

The Tribunal had to take into account the 'principles' of the Treaty; these were not defined in the Act and had to be determined by the Tribunal. The 'meaning and effect' of the 1840 agreement were to be considered, drawing on both the Maori and English texts. The Tribunal could refuse to inquire into a claim that it considered 'frivolous or vexatious', or if the subject matter was 'trivial'. Tribunal reports would go to the claimant, the Minister of Maori Affairs and any other appropriate persons. The Tribunal could also report on whether any provisions in proposed legislation were 'contrary to the principles of the Treaty'.

The 1975 Act initiated a process that before long would bring the Treaty into the very forefront of the political arena. But its beginnings were inauspicious. Although the Act acknowledged the Treaty, the Treaty itself was only appended as a schedule to the Act and therefore had no legal force. Although Maori had sought a statutory recognition of the Treaty, many were concerned that as part of a statute the Treaty itself might be vulnerable to being repealed. Most of all, the limitations placed on the Tribunal reduced its impact dramatically. The need for the Tribunal had arisen from the past record of the Crown and the inimical effect of some legislation on Maori interests (as submissions to the select committee on the Treaty of Waitangi Bill had recorded). Rata had hoped that the Tribunal's powers would be retrospective, at least to the start of the twentieth century (the Maori Council had suggested 1905). But, in the event, the Tribunal's jurisdiction applied only to claims arising after the legislation

[previous page] Matiu Rata, MP for Northern Maori (1963–80) and Minister of Maori Affairs (1972–75), outside Parliament in October 1975, with a number of supporters. DOMINION POST

The 1975 land march, or hikoi, began at Te Hapua in the far north and ended in Wellington, where a petition was presented to Prime Minister Bill Rowling at Parliament. The petition and an accompanying memorial of rights were directed at the Town and Country Planning Act and other legislation that impacted adversely on Maori land. The march was a dramatic expression of Maori discontent over loss of land and of determination to part with no more. The march coincided with the passage of the Treaty of Waitangi Bill through its last stages. AUCKLAND STAR, 17 SEPTEMBER 1975

had been passed. There was also no retrospective review of legislation already on the statute book. Above all, the Tribunal had no power to enforce its recommendations.

For a time, the legislation appeared to be a piece of government 'window-dressing', a suspicion that gained substance at the end of 1975 when the incoming National government delayed setting up the Tribunal. After an initial burst of activity in 1977, with hearings that opened in the incongruous setting of the plush ballroom of Auckland's Intercontinental Hotel, potential claimants seemed to lose interest. The Tribunal went into recess. An amendment in 1977 transferred its administration from the Department of Maori Affairs to the Department

Marchers were allowed to cross the Auckland Harbour Bridge on foot and the numbers swelled as they advanced – with the Auckland city skyline at the rear. CHRISTIAN HEINEGG, ALEXANDER TURNBULL LIBRARY, PA-15-06

of Justice. Claims were few, and both officials and Maori turned their attention for a time to the incorporation of Maori rights within human rights legislation.

It would be another five years before the Waitangi Tribunal began to fulfil some of the purposes envisaged by Matiu Rata and his supporters. Maori demands for political change, meanwhile, took other, more assertive forms.

A wave of protest

The continuing loss of land and other problems were drawing Maori – both young and old – together. This sense of unity was demonstrated in September and October 1975 by a massive land march. Led from Te Hapua in the far north by Te Rarawa kuia Whina Cooper, the march took a month to reach Parliament, stopping at many marae on its route. It coincided with the final passage of the Treaty of Waitangi Bill through Parliament, and raised both Maori and Pakeha awareness of the issues at stake.

There was a new note of resolve in the protests of the late 1970s. The stands Maori took over land disputes at Auckland's Bastion Point in 1977–78 and at Raglan in 1978 were emphatic and challenging. And, in 1979, Matiu Rata resigned from the Labour Party to set up the Mana Motuhake Party, aimed at self-determination for the Maori people within the existing framework of government.

On the last day, the hikoi filled Lambton Quay on its way through Wellington to Parliament. RAY PIGNEY, AUCKLAND STAR, 13/14 OCTOBER 1975

Large-scale immigration from the Pacific Islands brought fresh complications to race relations. The Treaty began to be seen by officials as the unifying symbol of an emerging multicultural society. Keith Holyoake, Governor General in the late 1970s, looked forward to the complete fulfilment of 'He iwi tahi tatou' by eliminating 'any form of distinction' between Maori and Pakeha. Many Maori interpreted this to mean the complete loss of a Maori identity. They pointed out that, until Pakeha accepted the full implications of biculturalism, national aspirations to multiculturalism were premature.

Waitangi Day now provided a forum for a new phase of protest. Challenges had originated with urban Maori groups in the 1970s; strident protest dominated the Waitangi ceremonies, particularly between 1979 and 1983. Young educated Maori were ready to articulate grievance forcefully; many were informed about protest movements in other parts of the world. A succession of groups began to challenge the Pakeha record in fulfilling Treaty promises – Nga

CHAPTER SIX: NEW DEPARTURES 147

Filling Parliament grounds at the end of the march, 13 October 1975. CHRISTIAN HEINEGG, ALEXANDER TURNBULL LIBRARY, PA7-15-12

Tamatoa, Kotahitanga (revived in the 1960s), the Maori Organisation of Human Rights and, by the end of the 1970s, the Waitangi Action Committee and associated groups.

The demand of the modern protest groups was initially for greater Pakeha awareness and acceptance of Maoritanga – the whole complex of Maori culture and identity – which they claimed the Treaty had guaranteed. By 1980, the cry was for recognition of the Maori people as tangata whenua, the people of the land, and for an end to the loss of land from Maori ownership. Some called for Pakeha to acknowledge Maori sovereignty. There was little talk of the Treaty as a sacred compact, a concept that some regarded as suspect.

In response, the government became more cautious in pressing the 'one people' theme, and moved away from the concept of Waitangi Day as a Maori-Pakeha 'celebration'. Instead, it would be the 'celebration of an historical event'. But this was an official evasion of Treaty issues, and a number of Pakeha (including church leaders) became increasingly reluctant to follow the official celebratory line at Waitangi Day ceremonies.

Whina Cooper, who was in her eightieth year, speaks to the hikoi at Parliament on 13 October; she had started the march a month earlier at Te Hapua. DOMINION POST, 13 OCTOBER 1975

By the mid 1980s, the major churches were reappraising the role of the Treaty, through individual and group study. Most reviewed their leadership and structures to reflect bicultural principles; some also reassessed the validity of holding land gifted by Maori for specific purposes for which it was no longer being used. New Zealanders generally, however, seemed more bemused and irritated by ongoing protest – although a random sampling of opinion in March 1983 indicated that most wanted to retain a day commemorating the Treaty signing.

In the early 1980s, Maori opinion on the Treaty was possibly more diverse than Pakeha. Activists were calling for 'ratification' of the Treaty, by which they usually meant greater legislative recognition, and for a 'boycott' of Waitangi Day ceremonies. By word and action, they challenged Maori to rethink long-held assumptions. For the elders of Te Tii marae at Waitangi, thrust into the public eye by protests, the challenge was not easy to accept. Protesters and police clashed at the marae in 1981, when one protester rushed on to the rostrum during the investiture of Whina Cooper and Graham Latimer. Maori leaders felt that the young were

[1] The Maori Affairs Department consulted with kaumatua around the country as its policies were reshaped in the 1980s. Hemi Te Wau-Peita, from Panguru, and Ephraim Te Paa, from Ahipara, attended a hui at Waiwhetu marae in Lower Hutt, as part of these developments in central government.
IAN MACKLEY, EVENING POST, 1 APRIL 1982. DOMINION POST COLLECTION, ALEXANDER TURNBULL LIBRARY, EP-1982-0981-14A

[2] Northern elder Simon Snowden speaking at a Waitangi ceremony in 1988. Protests by young Maori were not always easily accepted by elders, who regarded the Treaty as the special work of their ancestors. NORTHERN ADVOCATE

'trampling on the mana of their elders' by their methods of protest and their criticism of the Treaty. Many elders considered that the Treaty itself was not at fault, only the way it had been ignored by government or used in ways detrimental to Maori welfare.

The Tribunal's first reports

The Waitangi Tribunal, however, now held some promise. It had become active in the early 1980s under the chairmanship of Chief Judge Edward Durie. The National government's 'Think Big' projects of the 1970s (such as making methanol out of natural gas) had exacerbated Maori concerns about the environment, and the Tribunal heard several major claims involving environmental issues. Its findings and reports attracted considerable public attention: in 1983, a report on a claim by Te Ati Awa of Taranaki (known as the Motunui-Waitara Report), over the pollution of offshore fishing reefs by chemical discharge; in 1984, a report on a claim

Eva Rickard mounted protests in the 1970s over the Raglan golf course, where she staged an occupation resulting in her arrest in February 1978. Here she points out the land to Venn Young, Minister of Lands. The golf course was on Maori land that had included a village and urupa (burial ground). Taken compulsorily under the Public Works Act during the Second World War as an emergency landing strip for aircraft, the land was not returned after the war but was leased out by the local council as a golf course. Plans to expand the course prompted Rickard's campaign to attract public attention to this injustice. In 1984, the government made an agreement to return some of the land, part of which the golf course continued to lease.
NEW ZEALAND HERALD, 12 FEBRUARY 1978

concerning the discharge of sewage into the Kaituna River; and in 1985, a report on the Manukau Harbour that involved extensive fishing and usage rights.

The Crown had only to consider the Tribunal's recommendations – there was no obligation to act. But media coverage of Tribunal hearings built up public support, and this forced Prime Minister Robert Muldoon to reconsider his initial decision to ignore the findings. Solutions were found. Te Ati Awa's grievances were partially met: the right of Syngas to discharge effluent was cancelled, and provision made for its discharge through the Waitara Borough Council's upgraded sewerage system. Crown funding met a substantial part of the associated

[1] Protest at Takaparawha (Bastion Point), Auckland, began in the 1970s, as Ngati Whatua struggled to regain possession of their land. An occupation lasting 506 days ended when police evicted protesters from the Orakei site on 25 May 1978.
NEW ZEALAND HERALD, c. 26 MAY 1978

[2] Police guard Takaparawha as a child looks on.
NEW ZEALAND HERALD, ARCHIVES NEW ZEALAND/TE RUA MAHARA O TE KAWANATANGA, WELLINGTON OFFICE [AAMK W3495, 25/I]

The Bastion Point occupation was commemorated as protest over Ngati Whatua land rights continued into the 1980s. This 1982 banner reads: 'Stick to the Point: Reoccupy'. The Waitangi Tribunal's report in 1987 suggested a solution for the disputed land, and led to legislation in 1991. GIL HANLY

costs. In response to the Kaituna claim, a scheme for an improved sewage treatment plant and land disposal of the effluent ended the discharge into Lake Rotorua. The Manukau Report identified the need for comprehensive planning measures that involved various Crown, local and private bodies. Although work began in the latter part of the 1980s, it was recognised that a satisfactory resolution of the problems in Manukau Harbour would take years.

These were the first major reports from the Tribunal, and they made both politicians and the public much more aware of the Treaty. While showing some caution, the reports were also exploring the extent to which the Tribunal could test the terms of the 1975 Act. As law professor Jane Kelsey observed in her 1990 book *A Question of Honour?*:

> When reading the reports it is essential to bear in mind the tribunal's two distinct powers – one to interpret the Treaty and the other to investigate claims and recommend redress based on the 'practical application' of the 'principles of the Treaty'. With the first the tribunal was free from constraints. The second was intended to produce solutions within the political and economic status quo.

As a result, the Tribunal's recommendations were moderate, while its discussion of the Treaty principles tested the boundaries. The Motunui-Waitara Report used the conventions of international law to suggest that, where there was conflict between two texts, a treaty should be interpreted against the party that drafted the document. In the Kaituna Report, the Tribunal

Sally Mana Te Noki Kerena and Netta Wharehoka quietly work away during a Waitangi Tribunal hearing on the Motunui-Waitara claim at Owae marae in 1982. The claim, lodged by Aila Taylor on behalf of Te Ati Awa iwi, concerned discharge of sewage and industrial waste on the coast between New Plymouth and Waitara. Some 35 miles (56 kilometres) of the tribe's fishing reefs and a valuable food source had been adversely affected or polluted. The claim was brought to the Tribunal when further development threatened the Motunui reef, one of the few safe reefs left for collecting seafood. FIONA CLARK

discussed the relationship between 'kawanatanga' and 'sovereignty', as used in the Maori and English versions. In the Manukau Report, the Tribunal discussed the rights and limits involved in Maori cession of kawanatanga; one of those limits involved Crown ownership of harbours and the sea, which the Tribunal noted had not been ceded in the Maori text.

However, these challenges to the Crown's authority were not reflected in the recommendations, which acknowledged the Crown's legitimacy to govern and looked to redress based on the 'practical application' of the principles of the Treaty. This resort to the principles avoided confronting issues of sovereignty and tino rangatiratanga, but it brought into the public arena a discussion of the powers ceded and confirmed in the Treaty. The Tribunal's approach indicated caution about responses from both government and the public. Also, as a government-appointed body, the Tribunal was bound to operate within certain constraints.

David Doorbar, chairman of the Te Atiawa Iwi Authority, seen here with Jim and Chris O'Carroll, argued that this sacred place had been desecrated by mining, pipelines and river diversion. EVENING POST, 6 JULY 1996, DOMINION POST COLLECTION, ALEXANDER TURNBULL LIBRARY, E-571-Q-037-2

The Tribunal's reports and the protests at Waitangi triggered public debate on the Treaty and its place in modern New Zealand. They were significant, too, in opening up divisions among Maori. By the end of 1983, the Maori Council of Churches and Maori MPs were so concerned that they met to seek ways of reconciling differences. A hikoi of around three thousand people, including key representatives of religious groups, made its way to Waitangi for the February 1984 commemoration. As a way of drawing public attention to Treaty matters, the hikoi was highly successful, although it failed to present a unified front to the Governor General, David Beattie, who waited in vain to receive a deputation.

Debate and protest had an impact in the political arena as well. Labour in opposition was eager for Maori support, and hoped to give Maori concerns a fairer hearing. Announcing its Treaty policy in February 1984, Labour promised (if elected) to look into the unsatisfactory Waitangi Day 'celebrations', to consider incorporating the Treaty into a proposed Bill of Rights, and to extend the Tribunal's mandate to cover grievances arising since 1840. The promises were repeated before the snap election of July 1984, which Labour won.

Leaders of the fourth Labour government: Geoffrey Palmer, Minister of Justice and Attorney-General (1984–89), and David Lange, Prime Minister (1984–89). Palmer was Prime Minister from 8 August 1989 to 4 September 1990.
DON ROY, *DOMINION POST*, 21 DECEMBER 1988

The fourth Labour government

In government, Labour immediately and dramatically accelerated the pace of change on Treaty issues, with effects that would last long after its two terms (1984–90). Implementing the commitment to acknowledge the Treaty was to have a huge impact, not only on the work of the Tribunal but also on legislation and ultimately on most government structures. The policy would also come into conflict with other radical changes proposed by Labour that aimed at economic 'efficiency'. These consequences do not seem to have been fully appreciated by Labour leaders, either before the 1984 election or for some time afterwards.

The new Labour government gave Maori affairs a relatively high profile, and Maori expectations were raised accordingly. In September 1984, the Maori Council of Churches and a wide range of Maori organisations called a hui at Turangawaewae, in Ngaruawahia, attended by a thousand people. The aim was to produce a consensus on the Treaty; the general thrust was the political position of the Maori people. Resolutions covered the well-worn territory of earlier Maori requests for government action, including constitutional reform, and stressed in particular the desire for mana Maori motuhake (self-determination); the hui also sought a revamped ceremony at Waitangi. The official response seemed to be positive.

A second hui, held with government assistance at Waitangi on 5–6 February 1985, called for no further Waitangi 'celebrations' until the Treaty had been honoured. Only people from Tai Tokerau, for whom the Treaty remained a special cause associated with tribal mana, dissented. The hui acknowledged that the major challenge for the government in 'honouring' the Treaty (a term much used thereafter) was to find a way of satisfying all interested parties – not an easy task.

One election policy that was not well received by Maori was the proposal for a Bill of Rights. The Ngaruawahia hui made clear its opposition, and its preference for constitutional change that would recognise the Treaty and tino rangatiratanga. But the Deputy Prime Minister and Minister of Justice, Geoffrey Palmer, was committed to a Bill of Rights. When a white paper began to circulate for discussion in 1985, there was a great deal of suspicion among Maori. Leaders pointed to a number of possible outcomes if the Treaty were incorporated in a Bill of Rights (as the white paper proposed): the Treaty's mana would be diminished, for the Treaty was itself a Bill of Rights; the provision for a referendum, by which amendments could be made to the Bill of Rights in future, set the Treaty at risk of being altered; and, finally, a Bill of Rights would be interpreted in the legal system according to Pakeha legal norms, a situation that was unacceptable to Maori.

The Treaty did not find a place in the Bill of Rights legislation finally passed in 1990. Throughout the Labour period, however, the debate about tino rangatiratanga – its definition and its relationship to Crown sovereignty – continued. More than any other issue (and there were many), Maori insistence on tino rangatiratanga challenged the long-standing Crown assertion of sovereignty and the absolute right to govern; by the end of the Labour period, it would draw a firm response from government.

1985 – extending the Tribunal's mandate

Within months of taking office, the Labour government pushed ahead with drafting the promised changes to the Treaty of Waitangi Act 1975. The Treaty of Waitangi Amendment Bill was introduced in December 1984, although its third reading was not until 3 December 1985. In a radical step, the new Act enabled the Waitangi Tribunal to investigate claims referring back to 6 February 1840.

As the Tribunal's early reports had shown, the real problems affecting Maori were rooted in pre-1975 events and legislation: backdating claims to 1840 was a measure of justice welcomed by those who were aware of long-standing Maori efforts to have their grievances heard and remedied. But it seems that the government had underestimated its full impact. Opening up the whole historical record to investigation was likely to release a flood of claims,

In February 1984, Kotahitanga was revived in a hikoi to Waitangi in protest against 'celebrating' the day. Waiting for the march were Race Relations Conciliator, Hiwi Tauroa, the Governor General, David Beattie, and Northland elder James Henare. Several national hui to discuss Maori issues followed the hikoi. NEW ZEALAND HERALD

as some Opposition members pointed out during the passage of the Bill. A few historians and lawyers were also aware of the implications, and may have drawn the government's attention to them; if so, their cautions were ignored.

The Act also expanded the Tribunal to six appointees (of whom at least four had to be Maori), with the Chief Judge of the Maori Land Court as chairperson. Seven other people could be appointed as deputies or alternatives for these members; a quorum consisted of the chairperson and three other members. There was now provision for the Tribunal to appoint its own support staff and contract researchers, and to commission research on any claim; lawyers could be appointed to support the Tribunal's work or to act for claimants.

The amendment laid the foundations for the Tribunal as it now operates. Previously, claims had been heard and reports written by the few Tribunal members, with some assistance from

On 6 February 1984, the hikoi was stopped by police for three hours on the bridge at Waitangi before being allowed to proceed to the Treaty House grounds. Eva Rickard stands in the centre of the front row, with Bishops Whakahuihui Vercoe and Paul Reeves to the right. Titewhai Harawira is partially obscured behind the official's hat. GIL HANLY

Justice Department staff; a proper support infrastructure would now be established. But all this took time. With the passage of the 1985 amendment, the Tribunal constituted under the 1975 legislation came to an end; but more than nine months would elapse before the new Tribunal was appointed and fully in operation. As some Tribunal members were only part-time, there would be ongoing difficulties in scheduling hearings and completing reports.

Yet the floodgates had been opened, and many were affected as well as the Tribunal itself. The Crown Law Office (which defends Crown interests in claims hearings by responding to the evidence presented) was suddenly dealing with a vast amount of new research. And Maori, who had long wanted the Tribunal to become a forum for resolving historical grievances, had probably not anticipated the full extent of the task ahead, in researching and hearing such claims. No one, in fact, had seen how long it would take to deal with the range

CHAPTER SIX: NEW DEPARTURES 159

Tuhoe leader John Rangihau talks here with the Minister of Social Welfare, Ann Hercus, at a hui to discuss his 1986 report on the Department of Social Welfare's dealings with Maori matters. The report was largely accepted by Labour. DOMINION POST, 7 JUNE 1986

of issues in the new claims; nor had they expected the rapid increase in the number of claims lodged. In May 1986, there was a backlog of fewer than two dozen claims; by the end of 1989, there were 102 registered claims, each with an identifying WAI number.

The Tribunal in its new form would develop its research and other processes only gradually, and would face new complexities before the end of the 1980s. Expectations of a speedy process for hearing and resolving claims would be disappointed. The costs for claimants – as well as for government agencies – were going to be considerable. It appears, too, that the overall outcome or objective of the claims process had not been clearly defined. As the Tribunal evolved, it provided a forum for the expression of grievances; but it did not (and could not) guarantee prompt and satisfactory settlements. Even if the Crown accepted the Tribunal's recommendations (and it was not obliged to do so), the process for negotiating a settlement was separate from the Tribunal's jurisdiction and did not provide a certain outcome for claimants. In fact, for some years there was no government strategy in respect of settlements, and no sure process for negotiations leading to them. In short, a major change had been set in motion without a clear policy direction, structures or funding for settlements.

The Maori language and a Maori voice

The early Tribunal claims had concerned specific tribes and the public in certain areas; in 1985, a claim brought by Huirangi Waikerepuru and the Maori Language Board of Wellington made New Zealanders realise that the Tribunal's work could affect everyone, Maori and Pakeha. The claim asked for te reo Maori to be recognised as an official language of New Zealand, and sought protection for the language under the Treaty. The Tribunal's report, released in 1986, noted that taonga (guaranteed by Article 2) included intangible as well as tangible things — all treasured aspects of being Maori were to be covered. Following the report's recommendations, the Maori Language Act 1987 recognised Maori as an official language and established the Maori Language Commission/Te Taura Whiri i te Reo Maori; judicial proceedings could now also be conducted in Maori. These shifts — radical at the time — would bring in their wake a claim for a fair allocation of radio frequencies, the setting up of Te Mangai Paho/The Maori Language Broadcasting Funding Agency, and the development of iwi radio.

The Maori language claim created a degree of public unease. At the same time, however, the appointment of New Zealand's first Maori Governor General, Anglican Bishop Paul Reeves, in late 1985 was seen as fitting recognition of the nation's bicultural character. Maori leaders in general were expressing a right to a stronger voice in government circles. This was apparent in June 1986, when a departmental advisory committee chaired by John Rangihau submitted a report, *Puao-Te-Ata-Tu: Report of the Ministerial Committee on a Maori Perspective for the Department of Social Welfare*. This not only suggested changes to the Department of Social Welfare, but also recommended that a comprehensive approach be adopted in all government dealings with matters affecting Maori, and that the initiative of the Maori people and the New Zealand community at large be harnessed to help address problems. Ann Hercus, then Minister of Social Welfare, adopted the report and initiated a programme of change in her department. Maori claims and subsequent reports from the Tribunal, coupled with government moves to recognise the Treaty, all brought the Waitangi agreement more forcibly into the public consciousness over these years.

1986 – a crucial year for Treaty issues

For some New Zealanders, events relating to the Treaty of Waitangi were moving too fast for comfort. Nonetheless, move they did in 1986. Government ministers – Geoffrey Palmer, Koro Wetere and Russell Marshall – had been considering ways to recognise the Treaty and to build it into legislation. The Environment Act 1986 and the Conservation Act 1987 both did so: the former incorporated 'the principles of the Treaty' into its long title, the latter into section 4. Palmer would explain, in his 1992 book *New Zealand's Constitution in Crisis*, that statutory incorporation was designed not to give Maori enforceable rights but to require decision-makers exercising powers under various pieces of legislation to give the Treaty proper consideration. In short, they could not ignore it.

These moves marked a radical change, and opened up new possibilities for Maori and the Treaty. The government and its agencies were only partly aware of the likely impact on their work. And it appeared to Palmer that the bureaucracy was for the most part ignoring Treaty issues. On 23 March 1986, therefore, ministers were confronted with a Cabinet paper (prepared by Palmer and Wetere) outlining the implications of government recognition of the Treaty. After lengthy review, the paper went out on 23 June to all ministers and heads of government departments. It stated that 'all future legislation referred to Cabinet at the policy approval stage should draw attention to any implications for recognition of the principles of the Treaty of Waitangi'. Cabinet also agreed 'that departments should consult with appropriate Maori people on all significant matters affecting the application of the Treaty'. That these commitments would require significant resources was acknowledged.

The far-reaching implications of this Cabinet directive were not at first apparent; nor was there a clear ministerial strategy. Unclear what to do, government departments tended to put the directive to one side – a tendency evident later with legislation incorporating the Treaty principles. The public service was largely monocultural, with no great knowledge of New Zealand's history and little appreciation of Maori values. Various training courses had created some awareness of Treaty issues among senior managers; a few, therefore, recognised the need for departments to obtain information and develop a coordinated plan of action. Some departments – Treasury in particular – realised early that there were major implications for policy and practice, and that various departmental interests could be adversely affected. Treasury's work through this period, therefore, was significant in attempting to assess and restrict Crown liability in the settlement of Treaty claims.

At the same time, the Labour government was introducing dramatic economic reforms, which were potentially at odds with its Treaty policies. The conflict came to a head in 1986.

The State-Owned Enterprises Act 1986

On gaining office in 1984, Labour had set out to restructure the economy in order to promote efficiency and growth. Sooner or later, this aim was bound to clash with its commitment to resolving Treaty claims, which usually involved the return of land. The conflict would be most obvious in relation to land, fisheries, water and minerals – the management and ownership of resources. In its proposed reforms, the state was preparing to relinquish the very resources it might use for remedy, and Maori feared there would be no land to return. Government policies and moves to implement them were on a collision path with Maori interests and the Treaty. The crunch came when the State-Owned Enterprises (SOE) Bill was introduced into Parliament at the end of September 1986.

The object of the legislation was to create a group of state-owned commercial enterprises to replace a number of government departments on 1 April 1987. The nine new corporations would cover land, forestry, electricity, telecommunications, coal, the airways, the Post Office Bank, the Post Office and Government Property Services. Certain Crown assets would be transferred to the new enterprises, including extensive land holdings. That this might be a forerunner to full privatisation of these operations – and their assets – was denied at the time.

Officials realised only gradually the Treaty implications of the SOE Bill. The alienation of land and resources into private ownership would have a massive impact on the government's ability to settle Treaty claims. Further, the economic impact of this legislation would fall particularly on Maori, who would be disproportionately affected by the staff reductions proposed. Unemployment – already a spectre for Maori communities – would increase dramatically, and devastate some rural areas. The government's efforts to improve economic well-being for Maori, as a Treaty obligation, were being undermined by its own legislation. Officials suggested that the Crown should not be relinquishing ownership of the land but only usage rights, but this was not accepted by ministers.

The Muriwhenua claim

The Waitangi Tribunal soon saw the consequences of the SOE Bill for Maori. In early December 1986, Tribunal hearings were to open on the Muriwhenua claim, which involved the five tribes of the far north of the North Island. The claim covered land and fishing rights in the area from Whangape Harbour on the west coast, up the Aupouri Peninsula (including Ninety Mile Beach), and down the east coast as far as Whangaroa Harbour. Large areas of Crown land were involved, as well as fisheries, minerals and other resources. The claimants' lawyers pointed out that the SOE Bill would remove from Crown control assets that claimants sought to have returned. Moreover, land had sometimes been given up for forestry development in return for employment opportunities; many places were also identified as wahi tapu (sacred sites or cemeteries).

On 8 December 1986, the Tribunal made an interim report asserting that the SOE Bill was in breach of the principles of the Treaty. Maori tribal groups, led by Hepi Te Heuheu of Ngati Tuwharetoa and Tipene O'Regan of Ngai Tahu, lobbied with some result. Section 9 was added, but this was only a general declaration: 'Nothing in this Act shall permit the Crown to act in a manner that is inconsistent with the principles of the Treaty of Waitangi.' Further pressure led to section 27, which made special provision for lands subject to a claim before the Waitangi Tribunal on the day the Act became law (18 December 1986).

The protection of Maori interests was by no means secured. For example, tribal groups were concerned that the transfer of Crown land to Landcorp (an SOE) would make the land unavailable for possible recommendations by the Tribunal, because section 27 covered only claims to Crown land made *before* 18 December 1986. Claims made *after* that date might find that the land had already passed into private ownership through Landcorp selling to a third party.

In the first months of 1987, tribes struggled to secure information from government departments and to gauge the impact the SOE Act would have. Several major tribal groups sought undertakings that Crown lands in their areas would be withheld from corporatisation

During the Court of Appeal hearings, a large number of Maori attended in the court's public gallery, among them Whina Cooper (front right). In late June 1987, the court was full to hear the Court of Appeal's decision – which confirmed that government-owned land subject to a Treaty claim could not be transferred to state-owned enterprises. The case, brought by the New Zealand Maori Council, set a precedent that gave new life to the Treaty. DOMINION POST, 5 MAY 1987

while claims were being worked out. The Maori Council, however, came to the conclusion that no area would be unaffected by the Act, and that it needed to take legal action to protect tribal interests everywhere.

The Court of Appeal case, 1987

On 30 March 1987, the Maori Council applied to the High Court in Wellington for an interim order preventing the transfer of any Crown asset to an SOE, and for the case to be referred to the Court of Appeal. Hearings were held in May. The case turned largely on whether the special provisions of section 27 were the sole protection under the Act for Maori land claims, or whether the general declaration (section 9) gave more protection. On 29 June, the court gave

Robin Cooke, President of the Court of Appeal, led the team of five judges for the case brought by the New Zealand Maori Council and heard in 1987. The case was the first judicial consideration of Treaty principles.
DOMINION POST, 2 MAY 1986

its judgement. The five judges each reported separately, but were unanimous in their decision. The President of the Court of Appeal, Robin Cooke, stated that 'the principles of the Treaty of Waitangi override everything else in the State-Owned Enterprises Act'. The Crown was now required to work out a scheme safeguarding known and reasonably foreseeable claims, submit it to the Maori Council for agreement or comment, and finally send it to the Court of Appeal for approval.

The Court of Appeal's report discussed the principles of the Treaty in some detail. It noted that the principles 'require the Pakeha and Maori Treaty partners to act towards each other reasonably and with the utmost good faith', and that cooperation had to be at the heart of the agreed relationship between the Treaty signatories. Negotiations, therefore, were to be an important factor in Crown–Maori relationships. In particular, the judges stressed that the Treaty created a relationship 'akin to a partnership', which they saw as the central principle of the Treaty. As commentators noted, the precise terms of such a partnership had yet to be worked out in practice. For the Crown, there was a duty actively to protect Maori interests, using the Tribunal to ensure redress, and to ensure that Crown decision-making was adequately informed with respect to policies affecting Treaty rights. In return, Maori had a duty to be loyal to the Queen, to accept her government, and to provide reasonable cooperation.

The Maori Council case thus provided the first judicial consideration of Treaty principles as incorporated in a statute. The Court of Appeal's decision was to become a landmark, setting a precedent that gave new life to the Treaty. Previously, the country's law courts had been unable to give legal effect to the Treaty unless legislation incorporated a reference to the Treaty or its principles. For years this had prevented Maori claimants from successfully arguing Treaty rights in the courts. As the judges' report observed, it was not only in the context of the SOE Act but also in 'any other Acts in which the principles apply, [that] these duties will be enforceable if necessary by the Courts'.

The media covered the case extensively, stressing the liberal, conciliatory nature of the judgement and noting that the Maori Council had been 'vindicated' in bringing the case to the Court of Appeal. What was not so obvious at the time was that, in accepting the court's decision, Maori were accepting that sovereignty was held indisputably by the Crown: the Court of Appeal was exercising authority derived from sovereignty. The struggle for tino rangatiratanga would continue in other forums.

The Treaty of Waitangi (State Enterprises) Act 1988

Meanwhile, the government had already pushed ahead with its SOE policy, and corporations were operating under interim agreements. The vast range of Crown assets made the agreement on safeguards for potential Maori interests extremely difficult. Negotiations between the government and the Maori Council from July to December 1987 were fraught with tension as proposals and counter-proposals were exchanged. The Maori Council's key concern was that all Crown land and other assets should be screened before any transfer was made to SOEs; claims and potential claims involving SOE land had to be protected. The government wanted options for various kinds of land and other assets, and a cut-off date for any new claims that might involve such assets; these proposals were unacceptable to the council. By September, the government felt its SOE policy was in jeopardy. It was also under pressure on other fronts: Maori legal action was threatened with respect to fisheries, and Tainui were promising litigation if the government did not halt Landcorp moves to sell Crown assets that were involved in claims relating to nineteenth-century confiscations.

The Treaty of Waitangi (State Enterprises) Bill, introduced in December 1987, passed into law in mid 1988. The Act provided for the transfer of Crown assets to the SOEs with a right to on-sell, but gave the Tribunal increased powers in respect of land covered by the Act: when privatised, the land would have a memorial on its title and, if a Tribunal hearing found that the land had been acquired in breach of the Treaty, the Tribunal could make an order binding the government to acquire the land again and return it to claimants; the government would be responsible for compensation. The parties did, however, have the opportunity to negotiate an alternative settlement. The Act also allowed for the anticipated increase in research needs at

Tainui turned out in numbers at the Court of Appeal on 28 August 1989 to support the Tainui Maori Trust Board's bid to stop the sale of Coalcorp. Robert Mahuta sits to the right. DOMINION POST COLLECTION, ALEXANDER TURNBULL LIBRARY, EP/1989/3161/14

the Tribunal, the appointment of a Tribunal unit director, a mediation process, and the further provision of legal aid for claimants.

In practice, the Tribunal would use its binding powers very sparingly, partly because there was little need, and partly because, by the mid 1990s, the National government was threatening to alter the Act if the provision was used.

The Waitangi Tribunal expands

The speed with which Treaty issues were emerging made change in the Waitangi Tribunal essential. By the late 1980s, the Tribunal was struggling to meet the demands of its rapidly increasing body of work. The 1985 amendment, giving the Tribunal retrospective powers of investigation to 1840, had increased the number of claims lodged; so, too, had the court action over the SOE Act 1986. Tribes were anxious to put a halt to government moves before they went too far. Hearings on the Muriwhenua claim (from late 1986) and the Ngai Tahu claim

Matiu Rata, previously MP for Northern Maori and Minister of Maori Affairs, continued the battle for Maori rights in fisheries and other areas until his death on 25 July 1997. AUCKLAND STAR, 31 JULY 1997

(from 1987) were progressing and had to be supported; at the same time, reports on earlier claims were being completed. The Ngai Tahu hearings, in particular, brought new demands, as the claim involved most of the South Island and covered a vast range of issues. The research needs of both the Tribunal and the claimants were immense, and far more diverse than for any previous claims. The Crown Law Office also began to employ its own historical research and support staff.

The Tribunal and its supporting office unit both expanded. The Treaty of Waitangi Amendment Act 1988 allowed for sixteen full members (raised to seventeen in 1989) and did away with the provision for deputy members. It also eliminated the requirement for a majority of Maori members at hearings, although in appointing members the Minister of Maori Affairs had to 'have regard to the partnership between the 2 parties to the Treaty' and also the knowledge and experience needed in a range of matters that were likely to come before the Waitangi Tribunal. Under the amendment, a maximum of seven members and a minimum of three were required at any one sitting. These steps allowed more than one claim hearing to be held at the same time.

The Tribunal's support staff grew rapidly. The small team set up under the 1985 legislation became a full unit, with funding for additional costs. Under Wira Gardiner, the Tribunal's first director from 1988, researchers were appointed, office systems improved, and a document bank on confiscated land created. These developments would continue under Buddy Mikaere, appointed director in 1990.

Fisheries and the Treaty

In both the Muriwhenua and Ngai Tahu claims, the issue that was to prove most complex, divisive and difficult to resolve was that of fishery rights. Under Article 2 of the Treaty, Maori are 'confirmed and guaranteed' the 'full, exclusive and undisturbed possession [rangatiratanga] of their lands and estates, forests, fisheries and other properties [taonga]'. The Crown has a responsibility to protect this right, but fishery rights are also involved in the Crown's exercise of sovereignty, as well as in the rights of all citizens at common law to fish.

After the release of the Motunui-Waitara Report, the government began to appraise the situation. An interdepartmental committee was set up in 1984 to assess whether the law relating to fishing rights acknowledged the interests of the Maori people, 'having regard to the principles of the Treaty of Waitangi'; its report, released a year later, revealed how little was known about Crown treatment of Maori fishing rights, and how muddled it all was.

In May 1986, the Minister of Justice asked the newly appointed Law Commission 'to consider and report on the law affecting Maori fisheries'. A draft report, in limited circulation from early 1987, documented the continuous Maori exercise of fishing rights since 1840; Maori struggles to maintain those rights against incursions by early settlers and later statutes and regulations; and the extent of long-standing Maori protest to government. The evidence, supported by numerous quotations dating from the colony's first decades, was undeniable. Settlements in the 1920s had achieved limited recognition of freshwater fishing rights in Lakes Taupo and Rotorua, but coastal sea fisheries were a different matter. The report, held back for fear that the Law Commission would appear to favour Maori unduly, was finally released in March 1989, by which time evidence of the history of Maori fishing rights was publicly available elsewhere.

Commercial and traditional fishing rights

As the Law Commission was starting to research Maori fishing rights, the Ministry of Agriculture and Fisheries (MAF) was introducing a quota management system (QMS) under the Fisheries Amendment Act 1986. This new system, designed to protect seriously depleted

The Law Commission Report on Fisheries

Among its conclusions, the report stated that:

> The Maori people have never accepted the official view of their fishing rights, or been reconciled to the rejection of their claims. They saw the actions of governments, and by implication the decisions of courts, as a breach of the promises made to them in 1840. They consistently used the ordinary procedures available to them for the redress of grievances with little success. Current claims and protests have simply been more sharply expressed and directed and have had the benefit of wide publicity. This is at least in part the product of the greater opportunity created by the establishment of the Waitangi Tribunal.

SOURCE: *THE TREATY OF WAITANGI AND MAORI FISHERIES*, LAW COMMISSION, WELLINGTON, 1989, P.181

national resources, was based on the allocation of individual transferable quotas (ITQs) to those engaged in the fishing industry. The ITQ for each species was to be allocated on the basis of catch history, which effectively excluded part-time fishers. Many were Maori who took part in commercial fishing on a seasonal basis, which the previous licensing system had allowed. In effect, creating these tradeable, harvesting rights in perpetuity privatised the fisheries and ignored Maori fishing rights, recognised in Article 2 of the Treaty. These, Maori claimed, had never been relinquished.

Some admission of Maori rights had long been made in legislation – in the form of a series of regulations providing for Maori to take fish in certain locations and quantities for tribal needs. The Fisheries Amendment Act 1986 (which set up the ITQ scheme) and the main Fisheries Act 1983 both recognised Maori interests. Section 88(2) of the 1983 Act, for example, provided that nothing in the Act 'shall affect any Maori fishing rights'; this had been interpreted by MAF to mean specifically traditional – that is, non-commercial – fishing.

That traditional rights *did* involve a commercial aspect and that Maori had *not* relinquished any fishing rights confirmed by Article 2 of the Treaty were among the arguments presented in the Muriwhenua and Ngai Tahu claims. These arguments, supported by strong historical evidence, were to influence court judgements. After the first Muriwhenua hearings in early December 1986, there were moves to put the proposed quota management system on hold. Maori fishing interests would be adversely affected, the claimants said, but they also feared that the ITQ scheme would alienate fisheries from Crown control for ever. The Tribunal agreed, and warned the government formally on 10 December that further allocations of ITQs would prejudice the Tribunal's ability to make recommendations, and could lead to major demands for compensation. The Tribunal requested that the quota management system, then being introduced on a species-by-species basis, be halted. The gazetting of quota management areas covering twenty-two species went ahead nonetheless on 23 December.

170 AN ILLUSTRATED HISTORY OF THE TREATY OF WAITANGI

Drying eels at Lake Wairewa (Lake Forsyth) in 1948. Harvesting and preserving food was a crucial activity for Maori communities through the nineteenth century and into the twentieth century.
ARCHIVES NEW ZEALAND/TE RUA MAHARA O TE KAWANATANGA, WELLINGTON OFFICE (ALEXANDER TURNBULL LIBRARY, F4004/½ (AAQT 6401, A6120))

Maori concerns about the QMS led to court proceedings in 1987, even as hearings on the fisheries aspects of the Muriwhenua claim continued to take place. By September, the Tribunal was still not ready to issue its report on Muriwhenua fishing; the Minister of Fisheries meanwhile was determined to proceed with the allocation of quota in new species. Maori interests then sought an interim injunction to prevent further species being brought under the ITQ system. They argued that the quota management system was *ultra vires*, or outside the powers of the Minister of Fisheries: that contrary to the terms of section 88(2) of the Fisheries Act 1983, the QMS affected Maori fishing rights guaranteed by the Treaty; and that, to the extent that it affected coastal tribes, it was unlawful. An injunction was granted that halted

The Te Weehi Case

A landmark case in 1986 was seen as upholding traditional Maori fishing rights. In August that year, in the Christchurch High Court, Justice Williamson quashed a conviction against a Maori fisherman, Tom Te Weehi, caught with under-sized paua in January 1984. The judge cited section 88(2) of the Fisheries Act 1983, which stated that 'Nothing in this Act shall affect any Maori fishing rights.' Reviewing legislation and case history regarding traditional Maori fishing rights, he observed that the case before him was not based on ownership of land, or on an exclusive right to a foreshore or river bank; the claim was a 'non-territorial' one, and the right was limited in this particular case to Ngai Tahu and the iwi's authorised relatives for personal food. The decision, nevertheless, was seen by disconcerted fishing industry officials as a landmark judgement that could put Maori fishermen outside fishing controls and make industry management pointless.

extension of the quota management system; temporary arrangements allowed commercial fishing to continue.

Justice Greig, who had read the interim findings on the Muriwhenua claim, heard the application. He found that Maori fishing rights, including commercial aspects, existed prior to the Treaty and had not been extinguished by statute; the effect of section 88(2) was to preserve any Maori fishing rights with that commercial element, but subject to proof of their existence, scope and extent. Uncertain of the legal implications, the government feared the courts might decide that Maori had exclusive rights to the 200-mile fishing zone around New Zealand; court investigation of the extent of such rights would be a lengthy business. Faced with these possibilities, and the prospect of a court case on the legality or otherwise of the QMS, the government decided in December 1987 to start negotiations.

A joint working group on fisheries was established, with four Crown members and four Maori representing Muriwhenua (Matiu Rata), Ngai Tahu (Tipene O'Regan), the New Zealand Maori Council (Graham Latimer) and Tainui of Waikato (Denese Henare). To assist with negotiation costs, $1.5 million was made available to the Maori side. The negotiations were detailed, involved and prolonged. The Maori negotiators were claiming the Treaty guarantees of rangatiratanga and Maori ownership of the fisheries; as they firmed up their case, they argued that, while Maori would be justified in claiming exclusive rights, they were seeking a fifty-fifty partnership, covering ownership, profits and management. Pending a negotiated settlement, the Maori team was prepared to accept an interim arrangement and to allow a substantial period for the Crown to return property rights in fisheries. Above all, the negotiators were concerned that fisheries allocated under the QMS should not become permanently alienated property rights.

The Muriwhenua Fishing Report 1988

The Muriwhenua claim linked evidence of traditional usage to grievances arising from recent government policies. Claimants said that, from time immemorial, they had fished their coastal and deep-sea waters, but that government policy, especially in the preceding fifty years, had gradually forced them out. Then, early in the 1980s, a new fishing policy limited commercial fishing to those who could prove that they derived 80 per cent of their income from that source. This excluded most Maori fishermen, who tended to engage in part-time fishing to augment their income as seasonal workers and small farmers. Claimants sought remedial action and compensation. It was evident that the policy's impact on Maori communities had been severe and had added to the search for employment in urban areas. By the end of 1985, fewer than two thousand Maori were left in the fishing industry. The way the ITQ system operated also made it difficult for newcomers to buy in to the system. This and the initial ITQ allocation favoured the big fishing firms.

The Crown, on the other hand, was seeking to accommodate some Maori rights within an economically efficient structure for the fishing industry – one that would provide revenue to the government and confirm its authority over the fisheries resource. The historical basis for the Maori stand was probably understood by very few. The negotiations, often strained, were scheduled to reach agreement in principle before 30 June 1988, but failed to do so. All were waiting on the release of the Muriwhenua report on sea fisheries.

The Muriwhenua hearings drew to a close in April 1988. An interim report in June concluded that: 'The Treaty guaranteed to Maori full protection for their fishing activities, including unrestricted rights to develop them along either or both customary or modern lines.' To give that protection, the Crown had an obligation to support Maori economic initiatives in fishing; in Muriwhenua, this extended to deep-sea, offshore fisheries, and included the whole of the adjacent continental shelf. The Crown, therefore, 'must bargain for any public right to the commercial exploitation of the inshore fishery'. The report's only recommendation was that the Crown should meet the 'Maori party's reasonable costs' of negotiation, including the costs of legal and technical assistance.

The 1988 commercial fishing season was due to open on 1 October – the new date set for a negotiated settlement from the working group on Maori fisheries. Public opinion was growing hostile. Non-Maori fishing interests kept up pressure on the government and fired up the public with full-page advertisements warning of 'an end to fishing in New Zealand'. Maori negotiators, under considerable pressure from their own tribal groups, held to a fifty-fifty settlement and threatened a return to court action (which was partly in abeyance). The government considered ways in which some justice could be delivered to Maori, at minimal cost and without sacrificing the quota system or further alienating the general public.

Mac Taylor from Tai Tokerau (Northland) leans forward thoughtfully, as Waitangi Day proceedings unfold in 1987.
DOMINION POST COLLECTION, ALEXANDER TURNBULL LIBRARY, EP/1987/0630/25

The issue had become a very hot potato, and a solution had to be found. Through this time, several versions of a Maori Fisheries Bill had been before Parliament but none had proceeded to legislation. A proposal from Geoffrey Palmer eventually resulted in the Maori Fisheries Act 1989.

Maori Fisheries Act 1989

The stated purposes of the Act were 'to make better provision for the recognition of Maori fishing rights secured by the Treaty of Waitangi'; it was also 'to facilitate the entry of Maori into, and the development by Maori of, the business and activity of fishing'; and to make provision for the conservation and management of the rock lobster fishery. A seven-member Maori Fisheries Commission (with $10 million in funding) would be established, to receive 10 per cent of all ITQs; this transfer was to be completed by the end of October 1992. The commission could allocate some of this quota to tribes or individuals on a lease arrangement, but 50 per cent of its quota allocation had to go to Aotearoa Fisheries Ltd, a company to be set up by the commission. The commission would hold all the company's shares and would distribute dividends, but quota could be assigned and used as Aotearoa Fisheries determined.

The Maori Fisheries Act also addressed customary fishing rights in estuaries or waters close to the coast. Fishing grounds in these waters that had spiritual or cultural significance or were valued as a food source could, subject to certain requirements, be declared a taiapure or local Maori fishery, which would be managed by an appointed committee representing the local Maori community. This offered some recognition of Maori authority and tribal rights, although Maori resented the constraints it placed on tribal authority. This was not, as the wording of the Act might suggest, a recognition of rangatiratanga. Nonetheless, regulations for taiapure would be established first for the South Island and eventually for other areas, in a gradual, ongoing process.

The Maori Fisheries Act 1989 did not repeal section 88(2) of the Fisheries Act 1983. And Maori still had the option of going back to court to secure a judgement on the extent of their rights in fisheries. The injunctions halting the introduction of the QMS had been lifted, but the case brought against their introduction and the legality of the system was effectively put on hold for about three years. The 1989 Act was thus an interim arrangement, not a final settlement. It deferred the resolution of complex issues for a time; within a few years, negotiations between Maori and the Crown would lead to a different settlement. And ahead lay intense and bitter wrangles between Maori and Maori over fishery rights, quota allocation and the Maori Fisheries Commission.

CHAPTER SEVEN

The Roller-coaster Years
— 1987 to 1990

Tribunal members find proceedings on 13 March 1989 amusing – Bishop Manuhuia Bennett and Monita Delamere, with Gordon Orr and Mary Boyd partly obscured at the rear. MARTIN HUNTER, *DOMINION POST*, 13 MARCH 1989

As the Labour government forged ahead with the sweeping changes of the mid 1980s, it was repeatedly confronted by unresolved issues relating to the Treaty. The key questions were: the relationship between the Crown and the Maori people; the position of Maori in New Zealand society; and how an agreement made in 1840 could be translated into modern terms of reference. These challenges might have been anticipated, but apparently were not – at least not in practical terms. Perhaps the effects of change at this time were simply so extensive, complex and diverse (and sometimes so closely interrelated) that they defied precise planning.

The clash between recognition of the Treaty and Labour's economic reforms was, however, apparent as soon as restructuring began. The government recognised the need to address the Waitangi Tribunal's recommendations (arising from claim reports), but nothing coherent in the way of policies or structures emerged. No minister was in charge of Treaty issues; no one department was responsible for developing Treaty policy or for coordinating and implementing it, and no specific budgetary provision was made for settlements. Geoffrey Palmer was Attorney-General and Minister of Justice from 1984 to mid 1989, and Prime Minister from

[previous page] Edward Taihakurei Durie, Chair of the Waitangi Tribunal from 1981, leaves a meeting. Durie had a great influence over Treaty issues in the following decades. *DOMINION POST*

New Tribunal members line up in March 1989. Left to right: Joanne Morris, John Kneebone, Ngapare Hopa, Mary Boyd, Erihana Ryan and Evelyn Stokes. DOMINION POST, 14 MARCH 1989

early August 1989 to September 1990; with Treasury, he endeavoured to handle a messy and complex situation. By the time Labour began its second term in 1987, sorting out policy and process was an urgent priority.

Waitangi Tribunal reports, legislative changes and court actions made a potent mix for the media over these years. Barely a day passed without news breaking on some aspect of Treaty matters, often in dramatic or sensational style. Bemused, or simply confused, the public could be forgiven for thinking — as many did — that the Treaty had sprung from nowhere, and that the nation was on a roller-coaster with no brakes. As Labour pursued its policies, a high level of public disquiet developed. Much was directed at the Waitangi Tribunal, perhaps because it was the government agency most readily identifiable with the Treaty. The Treaty's impact in other areas was probably harder to grasp.

Orakei and Waiheke

In 1987, the government faced an election. The Waitangi Tribunal was due to release several reports, and other claims were in progress. All were covered widely in the media. Labour was anxious that public opinion was not rocked too hard by the reports, but this was inescapable.

Members of Ngati Paoa occupied land on Waiheke Island in 1984. The Tribunal's Waiheke Island Report on a claim brought by Ngati Paoa was released in June 1987 and a settlement followed in 1989. GULF NEWS

Two of the reports involved Auckland, the country's largest centre of population, and the tribal groups Ngati Paoa and Ngati Whatua. As W. H. Oliver observed in his 1991 book, *Claims to the Waitangi Tribunal*, the two claims had similarities:

> Each came from a virtually landless tribe; each asked for small but significant pieces of land on which to re-establish a standing place, some economic viability and tribal mana ... Each was concerned with land which had become Crown land, some of it passing into other hands. Each, finally, illustrates the complex history through which the Tribunal had to find its way, the impossibility of finding simple solutions and the inevitable disproportion between any conceivable remedy and the loss suffered.

The reports attracted considerable public attention and media debate. Both claims had also involved demonstrations and protests, ending in prosecutions and convictions; this added to Maori sensitivity over the claims and to public interest in the outcomes.

The Ngati Paoa claim concerned Waiheke Island. One of the larger islands in the Hauraki Gulf, with a growing permanent population, this was a popular resort for Aucklanders. The

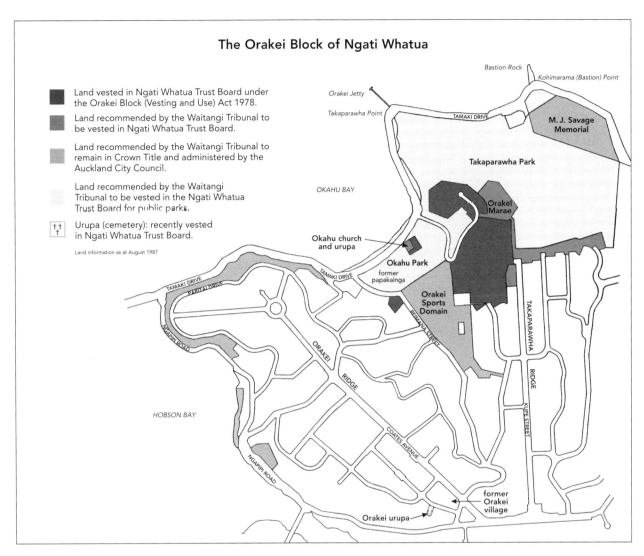

This map of land involved in the Orakei claim (from the Orakei Report 1987) shows the Waitangi Tribunal's recommendations. Negotiations resulted in the Orakei Act 1991 and other agreements that provided for the claim's resolution. Land was returned to the Trust Board for Ngati Whatua's care and use in 1991. A larger area – Okahu Park (and the beach above the high-tide line) and Takaparawha – was vested in the tribe for their benefit and that of the people of Auckland. This reserve is jointly managed by Ngati Whatua and Auckland City Council. WWW.WAITANGI-TRIBUNAL.GOVT.NZ/REPORTS/NORTHISLANDNORTH/WA19/APP03.PDF

claim covered early alienations of tribal land. The Waiheke Island Report, released in June 1987, stressed the Crown's duty under the Treaty to protect tribes from total alienation in order to ensure their future needs. For the first time, the Tribunal recommended the return of land, preferably in the form of a farm owned by the Crown; in the final settlement, the land was transferred to the Ngati Paoa Development Trust Board, with funding for the purchase of stock. The overall cost was $1.03 million, and the trust settlement was finalised in 1990. However, the government was not willing to provide funds for tribal land endowments, as the report had recommended, because it would set a precedent for other settlements.

CHAPTER SEVEN: THE ROLLER-COASTER YEARS   181

Radio Frequencies, Broadcasting Assets and the Radio Spectrum

When the Radiocommunications Act was passed in 1989, the government went ahead with its plans to sell off the different sectors of the radio broadcasting system. The New Zealand Maori Council and Nga Kaiwhakapumau i te Reo Inc. (Maori Language Board) lodged a claim with the Tribunal saying that the consultation process had been inadequate. Further claims through the 1990s involved broadcasting assets and management rights to the 2GHz range of the radio spectrum. The process has included lengthy legal battles.

The Orakei claim was more complex. Ngati Whatua had invited the first Governor to set up the capital at Auckland, and had sold land willingly. But, by 1854, the tribe held only the 700-acre (280-hectare) Orakei block – all that remained of their thousands of acres on the isthmus. More would be lost later. The claim traced the Crown's actions and inactions that had whittled the land away between 1840 and the 1970s. These lay behind the 1977–78 occupation of Crown land on Bastion Point (part of the Orakei block), a prominent vantage point over-looking the Waitemata Harbour and surrounded by prime residential land. But the spark that fired the occupation was the 1976 Crown proposal to develop the unused Crown land for high-income housing and parks. Some Ngati Whatua, calling themselves the Orakei Action Committee, took direct action, which caused a split in tribal ranks.

The Tribunal's Orakei Report, released in November 1987, explored the principles of the Treaty and its interpretation, particularly with respect to Ngati Whatua. According to Oliver:

> It emphasised especially the Crown's obligation to leave Maori enough land for their economic and social well-being and to refrain from buying land they wished to keep. The Crown had failed in this duty by allowing the Native Land Court and other bodies to bring about the very opposite result.

The Orakei Report recommended that, in addition to returning the 40 acres (16 hectares) agreed after the Bastion Point occupation, 50 acres (20 hectares) of Crown land be returned, together with a $3 million endowment to support its development. The Crown decided not to contest the claim, but the government hesitated for three years before acting on the Tribunal's recommendations. In 1991, the Orakei Act implemented the Tribunal's recommendations, and empowered the Ngati Whatua of Orakei Trust Board to act with full tribal authority. It was an outcome that went some way to reviving the mana of Ngati Whatua.

The Orakei Report established an important feature of the claims process: that although the Tribunal emphasised the loss of land and other property and the need for reparation, it did not recommend full legal compensation for the value of the land lost. It recognised that, if compensation were paid on that basis in the two Auckland cases and extended nationally, the financial burden on the country would be unsustainable. Governments would not be able to

Ready to enter the Downing Street, London, offices of the Privy Council in 1992 are New Zealand counsellors (from left) Eugenie Laracy, Martin Dawson and Sian Elias. A number of cases have been argued before the Privy Council, including the Broadcasting Assets case. Nga Kaiwhakapumau i te Reo and the New Zealand Maori Council argued that, by selling TVNZ assets to a state-owned enterprise, the Crown could not fulfil its Treaty obligation to protect the Maori language.
NEW ZEALAND HERALD

accept this. Moreover, where payments were uneven – as could be expected, given the variation in claims – they would create resentment among tribes, and between Maori and Pakeha. The Tribunal's report writers were evidently 'feeling their way' with recommendations that would be acceptable to government and to claimants. However, the Tribunal's move to recommending specific actions, as it did for the Orakei claim, was short-lived; it soon reverted to recommending negotiations.

Treasury and settlement

The task of funding settlements lay with Treasury. From early in 1987, Treasury tried to establish a strategy, but there were distractions and disagreements. In May 1988, a comprehensive paper outlined Treasury's assessment of government liability and attempted to work

 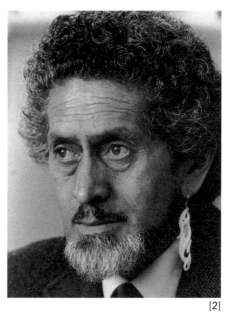

[1] Graham Latimer, a long-time battler for Maori rights, was a key participant in the Court of Appeal case brought by the New Zealand Maori Council on the State-Owned Enterprises Act in 1987. Latimer has held many influential positions over the years. He is chair of the CFRT Board of Trustees. NEW ZEALAND HERALD

[2] Huirangi Waikerepuru lodged the claim on te reo Maori (the Maori language) that led to the establishment of Te Taura Whiri i te Reo Maori (Maori Language Commission). His drive to secure resources for te reo continued through the 1990s and into the twenty-first century. DOMINION POST

out a formula for determining redress. The paper asserted a limited view of tino rangatiratanga deriving from the Treaty: the Crown could engage in sharing power insofar as that meant consultation, and was obliged to do so, but only in those areas explicitly protected by the Treaty. Settlements were to aim at redress for injury to tribal mana and at establishing an economic base.

Some options were laid out: claims could be settled on the basis of the claimant iwi's needs; or compensation could be calculated on the basis of past losses (an expensive option, and difficult to quantify). Other problems were indicated. To whom or to what body was compensation to be paid? And what account was to be taken of the national interest in allocating taxpayers' money? For a time, the notion of a 'grand slam' solution circulated within Treasury: the existing policy of dealing with individual claims would be discontinued; instead, claims would be settled on general principles applicable to all tribes, with the Tribunal's role possibly reduced to advice on matters such as legislation. But the Justice Department did not agree, believing that claimants needed the Tribunal as a forum.

Treasury concluded that determining fair and appropriate compensation would ultimately be a political decision resting with ministers. Through 1988 this question was debated within government, but by mid 1989 there was still no clear strategy on the settlement of historical land claims.

The Treaty of Waitangi Policy Unit

In the latter part of 1988, the government set up the Treaty of Waitangi Policy Unit (TOWPU) within the Department of Justice. Its brief was to develop and coordinate government policy on Treaty issues, to advise government, and to negotiate with Maori on claims. The initiative was long overdue, but by mid 1989 the unit was still under-resourced, with a tiny handful of staff.

In addition to the numerous Tribunal hearings, Treaty-related business was increasing in leaps and bounds. Many sections of government were involved – the executive, the legislature and more than a dozen departments. The judiciary, too, was being drawn into cases involving Treaty rights in fisheries, forestry and coal, and (through a claim about radio frequencies) broadcasting. TOWPU's work thus covered a wide range of policy issues. The unit also advised the Crown Law Office on its defence of the Crown's position in claims hearings. To some degree, too, TOWPU operated as a think-tank, which proved valuable to Geoffrey Palmer in establishing priority for some issues. There was plenty to do – probably the difficulty was knowing where to start.

Crown Forest Assets Act 1989

Labour's economic restructuring continued to clash with Treaty obligations. The policy of commercialising Crown assets now began to affect forests (much as it had fisheries earlier). Under the SOE Act 1986, the government intended to transfer about 700,000 hectares of forest land (550,000 hectares in stocked forest) to the Forestry Corporation. But following the Court of Appeal's decision on the SOE Act in June 1987, the government was obliged to deal with the sale of these Crown forests (along with other SOE land) according to Treaty principles. This led to the passing of the Treaty of Waitangi (State Enterprises) Act in June 1988.

However, the government announced in July 1988 that the forests were to be sold not to the Forestry Corporation but directly to the private sector – thereby possibly bypassing the provisions of the Treaty of Waitangi (State Enterprises) Act. The New Zealand Maori Council sought an injunction to prevent the sale of any of the Crown's forests. The council reasoned that Crown forest land might be needed as part of a settlement, or might be shown by a Tribunal investigation to have been acquired in breach of the Treaty. The government and Maori representatives (the Maori Council and the Federation of Maori Authorities) decided to negotiate. On the one hand, there was a need to protect Crown interests and to develop commercial forestry (with its long lead-time). On the other hand, there was a need to protect potential Maori owners of the land and to make provision for determining any Maori claims to such land.

In July 1989, the negotiators came to a formal agreement, which was given a statutory basis in the Crown Forest Assets Act 1989. It was assumed that Maori could own the land when a forest was privatised. The Act made provision for this eventuality by empowering the Waitangi Tribunal, if such a claim came before it, to determine ownership and recommend the action to be taken. Meanwhile, the Crown could sell the trees and grant a right (in the form of a Crown forestry licence) to the purchaser to use the land on which the trees stood.

CHAPTER SEVEN: THE ROLLER-COASTER YEARS   185

Augusta Wallace (the Tribunal's Presiding Officer for the Kaipara claims hearings), with Tribunal member Areta Koopu to the left, leading a field trip to the Poutu forest in 1997. Te Uri-o-Hau claimants sought the return of the forest from the Crown. The Kaipara Interim Report 2002 led to a settlement of cash and Crown-owned land to a value of $15.6 million. The properties selected included two on which Crown-licensed forests are found; Te Uri-o-Hau would receive over $1 million in accumulated rentals. In July 2004, as part of the settlement agreement, Prime Minister Helen Clark made an historic apology to the tribe.
MANA, OCTOBER/NOVEMBER 1997

The Act provided for the Crown to establish a trust to receive licence fees from the use of the land; interest on the trust's holdings would be made available to assist Maori in pursuing claims in relation to Crown forest land. If a claim involving a particular piece of land was successful, the Maori owners would receive the accumulated rentals relevant to that land. If the Crown's title was confirmed, the Crown would get the accumulated rentals for the land. If the Tribunal recommended that a piece of land subject to a Crown forestry licence be returned to Maori ownership, the Maori owners would be paid compensation (determined by the Tribunal) for the fact that occupation was not immediately available. If the Tribunal recommended that land was not liable for return to a Maori claimant, there could be no more claims asking for its return.

The agreement and the legislation were designed to work to the advantage of both Maori and Pakeha interests, and were considered at the time an important advance in honouring Article 2 of the Treaty. But the Crown Forest Assets Act was introduced with the expectation that the Tribunal could move more quickly than it has been able to. With the risk of alienating government, the Tribunal has been notably cautious in its recommendations in this area. The

Willie Wright, claim manager for Te Uri-o-Hau, with Crown Forestry Rental Trust staff member David Armstrong (on left), at Poutu marae in 1997. STEPHEN COOK, NORTHERN ADVOCATE/MANA

question of mandate also creates particular difficulty with Crown forest lands: it is often hard to establish with certainty which group of Maori claimants is the appropriate recipient of any allocation. Expectations, sometimes unrealistic, would lead in time to dissatisfaction with the Act and its results. Meanwhile, the Crown Forestry Rental Trust (CFRT) was established in 1990 and began to fund research for claimants in 1991.

Devolution and Maori Affairs

As the decade drew to a close, change continued at a cracking pace. More legislation and new structures were set in place. Up for reform, inevitably, was the Department of Maori Affairs: its responsibility for providing a wide range of services to Maori was now felt to lie more properly either with mainstream government departments or with iwi. Some moves towards devolution of government responsibilities to iwi had already begun, with mixed results. In April 1988, the government began to circulate *He Tirohanga Rangapu: Partnership Perspectives*, a discussion paper proposing substantial devolution of powers to iwi.

Through the nineteenth and twentieth centuries, Maori leaders had argued for the right to exercise authority over their affairs, independent of government and official policy. The recognition of te tino rangatiratanga (as in Article 2 of the Treaty) has been at the core of

Huge plantations of *Pinus radiata* created a multi-million dollar industry later in the twentieth century. Forestry provided work for rural Maori until the economic restructuring of the 1980s, when massive layoffs brought unemployment to many communities. These plantations are in the Kaingaroa area. DOMINION, 26 MARCH 1969

many Maori protests, and remains a concern. But finding a way to give formal status to tino rangatiratanga is no simple matter – as the Labour government discovered. Shrewd Maori observers soon concluded that Labour's 1988 proposal stemmed from its policies of economic rationalisation and devolution across many fields, rather than from a genuine commitment to power-sharing on the basis of some kind of partnership.

In 1989, the government began its moves towards devolution. On 1 July, a policy-oriented ministry replaced the old Department of Maori Affairs, and the 112 staff of the Maori Land Court moved to the Department of Justice. For an interim period, an Iwi Transition Agency would assist tribal groups in running state-funded resources. These moves were presented as part of the government's Treaty policy, and appeared – to the public at large and to some Maori – to be a step towards the recognition of rangatiratanga. A Runanga Iwi Bill, introduced in December 1989, aimed to identify the tribal bodies – perhaps about fifty – that would speak authoritatively for Maoridom. Each tribe would have a runanga council, which would manage government funding and resources (as well as tribal resources). It was clear, however, that accountability for government funding would intrude on tribal authority and independence;

Hepi Te Heuheu, seen here with his wife Pauline Hinepoto (Tuutu) Te Moanapapaku, led the central North Island iwi Ngati Tuwharetoa for many years. He played a key role in holding major hui on Maori political and cultural matters.
PRIVATE COLLECTION

thus those who sought absolute independence did not see devolution on these terms as an answer to the long-standing call for rangatiratanga.

Also causing disquiet was the need to define the characteristics of an iwi and its boundaries, and to make provision for individuals with several tribal affiliations. At several dozen hui in late 1989, Maori were urged to start planning. Maori, however, made it clear that if iwi were to be responsible for their own development they needed resources, and no budgetary provision had been made. Despite obvious practical difficulties (articulated clearly by Maori Labour MPs), the legislation was enacted in late 1990. The Iwi Transition Agency had already begun to implement devolution. Although not uncritical of the old Department of Maori Affairs, Maori were accustomed to the services it provided and regretted its demise.

In mid 1989, an independent national organisation – the Maori Congress – began to emerge. Formally established in July 1990, with representatives of over forty iwi, the congress aimed to provide a unified voice for iwi; its role would include the monitoring of legislation, or proposed legislation. Support for the congress was indicated by its first presidents: Ngati Tuwharetoa leader Hepi Te Heuheu; the Maori Queen, Te Atairangikaahu; and Ratana leader Te Reo Hura.

Local government

Labour's policy of devolving authority from central government included areas such as local government, resource management and education. Aimed at increasing public responsibility, these reforms affected New Zealanders at large, but had particular implications for Maori. Once again, Treaty obligations were threatened by the proposed transfer of responsibility for natural resources from the Crown, in this case to local and regional authorities. Each set of reforms involved Treaty rights and obligations, in different and complicated ways; collectively, the moves kept leaders in both the public sector and Maoridom extended to the full, and many in the wider Maori community much agitated.

New Zealand's system of local government has evolved from the Constitution Act 1852, which set up six (later nine) provinces with separate political and administrative structures. In 1876, the provincial system was abolished in favour of a multiplicity of boroughs and counties. Over the next century local bodies proliferated, despite efforts to rationalise them; by the mid 1980s, there were between six and seven hundred local bodies and organisations. Initially, Maori were largely excluded from political life by franchise qualifications (which required individualised property title). All adult Maori males received the vote in 1867 (ahead of their Pakeha counterparts), but in most districts Maori remained outside local body politics. Battles with local government over a wide range of issues have been a source of constant irritation to Maori. And many local bodies have failed to take account of Maori interests and values, leading sometimes to breaches of the Treaty. Long-standing problems of non-payment of rates have dogged some councils. Grievances and protest have been an inevitable consequence of these relationships.

Under the Minister for Local Government, Michael Bassett, Labour sought a major reform of local government. In its final form, the new structure would have three tiers: regional authorities, territorial authorities and special purpose boards. Facing a multitude of interest groups that could have stalled the process, Bassett was determined to drive the changes through. Little provision was made for Maori input on advisory committees, and consultation was minimal. Local government reform was running parallel to related reform in the resource management arena, and both involved Maori interests.

Over an eighteen-month period, as officials and committees batted proposals to and fro, it became clear that Bassett wanted to avoid incorporating the Treaty or reference to its principles in any local government legislation; at most, provision for Maori involvement could be deferred, or incorporated in the resource management legislation. The commonly held view of local authorities was that the Treaty had no place in local government and was an issue for central government to resolve. While Maori leaders generally accepted that the Treaty was with the Crown (now central government) and not with local government, some were concerned at the absence of any reference to the Treaty in local government legislation, and pressured the government to remedy the omission.

Opinions were locked particularly around the question of tino rangatiratanga: how it should be interpreted, and how it should sit within a democratic local body structure. At one extreme, some Maori leaders made a bid for a fifty-fifty partnership in the sharing of authority

This sign draws the public's attention to the fact that the land is an urupa, or burial ground. Similar sites, often unmarked, have been affected by developers and the public in ways that give offence. DOMINION POST

within local government. It is hardly surprising that this was unacceptable, not only to the government but also to the Opposition and most in the wider community. The reforms moved speedily, with the Local Government Amendment (No.3) Act 1988 directing the Local Government Commission to prepare schemes for local government restructuring.

The final legislation – the Local Government Amendment (No.2) Act 1989 – was silent on Treaty matters. It made no provision for Maori representation on local bodies; there would be involvement with Maori, but local bodies were not bound to accept Maori views. (A separate draft Bill to create Maori advisory committees lapsed with the 1989 election.) Some Maori feared – with some justification – that their battles with central government over Treaty rights would be multiplied by the need to deal with many local bodies, whose understanding of Treaty issues would be as variable as those held by the general public. The outcome was a blow for those who hoped to increase Maori participation in power-sharing. The local government reform also left unresolved the question of whether the Crown could devolve its Treaty powers to local bodies, and what exactly constitutes local body obligations in respect of the Treaty. These issues would remain a matter of debate.

Resource management

When the reform of resource management law began in 1988, it also created alarm among Maori and some Pakeha groups. A Bill introduced in December 1989 gave the community responsibility for the direction and progress of environmental protection. The central purpose of the legislation was to promote the sustainable management of natural and physical resources. Although the Bill stated that the Treaty and tribal concerns were to be considered, differences between local authorities and Maori authorities were anticipated. Maori at first focused on the question of how those differences would be resolved and what structures would be set up to ensure that the solutions would be satisfactory. However, local authorities were clear that they should have no responsibility for Treaty matters, and were not Treaty partners.

The Resource Management Act, as finally passed in 1991, replaced some seventy statutes relating to resource management. The Act required local authorities to recognise and provide for the relationship of Maori with their ancestral lands, water, significant sites, wahi tapu (sacred places) and other taonga (section 6(e)); to have regard to kaitiakitanga, or guardianship (section 7(a)); and to take into account the principles of the Treaty (section 8). Local authorities were also required to consult with tangata whenua through iwi authorities and tribal runanga when preparing or changing their policy statements and plans.

However, the cooperation of councils and tangata whenua was not assured by the Act, because it provided no certainty that Maori *would* be effectively engaged in decision-making processes. Maori wanted to be proactively involved at all levels, including planning and policy. Their experience had made them keenly aware of the conflict that could arise between the interests of tangata whenua and those of the general public, particularly where development was the issue. Reconciling these conflicting interests was often a fine balancing act, and Maori knew that they had to be able to participate in the decision-making process if their interests

A lively kohanga reo class. Kohanga reo, or language nests for pre-schoolers, were first established in the early 1980s. Later, schooling in Maori at higher levels developed in kura kaupapa. TYRONE KALLMEIER, *DOMINION POST*, 12 FEBRUARY 1991

were to be protected. Through the 1990s, the Ministry for the Environment and other government institutions published a series of guidelines for Maori and local bodies as they developed a new relationship in local government.

Education

Maori pressed hard for recognition of Treaty rights in education. In 1989, a new Education Act acknowledged the principles of the Treaty of Waitangi and brought significant institutional change. The Act required state-funded educational institutions, in consultation with their communities (including Maori), to draw up charters with mandatory goals. Under these, schools were to address 'equity issues', including the position of Maori people within the education system. A separate mandatory goal called for the implementation of the Treaty of Waitangi through the provision of Maori language to those students whose parents request it, and bicultural curricula to all students.

A group engaged in education on Treaty issues and conservation decided to walk the Wellington coastline on Waitangi Day 1988. The discharge of effluent on the coast has been a source of contention.
DOMINION POST COLLECTION, ALEXANDER TURNBULL LIBRARY, EP/1988/0626/11A

Meanwhile, the pre-school kohanga reo (language nests) initiated by Maori in the early 1980s were in financial difficulty; in the 1988/89 financial year, the government lifted their funding to $11 million, although this was still inadequate for their needs. By the end of the decade, children who had come through the kohanga were entering the school system with a grounding in the Maori language. The compelling need to extend Maori-language teaching led some schools to establish bilingual courses in basic subjects.

In late 1989, government support was requested for six schools that had been set up with the aim of teaching all subjects in a totally Maori-speaking environment. These kura kaupapa valued their degree of independence and achieved good results with their students; nonetheless, their organisers believed they were entitled – as indeed they were – to public funding. Maori educators, however, had some reservations about accepting a level of control from education authorities as a prerequisite for funding. This would raise debate on the need to strike a balance in the relationship between the Crown and Maori, and the need for structures that would allow Maori to exercise tino rangatiratanga over their affairs.

The principles of the Treaty

By mid 1989, the Labour government was under pressure to define its policy on the Treaty. There was tension about the Treaty within the public service, and in Labour's own ranks. Growing public confusion led all too frequently to anger. Maori, meanwhile, were forcing the government to clarify its position. The position of some Maori leaders was seen as increasingly extreme on a number of issues, especially tino rangatiratanga. This was evident in a range of government work involving Maori – notably, local government and resource management reform, fisheries and other Treaty-related business. Perhaps most irritating to the Minister of Justice were proposals by Moana Jackson, commissioned by Palmer himself, for a separate but parallel criminal justice system for Maori (who at the time made up around half of the prison population). A divergence of views on the relationship between Maori and the Crown – never entirely absent from Treaty debates – was exacerbated through this period.

The Minister of Justice, Geoffrey Palmer, probably considered it timely, in any case, to establish a set of working principles to guide the Crown. In July 1989, the government released *Principles for Crown Action on the Treaty of Waitangi*. Initiated by the Treaty unit of the Department of Justice (TOWPU) and developed by a small group of officials, the publication set out five principles. A summary identifies these as:

- The Principle of Government/The Kawanatanga Principle: the government has the right to govern and to make laws.
- The Principle of Self Management/The Rangatiratanga Principle: the iwi have the right to organise as iwi and, under the law, to control the resources they own.
- The Principle of Equality: all New Zealanders are equal under the law.
- The Principle of Reasonable Cooperation: both the government and the iwi are obliged to accord each other reasonable cooperation on major issues of common concern.
- The Principle of Redress: the government is responsible for providing effective processes for the resolution of grievances in the expectation that reconciliation can occur.

'They are not an attempt to rewrite the Treaty,' stated Prime Minister David Lange in the foreword, but critics saw it as just that. The full statement of principles, each with a lengthy commentary, was a clear signal that the government held its sovereign rights (kawanatanga as ceded in Article 1 of the Treaty) to be unassailable, although qualified by the need to accord 'an appropriate priority' to the Maori interest specified in the Treaty's second article. On these terms, the rangatiratanga of Article 2 enabled tribes merely to hold authority over their own resources. This assertion of absolute Crown authority was seen (perhaps unfairly) as a retreat from the commitment of the first years of the fourth Labour government.

Predictably, the principles drew attacks from those who held that the Treaty in 1840 had left the sovereignty of the country essentially in Maori hands. This definition of rangatiratanga would not meet the demands of Maori who called for 'absolute' and independent authority. Critics noted that there had been no consultation with Maori leaders, and that the Waitangi Tribunal was already engaged in defining the principles of the Treaty (a task for which it had special responsibility). A statement on Treaty principles had also emerged from the 1987

Court of Appeal case on the State-Owned Enterprises Act, where the court had the duty to determine the principles of the Treaty with which the Crown's actions had been inconsistent.

Thus, there were at least three sources that spelt out the principles of the Treaty in the late 1980s. Although they differed in detail, there was a common core recognising that the government had the right to govern. But critics argued that, whereas the Waitangi Tribunal and the Court of Appeal gave prominence to the Crown's responsibility to protect the Treaty rights of Maori in return for their gift of the right to govern (thus emphasising the reciprocal nature of the agreement and allowing for a more open definition of rights), the Labour government's set of principles seemed more limiting. Its first two principles asserted the government's right to govern and make laws, while Maori tribal authority was applicable to tribal self-management. The Tribunal and the court, however, saw the Treaty as signifying or establishing a relationship akin to a partnership. The government's principles were hedged around with cautious explanations: the Treaty's first and second articles were 'strong statements which necessarily qualify one another', but '[t]he working out in practice of the balance between the two articles must depend upon a case by case consideration.'

Important as the principles were, as the government's statement of Crown responsibility to Maori under the Treaty, they did not concede too much. The government seemed to be backing off from a position in which 'partnership' might suggest a Treaty relationship in which the Crown conceded residual pre-1840 sovereign rights and, by doing so, might admit obligations to devolve broader authority to Maori. At the same time, however, the principle of partnership was being well established in Treaty jurisprudence. And 'partnership' was a term that would increasingly be used across many departments, and more broadly in community groups, in efforts to give contemporary meaning to the reciprocal nature of the Treaty's first and second articles, and consequently, in the broadest sense, to the relationship between Maori and Pakeha in New Zealand.

In all cases at all levels, however, giving substance to the principle of partnership has been difficult; it remains an ongoing source of debate, as well as an avenue whereby relationships can evolve. Despite initial criticisms of the principles issued in 1989, these would remain a touchstone for the government and the community in developing the Treaty relationship. And the need to take the principles of the Treaty into consideration would continue to have a significant role in the formation of legislation.

Tainui and Coalcorp

In trying to define the relationship between the Crown and Maori, the Labour government was clearly hoping to calm public fears and curb Maori aspirations. The Treaty principles of reasonable cooperation and redress were soon tested, as Labour pushed ahead with its economic policies. This time it was the Tainui people of the Waikato who sought to negotiate with the government, over the sale of the state-owned enterprise Coalcorp. The government argued that only Coalcorp's assets and mining licences were being sold, and that the land would be protected under the Treaty of Waitangi (State Enterprises) Act. But Tainui were not so

On 28 August 1989, Tainui women against the sale of Coalcorp sing outside the Court of Appeal, while the case is heard.
DOMINION POST COLLECTION, ALEXANDER TURNBULL LIBRARY, EP-ETHNOLOGY-MAORI LAND FROM 1976-03

confident; with no negotiated solution in sight, they obtained an injunction stopping the sale of Coalcorp shares or assets, including mining licences. The Court of Appeal supported Tainui in ruling that the mining rights were legally interests in land and should, therefore, be subject to the claw-back provision of the Treaty of Waitangi (State Enterprises) Act. The court also ordered the Crown to produce a scheme to safeguard Maori interests in surplus lands managed (although not owned) by Coalcorp.

The government was being urged to negotiate, but Geoffrey Palmer threatened to take the case to the Privy Council, a proposal he later dropped. However, he was concerned about observations made during the Court of Appeal Coalcorp case, which had seemed to suggest that the courts had the final power to rule on solutions to Maori grievances. Palmer's uneasiness was reflected in a paper he gave on 14 December 1989 to the Wellington District Law Society. Although the government accepted that the Court of Appeal had 'correctly decided the actual points of law before them', Palmer expressed reservations about the way the courts might usurp powers he considered were entrusted to an elected government.

New structures or last-ditch organisation?

In 1989, the Crown Task Force on Waitangi Issues was announced — another move to clarify the government's position. One of a string of Treaty-related committees that had come and gone in the Labour period, this was to comprise a standing committee of Cabinet members, a core group of officials, and strengthened units in the Department of Justice (the Treaty of Waitangi Policy Unit) and the Ministry of Maori Affairs (where a Treaty Issues Unit had operated for some time). The task force would be responsible for developing the Crown's position with regard to Waitangi Tribunal hearings, for negotiations and court proceedings, and for ensuring the implementation and coordination of government responses. The aim was to set up procedures in the appropriate departments to handle claims efficiently and effectively, with a 'negotiations register' putting claims in priority order. The task force was also to monitor public awareness of Treaty issues. (Polls in late 1989 were indicating the public's lack of understanding and a non-acceptance of the justice of settling land claims.)

It was a belated and ad hoc move; the government needed to advance the settlement process, and the approaching year held not only an election but also the 150th anniversary of the signing of the Treaty. Thus there was more than a hint of damage control in the press release with which Geoffrey Palmer greeted the new year on 2 January 1990:

> The Crown has obligations under the Treaty of Waitangi. No Government in the history of New Zealand has done more to honour those obligations than the present one.
>
> We have set up mechanisms for hearing grievances and provided the means for finding remedies. The process is slow and not without pain. It has been nurtured and sustained by goodwill and mutual respect between New Zealanders of both Maori and non-Maori descent.
>
> The results of this process will not be nearly as dramatic as some Maoris expect nor as some non-Maoris fear. Further progress in these matters depends not only on co-operation between Maoris and the Crown, but also on maintenance of the balance between the three branches of Government — Parliament, the Executive and the courts.
>
> The Crown, represented through the Executive, has obligations. Its actions must be scrutinised, tested, and finally agreed to by Parliament. The courts have the obligation of interpreting the legislation which Parliament passes. They must do justice in individual cases. But there has arisen in New Zealand a feeling that somehow all the fundamental decisions about how the Treaty of Waitangi will be honoured will be made by the courts. That is not the case. It cannot be so.
>
> The courts are an essential part of New Zealand's constitutional arrangements. They have provided in recent years justice for Maori claims against the Government. Some imaginative and constructive resolutions have been achieved.
>
> These should not be forgotten, nor should they be rejected. The courts are important. They will continue to be important. But the courts interpret the law, they do not legislate, they do not govern. The Executive governs ... It must be made clear that the Government will make the final decisions on treaty issues.

A 1990 commemoration poster tried to capture the spirit of the two peoples, Pakeha and Maori, in one nation.
DOMINION POST COLLECTION, ALEXANDER TURNBULL LIBRARY, EP-ETHNOLOGY-MAORI LAND FROM 1976-02

The Prime Minister, on behalf of the Labour government, was rightly claiming some credit for the measures taken to honour Treaty obligations and handle claims. But he was clearly cautioning Maori and non-Maori about limitations to the power of the courts, and about the government's authority to govern and determine Treaty issues: these were political matters.

The 1990 commemoration

The government's first challenge in 1990 was to make the sesquicentennial commemorations a success. Set up in June 1988, the 1990 Commission had identified dates throughout the year that were considered markers in the country's history. Anniversaries of the first settler arrivals fell in January for both Wellington and Auckland, with Waitangi Day following in early February. The commission produced an impressive diary of events – big and small – in which all New Zealanders might find cause for enjoyment and celebration.

The promotion of national identity was a major feature of the commission's work. The Treaty was presented as the nation's founding document, a view (according to the opinion polls) that had gained considerable support in the community by 1990. Many of the nation's leaders, both Maori and Pakeha, encouraged New Zealanders to consider aspects of their country and way of life that they shared and could be proud of. The government had decided against holding an official ceremony at Waitangi in 1989, instead maintaining goodwill to ensure a protest-free Waitangi Day in 1990.

The year opened with festivities at historic sites such as Cook's first landfall in 1769 at Gisborne. The focus then shifted north, especially to the Auckland area where many thousands of people were caught up in a series of events — one of Kiri Te Kanawa's 'homecoming' concerts, the 14th Commonwealth Games (from 24 January to 3 February), and, on 4 February, the departure of the Whitbread yachts on the third leg of their round-the-world race, escorted by a great flotilla including several tall sailing ships that were part of the 1990 celebrations elsewhere.

Further north, in the last week of January, festivities began at Waitangi, where the Aotearoa Maori Arts Festival drew thousands of participants and spectators. By 4 February, over twenty waka had arrived and were drawn on to Waitangi Beach, adjacent to an enormous tent city at the historic Te Tii marae. The canoes, most of them constructed and carved by tribal groups especially for 1990, were a source of wonderment and deep satisfaction, not only for the Maori involved but also for visitors, Maori and Pakeha alike. Te Tii marae, where discussions on the Treaty had been held since 1840, became once again a focal point for a range of meetings and activities, including the erection of pou (poles) on the site, known as tau rangatira, where the chiefs had debated the Treaty on the night of 5 February 1840.

Waitangi Day 1990

The Treaty House had been handsomely refurbished for the event, and the grounds upgraded. The organisers of the commemoration worked hard to ensure that the event was fitting. From 1985 to 1989, the Labour government had treated Waitangi Day commemorations with caution, and the emphasis on Waitangi itself had been less marked. But in 1990 the mood was different. Thousands converged on the Bay of Islands to share in the events of 5 and 6 February.

On 6 February, Queen Elizabeth II visited Waitangi. In brilliant sunshine, her launch was accompanied to shore by the waka and other craft, led by the canoe *Ngatokimatawhaorua*, which had been built for the 1940 celebrations. The Queen was at Waitangi as the great-great-granddaughter of Queen Victoria, one of the parties to the Treaty; at her request, she met some descendants of chiefs who had signed it. As in 1940, a re-enactment of the signing took place. It was a gala occasion, marked by a spirit of openness and hope for the future. Both were reflected in the speeches.

The Queen observed that people were strong enough and honest enough to admit that the Treaty had been imperfectly observed. She noted that the original signatories had seen the Treaty as a charter for their future; she looked on it as a legacy of promise. 'Working together, the people of New Zealand can make a country which is strong and united, and unique among the nations of the earth.'

A mere-wielding warrior in a haka at the re-enactment of the Treaty signing at Waitangi, 6 February 1990.
NORTHERN ADVOCATE

Protest, however, was not entirely absent, and some came from an unexpected quarter. The Anglican Bishop of Aotearoa, Whakahuihui Vercoe (who spoke before the Queen), had been startlingly frank:

> Some of us have come here to celebrate, some to commemorate, some to commiserate, but some to remember what … our tupuna said on this ground: that the treaty was a compact between two people. But since the signing of that treaty … I want to remind our partners that you have marginalised us. You have not honoured the treaty. We have not honoured each other in the promises we made on this sacred ground. Since 1840 the partner that has been marginalised is me – the language of this land is yours, the custom is yours, the media, by which we tell the world who we are, are yours.

Waitangi Day, 1990. Protesters take to the water outside Te Tii marae to display their banner more clearly to the official party approaching by launch. NORTHERN ADVOCATE

This was a pointed reminder to the majority partner – the non-Maori New Zealander – that the mana of te tino rangatiratanga was still the main issue. A large number of Maori people continued to look to the government to develop a working compact between kawanatanga and rangatiratanga. This would involve the nation, too, because acknowledging the special position of Maori required the non-Maori partner's recognition and acceptance. Many New Zealanders would need to change their attitudes, and this would not be easy to achieve.

The Prime Minister, Geoffrey Palmer, spoke against background noise from a small group of protesters, and readily admitted there were problems:

> It is a testing time for us. Because this generation will be judged by its successors on the way we managed to deal with the issues raised by the document whose signatures we mark today … I want this generation of New Zealanders to be able to say that it put in the hard work, it saw what was needed to be done to address injustice and inequality, it sought settlements acceptable to all and it helped produce a land fit for our grandchildren to inherit. That will not happen of itself. It will not happen purely through action by the Government. Settlements must have the support of the nation.

Waitangi Day 1990: protester and policeman in a close exchange. DOMINION POST

Palmer was clearly making an appeal to a sense of justice and fair dealing in New Zealanders. He, too, was acknowledging that the nation as a whole had a role to play; and that, in the final event, a government is circumscribed in its actions, since it is subject to the ballot box – an important consideration in an election year.

Educating the public

The 1990 celebrations stimulated a small flood of publications on the Treaty, and more broadly on race relations and colonial history. As the Treaty gained a hold on public attention in the 1980s, church groups and organisations such as Project Waitangi had taken the initiative in providing information on the Treaty for the wider community. There were parallels in the public sector. In July 1987, for example, the Royal Commission on Social Policy widely distributed a small discussion booklet on the Treaty and social policy. The commission's report, released in April 1988, explored the issue further. From 1988 through into 1990, the Treaty and its implications were studied at seminars sponsored by government departments, the New Zealand Planning Council, the State Services Commission, and by many other public and private bodies. The work of historians, lawyers and Maori leaders stimulated new writing on the Treaty. Groundbreaking research made its way into books selling widely in the general market; for many New Zealanders, it was the beginning of a journey of personal discovery. In

Ranginui Walker, writer and historian, has published several books and written widely for the media, to express and clarify Maori concerns. PRIVATE COLLECTION

the populace at large, however, there was considerable antagonism to Maori claims in such areas as fisheries, and in the absence of a government education or information programme (a need recognised but not acted upon), public opinion was largely shaped by the media.

Through 1990, the National Opposition in Parliament enjoyed the government's discomfort over the clash between its Treaty policies and other reforms. Good political mileage was also gained from several 'scandals' involving Maori leaders. National Party MP Winston Peters fired public hostility further with comments about Labour's Treaty initiatives and its recognition of the Treaty principles in legislation (which, he said, should be repealed), and with threats to scale down the Waitangi Tribunal. Naturally, all were well aired in the media. So, too, was National's message to the public – broadly speaking, 'one nation, one law' for all – which had considerable appeal.

Political commentators in New Zealand and overseas predicted that the Pakeha backlash over the Treaty might be a determining factor in bringing Labour down at the coming election. Support for Labour among Maori was also at risk. Labour's record in the 1980s left large numbers of Maori disappointed: economic restructuring had hit Maori hard, and there was as yet no viable settlement process for Treaty claims. The Maori Council of Churches also promoted a 'Don't Vote' campaign. These factors may have contributed to the lower than usual turnout of Maori at the polls.

Members of the Opposition at Waitangi on 6 February 1988. From right to left: Bill Birch, Winston Peters and Jim Bolger (Leader), with Joan Bolger. NORTHERN ADVOCATE, HELD BY DOMINION POST COLLECTION, ALEXANDER TURNBULL LIBRARY, EP-ETHNOLOGY-MAORI LAND FROM 1976-01

In its two terms in government, Labour had established the legislative basis for major changes on Treaty issues, and had battled its way through the political and legal consequences. The 1985 extension of the Tribunal's jurisdiction to 1840 had led to substantial research and findings, particularly in the two major claim hearings of Muriwhenua and Ngai Tahu (the Ngai Tahu Report was not released until 1991, but its substance was widely known earlier through media coverage of the claim's extended hearings). In the 1980s, the Tribunal had built a new jurisprudence; it had developed the reasoning and approaches taken up by the courts. As a result, Maori had secured a protection of rights despite being outnumbered in the legislature. In the public service, too, there was a greater awareness of Maori and Treaty issues, although the degree to which this had permeated all levels of staff was uneven.

Only late in the day, however, had the Labour government started to develop a set of proposals for settling Treaty claims. The task would be taken up by National when it won the October 1990 election. Labour now found itself in opposition for nine years.

CHAPTER EIGHT

A Decade of Claims
— the 1990s

The October 1990 election returned a National government under the leadership of Jim Bolger. The Maori Affairs portfolio went to Winston Peters, a Maori MP who was antagonistic towards Treaty issues. In early 1991, he released *Ka Awatea*, a report that assessed the socio-economic position of Maori and proposed strategies for change, with a focus on improved health, education, training and economic development. With its pan-Maori approach, *Ka Awatea* was not well received by all Maori; nor was it completely acceptable to the government. By October 1991, Peters had been moved out of Cabinet.

Soon it was known that the Ministry of Maori Affairs/Manatu Maori would be replaced (on 1 January 1992) by the Ministry of Maori Development/Te Puni Kokiri, its role part policy and part operational. The Runanga Iwi Act, rushed through Parliament in 1990 before the election, was repealed and the work of the Iwi Transition Agency phased out. The Act, which recognised the Treaty's rangatiratanga (defined cautiously as the right of tribes to manage their own affairs), had had a mixed reception from Maori. Nonetheless, much time and money had been spent in preparing for devolution.

The new government's emphasis was on the delivery of services to Maori – as to all citizens. (This was referred to as 'mainstreaming'.) Maori advisers were employed in government departments and the delivery of services was monitored by Te Puni Kokiri (commonly known as TPK). This approach depended on the commitment made by each department; TPK did not have the powers to enforce compliance, and its monitoring role would remain a difficult one.

That these policies did not improve the situation for Maori was soon apparent. A population disproportionately represented among the unemployed and the unskilled labour force would be severely affected by tighter controls for welfare, lower benefits, market rentals for state housing and reduced access to housing loans for low-income earners. (Although an accommodation supplement was introduced, it was of little assistance to those on benefits.) National also put an end to lending on Maori land with multiple owners.

Still reeling from the impact of Labour's market liberalisation through the 1980s, Maori continued to have devastating records in health, employment, poverty and education. In the first quarter of 1992, for example, Maori unemployment was recorded by Statistics New Zealand at 27.3 per cent, in contrast to the overall rate of 8.4 per cent. It seems, however, that the government ignored departmental warnings and surged ahead with its policies.

A new turn on Treaty matters

In its pre-election manifesto, National had signalled that it would settle all genuine and major Treaty claims by the turn of the century; it would also establish better public understanding of the Treaty and a consensus on its future role. This highly ambitious pledge was in part

[previous page] Ngati Ruanui representatives sign the heads of agreement with the Crown on 7 September 1999. From left to right: Pat Heremaia, Haimoana Maruera and Hoani Heremaia, watched by MPs Doug Graham and Georgina Te Heuheu. Doug Graham said that the signing marked a new beginning for a proud iwi that had suffered greatly during the last century: 'More than 83,000 hectares of land were unjustly confiscated following Ngati Ruanui's support of other iwi of Taranaki as they attempted to retain their traditional lands.' DOMINION POST

208   AN ILLUSTRATED HISTORY OF THE TREATY OF WAITANGI

Signs of poverty grew in the last decades of the twentieth century. Unemployment and long-standing urban housing shortages impacted on many groups, and particularly on Maori. Over-crowded flats, garages and caravan parks (like this one in South Auckland) were sometimes the only accommodation available for poor families.
ALISTER BARRY, *IN A LAND OF PLENTY: THE STORY OF UNEMPLOYMENT IN NEW ZEALAND*, COMMUNITY MEDIA TRUST/VANGUARD FILMS

an election pitch to satisfy public opinion, and its time-frame was unrealistic. Nonetheless, National was committed to resolving claims more speedily, and through the 1990s would reaffirm its aims.

In May 1991, Doug Graham became responsible for Treaty negotiations, initially as Minister of Justice and, from 1993, as Minister in Charge of Treaty of Waitangi Negotiations (a separate portfolio). The first step was to develop a strategy for advancing the claims process. In *Trick or Treaty?* (1997), Graham identified the key factors: consistency in addressing the many claims lodged; a clear tribal mandate for each claim; a means of dealing with generic claims (claims not specific to one tribe but affecting all Maori); adequate and appropriate consultation; a formula for compensation; and an assessment of the possible forms of redress. There was also a need for settlements to be 'final', for coordination of government agencies, and for public education on Treaty matters.

Graham also identified aspects of the Maori community that the government had to take into account: the lack of an effective structure that enabled Maori 'to speak with one voice';

Maori made up around 50 per cent of those in prison in the 1990s, although they represented less than 15 per cent of the total population. Courses focusing on tikanga Maori were introduced in many prisons. DEPARTMENT OF CORRECTIONS

strong independent tribal identities; the lack of leadership in some iwi; conflicts between old and young; the difficulty of determining tribal membership and individual entitlement; and the lack of resources for researching claims. Some Maori also were not ready to concede that interest in Treaty matters extended beyond the Crown and Maori, and that other groups (such as conservationists) had to be consulted.

In some Maori claimants, Graham perceived a reluctance to settle a claim, since this would mean taking on the burden carried by their ancestors, as well as the needs of future generations. This was not an unnatural response, but it had the potential to inhibit negotiations. Shrewdly, Graham observed what was becoming evident in claims reports and in Maori attitudes towards settlements – that redressing tribal mana was often as significant to Maori as financial or other compensation. The reports were also revealing a range of attitudes to the tino rangatiratanga of the Treaty – to the concepts of self-determination and autonomy, and the ways these might be expressed in different contexts.

With Tribunal reports now being released regularly, Maori demanded an urgent response from the government. And the Crown was vulnerable: iwi could apply to the Waitangi Tribunal for mandatory orders for the return of assets under the State-Owned Enterprises Act and the Crown Forest Assets Act, with an outcome potentially less favourable to the government than a negotiated settlement. Doug Graham was keen on direct negotiations, with a gradual development of policy. By late 1991, discussions on two major claims were under way. Negotiations on

The need for concerted action on Maori health was evident in statistics. This Maori asthma review team (photographed in 1991) became the nucleus of the Health Research Council's first Maori Health Committee. From left: (standing) Hohua Tutengaehe, Eru Pomare, Neil Pearce; (sitting) Makere Hight, Irihapeti Ramsden.
LYNETTE SHUM/NEIL PEARCE; MANA, OCTOBER/NOVEMBER 2002

the Waikato-Tainui claim (lodged in 1985) had been initiated by Labour late in its term and stalled with the change of government; now they began again. This claim proceeded without any Tribunal hearing. In October, negotiations started on the Ngai Tahu claim, based on the massive Tribunal report released in 1991. Both sets of negotiations were clearly going to take some time to resolve: their progress was affected in 1992 by an unexpected development in fisheries.

The Sealord deal

The Maori Fisheries Act 1989 (an interim settlement of fisheries claims) had allowed for a transfer to the Maori Fisheries Commission of 10 per cent of the total commercial quota over a four-year period (starting in 1990) and $10 million to develop the Maori fishing industry.

Eleven Hauraki marae banded together in 1986 to launch a marine farming venture south of Coromandel. The team is engaged here in harvesting mussels in early 1995. The business was employing six full-time workers and had an annual turnover of about $1 million. BILL GIBSON, MANA, FEBRUARY/APRIL 1995

Maintaining their claim to a substantially greater share of the total quota, Maori had continued negotiations with the Crown; an increasing number of court cases were on hold, awaiting decisions.

In August 1992, the influential Ngai Tahu Sea Fisheries Report was released – the first major fisheries report since 1988. The Tribunal found that Ngai Tahu had an exclusive right to the sea fisheries to a distance of 12 miles from the shore of all the tribe's land boundaries; and, within the 200-mile exclusive economic zone, a right to a reasonable share of the deep-water fisheries. It noted that, in determining the share, allowance should be made for the serious depletion of Ngai Tahu's inshore fishery. The report's principal recommendation was that the Crown and Ngai Tahu should enter into negotiation to reach settlement on the claim. The report generated a frenzy of media comment, much of it inaccurate.

At this point, Carter Holt Harvey decided to sell its interest in the commercial fishing venture Sealord Products Ltd, which amounted to 24 per cent of the total commercial fisheries quota. To Graham, this 'provided a one-off chance to acquire substantial quota for Maori'. He aimed to reach a pan-Maori settlement by negotiating with several Maori leaders, seeing this as the only way to achieve a decision in the time-frame allowed by Sealord. The negotiators on the Maori side were Tipene O'Regan, Matiu Rata, Robert Mahuta, Whatarangi Winiata, Graham Latimer and Dick Dargaville.

Within a few weeks, an agreement was struck. The Crown would provide the Maori (later Treaty of Waitangi) Fisheries Commission/Te Ohu Kai Moana with an advance payment of

The signing of the Maori commercial fisheries settlement, September 1992. From right: Don McKinnon (Acting Prime Minister), Tipene O'Regan, Doug Graham and others who had been involved in the negotiations. Aquaculture and marine farming were not part of the settlement. MICHAEL SMITH, DOMINION POST

$150 million. It was to be used to increase Maori involvement in the fishing industry; this would include the purchase of 50 per cent of the Carter Holt Harvey shares in Sealord, with Brierley Investments Ltd holding the other 50 per cent. The Sealord deal would take Maori interests in commercial fishing from the 10 per cent already agreed to 22 per cent; it was expected that, with good management of the asset, this could be increased to 50 per cent (which by 1997 was the case). The Crown would assign to the commission 20 per cent of the quota for each new species coming into the quota management system; it also agreed to ensure Maori participation in statutory bodies dealing with fisheries.

Taiapure (customary fishing areas) were recognised under new legislation in the 1990s. Haami Te Whaiti (left) and Dick Te Whaiti of Ngati Hinewaka look over one of the first taiapure, established in Palliser Bay, South Wairarapa, in 1995. MELANIE BURFORD, *DOMINION POST* COLLECTION, ALEXANDER TURNBULL LIBRARY, EP/1995/1597/29

Shane Jones (right), chair of the Waitangi Fisheries Commission/Te Ohu Kai Moana, delivers the commission's report on a settlement model to Peter Hodgson, Minister of Fisheries, in May 2003. The Fisheries Commission had battled for thirteen years to reach agreement on a model that would determine the allocation of over $700 million worth of fisheries assets. A Maori Fisheries Bill was introduced to Parliament in November 2003. DOMINION POST, 10/11 MAY 2003

For their part, the Maori people were to relinquish all customary rights over commercial sea fisheries. Legislation would extinguish all statutory, common law and Treaty rights to commercial fishing, and there could be no further claims asserting rights other than those included in the agreement. Section 88(2) of the Fisheries Act 1983, which acknowledged Maori fishing rights under the Treaty, was to be repealed. Maori also had to accept that non-commercial fishing rights would no longer have any legal effect or legislative recognition, although such rights would continue to be subject to the principles of the Treaty. Maori had to endorse the quota management system, and desist from pursuing litigation.

These were substantial concessions, for which the negotiators were soon severely criticised by many Maori. Tribes dissenting from the agreement mounted a legal challenge, which failed. The support of the Tribunal was enlisted; it supported the deal, but the changes it recommended were not included in the agreement. The Deed of Settlement was signed in September 1992 by over eighty tribal representatives and was confirmed in December that year by the Treaty of Waitangi (Fisheries Claims) Settlement Act (commonly known as the Sealord deal).

Settlement Principles (1994)

- The Crown explicitly acknowledges historical injustices.

- In attempting to resolve outstanding claims, the Crown should not create further injustices.

- The Crown has a duty to act in the best interests of all New Zealanders.

- As settlements are to be durable, they must be fair, and sustainable, and remove the sense of grievance.

- The resolution process is consistent and equitable between claimant groups.

- Nothing in the settlements will remove, restrict or replace Maori rights under Article 3 of the Treaty, including Maori access to mainstream government programmes.

- Settlements will take into account fiscal and economic constraints and the ability of the Crown to pay compensation.

SOURCE: *CROWN PROPOSALS FOR THE SETTLEMENT OF TREATY OF WAITANGI CLAIMS*, DEPARTMENT OF JUSTICE, WELLINGTON, 8 DECEMBER 1994

Before the legislation was introduced, a final adjustment made allowance for the protection of customary, non-commercial fishing rights. Statutory regulations were gradually introduced.

The fisheries settlement appeared to offer significant economic advantages to Maori; yet it led to years of bitter debate. Maori protest had long been based squarely on customary rights being *confirmed* by the Treaty and never extinguished; the fisheries settlement not only extinguished those rights but ignored the cultural and spiritual relationships of Maori with the sea. Many objected strongly to the speed of the deal and the limited number of negotiators who were recognised as speaking for Maoridom.

Implementing the agreement also caused difficulty. While the settlement stated that the deal was for 'all Maori', the quota was to be distributed through iwi. Questions about the nature of an iwi, appropriate representation, and the basis for allocating quota have involved several legal actions. In 1996, a decision from the Court of Appeal recognised the rights of urban-based Maori, who had challenged the traditional definition of an iwi. But legal battles and disputes over urban Maori rights would continue. Conflict over models for allocating quota – on the basis of coastline or population, or combinations of the two – proved difficult to resolve, and dogged the commission into the twenty-first century.

Fast, shrewd negotiation had secured a great commercial asset that could be utilised for Maori economic development. But with this came new problems that divided Maori, in the courts and elsewhere. Meanwhile, Maori and the Crown worked to ensure that provision was made to protect customary fishing rights. The ability to establish taiapure (local fisheries) and mataitai reserves (traditional fishing grounds) is protected under the Fisheries Act 1996. Two sets of customary fishing regulations became law in 1998: regulations for the North Island and for the South Island. Establishing each of these provisions has taken some time, and work continues on all of them.

Types of Claim

Historical

- the land confiscations (raupatu) of the nineteenth century

- Crown purchases between 1840 and 1865 under Crown–Maori negotiations

- transactions under the Native (Maori) Land Court system

- land takings for public works

Contemporary

- Maori language

- Maori electoral roll

- immigration policies

- education policies

- cultural and intellectual property rights

SOURCE: *CROWN PROPOSALS FOR THE SETTLEMENT OF TREATY OF WAITANGI CLAIMS*, DEPARTMENT OF JUSTICE, WELLINGTON, 8 DECEMBER 1994

Crown proposals for settlement

The Sealord deal emphasised the need for clear policy on Treaty claims. As Doug Graham explained in *Trick or Treaty?*, 'somehow we had to estimate how much in raw dollar terms the settlements were likely to cost and over what period'. Relativity between settlements was another vexed issue: it was essential 'to set a parameter to enable the first claimant group to assess the fairness of any settlement proposal'. This would help to curb the expectations of Maori claimants and their advocates: 'If we were to be consistent and fair, then ideally a bench-mark would be set by a large settlement and all the other settlements could flow from that.'

From the outset, there were problems in deciding on a total figure and in establishing relativity between claims. Various estimates for a settlement fund were advanced by Treasury and the Ministry of Maori Development/Te Puni Kokiri (the former being rather less generous than the latter); unofficial estimates came close to $2 billion; some Maori estimates were many times that amount. The difficulty in achieving relativity between settlements would emerge more clearly as claims were negotiated.

As government policy developed, it filtered quickly into the Maori community. The idea of a 'fiscal cap' on settlements was in circulation as early as 1992. A clause in the Treaty of Waitangi (Fisheries Claims) Settlement Act 1992 provided that the fisheries settlement would be a first charge on any settlement fund, if one were subsequently established. Initially denied, the fund with its 'fiscal cap' was soon approved by Cabinet. From early 1994, Doug Graham began discussions with Maori and started to release information on Treaty strategies to the public; he was seeking to conclude negotiations on several large claims (often referred to as

[1] Pita Sharples, a driving force behind the Hoani Waititi marae in West Auckland, urges on a group of performers in early 1997. The marae has become a base for many employment, social and educational programmes. Along with Tariana Turia and others, Pita Sharples became a leading member of a new Maori political party formed in June 2004.
KIM REED, MANA, SUMMER 1996

[2] John Tamihere moved from law to head an urban Maori authority, Te Whanau o Waipareira Trust. A Member of Parliament from 1999, he is an active and articulate spokesman for urban Maori interests. MANA, SUMMER 1996/97

the 'mega-settlements'), leaving the rest to be dealt with in due course. Late in 1994, Cabinet approved a set of policy proposals, which were published as *Crown Proposals for the Settlement of Treaty of Waitangi Claims*. At the heart of these lay the concept known as the 'fiscal envelope' or 'fiscal cap': total settlements would be limited to $1 billion over ten years.

The government launched the proposals at Premier House on 14 December 1994. The assembly was small, but included senior tribal leaders and a handful of Pakeha. Most were probably already familiar with what they were about to hear. Introduced by the Prime Minister, Jim Bolger, and Doug Graham, the proposals were briefly outlined and comments invited. The responses from Maori were icily calm but clear. The government was presenting what appeared to be a non-negotiable package: where was the partnership, and what justice did this amount to? Speakers voiced their objections to key points in the proposals but also to the manner of their release. There had been little Maori involvement or consultation.

As Graham later explained in *Trick or Treaty?*, the proposals were based on certain general principles. They outlined criteria for settlement and set a limit within which settlements could be negotiated. A cut-off date of 21 September 1992 would establish which claims fell within or outside the limit. Claims arising as a result of a Crown action or inaction on or before 21 September 1992 would be classed as 'historical claims', and would fall within the limit; claims that arose from 'actions or omissions after that date' would be classed as 'contemporary claims',

The Waipareira Trust has a number of economic activities and runs a range of health, education and social services. Shown here in 1997, Waipareira Corporate Building is the base for a call-centre operation and a joint-venture English-language school. WAIPAREIRA CORPORATE

and would fall outside the limit. (Graham hoped that, in future, government departments would provide less cause for Maori to bring contemporary claims against the Crown.) The date of 21 September 1992 was chosen because it was the day Cabinet agreed on the general principles for settling Treaty grievances, and concluded the Sealord settlement. Establishing a cut-off date also allowed for consistent comparisons in levels of redress provided to different claimants.

The proposals also outlined the government's Treaty policy in relation to the conservation estate, natural resources and gifted land. The last of these provoked little debate. It was clear that land given to the Crown for public purposes such as schools but now surplus to requirement should be returned to the donors (Maori or non-Maori), where this could reasonably be done. The government was already addressing this. But the other two issues were much more complex.

Public interest in the conservation estate made this a highly contentious area. During Tribunal hearings on the Ngai Tahu claim, the government had been intensively lobbied by organisations such as the Federated Mountain Clubs over the need for the Crown to retain control of the conservation estate; tension between conservationists and high-country farmers on one side and Maori on the other had been high. Now the proposals stated that conservation estate land should not be used to settle claims; the Crown held responsibility for the natural and historic values of the land, and the rights of public access should not be affected by Treaty claims. Certain categories of land, however, might be considered as part of a settlement – specifically, sites of particular significance to Maori – for which special provision would be made.

Natural resources were even more problematic. These included water, river and lake beds, foreshores and seabeds, geothermal energy, minerals (such as coal, gold, gas and petroleum) and gravel. The Crown proposed that Treaty claims involving natural resources should focus on their uses and their spiritual and cultural value, rather than 'ownership'. While accepting that Maori used and valued a number of resources at the time the Treaty was signed, the Crown did not consider 'that Article II of the Treaty guaranteed to Maori the ownership of natural resources in 1840'. The Crown held that, where the national interest required the government to own or control a resource, then it would do so, although in practice there was some flexibility, and each case would be judged on its merits. In effect, the proposals said that natural resources were not available for negotiation.

A number of claims before the Waitangi Tribunal involved conservation land or natural resources (or both); claimants based their cases on the Treaty's second article, which confirmed and guaranteed tino rangatiratanga over land, forests, fisheries and other taonga. At issue were interpretations of both the second article and the first (ceding sovereignty and the right to govern). The Crown's proposals thus encapsulated the tensions over sovereignty and tino rangatiratanga in the Treaty, and over what each stood for in the contemporary world.

From the government's viewpoint, the proposals were an attempt to deal with the totality of the Treaty claims process in a rational way. From the Maori viewpoint, however, the proposals exemplified the long-standing Maori battle with the Crown to assert Treaty rights. This viewpoint was articulated at a major hui, held under the auspices of the Ngati Tuwharetoa leader, Hepi Te Heuheu, at Hirangi marae in Turangi on 29 January 1995. About a thousand Maori attended the gathering, which roundly rejected the Crown's proposals and called on the government to put forward a policy that gave the Treaty a more secure constitutional position. Several models were advanced: a separate Maori parliament; a Maori assembly to draft policy for Parliament's consideration; and a Maori House (perhaps even an Upper House) within the present Parliament, a model that had evolved within the Anglican Church.

Mason Durie, deputy chair of the Maori Congress, noted that a debate on possible constitutional changes was timely (the Prime Minister had just sparked debate on republicanism): lasting solutions to Treaty issues would be found only when Maori had a greater say in running their affairs. When Doug Graham heard of the hui's resolutions, he dismissed the idea of a 'separate parliament' as unrealistic. Treaty settlements and Maori self-determination, he said, were separate matters. Seeking constitutional reform was, in his view, too extreme. Graham had devoted much personal effort to the proposals, and was disappointed at their reception.

The Waikato-Tainui settlement

The Waikato-Tainui claim was one of the largest before the Tribunal at the time. It was based on the confiscation (raupatu) of Waikato land by the Crown after the wars of the 1860s: 1.2 million acres (480,000 hectares) were taken from the Tainui people as punishment for their

A group of Tainui in the public gallery of Parliament on 20 October 1995 mark the passage of the Waikato Raupatu Claims Settlement Act 1995 through its last stages. CRAIG SIMCOX, *DOMINION POST COLLECTION*, ALEXANDER TURNBULL LIBRARY, EP/1995/4228/4A

so-called rebellion. Although a third of the confiscated land was returned to Maori who had not 'rebelled', most had soon been purchased under individual title. The injustice had been acknowledged by the Sim Commission in the 1920s; in 1946, Waikato reluctantly accepted a compensation payment of £6,000 a year, which was later indexed to inflation. As Graham observed, the confiscation was well documented and 'the wrongs done could not be refuted'; the Crown accepted that it had acted unjustly. A Tribunal hearing was not considered necessary, and so negotiations on the Waikato-Tainui claim proceeded more swiftly than those on the Ngai Tahu claim.

At the heart of Tainui was the King movement or Kingitanga, which had remained a powerful force among the people after the 1860s wars. Robert Mahuta was the main negotiator for thirty-three hapu who sought the return of Crown land in compensation for the lost Tainui land. The return of land was the crux for Tainui, but only a small amount of Crown land was available. In 1989, negotiations had started but then stalled. As negotiations resumed in 1992, the Hopuhopu military camp near Ngaruawahia was returned as a mark of goodwill. In December 1994,

The Waikato Raupatu Claims Settlement Act 1995 received the Royal Assent from Queen Elizabeth II, shown here with the Maori Queen, Te Atairangikaahu, and flanked by the Prime Minister, Jim Bolger, at left, and at right by the Minister in Charge of Treaty Negotiations, Doug Graham. Part of the settlement was an apology in which the Crown acknowledged the Treaty breach in its dealings with the Kingitanga and Waikato, and expressed regret for the loss of lives from the invasion and resulting devastation of property and tribal life. DOMINION POST

the main points of agreement were reached, and details were hammered out over the next six months. In May 1995, the Deed of Settlement was signed by the Maori Queen, Te Atairangikaahu, and the Prime Minister, Jim Bolger. The Waikato Raupatu Claims Settlement Act 1995 gave effect to the settlement. The Crown's formal apology to Tainui was given special meaning by Queen Elizabeth II signing the Act, which included the apology. The significance of the settlement was made clear to the House and the New Zealand people by the response of Tainui people in the public gallery as the Act went through Parliament.

The Tainui settlement included the return of around 40,000 acres (16,000 hectares) of land, much of it rented, and monetary compensation. Over five years, around $65 million would be placed in a Tainui-controlled land acquisition trust. The total settlement value was about $170 million. The 'fiscal cap' had been announced in December 1994, and the Tainui settlement was 17 per cent of the $1 billion 'settlement fund'. However, the Tainui agreement included a provision that, if the total settlement of claims went beyond $1 billion in the next fifty years, Tainui would be entitled to 17 per cent of the additional amount. The 'relativity clause' cemented the negotiations but would cause problems with other settlements later.

Among a number of conditions, Tainui had to accept that the settlement was full and final; no further claims would be allowed in respect of the confiscation. (This excluded any claim to

Robert Mahuta, the main Tainui negotiator for claims arising from the 1860s confiscation of Waikato lands. In 1994, the tribe reached an agreement on the $170 million settlement. Mahuta's health declined in 2000, and he died in February 2001. NEW ZEALAND HERALD

the Waikato River and harbours on the west coast, which would be pursued later, together with any other historical grievance not related to the confiscation.) They also had to withdraw their legal action on coal; minerals, including coal, would remain in Crown ownership.

A postal ballot of Tainui's constituents secured agreement to the settlement, but revealed some disagreement over terms. Some hapu felt that they had suffered more acutely than others, and that a 'global' payment failed to recognise this. There was also some disquiet about the structure constituted to receive and manage the settlement; its membership did not (some argued) reflect the wide relationships within the Kingitanga.

Once the Waikato Raupatu Claims Settlement Act 1995 went through, there were setbacks; some investments turned out badly, and there was inevitable controversy. The untimely death of Robert Mahuta, a central figure in both Tainui and the Kingitanga, in 2001 was a blow to the people. But the settlement enabled Tainui to move forward in its own way, using funds for the iwi's development, including upgrades to marae, training and educational grants, and health services. Any remaining differences over the settlement would have to be resolved by the Kingitanga.

The Ngai Tahu settlement

Negotiations on the Ngai Tahu claim started in October 1991, and continued over six years. The claim dealt with most of the South Island (more than half of New Zealand's total land mass). Lodged in 1986 by the Ngai Tahu Maori Trust Board, the initial statement of claim was followed

Ngai Tahu leader Charles Crofts and Doug Graham exchange a hongi at the settlement of the Ngai Tahu claim, September 1997. DOMINION POST, 24 SEPTEMBER 1997

by seven amending claims. The tribe's grievances arose from the Crown's purchase of the South Island in about a dozen land sale transactions dating from 1844 to 1865. At the Tribunal hearings, which spanned several years in the late 1980s, an immense amount of research was presented, covering almost every matter that would be likely to come up in a claim.

The Tribunal's three-volume report, released in 1991, told a sorry tale of government ineptitude, lack of care and appalling injustice. Twenty-five years after the signing of the Treaty, Ngai Tahu were an impoverished people, largely subsisting on uneconomic plots of land, on the margins of a developing European society, and neglected by both national and provincial governments. Reserves were either non-existent or inadequate; many food resources (mahinga kai) had been lost as settlement expanded; the promised hospitals and schools had not been provided; and pounamu (greenstone) had not been protected (as undertaken in the Arahura purchase).

Ngai Tahu's protests had begun informally in the 1840s and more formally in the 1860s; they had continued for well over a hundred years. Several commissions of inquiry into the tribe's landless state had been held from 1886, but successive governments had failed to deal effectively with the issues. In 1944, a settlement of £10,000 a year for thirty years had been accepted, albeit reluctantly. Changed in 1973 to $20,000 a year in perpetuity, this sum created the fund to take the claim to the Tribunal.

An emotional moment for Ngai Tahu as the Ngai Tahu Claims Settlement Act 1998 passes its last stages in Parliament. From left: Kuao Langsbury, Charles Crofts, Tipene O'Regan and Mark Solomon.

CRAIG SIMCOX, DOMINION POST COLLECTION, ALEXANDER TURNBULL LIBRARY, EP/1998/0025/00

The Tribunal's report focused on the Crown's failure to fulfil its Treaty obligation to ensure that Ngai Tahu were left with sufficient land for their immediate and long-term needs, and its failure to carry out its contractual obligations in a number of land purchases. At the request of both the Crown and the claimants, the Tribunal did not recommend avenues of redress, but suggested that a mix of remedies was likely; however, recommendations were made on specific matters that the Tribunal felt should be dealt with immediately. During the Tribunal hearings, many additional grievances emerged; these formed ancillary claims covered in a later report.

Negotiation meetings on the major report were held each month from late 1991, but were complicated by negotiations over fisheries and by legal actions Ngai Tahu took over forestry lands and other issues. Suspended for a while, negotiations finally reached a conclusion: in 1997, Te Runanga o Ngai Tahu was established to receive the settlement, which was formalised in the Ngai Tahu Claims Settlement Act 1998. The settlement had a value of around $170 million and included a relativity clause; it comprised a mix of Crown land, forestry land, and title to certain valued sites and specific reserves.

The settlement contained symbolic and cultural elements, the most important being a public apology to Ngai Tahu. The tribe's suffering was acknowledged, along with the injustice that had impaired its economic, social and cultural development. Ngai Tahu's special relationship with certain places was recognised. Ngai Tahu would regain the title to Aoraki/Mt Cook, and then would eventually gift the mountain to the nation; the tribe also had statutory representation on conservation bodies. Rights to Crown-owned greenstone in the Arahura Valley were established in the Ngai Tahu (Pounamu Vesting) Act 1997.

Settlement had to be full and final; Ngai Tahu could make no further claims based on the Crown's failings in the nineteenth century. The Ngai Tahu and Waikato-Tainui settlements would be the only ones with a relativity clause.

Rangahaua Whanui

By the early 1990s, the number and scope of claims were challenging the resources of the Waitangi Tribunal and its support unit. The demand for historical knowledge and for research skills was huge. It was hard to find enough trained historians, and claims investigation would often take researchers into new areas, where little historical work had been done. The extent of existing research was also often difficult to establish.

So, in 1993, the Tribunal initiated the Rangahaua Whanui Project in order to rationalise research and create a resource that claimants, the Tribunal and the government could draw on as a base for direct negotiation. The project, which had the encouragement of Doug Graham, set out to provide a broad and systematic coverage of the country's history as it affected Maori. Historians started work on fifteen geographic regions and fifteen major themes, such as the rating of Maori land; Alan Ward provided an overview, drawing the bulky studies together. The undertaking was ambitious and somewhat underfunded; inevitably, the quality of the individual reports varied. But, even in progress, this work began to provide the basis for Tribunal submissions and for negotiations.

The Office of Treaty Settlements (OTS)

From 1991, the Treaty of Waitangi Policy Unit (TOWPU) assisted government with the settlement process. Set up first in 1988 within the Justice Department, TOWPU was reconstituted in 1995 as the semi-autonomous Office of Treaty Settlements (OTS); its director reported to the Minister in Charge of Treaty of Waitangi Negotiations.

The primary role of OTS was to support the negotiation and settlement of historical claims with claimant groups, under the direction and guidance of Cabinet. The office was responsible for coordinating the government departments involved, providing advice to the Minister and implementing the settlements. Increasingly, it provided policy advice to the Crown on generic

Protection Mechanism and Land Banks

A matter of long-standing concern to Maori was the sale (or threatened sale) of surplus Crown land. Each year, the Crown sold many blocks of surplus land to private buyers. This meant that the opportunity to include such land in a claims settlement might be lost. The government, therefore, set up a mechanism to enable Maori to acquire surplus land in settlement of a claim.

The protection mechanism applied to surplus land owned by government departments, and to land that became surplus when it was transferred to Crown entities (such as Crown Research Institutes and Crown Health Enterprises) at the time of incorporation. The Crown also instituted land banks in order to hold land for a claimant group pending settlement, and made similar provision for holding land within raupatu (confiscated) areas. There might also be memorials on titles where land was transferred to SOEs and tertiary education institutions when they were incorporated. This enables the Crown to re-acquire any land that may have been sold by an SOE to a third party if the land is subsequently required for settlements.

These arrangements for various types of protection have been modified over the years, but have continued to operate.

Treaty settlement issues and on individual claims. OTS was also responsible for the management of Crown property assets identified for potential allocation in settling claims.

Several Tribunal reports were issued through the 1990s, and negotiations based on their recommendations were opened with the Crown. But it was also expected that claimants might bypass the Tribunal and go straight into negotiation with the Crown. Doug Graham was keen to move to settlement in cases where claims could readily be identified as valid, he saw the benefits of compensation for claimants as providing an economic base that they could control, and the restoration of tribal self-respect. OTS's central role over this period led to significant expansion in the unit.

Te Roroa and private land

One Tribunal report caused disquiet in many quarters. A claim brought by Te Roroa, a tribe from the north of Kaipara Harbour, covered several matters, including the Department of Conservation's management of the Waipoua forest. When the Tribunal reported on this in 1992, one recommendation eclipsed all others: land on a privately owned farm (about 37 of the total 660 hectares) should be recovered at any cost and returned to the claimants. An investigation in 1946 had made the same recommendation; this land, which included a burial site, should have been reserved to Te Roroa when surveys were made.

Hostilities flared up. Maori threatened to occupy the land; confrontations between Maori and the farmer (Allan Titford) were well publicised; public emotion ran high. Successive governments had assured the public that private land could not be taken; in fact, the whole claims process was based on an understanding that Maori claims were against the Crown and that the Crown would have to find remedies that did not involve private property.

The government finally bought the land to hold as possible redress for Te Roroa, but resolved to forestall a repeat performance. It could not afford to be so vulnerable to manipulation by both landowners and Maori, and the credibility of the Tribunal process was at risk. Public alarm about Treaty claims was fuelled again when a mysterious fire gutted a Titford house.

A 1993 amendment to the Treaty of Waitangi Act prevented the Tribunal from making recommendations over private land, either for its return or for its acquisition by the Crown for return. This included lands under local body control, a matter that irked Maori since such land could involve areas of great significance. Under the amended Act, the Tribunal was still entitled to make recommendations on former SOE land that had passed into private ownership and was tagged with a memorial known to the purchaser.

A turbulent year

Despite the progress toward two 'mega-settlements' and action on a number of other claims, 1995 was set to be a turbulent year. Maori resistance to the 'fiscal cap' strategy announced in late 1994 should have warned the government that there could be trouble on the following Waitangi Day – by now a reliable weathervane for the nation's attitudes to the Treaty and for Maori responses to government policies.

In National's first two years in government, the commemorations had gone reasonably well. The formal programme at Waitangi stressed the Maori–Crown partnership, while the entertainment reflected the broader relationship of tangata whenua and tangata tiriti. The latter term gained currency in the late 1980s; it acknowledged that non-Maori had a right to be in New Zealand as a result of the 1840 Treaty. The concept did not sit comfortably with everyone, however. By early 1993, a multitude of Treaty-related issues were disturbing many Maori and creating divisions among both Pakeha and Maori. The events at Waitangi in February 1993 revealed a hardening of anti-government attitudes among both Maori elders and activists. Cabinet reviewed its options, and a new working group was established for Waitangi Day commemorations; the Crown and northern Maori (including protest groups) were represented, and the group was co-chaired by Deputy Prime Minister Don McKinnon and northern Maori representative Pita Paraone. The 1994 programme featured a forum on Te Tii marae for government ministers and Maori to exchange views on Treaty issues, and a sports-cum-cultural festival in the Treaty House grounds. The revamped programme was fairly successful, and protest was low-key. But the release of the Crown proposals in December 1994 opened the floodgates for protest.

On 6 February 1995, offensive behaviour on Te Tii marae towards the Governor General, Cath Tizard, and other dignitaries led to the cancellation of the forum. When protest flags

With disruption at Te Tii marae and Maori flags raised on the flagpole in the Treaty House grounds, formal proceedings at Waitangi were cancelled in 1995. FOTOPRESS LTD

were hoisted on the Treaty House grounds and public security appeared to be at risk, the formal ceremonies were also cancelled. Maori and Pakeha throughout the country were outraged by these events. The Prime Minister, Jim Bolger, probably spoke for most New Zealanders when he observed that the day could no longer be commemorated as it had been. For the rest of the decade, the government marked Waitangi Day with a formal event in Wellington and a limited official presence at Waitangi. But protest, though muted, was not silenced; it remained an effective way for Maori to draw attention to Treaty-related issues.

In the first few months of 1995, the Crown's proposals for the settlement of claims (and the 'fiscal cap') were presented at hui around New Zealand, organised by the Ministry of Maori Development/Te Puni Kokiri. No doubt Maori and government perceptions of the events as

Kia Kingi practises flax plaiting beneath the damaged statue of John Ballance, a nineteenth-century politician, in Moutoa Gardens. For Maori, the Wanganui park was a traditional fishing place, called Pakaitore. An occupation lasting eighty days, from 28 February to 18 May 1995, drew attention to Maori claims for rights relating to the Whanganui River. During the protest, the head of the statue was replaced with a pumpkin.

PHIL REID, *DOMINION POST* COLLECTION, ALEXANDER TURNBULL LIBRARY, EP/1995/0789/15A

they unrolled were very different. Wira Gardiner, head of TPK at the time, recorded his impressions in *Return to Sender* (1996).

At Doug Graham's insistence, Treasury and other officials were asked to attend the hui. It was to be a wounding experience for the government, a learning experience for the officials involved, and something of a public relations disaster. The government's loss of credibility in the eyes of Maori was considerable; in particular, the middle ground of Maori support was lost. Protest was inevitable. Maori attending the hui used the opportunity to put forward submissions, often presenting them with theatrical skills that drove the point home. The proposals were rejected by all.

Cilla Hamiora prepares lunch at Pakaitore, 18 March 1995. The camp had to feed not only the occupiers but a multitude of visitors and supporters. PHIL REID, *DOMINION POST* COLLECTION, ALEXANDER TURNBULL LIBRARY, EP/1995/0792/10

To the general public, the positions taken by some Maori at the hui appeared radical. Yet the submissions often repeated long-standing grievances: there had been no joint process in developing the proposals; they had been presented as a 'take it or leave it' package; and certain aspects constituted an attack on Treaty rights. Such arguments were reasonable, but it seemed to some sections of the public that nothing the government did would ever be acceptable to Maori. This impression proved hard to budge.

Even as the proposals were being discussed at hui around the country in February and March 1995, a number of land occupations had begun, the most publicised one at Moutoa Gardens (or Pakaitore) in Wanganui. Lasting for nearly eighty days, the protest focused attention on Maori issues and greatly increased public tension. Several other occupations and protests took place through the year, including a chainsaw attack on the lone pine tree on Auckland's One Tree Hill. Extensively covered by the media, these highly visible actions added to public unease and alienated some who, in less tense times, might have accepted the validity of the underlying issues. Occasionally, authoritative commentaries or articles by historians or lawyers were published in the mainstream press, but their moderating influence was hard to gauge.

The opposition parties – Labour, the Alliance and New Zealand First – had rejected the concept of the 'fiscal envelope' before the proposals were released. Doug Graham had indicated that he was prepared to reassess the proposals if there was overwhelming opposition. But

Ken Mair (left) and Nico Tangaroa hold the eviction notice served on the protesters occupying Pakaitore, in May 1995. In February 2001, an agreement was made between the Wanganui District Council, the Crown and the local iwi Te Ati Haunui-a-Paparangi: there would be a joint management board to take care of the historic reserve; the Ballance statue and a second sculpture would be restored. DOMINION POST

despite Maori objections, the government proceeded on the basis of the proposals, although the fiscal envelope was subsequently referred to as a 'guideline' rather than an absolute 'cap'. In 1996, it was dropped, having served its purpose; the existing settlements would be used as benchmarks in future negotiations. In 1997, additional non-commercial options for redress were developed for claims involving natural resources.

The extent of Maori unrest and public disquiet during 1995 spurred the government to work on damage control. In April, the Prime Minister, Jim Bolger, announced that the government might provide support for an elected national organisation if Maori wanted this. The challenge was accepted, but divisions within Maoridom appear to have stalled the idea. The Prime Minister also sought the views of Hepi Te Heuheu on a possible working party of Crown and iwi representatives to consider submissions on the proposals for settlement, but the invitation was declined.

For his part, Doug Graham gave repeated assurances that there would be action on settlements where the Tribunal had reported or where negotiations had reached a satisfactory conclusion. That year, several Tribunal reports were released, covering Ngai Tahu's ancillary claims, claims on Napier's inner harbour (Te Whanganui-a-Orotu Report) and Turangi township, and other claims. A second report on Turangi proposed remedies – and for the first time interim orders were included, which could mature within ninety days and bind the Crown. In the last quarter of the year, the Tainui settlement was drawing to a conclusion; more were in negotiation. A directive to heads of government departments asked for action in following up business arising from Tribunal reports and Treaty issues. It was a challenge, as a 1995 report by the Auditor-General admitted:

> The processes and functions for settling claims are complex and many and varied, and are located in a number of departments, Crown entities and other agencies. Tracking the funding allocated for administration and settlement costs is not a simple exercise. I have come to the view that only a limited number of people within government, or outside of it, have a good understanding of these matters.

The Auditor-General also noted the need for greater monitoring of government performance in Treaty settlements.

Reserved lands

Doug Graham also gave assurances of government action on Maori reserved lands, which appeared in many claims. Scattered around the country, these included land reserved for Maori in the New Zealand Company purchases, reserves in land purchased by the Crown, and some land returned to Maori from confiscations. Commissioners of Native Reserves had been appointed in the 1860s, and for several decades reserved lands were leased out. The Native Reserves Act 1882 brought the reserves under the Public Trustee. At that time, they included around 300,000 acres (120,000 hectares) in Taranaki – reserves and other land promised by the Crown. After investigation by the West Coast Commission in 1881–82, these became the West Coast Settlement Reserves. In 1920, responsibility for Maori reserved lands passed to the newly created Native Trustee.

A history of the reserved lands shows how administrators increasingly bowed to pressure from settlers. In Greymouth, Pakeha lessees demanded lower rentals and defaulted on payments; to avoid selling the land outright, Maori owners agreed to lease it in perpetuity with no revision of rent. A similar pattern occurred elsewhere – for example, in the Wellington central city area, and in the West Coast Settlement Reserves in Taranaki, where Parliament authorised the Public Trustee to grant leases in perpetuity and to sell in some circumstances. Crown protection guaranteed by the Treaty had been undermined by political pressure; the Crown had failed to ensure that the reserves were inalienable.

Government maladministration of reserved lands and the need for redress had been acknow-ledged by successive investigations over many decades. Around forty pieces of legislation, some dating back to the 1850s, were consolidated in the Maori Reserved Land Act 1955. Its key points were: perpetually renewable twenty-one-year leases, rent prescribed at 5 per cent of the unimproved value for rural land and 4 per cent for urban land, and rent fixed for the whole of each lease period. Official inquiries kept reaffirming that further reform was needed.

Priscilla and Adam Adamski, shown here with their son Peter, have for years farmed a leasehold property designated as West Coast Settlement Reserve Land. When government addressed long-standing Maori protest over inequitable lease terms on such lands, the Adamskis and other farmers feared their investment and livelihood were at risk. Settlers took up the leases believing that fixed lease terms were almost as good as ownership. Many had paid near-freehold prices and thought they would see their grandchildren farm the land. Legislation in 1997 and 1998 introduced new provisions for the lands that aimed to meet the interests of both lessors and lessees, and provide compensation if needed. For the Adamskis, the change meant an uncertain future in which the landowner might exercise a right to resume the land. DAILY NEWS/MANA, AUGUST/SEPTEMBER 1993

A ministerial review in 1991 led to proposals for a solution, released in 1993 for public discussion. It was acknowledged that the 1955 Act needed to be changed, and compensation paid for any losses incurred. The proposals were not well received by Maori owners (who considered that more attention was being paid to compensation for lessees) or by lessees (who occupied properties as various as private homes in Wellington, dairy farms in Taranaki, baches in Kawhia, and commercial premises in Greymouth and Motueka). Significant amounts of urban property was built on Maori reserved lands, and leased out.

Both parties agreed, however, that existing lease conditions were unfair to the Maori landowners (around four hundred of whom had already negotiated changes). Landowners needed to gain some control over their land, as well as obtaining commercial rents; lessees needed certainty about the status of their leases, and compensation if lease conditions were altered.

Maori Reserved Lands

By July 2002, of around two thousand leases scattered around the country, only a handful were still to be sorted out. The government had announced in May that it was addressing the issue of owners' historical grievances in relation to the leases, an intention signalled in the Maori Reserved Lands Amendment Act 1997. A one-off payment of $47.5 million was offered to Maori leasehold landowners, in recognition of the losses they had sustained through their inability to maintain market rents under the pre-1997 legislation. The agreement was made between the Finance Minister, Michael Cullen, the Minister of Maori Affairs, Parekura Horomia, and the chairman of the Federation of Maori Authorities, Paul Morgan. It was a good example of what could be achieved outside the Tribunal process and the formal Treaty settlement process.

After further negotiations, Doug Graham promised legislation, which was passed as the Maori Reserved Land Amendment Act 1997.

The key purpose of the Act was to enable Maori owners to gain physical possession of their land (albeit sometime in the future) if they wished. Other features included a provision for phased introduction of market rent reviews every seven years, unless the parties to the lease negotiated more frequent reviews. Landowners had a right of first refusal if lessees wanted to sell a lease; lessees had a right of first refusal if owners wanted to sell their land. (In both cases, certain provisions applied.) Various formulae provided for compensation to both owners and lessees. The process would take time to work through, some contention was inevitable, and there would be ongoing dissatisfaction in some quarters. But the Act and its 1998 amendment offered a solution to a long-standing breach of the Treaty.

Public works

Many claims to the Waitangi Tribunal in the 1980s and 1990s involved Maori land that had been taken compulsorily for public works – among them the claims covered by the Manukau Report (1985), the Te Maunga Railways Land Report (1994), and the Ngai Tahu Ancillary Claims Report (1995).

The history of compulsory seizure reaches back to the nineteenth century, and in most cases is complicated. From 1864, both the Crown and local bodies had taken land under a series of legislative provisions that gradually extended their powers. Actions taken under public works legislation tended to discriminate against Maori land, whether ownership was customary or Crown-granted. The tendency to select Maori land is borne out by Tribunal research, which indicates that the practice continued into the 1980s. Until 1928, up to 5 per cent of Crown-

The Taranaki Report 1995

Between September 1990 and June 1995, the Waitangi Tribunal held twelve hearings in Taranaki. The Crown did not make a case in response, so that the claim could move to negotiation as soon as possible. The Tribunal's report, released in 1996, dealt with twenty-one claims relating to the Taranaki district. It covered the Waitara purchase leading to the 1860s land wars and confiscations in the area, as well as the 1881 invasion of Parihaka and imprisonment of several hundred Taranaki Maori.

The conflict in Taranaki, more prolonged and intense than elsewhere, left a lasting grievance. The land involved in the claim was close to 2 million acres (810,000 hectares); the report noted that less than 5 per cent of their original lands remained in Taranaki Maori ownership and most of this was tied up in perpetual leases – a matter of ongoing protest and a major impediment to the resolution of grievance. The report proposed that settlement not be made with Taranaki as a whole, but with main hapu groups. In 2002, a number of those settlements were nearing completion. The leases were settled separately.

granted land, often in Maori ownership, could be taken for roading without compensation – and officials often argued that problems in collecting rates justified the taking of Maori land. Other legislation empowered local authorities to drain swamps, clear rivers and open up coastal lakes or lagoons – areas that Maori used for freshwater fisheries. These actions were usually taken without compensation.

Under the Public Works Act 1981, lands would be offered back to the original owners when they were no longer needed for public purposes. In 1996, the Crown proposed that the land be offered back to the original owner at current market value. But requiring the owner to buy back land does not appear to do justice to Maori for the loss of their land and resources. And there are other problems to be resolved, if the 'offer back' formula is to be effective.

The Crown does not recognise failure to offer back surplus land prior to 1981 as a breach of the Treaty, because until that date there was no obligation to do so under public works law. The Crown also declines to take responsibility for the actions of local or statutory bodies, which were often involved in the taking of land.

The Crown now acknowledges as a general principle that, while it is necessary to take land in certain circumstances, there has to be proper consultation and compensation, and alternative sites must be considered. The Waitangi Tribunal has made the point more emphatically, stating that any compulsory acquisition of Maori land should be limited to 'exceptional circumstances and as a last resort in the national interest'. It would be preferable, the Tribunal added, for a leasehold interest or a licence to be acquired rather than a freehold interest, so that the land would revert to Maori without the present hindrance of the 'offer back' procedures.

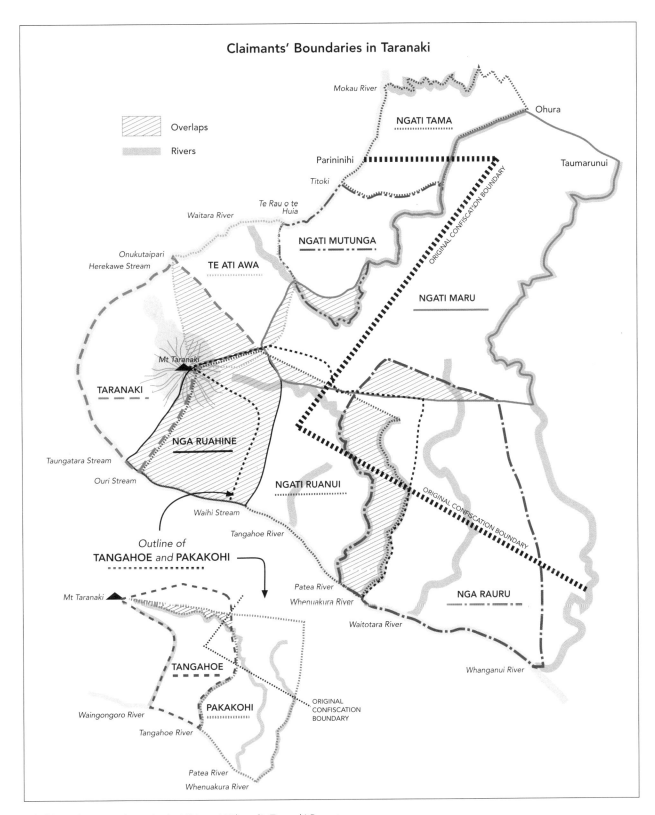

Tribal boundaries, as shown in the Waitangi Tribunal's Taranaki Report.
SOURCE: *THE TARANAKI REPORT: KAUPAPA TUATAHI*, WAITANGI TRIBUNAL, WELLINGTON 1995

Chief Judge Eddie Durie (second from left) was elevated to the High Court on 23 October 1998; Judge Joe Williams replaced him as acting Chief Judge of the Maori Land Court and Chair of the Waitangi Tribunal. DOMINION POST

In the mid 1990s, the Tribunal recommended a review of the Public Works Act 1981, which began in December 2000. The urgent need for a review was indicated by difficulties arising from the 1981 Act, court decisions, and uncertainty about the availability of some surplus land for settling claims. Review of the Act stalled after public submissions, but will lead in due course to new legislation.

Maori and political power

National's first term (1990–93) was marked by significant tension on Maori issues, and Maori support for the government did not increase when National was returned in 1993. In opposition, Labour generally supported National's policy on Treaty grievances (apart from the 'fiscal cap'), but attack from opposition parties grew as the 1996 election approached. The ACT leader, Richard Prebble, in particular levelled criticism at the whole Tribunal process, as well as the 'fiscal cap'. At the same time, many Maori were dissatisfied with the slow progress of claims, despite some major reports and key settlements. And government measures on the socio-economic front had severely affected Maori.

In the early 1990s, proposed changes in the electoral system provoked fiery debates about the four Maori seats in Parliament. The seats were introduced in 1867 as a temporary measure until Maori qualified for the individual property franchise, which would enable them

Government moves to change the electoral system led to considerable Maori interest in voting rights. Here, some voters consider the options. MMP was finally adopted for the 1996 general election. MANA, NOVEMBER/DECEMBER 1993

to register on the general roll. But the four seats had become a fixture, although they never fairly reflected Maori numbers in the population. Over the years, the system of Maori seats would be criticised for its inadequate representation of Maori interests. Since 1975, Maori have exercised the Maori electoral option; in a period of two months (changed in 1996 to four months) after each five-yearly Census, Maori can choose whether they wish to be registered on the Maori roll or the general roll. (A full Maori electoral roll was not instituted until 1949; secret ballot was introduced only in 1938.)

In 1986, the Royal Commission on the Electoral System recommended that New Zealand replace the first-past-the-post (FPP) system by mixed-member proportional representation (MMP). In 1992, the government held an indicative national referendum on the various options; if a majority supported change, a binding referendum would be held in 1993. The commission had argued that combining an electorate system with members selected from party lists under MMP offered better opportunities for Maori representation, with the proviso that any Maori

CHAPTER EIGHT: A DECADE OF CLAIMS   239

party should not be subject to the 5 per cent threshold for the party vote. (To qualify for seats in Parliament, a party has to win at least 5 per cent of all party votes or one electorate seat.)

As the government and opposition parties developed options in 1992 and 1993, Maori became aware of draft legislation that would abolish the four Maori seats. This, and the electoral reforms in general, sparked a great deal of debate in Maori communities. Was the abolition of the Maori seats a breach of the Treaty? How could Maori best achieve a rightful share of power in Parliament? The debate was often expressed in terms of securing tino rangatiratanga. Some Maori wanted to expand Maori strength in the mainstream through the increased allocation of seats in Parliament; others sought a separate parliament or a second (or upper) parliamentary chamber. A range of options in between was canvassed. In the event, Maori (and others) objected to the abolition of the Maori seats. When the Electoral Act 1993 was passed, the seats were retained, although the suggestion that a Maori party should not be subject to the 5 per cent threshold was dropped.

In their 1998 book, *New Zealand Adopts Proportional Representation*, political analysts Keith Jackson and Alan McRobie conclude:

> The 1993 Electoral Act established a process in law that gave Maori choice as to the form of representation they preferred. It provided, for the first time, guaranteed representation on a proportionate basis for as long as Maori wished it to continue, but it no longer provided them with a fixed number of seats, or any guarantee that the separate Maori seats would remain a permanent feature of the electoral system.

The Electoral Act 1993 provided for the number of Maori electorates to be based on the results of the Maori electoral option. Just before Christmas 1993, notice was given that the option would begin on 15 February 1994 and close two months later. The time-frame was short, and 16,000–50,000 Maori were estimated to be on neither the Maori nor the general roll. An information campaign was quickly under way.

Maori organisations, in particular the Maori Congress, were keen to encourage Maori to enrol. More Maori on the Maori roll would mean more Maori electorates. In early January, the Maori Congress, the New Zealand Maori Council and the Maori Women's Welfare League held a hui at Turangawaewae, and appealed to the Waitangi Tribunal for an urgent report on their claim that the process and funding for the Maori electoral option were simply inadequate. The Tribunal's report found that the level of funding did not protect Maori citizenship rights under Article 3 of the Treaty and breached Treaty principles. The Crown rejected the report, which led to a challenge in the courts. In the event, the campaign for a rerun of the 1994 Maori electoral option before the 1996 election was not successful.

The 1996 election and National's third term

The 1996 election showed how MMP might work to Maori advantage. With larger numbers on the Maori roll (a net increase of 32,294), Maori seats increased from 4 out of 99 electorates under the previous system to 5 out of 65 under MMP. All were taken by New Zealand First,

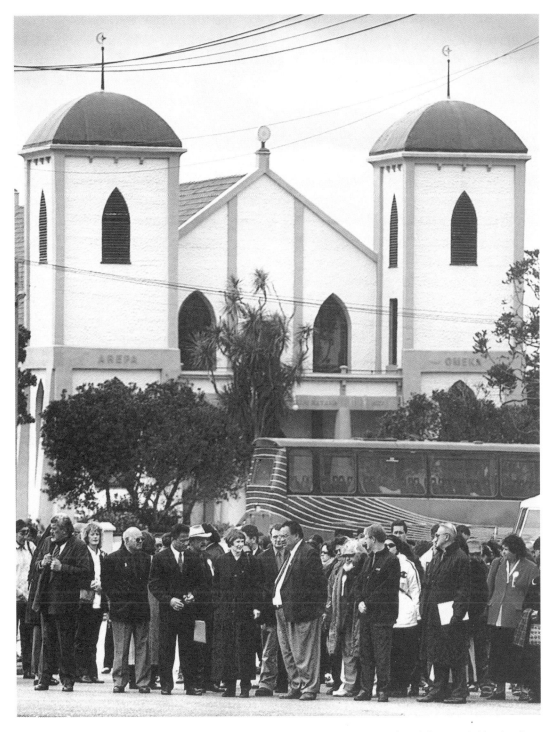
Labour leader Helen Clark is welcomed at Ratana headquarters, near Wanganui, to launch her party's Maori policy in October 1999. MARK ROUND, *DOMINION*, 16 OCTOBER 1999

CHAPTER EIGHT: A DECADE OF CLAIMS 241

a new party led by Winston Peters. The result was a paradox: Maori had opted for strong Maori political leaders and ignored the fact that New Zealand First's leader courted his Pakeha constituents with markedly anti-Treaty rhetoric. A coalition government was formed by National and New Zealand First, with Maori in key positions: Peters as Deputy Prime Minister and Treasurer, John Delamere as Associate Treasurer, Tau Henare as Minister of Maori Affairs, and several others in lesser posts.

With additions from the party lists, there were now fifteen Maori in Parliament. It seemed that MMP promised a greater degree of power-sharing and a measure of leverage in Parliament, although political analysts were cautious. Much depended on how the political parties selected and positioned their candidates. Meanwhile, debate on power-sharing would continue. Securing tino rangatiratanga under the Treaty was an ongoing issue; as some Maori commentators noted, MMP did not deal with the fundamental constitutional changes required to put the two Treaty parties on a more equal footing.

The coalition government was committed to continuing the settlement of Maori grievances. It gave an assurance that the 'fiscal cap' – the total amount of money available for settlement of historical Treaty claims – was being abandoned. But any suggestion that this might mean an expansion in funds available was quickly scotched; the government considered that sufficient benchmarks had been struck for a cap (or 'quantum') to be effectively in place. The relativity clause in the Waikato-Tainui and Ngai Tahu settlements (the latter finalised in 1998) also tended to inhibit any expansion of the quantum.

From 1992, Doug Graham had encouraged Maori claimants to seek direct negotiation with the Crown as an alternative to a full hearing before the Waitangi Tribunal. In late 1998 and early 1999, the government went further: the Crown accepted that a prima facie breach of the Treaty existed where claims related to pre-1865 land sales, confiscation or the operations of the Native Land Court. Graham hoped that this might expedite negotiations and settlements, but it failed to do so. The message had in general been conveyed informally, and perhaps this created suspicion. But the obstacle in all negotiations was the difficulty Maori had in establishing among themselves a mandate to negotiate – a problem that would continue to slow down the settlement process.

Perhaps it was no coincidence that, as the coalition government broke up in August 1998, Doug Graham made public his intention not to stand for Parliament in the 1999 election. He had been the first Minister (apart from Ministers of Maori Affairs) to throw his energies wholeheartedly into establishing processes for the settlement of Treaty claims, and he acknowledged that the work had taken its toll. As well as building relationships with Maori, he had worked to establish broad political support for Treaty policies. His warm personality, generous dedication of private time, and personal commitment to reconciliation between the Crown and Maori had taken the settlement process a significant step forward. In this he had the full support of the Prime Minister, Jim Bolger; by late 1997, when Jenny Shipley succeeded Bolger as Prime Minister, Cabinet and National Party support for Treaty settlements was waning.

As Graham himself observed, it was time to allow those with new energy to take over the task of advancing Treaty issues. In the forthcoming election, that challenge would fall to Labour.

Jenny Shipley, Prime Minister from 8 December 1997 until just after the 27 November election in 1999, reads the formal Crown apology, part of the Ngai Tahu claim settlement, at Onuku marae, Banks Peninsula, on 29 November 1998. THE PRESS, CHRISTCHURCH

CHAPTER NINE

Into the Twenty-first Century

On Waitangi Day 2000, Prime Minister Helen Clark avoided Waitangi and went to Onuku marae near Akaroa, with two previous Governors General: to the left, Cath Tizard with Parekura Horomia, Minister of Maori Affairs, and, to the right, Paul Reeves with MP Mahara Okeroa, far right, and Peter Davis (partly obscured). THE PRESS, CHRISTCHURCH

The Labour-Alliance government formed after the 1999 election soon ran into trouble in its handling of Maori affairs. A key new policy was announced: called 'closing the gaps', it aimed to improve the socio-economic welfare of Maori citizens at the low end of the income scale. There was a public outcry, from people opposed to the idea of special treatment for one group in the population. The 'closing the gaps' title was dropped, although most of the policies continued on the basis of need. (In 1999, Maori unemployment was over 17 per cent.) Not for the first time, public criticism made it difficult for the government to sustain actions tagged specifically for Maori.

The new government began with a low profile on Treaty issues. The Minister with responsibility for Treaty negotiations was the Attorney-General, Margaret Wilson. For some time,

[previous page] At Parihaka in 2003, Huirangi Waikerepuru speaks to representatives of the Crown – on this occasion, the Prime Minister, Helen Clark, and the Minister of Maori Affairs, Parekura Horomia. ROB TUCKER/MANA, APRIL/MAY 2003

Protesters at Waitangi make a stand and then depart, February 2000. NORTHERN ADVOCATE, 7 FEBRUARY 2000

Wilson was heavily involved in seeing through legislation on employment relations and other major issues. But, by the middle of 2000, the policy framework for the settlement of historical claims that had developed since 1992 had been reviewed and largely confirmed. In a July press statement, Wilson affirmed the Crown's objective that settlements of historical claims had to be 'fair, durable, final and occur in a timely manner'; she also announced a set of principles for settlement. There would be no more relativity clauses: each claim would be 'treated on its merits' and would not have to be 'fitted under a predetermined fiscal cap'. There did, however, need to be 'fairness' in the treatment of claimant groups – similar claims would receive similar levels of redress. These principles would stand as guidelines for the Crown's settlement of historical claims under the Treaty. But, as the new Minister made clear, they formed only one part of the government's wider commitment to restoring and improving the relationship between the Crown and Maori.

Over preceding years, there had been considerable action on Treaty issues: a substantial number of claimant groups had passed through the hearings and report stages; some major claims had been settled, as well as smaller ones; and several were at different stages in the negotiation and settlement process. Although committed to moving along the settlement of Treaty claims, the government wanted to make a careful assessment of the Treaty sector. This was by

Former law professor Margaret Wilson became Minister in Charge of Treaty Negotiations and Attorney-General when Labour won the election in November 1999.
DOMINION POST

now fragmented: several ministers shared responsibility for the Treaty, and work was carried out by a number of key agencies, each created for different reasons. The two main participants were the Waitangi Tribunal and the Office of Treaty Settlements (OTS). The Tribunal was in the Department for Courts (moving from Justice in 1995, and returning in 2003), while OTS was in the Ministry of Justice. The other key organisation involved was the Crown Forestry Rental Trust (CFRT). The Tribunal, OTS and CFRT all now reviewed their work.

The Waitangi Tribunal in 2000

The year 2000 was an occasion for marking the work of the Waitangi Tribunal: the twenty-fifth anniversary of the Treaty of Waitangi Act 1975 (which established the Tribunal) fell in October. Since 1985, the Tribunal had published thirty major reports: ten or more had dealt primarily with land, and two with fisheries (Muriwhenua and Ngai Tahu); others covered an ever-widening range of subjects. By the end of the 1990s, several Tribunal hearings were running concurrently, and preparatory research was under way on a number of other claims.

This was a massive amount of work within a relatively short time-frame. As historian Alan Ward noted in *An Unsettled History* (1999):

> Given that the nation has embarked on nothing less than a review of its entire colonial history, remarkable progress has been made in researching and reporting claims ... In the space of about 12 years the Tribunal, the Crown Forestry Rental Trust, and claimant and Crown researchers have built up a formidable information-base on issues ranging from customary Maori rights in land and waters, and early interactions between Maori and settler, to the role

Principles for the Settlement of Treaty of Waitangi Claims (2000)

Good faith: The negotiating process is to be conducted in good faith, based on mutual trust and cooperation towards a common goal.

Restoration of relationship: The strengthening of the relationship between the Crown and Maori is an integral part of the settlement process and will be reflected in any settlement. The settlement of historical grievances also needs to be understood within the context of wider government policies that are aimed at restoring and developing the Treaty relationship.

Just redress: Redress should relate fundamentally to the nature and extent of breaches suffered, with existing settlements being used as benchmarks for future settlements where appropriate. The relativity clauses in the Waikato-Tainui and Ngai Tahu settlements will continue to be honoured, but such clauses will not be included in future settlements. The reason for this is that each claim is treated on its merits and does not have to be fitted under a predetermined fiscal cap.

Fairness between claims: There needs to be consistency in the treatment of claimant groups. In particular, 'like should be treated as like', so that similar claims receive a similar level of financial and commercial redress. This fairness is essential to ensure settlements are durable.

Transparency: First, it is important that claimant groups have sufficient information to enable them to understand the basis on which claims are settled. Second, there is a need to promote greater public understanding of the Treaty and the settlement process.

Government-negotiated: The Treaty settlement process is necessarily one of negotiation between claimant groups and the government. They are the only two parties who can, by agreement, achieve durable, fair and final settlements. The government's negotiation with claimant groups ensures delivery of the agreed settlement and minimises costs to all parties.

SOURCE: *HEALING THE PAST, BUILDING A FUTURE: A GUIDE TO TREATY OF WAITANGI CLAIMS AND NEGOTIATIONS WITH THE CROWN*, OFFICE OF TREATY SETTLEMENTS, WELLINGTON, 2002, P.30

and functions of modern agencies such as the Maori Trustee. Many issues never previously examined, or only superficially so, have been explored in depth, and Maori understandings of historical experience revealed.

It seemed appropriate now to review and evaluate the Tribunal's processes. In 1996, under a new director, Morrie Love, the Tribunal had initiated a system of 'district inquiries'. By focusing on claims district by district, the Tribunal could hear multiple claims within a common geographical area. A casebook of evidence was compiled for each district inquiry, using the Rangahaua Whanui research reports as a starting point. The casebook contained all the research reports that the claimants relied on in the hearings, as well as the research reports and

The Waitangi Tribunal at one of the hearings on the Hauraki claim in 2001: from left, John Kneebone, Te Wharehuia Milroy, Augusta Wallace (Presiding Officer), and Evelyn Stokes. A Tribunal sitting has a presiding officer and usually between two and four other members (at least one of them Maori). Members are chosen for their knowledge of the issues likely to come before the Tribunal, and have included business people, academics and legal experts. WAITANGI TRIBUNAL COLLECTION

documents that the Tribunal considered relevant. Hearings began when a casebook was ready, which could take eighteen to twenty-four months. For a major hearing involving a number of claims, a casebook might be thousands of pages in length. The first casebook to be completed was for the Mohaka-ki-Ahuriri claim in northern Hawke's Bay.

The 2000 review identified some problems in the Tribunal's process: the hearings took too long, the reports were not completed promptly enough, and the overall time-lapse meant that the claimants' mandate to progress the claim through hearings might collapse. (The mandate is the authority given by a claimant group to its representatives.) The review laid the groundwork for a new approach that would streamline the research, inquiry and reporting processes so that claimants could move on to negotiation and settlement. The Tribunal wanted not only greater efficiency but also a process that would drive the Crown and Maori more purposefully toward settlement.

The one-thousandth claim (WAI 1000) was registered at the Waitangi Tribunal in August 2002: Chief Judge Joe Williams (Acting Chairperson) with Tribunal Director Morrie Love and Assistant Registrar Jacqui Lethbridge. Many claims are grouped into district inquiries for hearings. When the full process of negotiation, settlement and legislation has been taken into account, historical claims should be finalised by 2020. WAITANGI TRIBUNAL, TE MANUTUKUTUKU, OCTOBER 2002

The new approach was implemented in 2001, in the Gisborne district inquiry under Judge Joe Williams, who became deputy chairperson of the Tribunal in 2000. Preparation for the Gisborne hearings included: conferences with all parties to identify and clarify the issues being contested, a clear mandate established, with full representation of the claimant groups; and deadlines set for all participants. Early in the hearings, the Crown was required to state its position on the claim's major issues, in order to focus the hearings on matters still in dispute (previously, the Crown had not been required to respond until it had heard all the evidence, and much time had been spent on aspects of the claim not in fact defended by the Crown). Reports were now to be drafted immediately after the hearings were completed; there was to be a smooth transition to negotiation, which could begin before the final report was released. The Tribunal estimated that the process from start of research to release of report should take three to four years for each group of claims.

The Tribunal aims to use this approach in all new district inquiries. It is an intensive process, requiring the active engagement of all parties – the claimants, the Tribunal and the Crown, as well as support agencies. The demands on resources are such that probably only two or three

CHAPTER NINE: INTO THE TWENTY-FIRST CENTURY   251

Treaty Settlements or Agreements (at 31 March 2004)

Settlements since 21 September 1992

Claimant Group	Year Settled	Value of Settlement ($)
Fisheries	1992/93	170,000,000
Ngati Whakaue	1993/94	5,210,000
Ngati Rangiteaorere	1993/94	760,000
Hauai	1993/94	715,682
Waikato-Tainui Raupatu	1994/95	170,000,000
Waimakuku	1995/96	375,000
Rotoma	1996/97	43,931
Te Maunga	1996/97	129,032
Ngai Tahu	1996/97	170,000,000
Ngati Turangitukua	1998/99	5,000,000
Pouakani	1999/2000	2,000,000[1]
Te Uri o Hau	1999/2000	15,600,000
Ngati Ruanui	2000/01	41,000,000
Ngati Tama	2001/02	14,500,000
Ngati Awa	2002/03	42,240,000
Ngati Tuwharetoa (Bay of Plenty)	2002/03	10,500,000
Nga Rauru	2003/04	31,000,000
Total settlement redress		679,073,645[2]

Heads of Agreement or Agreements in Principle (reached by 31 March 2004)[3]

Claimant Group	Year Agreed	Agreed Quantum ($)
Ngati Mutunga (Taranaki)	1999/2000	14,500,000
Rangitane o Manawatu	1999/2000	8,500,000
Te Ati Awa (Taranaki)	1999/2000	34,000,000
Te Arawa Lakes	2003/04	10,000,000

1. Includes $650,000, paid in advance of settlement in 1990.
2. Additional expenses of some $35,000,000 (relating to a variety of claims and settlement costs) are not included in this total.
3. Still to reach signed Deed of Settlement.

SOURCE: FROM WWW.OTS.GOVT.NZ – QUARTERLY REPORT, 31 MARCH 2004

such district inquiries can be started each year (with up to fifteen in process at any one time). The focus on speed and efficiency brings clear benefits to all sides, but it may also limit an important aspect of the hearings. The Tribunal is a commission of inquiry, not a court; its purpose is investigation, and it is not intended to be adversarial. The opportunity for Maori to tell of their experience and their understanding of the relationship with the Crown is a significant element in resolving claims; hearings, often held on marae, allow emotions to be

Heni Sunderland speaking at Gisborne hearings of the Tribunal in 2002. The intensity of claims hearings is demanding for all involved.
WAITANGI TRIBUNAL COLLECTION

expressed, and the value of this is acknowledged by many who have participated, both claimants and Tribunal members.

After the hearings are finished, it may be one or two years – or sometimes longer – before the Tribunal's report is ready for release. This report represents a huge achievement for claimants, marking years of work and commitment. But it is only a halfway stage. Once the report is delivered to government and to claimants, the Crown must decide how to act on it, and claimants face a new challenge in moving to negotiation and settlement. Claimant resources are often depleted from the claims process; sometimes the mandate has fragmented, and needs to be re-established. Claimant groups are often daunted by the next phase. Funding has to be found to cover the cost of the negotiation period, and the relationship with OTS established.

The negotiation process

Settlements are negotiated between claimants and the Crown. The Crown in this case means the executive branch of government – Cabinet, the ministers particularly involved in Treaty issues, and their departments (Treasury, Te Puni Kokiri and the Department of Conservation). Other departments and ministers are often involved, too, including the Crown Law Office.

But the Crown's chief agency for negotiating settlements of historical claims is the Office of Treaty Settlements. For claimants, this is the main point of contact with the Crown during negotiations.

With a staff of over fifty in 2003, OTS reports directly to the Minister in Charge of Treaty Negotiations. In addition to negotiating settlements, it provides the Minister with advice on settlement issues and individual claims; it also funds the Crown Law Office to undertake research into historical claims, and to represent the Crown's position at Tribunal hearings. OTS also helps to coordinate the government departments and bodies involved in negotiations and settlements. It is responsible for overseeing the implementation of the settlements, and manages surplus Crown property assets held for potential redress.

Claimant groups can opt to bypass the Waitangi Tribunal and go straight into negotiation with OTS, but to date few have done so. Claimants usually decide to act on the basis of a Tribunal report. OTS also has a responsibility for helping claimant groups develop a mandate and prepare for negotiation.

It is OTS policy to negotiate with the largest natural grouping possible – usually an iwi and sometimes a hapu – and to make comprehensive settlements. This is seen as the most effective way of ensuring that a secure mandate is achieved, that cross-claims are avoided, that the scope of possible redress is maximised, and that finality is reached. It is recognised that a comprehensive settlement may not always meet the aspirations of all the claimant groups involved (and there are usually a number of groups in any settlement); there are often provisions for specific redress for one or more subgroups. Redress may involve protocols with government agencies that ensure that the basis for the relationship is understood and the agency is committed. Cabinet defined the process for establishing these protocols, which are legally enforceable, late in 1999.

A secure legal outcome is one of the key objectives of any settlement. As part of the settlement process, claimant groups need to establish an appropriate governance structure – a body that will receive and manage the settlement cash and assets. It is accepted that full compensation for all the economic losses of a claimant group is not an option; instead, negotiations aim at 'a fair level of redress'. The settlement package is usually a mix of commercial and financial redress, cultural redress, and an historical account and a Crown apology. The settlements vary considerably. Each takes a different path to full implementation, and includes new elements of redress. OTS is steadily developing further options.

The settlement is made between the Crown and the tribal group, whose representatives must agree to negotiations being confidential (except for necessary internal consultation on each side). The intention is that the financial component of the settlement will be used to build a strong economic resource, as the tribe sees fit. There is no fiscal cap in determining the total value of each settlement, although existing settlements do still serve as benchmarks. The factors taken into account by the Crown when making an offer are: the nature of the breach (raupatu, or confiscation, being considered the most serious); the size and proportion of the loss (for example, in relation to the land area left in claimant ownership); other settlements; and factors particular to the group (in which population size is only one consideration).

Property Portfolio Information

Three land banking mechanisms operate to protect surplus Crown, District Health Board and Crown Research Institute land for potential use in settling historical Treaty claims:

- **Claim-specific land banks** include properties that have been nominated for land banking by mandated claimants, and the land-banked properties are dedicated to that particular claimant group's eventual settlement. A financial cap applies.

- **The Crown settlement portfolio** operates within former raupatu (confiscation) boundaries. All surplus Crown properties within these boundaries are land-banked. No cap applies.

- **Regional land banks** comprise areas not covered by the above two mechanisms. The boundaries coincide with the Waitangi Tribunal's Rangahaua Whanui regions. Properties are selectively land-banked, through the operation of the protection mechanism, but are not dedicated to any particular claimant group.

SOURCE: WWW.OTS.GOVT.NZ – QUARTERLY REPORT, 31 MARCH 2004

The negotiation of a settlement – from the first steps in negotiation to final legislation – usually takes four to seven years. This is not surprising, given the complexity of the Treaty settlement process. Many issues need to be resolved, and the claimants' representatives are usually chosen from many groups – mostly within an iwi, but sometimes across tribal groupings. The process also involves Parliament, ministers, government departments and other agencies. Settlements need to be full and final, and they must form a basis for good relations between the Crown and Maori.

In 2002, OTS set up a claims development team to assist claimants with the settlement process and advise on the ways in which divergent interests might be reconciled within an overall negotiation. This has arisen because claims reported by the Tribunal do not necessarily advance to the negotiation stage: sometimes the mandate for negotiation has broken down; or claimants are unwilling to join forces and undertake comprehensive negotiations; or cross-claims have arisen; or claimants are unhappy about the likely size of the settlement. Sometimes, too, claimants who have opted to bypass the Tribunal and initiate direct negotiations with OTS might revise this decision, and take their claim first through the Waitangi Tribunal. The Tribunal process can help to build a secure mandate and stronger tribal cohesion.

During negotiations, both the Crown and claimants face challenges. Sometimes third-party interests can delay a settlement. Heads of agreement are often contingent on the agreement of other agencies – for example, the Department of Conservation or local bodies. Settlement packages often include the return of significant places to tribal custody. Where these are reserves in the care of local councils, cooperation from the local body may be hard to obtain. A redress item that fails to get local body agreement can leave the tribe with a residual sense of grievance, despite the best efforts of OTS and much time spent.

Flow Chart for Claims Processes

- There are two distinct processes for addressing historical Treaty claims: the **Waitangi Tribunal inquiry process** and **negotiation with the Crown** (managed for the Crown by the Office of Treaty Settlements).

Tribunal inquiry process (right):
- If a claimant group chooses to go through the Tribunal process, it is nonetheless possible to move to negotiations at any point (except during a remedies hearing).
- Once the Tribunal has reported, the next step is for claimants and the Crown to move into negotiation, seeking agreement on the terms of settlement.

Negotiations (far right):
- Claimant groups can choose to bypass the Tribunal inquiry process entirely, and enter into negotiation with the Crown as soon as the claim is registered.
- Groups in negotiation with the Crown can move over to the Waitangi Tribunal process at any point. Negotiations are then suspended.

Settlement:
- Whichever process a claimant group chooses to address its claim, Deeds of Settlement (which may include a Crown apology, cultural redress, and financial and commercial redress) are possible only through negotiation between the claimant group and the Crown (far right).

Historical and contemporary claims:
- Crown acts or omissions before 21 September 1992 are covered by **historical claims**; those occurring after 21 September 2002 are covered by **contemporary claims**. The process for dealing with historical claims is outlined above. Contemporary claims are dealt with through the Waitangi Tribunal, the courts or relevant government departments.

SOURCE: BASED ON *HEALING THE PAST, BUILDING A FUTURE: A GUIDE TO TREATY OF WAITANGI CLAIMS AND NEGOTIATIONS WITH THE CROWN*, OFFICE OF TREATY SETTLEMENTS, WELLINGTON, 2002, PP.27, 39

The Inquiry Process at the Waitangi Tribunal (2004)

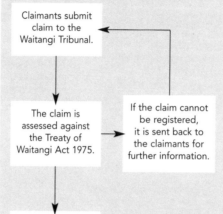

SOURCE: BASED ON WWW.WAITANGI-TRIBUNAL.GOVT.NZ/PREPARINGCLAIM/FLOWCHAQRT.ASP, ACCESSED AUGUST 2004-09-19

STAGE 3
Findings and recommendations

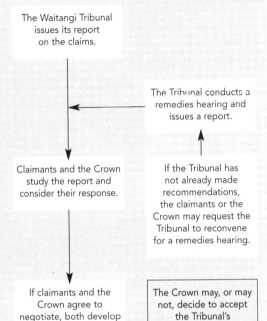

The Negotiation and Settlement Process (2004)

Managed for the Crown by the Office of Treaty Settlements.

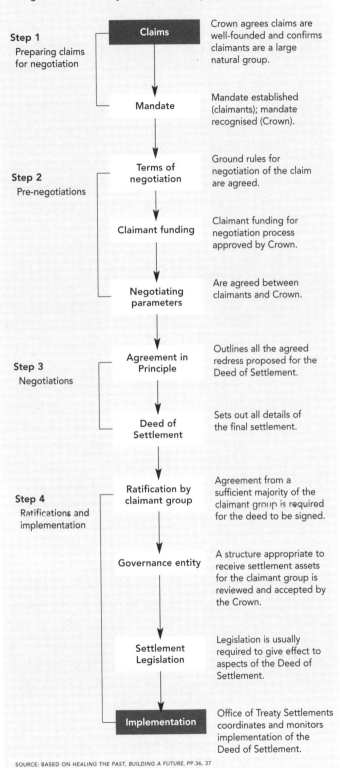

SOURCE: BASED ON *HEALING THE PAST, BUILDING A FUTURE*, PP.36, 37

More difficult to resolve are the issues that inhibit claimants either from coming to the negotiating table, or from finalising settlements. One is the Crown's adherence to comprehensive settlements with large natural groupings. OTS advances good reasons for maintaining this policy, but claimants do not always find it easy to comply. Each region has its own unique history, giving rise to specific problems; one system does not comfortably fit all.

All claimant groups have found that holding a mandate secure and keeping a large group together is a challenge. Tensions are bound to arise within claimant groups, for many reasons: because negotiations are confidential, it is difficult to maintain the support of the wider group; if the tribal group is scattered, it is hard for people to stay in touch; and the management of the post-settlement phase can present new and sometimes problematic issues for the claimant group. In general, it is clear that claimants need to move as briskly as possible to negotiation after receiving a Tribunal report, and they need to be well organised. Claimant groups also require substantial funds for both the Tribunal claims process and negotiations with OTS. These are hard to raise.

Funding Treaty claims

For everyone involved in Treaty claims, adequate funding is a major problem – and always has been. Legal and research costs are considerable, whether claims go through the Tribunal process and on to OTS for negotiation and settlement, or directly to OTS. By 2003, the Crown Forestry Rental Trust (CFRT) was meeting about 80 per cent of claimants' research costs.

CFRT was established in 1990 under the Crown Forest Assets Act 1989. Under the terms of its trust deed, CFRT receives the licence fees paid for the rental of Crown forest land. Fees amount to many millions of dollars each year; at the end of the 2002/03 year, the total licence fees held by the trust were about $350 million, and the interest generated that year was over $20 million. CFRT is able to use this interest to help Maori prepare, present and negotiate claims before the Waitangi Tribunal that involve (or could involve) licensed Crown forest land. In the 2002/03 year, CFRT provided over $3 million for research and over $4 million for other services for claimants, with around $5 million dispersed directly to claimants.

Reports funded by CFRT and written by (or under the supervision of) experienced research staff have greatly expanded the volume of historical research available for Treaty claims. Like the Waitangi Tribunal and OTS, CFRT has reviewed its policies, focusing its resources and aligning them with the Tribunal and OTS processes. CFRT is independent of both the Tribunal and OTS but aims to work with them in a coordinated way. Recently, CFRT policy has extended to encouraging claimants to cluster in groups for claims hearings, supporting claimants through the hearings and negotiation stages, and developing the tribal structures and expertise needed to receive settlements and make best use of them.

CFRT's access to funds is seen by many as giving forestry claimants an advantage over others. This has sometimes led to friction among claimant groups and criticism of CFRT. A review of the trust by the Maori Affairs Select Committee in 2002 and 2003 was critical of CFRT's wide interpretation of its trust deed, its alignment with Tribunal processes and Crown policies of

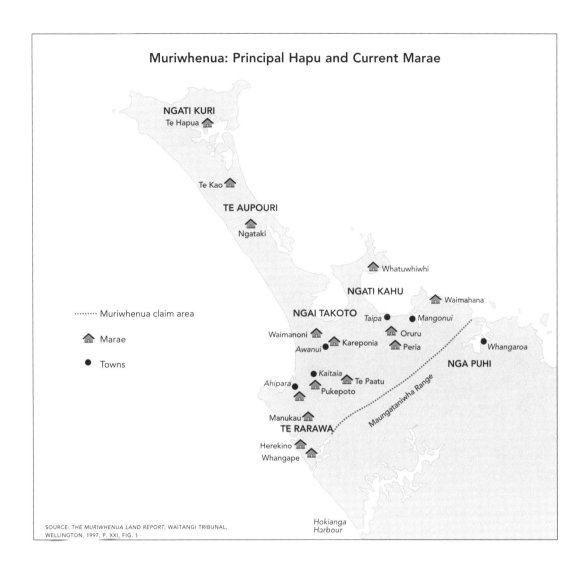

Muriwhenua Land Report 1997

This Waitangi Tribunal report relates to the land north of the Maungataniwha Range in the far north. The Muriwhenua claims involve five main tribes and deal with pre-Treaty private transactions from 1834, and government transactions from 1840 to 1865, together affecting around 430,000 acres (174,000 hectares). Maori saw these transactions – at least in part – as contracts for mutually beneficial social relationships; to European settlers and officials, they were simply land sales. By 1865, the tribes' economic and social status was in jeopardy; as land losses continued, the tribes were reduced to penury and dependence on the state, living on lands insufficient for traditional subsistence and inadequate for farming. The report suggested possible settlement options. Disputes over who should hold the mandate for negotiations delayed the process, but it was in train by 2003.

People from Te Whakatohea iwi ascend the staircase in the Beehive on 1 October 1996 – among them, Tuhiakia Keepa (centre foreground) and Mere Walker (centre right, carrying a kete). With other tribal members, they were present to witness the signing of a Deed of Settlement for the Whakatohea claim. However, the settlement offer was subsequently rejected in favour of new negotiations. DOMINION POST COLLECTION, ALEXANDER TURNBULL LIBRARY, EP/1996/2831/12

comprehensive settlements, the scope of historical research, and the size of its staff (over fifty in 2002/03). The review urged the devolution of research capability to claimants, and criticised the criteria for allocating funds. Government did not accept most recommendations, but nonetheless the trust was given a year to improve its management and performance. The CFRT unit was restructured, and work contracted out. The trust's independence, its substantial income, and its public profile in some large claims (for example, those concerning the forests in the central North Island) will continue to make it a target for comment – with the potential to fuel political and public unease about the Treaty process as a whole.

CFRT funding has proved essential to the Treaty process, however. In marked contrast, Tribunal funds available for research in each of the three years to 2002 amounted to about $500,000 for contract work, with a similar amount for research carried out by staff. As early as 1994, budgetary constraints were causing the Tribunal's chair, Chief Judge Eddie Durie, to

Research for Treaty Claims

Office of Treaty Settlements (OTS)
- Provides advice, but does not generally carry out primary research for claims.
- Assesses claimants' research, with assistance from the Crown Law Office.
- Does not provide funding for historical research by claimants.
- Instructs and funds Crown Law Office in researching and presenting the Crown case at the Waitangi Tribunal.

Claimant Group
- May undertake research on tribal history and oral evidence, including research on specific sites for cultural redress.
- May obtain funding from a range of sources, including CFRT and the Waitangi Tribunal.

Crown Forestry Rental Trust (CFRT)
- Provides research funding if the claim involves licensed Crown forest land.

Waitangi Tribunal
- Undertakes research for hearings and produces a report.
- A Tribunal report may be used as a basis for negotiations.

Claimant groups and the Crown may use CFRT and Tribunal research in negotiations, as well as their own research.

SOURCE: *HEALING THE PAST, BUILDING A FUTURE: A GUIDE TO TREATY OF WAITANGI CLAIMS AND NEGOTIATIONS WITH THE CROWN*, OFFICE OF TREATY SETTLEMENTS, WELLINGTON, 2002, P.43

---

note that there was a risk of the claims process being curtailed. Additional funding was allocated in the 1995/96 and 1997/98 financial years, but Durie continued to draw attention to the lack of resources. In 2002/03, the Tribunal had a staff of forty-eight and a total budget of $6,296,000.

The legal and research costs met by claimants themselves during the preparatory and hearings stages of a claim are usually substantial. The need to assist claimants with legal costs was recognised in the 1980s. Under an amendment to its 1975 Act, the Tribunal could assist claimants by appointing counsel, but this was a charge on the Tribunal's limited budget. The Legal Services Act 1991 made provision for Maori with a claim before the Tribunal to apply for legal aid. Applying through the Legal Services Agency, claimants, whether individuals or groups such as hapu and iwi, have to substantiate their need for legal counsel and for funding, and meet other criteria. (In the early 1990s, CFRT also contributed to claimants' legal costs but has ceased doing so.)

When claimants move into the negotiation and settlement phase, they can apply to OTS for funding (although this does not cover their research costs). OTS funding used to be deducted

Ngati Awa Raupatu Report 1999

This Waitangi Tribunal report was presented to Ngati Awa in October 1999. It deals with the raupatu aspects of Ngati Awa and Tuwharetoa ki Kawerau claims. The report's principal finding is that Ngati Awa territory was confiscated in 1866 without just cause and in contravention of the Treaty of Waitangi. The popular misconception is that the land was taken in response to the murder of a Crown official in Whakatane in 1865. However, the report makes it clear that the land was taken not for that civil matter, which was pursued through the courts, but for a supposed rebellion that occurred when the arresting party came to seize those responsible for the murder. The Tribunal found that no such rebellion had taken place, and that any resistance to the invading forces (comprised largely of Te Arawa, Ngati Awa's traditional enemy) was in self-defence.

from the claimants' negotiated settlement, but in 1997 funding became separate from redress. The level of funding varies according to the size of the claimant group, the complexity of the issues, and the stage reached in the negotiation process. Funding is not automatic – claimants must apply, and OTS applies stringent requirements with regard to mandate. In the six years to 31 March 2002, OTS paid out close to $10 million in various types of funding for claimants. In the 2002/03 financial year, OTS had a total budget of around $13 million, of which $2 million covered costs involved in representing the Crown before the Waitangi Tribunal, including the Crown's historical research.

The public debate

Treaty claims and settlements have been the focus of heated debate in New Zealand since the 1980s. A broad public consensus on the need to settle Treaty grievances is crucial to any government undertaking such an enterprise. But since the mid 1990s, this consensus seems to have weakened. Intense public interest in Treaty issues peaked in 1995, then eased off. New developments – especially the fisheries settlement of 1992 and its aftermath – have drawn Maori into disputes, and added to public unease about the feasibility of Treaty settlements. Within the community at large, there has been a surprising lack of understanding about the claims and settlement process; conflicting views on the meaning of the Treaty also abound.

In the 1990s, the debate was fuelled by the release of several major Tribunal reports, followed by apologies and settlements by the Crown. Media commentary tended to raise public antagonism towards what was often referred to as a 'grievance industry' or 'gravy train'. Bitter as the debate has sometimes been, public attitudes have changed radically since the early 1980s. Information about New Zealand history has been disseminated through Tribunal hearings and reports, and found its way into general histories; many people now accept that the Treaty was

Emotions have been heated at times in Taranaki as claims and settlements were worked through. Disagreement and discord have sometimes led to the kind of stance taken here at Manaia. MARK ROUND, DOMINION POST, 9 SEPTEMBER 2000

breached in various ways. Claims are often seen as justified; where questions are raised, they are mostly about the means of redress, its fairness to the nation as a whole, and the need for the government to 'get on with it'. But claims have also become more complex, and have moved into more contemporary matters such as the WAI 262 claim (known as the flora and fauna claim), which involves intellectual property rights. Claims now engage many areas of government and are often baffling to the public. They are also potentially threatening when they affect large urban areas, such as Wellington and Auckland.

It is clear, however, that many people lack confidence in the Treaty claims process and its eventual goals. Information on the process is available on the websites of the Tribunal, OTS and CFRT, but it is dense and detailed, targeted mainly at those involved. The Human Rights Commission also has responsibility for creating an awareness of the Treaty in the context of

CHAPTER NINE: INTO THE TWENTY-FIRST CENTURY   263

Ngati Ruanui signed a Deed of Settlement with the Crown in May 2000; this was finalised in legislation in 2003. The deed is being signed here by the Minister in Charge of Treaty Negotiations, Margaret Wilson, and Ngati Ruanui negotiatior Steve Heremaia, with Mate Carr (far right) and staff from the Office of Treaty Settlements looking on. DAILY NEWS

human rights law. In 2003, the government set up a Treaty information unit in the State Services Commission, with a three-year brief to improve public understanding; there were 1.8 million hits on the unit's website in its first eleven days in 2004. There is no doubt about the public's interest in the Treaty in the early twenty-first century.

Looking to the future

In 2002, the one-thousandth claim was registered with the Tribunal. To acknowledge this is to raise fears that claims will continue to multiply. The reality is less alarming. Many of these claims are now clustered into district inquiries, which the Tribunal is scheduling in hearings through to around 2010. When these claims move into negotiation, there could be fewer than a hundred

It is an emotional day for kaumatua Pat Heremaia and Tom Ngatai as they enter Parliament in May 2003 to hear the final stage of the $41 million Ngati Ruanui settlement. DOMINION POST, 2 MAY 2003

settlements. Allowing for the release of reports and for the negotiations that follow, the time-frame for the settlement of historical claims will probably reach out to around 2020. These are manageable goals, with achievable endpoints.

Dealing with Treaty matters will, for the foreseeable future, be a significant part of any government's work. But, although continued improvements to the process are essential, a long-term vision is also needed. The Tribunal, for example, has provided a valuable place for the expression of Maori concerns in the last twenty years; in researching and reporting on claims, it has built up a remarkable storehouse of knowledge and experience. Yet it is often assumed that, when historical claims are settled, there will be no further role for the Tribunal. This overlooks the fact that the Tribunal also deals with contemporary claims. In the longer term, the Tribunal could perform an important function as a court of appeal for Maori as new issues arise that are not addressed effectively by government, its agencies or other bodies.

It can also be noted that the Crown's commitment to the principles of the Treaty is now well established in legislation and throughout the entire fabric of government. This 'quiet revolution' may at the end of the day have as great an impact on the Treaty, and the position of Maori in the nation's future, as the settlement of historical grievances.

The principles of the Treaty

Over the last twenty-five years, the Treaty and Maori rights deriving from it have been recognised by the Crown in significant ways, but usually in terms of the principles of the Treaty. Differences between the English and Maori texts have led to different understandings of the Treaty. These differences, together with the need to apply the Treaty in contemporary circumstances (or in the modern world), have led Parliament to refer to the principles of the Treaty in legislation, rather than to the Treaty texts themselves.

Thus, the Waitangi Tribunal can inquire into claims by any Maori that the Crown has acted in breach of Treaty principles, and can make recommendations for redress; the Crown has accepted a moral obligation to resolve historical grievances in accordance with the principles; government departments and agencies are required by legislation to consider the principles; and the courts can apply the principles where legislation allows them to do so. The 1987 lands case, won by the New Zealand Maori Council over the State-Owned Enterprises Act in the Court of Appeal, was followed by several other major cases; the many court actions in the last two decades have led to the development of a Treaty jurisprudence.

However, since the government moved to reform health, welfare and education services from the late 1980s, Parliament has not been so ready to include legally contestable references to the Treaty or other Maori rights in social legislation. Maori point to the fact that the Treaty itself is still not enforceable in New Zealand courts; they remark that, although government agencies are required to heed the principles of the Treaty, much is still to be done to give effect to a relationship intended to be 'akin to a partnership'. A great deal depends on individuals at every level throughout the government and the community – on how well informed each person is, and on their willingness to exercise goodwill. In this respect, the government has a key role in facilitating, informing, encouraging and, if necessary (as it often is), legislating to bring about change.

The difficulty of interpreting Treaty principles was evident in government departments and among local bodies, as efforts were made to implement change in the 1990s. Legislation invokes Treaty principles without defining them, and their effect varies from one Act to another. The principles may be helpful as guidelines, but they leave plenty of scope for differences of opinion. Maori leaders sometimes observe that the principles allow the Crown to avoid the core issue of a partnership based on the 1840 agreement. Local government in particular can avoid partnership with Maori because the responsibilities devolved from central government do not include those of a Treaty partner.

The issues relating to the Treaty and its principles have perhaps been most clearly demonstrated with the Resource Management Act 1991 (RMA), which requires decision-makers to 'take into account' the principles of the Treaty. The RMA provides for Maori involvement, but in practice Maori participation has not always been achieved, nor have Maori interests been

Kaumatua gather at Manutuke marae near Gisborne for health checks by Turanga Health nurses, in 2002. Marae clinics aim to address major health problems such as diabetes, heart disease and asthma. TURANGA HEALTH

adequately protected. By early 1998, surveys showed that, although local bodies and Maori were developing relationships, there was great regional variation.

An impetus for change, however, has come from the Treaty claims process. Several Tribunal reports have focused on resource management – among them, the Mohaka River Report (1992), the Pouakani Report (1993), the Ika Whenua Report (1998) and the Whanganui River Report (1999). These have repeatedly brought up the issue of Maori participation in resource management. Where Treaty settlements require legislation (and many do), statutory requirements can be put in place to ensure that Maori can participate effectively in the local authority decision-making processes over specific resources. The Ngai Tahu settlement legislation demonstrates this.

At stake is the question of tino rangatiratanga – the right of Maori to be involved on their terms. Real participation in resource management will be difficult as long as the structures and culture remain essentially Pakeha. In building satisfactory Treaty relationships, much depends on the community as a whole, on elected bodies and on their openness to difference. When the benefits of setting up relationships in which Maori play an active role are recognised, significant change can occur.

Two examples make this clear. In July 1998, the Bay of Plenty Regional Council announced that it would create four Maori seats on the council, and the enabling legislation was passed in 2001. In Auckland, the Waitakere City Council recognises urban Maori authorities that might otherwise be omitted from consultation (despite the fact that the bulk of the country's Maori population is urban-dwelling); it also has a formal partnership agreement with tangata whenua, Te Kawerau a Maki and Ngati Whatua. In 1991, a Maori Perspective Committee (Te Taumata Runanga) was established, its members drawn from the city's key Maori groups, including local iwi; in 1993, the runanga became a standing committee of council. In addition, the council has made a commitment to liaise with Te Whanau o Waipareira Trust, a pan-tribal organisation that provides social services.

A decade after the Resource Management Act 1991, Treaty settlements and local initiatives have made an impact on the way the RMA works: Maori are now more fully represented in local body decisions about resources. But the change has been gradual and uneven; the difficulties have shown the need for legislation to be more specific about Treaty issues. Two recent legislative moves might meet this need. The Local Government Act 2002 requires that all councils adopt measures that proactive councils have already put in place — some specific provision (an agreement, an advisory committee or other mechanism) to allow Maori to consider and discuss council business on a regular basis. A 2003 amendment to the RMA further strengthens councils' obligations towards iwi, as well as elevating historic heritage to a matter of national importance. Although the changes go beyond consultation over particular resource management issues and include broader discussion on council services, the weight to be given to Maori views is still limited and will not necessarily determine outcomes. Widespread dissatisfaction about consultation indicates that a process needs to evolve that is acceptable to all parties – Maori, councils and the public. Councils need more examples of good practice; Maori need capacity-building; appropriate forms of compromise that offer genuine solutions need to be found.

Sovereignty and tino rangatiratanga

Despite the huge steps taken since 1975, defining a Treaty relationship 'akin to a partnership' remains central to finding the balance between sovereignty and tino rangatiratanga. Both National and Labour made it clear in the 1990s that sovereignty rested with the Crown and had been ceded in the first article of the Treaty. However, a number of Maori leaders and a few Pakeha academics have continued to reason that the use of kawanatanga in Article 1 ceded governance rather than sovereignty to the Crown, and that tino rangatiratanga should be understood as expressing more than the right to self-management.

Te tino rangatiratanga (in Article 2) has been defined in various ways: Maori sovereignty, mana motuhake, absolute authority, autonomy, self-determination, self-regulation and self-management. The underlying issue is the desire of many Maori for the recognition of Maori

Te Whanau o Waipareira Report 1998

This 1998 report from the Waitangi Tribunal inquired into the relationship between the Department of Social Welfare's Community Funding Agency (CFA) and the trust established by Te Whanau o Waipareira to provide social services to the West Auckland community. The Tribunal upheld the claim that the policies and operations of the CFA had prejudiced Te Whanau o Waipareira and were in breach of Treaty principles. The claim was ground-breaking because, although the Waipareira community is not a traditional tribe, the Tribunal found that, in the delivery of services, the Waipareira Trust exercises rangatiratanga in a modern setting. The report recommended that government protect the rangatiratanga of all Maori groups in contemporary settings (whether they are kin-based or not), where rangatiratanga is in fact exercised. It also recommended that the CFA negotiate with the trust to devolve sufficient authority and resources to enable the trust to undertake a coordinated and holistic approach to community development within the whanau. The report had a significant impact on CFA policy, and also led to legislative changes.

mana, for the restoration of resources to create a sound economic base, and for the recognition of Maori authority over them. More broadly, it is an issue of power-sharing throughout the political system. Not surprisingly, there are tensions around this question.

There is no unified Maori position on what might give effective expression to tino ranga-tiratanga. Some Maori look to indigenous structures elsewhere as models; some see long-term advantages in the more fluid opportunities offered by mixed-member proportional represen-tation (MMP); others see limitations in the political process and look to constitutional change. Many see aspirations to tino rangatiratanga as being satisfied through a combination of measures – political, economic, social and cultural – that empower Maori. Through the 1990s, for example, iwi groups were contracted by mainstream government departments to supply social and welfare services to Maori. As a means of acknowledging tino rangatiratanga, this is not the partnership some might wish for, but it is a valuable opportunity for some degree of self-management.

In the political arena, MMP has increased Maori representation and provided more oppor-tunities to influence policy. After the 1999 election, there were sixteen Maori MPs in Parliament. Labour took all six of the Maori electorate seats (a sixth Maori seat was added in 1997 after a further Maori electoral option). The new Labour-Alliance government had two Maori ministers inside Cabinet, and two outside; the Labour caucus included ten Maori MPs. This was a sub-stantial proportion of the senior government party. (There were two Maori MPs in the Alliance, two in New Zealand First, and one each in National and ACT.)

Political commentators, however, remained cautious about the extent to which MMP gave Maori a more effective voice in Parliament. The experience of MMP was too new, and the

Following the release of the Court of Appeal decision in June 2003, extreme statements from Maori and Pakeha fuelled a debate that continued for months. Five hundred Nelson people marched on 28 July 2003 to protest about Maori claims to the foreshore and seabed. Many Pakeha felt threatened by Maori claims of exclusive rights, and by a sense that the Treaty process was out of control. Maori had been battling for aquaculture space for years, and many were convinced that they were being locked out. In general, Maori felt that government moves were unjust. The strength of the public's reaction over foreshore and seabed issues alarmed many New Zealanders. NELSON MAIL

Mud thrown by a protester at Waitangi's Te Tii marae hits National Party leader Don Brash on 5 February 2004. The previous week, Brash had delivered a speech critical of the Treaty process and the privileges allegedly given Maori. It earned him, and National, widespread support, but brought controversy in its wake. The demotion of National's Maori spokesperson, Georgina Te Heuheu, for her refusal to support such comments added to public tensions. At the same time, the government's stand on the foreshore and seabed caused widespread reaction among Maori. Many assumed that the ruling was an admission that Maori already held customary rights to these areas, although this was not what the decision said. Extreme positions taken on all sides of the debate suddenly seemed to put at risk the vision of a fair and inclusive society. JOHN SELKIRK/DOMINION POST, 26 FEBRUARY 2004

political scene too unstable. No Maori caucus had emerged across the parties. Maori community leaders were also cautious. But the number of Maori MPs continued to rise. After the July 2002 election, there were nineteen Maori MPs (a seventh Maori seat was added before the election). In 2003, Maori MPs made up 15.8 per cent of Parliament, a figure comparable for the first time with their proportion of the population (14.7 per cent in the 2001 Census).

Public debate on tino rangatiratanga, with its various meanings, surfaces regularly. The debate may diminish over time as Treaty settlements enable tribal groups to establish an economic base, with continued growth in tribal identity. More generally, government policies may address the disparity between Maori and non-Maori in such areas as health, education, housing and employment. Some critics have argued that Treaty settlements should be used to fund social services, but these are basic rights of all citizens, Maori and non-Maori. The inequalities that continue to exist in New Zealand – and indeed were exacerbated in the late twentieth century – remain the responsibility of government.

Marlborough Sounds and Aquaculture

The foreshore and seabed debate was sparked off by the booming aquaculture industry in the Marlborough Sounds in the 1990s. With around five hundred marine farms in the Sounds, there was little suitable water left for expansion. Maori opposition on customary grounds to resource consent applications for marine farms had failed, and the few Maori applications had been turned down. Maori feared that the Crown intended to introduce a management system akin to the quota management system for wild fish, and that it would lead to the privatisation of large coastal areas in the Sounds. A group of South Island iwi brought a case to the Maori Land Court to determine Maori customary rights to certain land in the Sounds below the high-water mark. Judge Ken Hingston decided that, as a general principle, Maori customary rights in the foreshore and seabed in that area had not been extinguished. A series of judicial moves for and against this judgement led to the Court of Appeal decision (released in June 2003) affirming that the Maori Land Court held the jurisdiction to determine Maori customary rights in the foreshore and seabed.

2004 – a turning point?

Meeting that responsibility, as well as handling the broader dimensions of the government's role, is no easy task. This was evident in a series of events that began to unfold in 2003.

In June 2003, the Court of Appeal issued a controversial decision in the Ngati Apa case. It ruled that the Maori Land Court, established in the 1860s and now operating under the Te Ture Whenua Maori Act 1993, held the jurisdiction to determine Maori customary rights in the seabed and the foreshore (the land between high- and low-tide lines). Although this case was one of a series starting in the 1990s, the ownership of foreshore lands, including harbours and fishing areas, had been a source of contention since 1840. The Appeal Court noted that the transfer of sovereignty under the Treaty did not affect customary property rights, which encumbered the Crown's underlying (or radical) title and was preserved by common law, as modified by New Zealand conditions. Maori customary rights still existed, unless they had been specifically extinguished by legislation, and no Act had given a clear enough indication of this intention. The decision showed that investigation of customary rights by the Maori Land Court could lead to the court establishing freehold title in sections of the foreshore and seabed – although the Court of Appeal considered this would be established only in a few cases. The government was not so sure. The ruling challenged the long-held assumption that the Crown had overriding rights to the foreshore and seabed.

The decision triggered real and imaginary fears among the public. Access to the country's beaches and the surrounding seas is treasured by New Zealanders, and there was a tendency initially to think that this access was threatened: this was like a challenge to national identity. It became apparent that public ownership was already in question in some coastal areas. Two

This meeting at Whangara on the East Coast was one of several hui held around the country in August and September 2003 to hear the initial government proposals on the foreshore and seabed. Maori rejected the proposals at all the hui, seeing the government's moves as unjust. DOMINION POST, 5 SEPTEMBER 2003

documents released in August by the Minister of Agriculture, Jim Sutton, indicated that significant stretches of coastal land and foreshore were already in private ownership, and that public access was not guaranteed.

To complicate matters, marine farming was implicated. The government had previously announced proposals for aquaculture management reforms. A group of iwi (including Ngai Tahu, Ngati Whatua and Ngati Kahungunu) had lodged a claim alleging that the proposals would prejudicially affect their interests in aquaculture and marine farming. The Tribunal's Ahu Moana Report in 2002 urged consultation before any Bill was introduced. (When one was heralded in July 2004, it proposed an offer to Maori of 20 per cent of the marine farming industry.) Meanwhile, there was a two-year moratorium on new development (due to expire on 26 March 2004 but then extended to 31 December 2004).

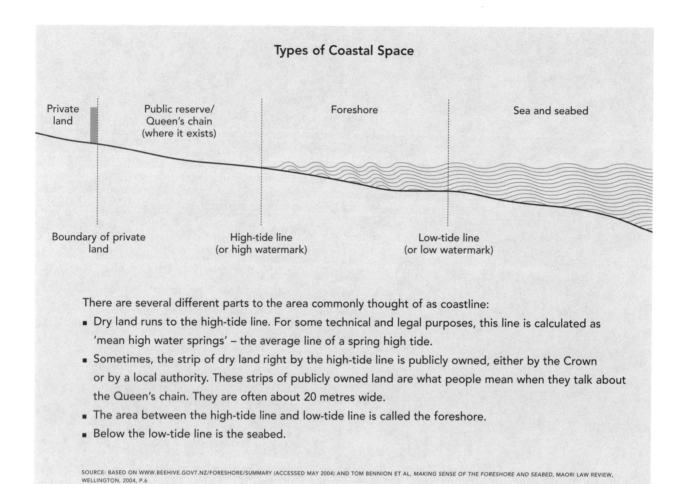

The implications of the Appeal Court's decision were a cause of serious concern to the government; local authorities also had fears about their powers under the Resource Management Act. Within days of the Appeal Court decision, the government declared it would legislate to ensure Crown ownership of the foreshore and seabed. A month later, its proposals were released: the foreshore and seabed would be 'public domain', with access and use ensured for all New Zealanders. The Crown would be responsible for regulating the use of both areas, and there would be certainty about the range of rights available to those who used, and those who administered, the foreshore and seabed. Maori customary interests should be acknowledged and specific rights protected. Six weeks were allowed for submissions.

Heated debate ensued throughout the country, and was amply covered by the media. It was evident that only Crown ownership would satisfy many New Zealanders. The 'public domain' concept was too vague and had no legal basis.

At ten consultation hui, Maori rejected the proposals: the Crown's move to block the due process of the law was considered unjust; if legislation extinguished or curtailed Maori customary rights, it would be a breach of the Treaty. Dozens of claims asserting rights to the

A hikoi starting in the far north crossed the Auckland Harbour Bridge on 28 April 2004. By 5 May, when it moved through Wellington to Parliament, the hikoi numbered over fifteen thousand. The carved pou that was symbolic of the 1975 hikoi over Maori land loss was again carried. Protest this time was about government legislation that would effectively prevent the Maori Land Court from awarding title if it found that Maori customary rights in the foreshore and seabed existed. The introduction of the Foreshore and Seabed Bill the next day seemed to many Maori a new form of confiscation, akin to nineteenth-century raupatu. The hikoi was driven by a sense of injustice and by the need for public affirmation of Maori strength in the face of widespread hostility over Maori claims. FOTOPRESS LTD

country's foreshores were lodged with the Waitangi Tribunal and the Maori Land Court; they indicated Maori intentions to fight for the principles involved, and at the same time reinforced public fears. Hearings were put on hold until a second policy statement (similar to the first) was issued in December. The government signalled that it would legislate in 2004; Crown ownership of the foreshore and seabed was clearly its intention. A Tribunal report in March 2004 found the government in breach of the Treaty, but its recommendations were dismissed. A Foreshore and Seabed Bill had its first reading in May.

CHAPTER NINE: INTO THE TWENTY-FIRST CENTURY 275

Treaty settlements provide iwi with an opportunity to develop a sound economic base. Iwi have taken different approaches, but most have commitments that range through investment in housing, education and health to tourism, fishing and other commercial ventures. Ngai Tahu is rapidly expanding its commercial arm. The Ngai Tahu Seafood business, with annual turnover approaching $90 million in 2003, has grown sales in both export and domestic markets (including retail and wholesale). The worker shown here at the Murihiku Seafood Processing Plant, Bluff, is preparing seafood for export. NGAI TAHU HOLDINGS GROUP

Meanwhile, other changes were brewing on the political scene. National's leadership had passed in September 2003 from Bill English to Don Brash, a former Governor of the Reserve Bank. In a speech to the Orewa Rotary Club on 27 January 2004, Brash argued that no special privileges should be given to Maori and that there should be 'one law for all'. Although his case lacked hard data, Brash's Orewa speech touched a nerve, and opened the way for violent expressions of public impatience over Treaty issues. It earned him widespread support. Brash's claims were countered by arguments that affirmative action was needs-based, and that Maori happened to be strongly represented in the most needy sector of the community. Brash also expressed irritation with Tribunal claims, and stated his intention to expunge mention of the Treaty principles from legislation. National's Maori Affairs spokesperson, Georgina Te Heuheu, refused to endorse such policies and was forced to relinquish her role. Mud flung at Brash during Waitangi Day events expressed Maori anger, but probably reinforced a widely held public view that Maori extremists had gone too far.

[1] In early 2000, *Mana* magazine interviewed several Maori about their fears and hopes for the future. Merimeri Penfold (Ngati Kuri) is a Maori-language teacher who had recently retired from the University of Auckland. She was concerned that the government had not done enough for Maori education, but hoped that 'in education, the arts and the economy, systems will be put in place to see that we succeed'. It was through the perpetuation of Maori institutions and values that Maori people would reach their potential. MANA, DECEMBER 1999/JANUARY 2000

[2] Lawyer Moana Jackson (Ngati Kahungunu, Ngati Porou) has worked for Maori rights for many years. In *Mana*, he spoke out against the ongoing poverty and violence that Maori experience, despite the political talk and activity of recent decades. 'Personally, I'd like to see my mokopuna grow up and not have to fight the same sort of struggles that my generation have. [But] I have confidence in our people to not just survive, but get stronger.' MANA, DECEMBER 1999/JANUARY 2000

The debate that raged for some months covered race relations, the Treaty and, at a deeper level, the place of Maori in New Zealand society. There was some considered discussion in the media, and published statistics justified affirmative action on Maori health and education. But the impact of this was offset by the continuing media focus on strongly expressed opinion, antagonistic to special rights for Maori. The response to Brash's speech showed that a substantial sector of the public was impatient with Maori concerns, and the government was placed on the defensive. Polls in the first half of 2004 indicated a rapid rise in National's popularity.

As the government moved to introduce the Foreshore and Seabed Bill on 6 May, a hikoi reminiscent of the 1975 land march arrived at Parliament on 5 May. Some fifteen thousand people marched through Wellington to express opposition to the government's moves. Within the ranks of Labour's Maori MPs there were divisions, with some supporting the Bill and others opposing it; dissatisfaction was expressed in the resignation of government Minister Tariana Turia and in moves to form a new Maori party. Select committee hearings began in July

2004, and could alter the Bill's provisions, but the government obviously intended to clarify the position across a broad spectrum of user rights.

An analysis of over two thousand submissions on the government's original 2003 proposals showed that everyone wanted certainty about their rights: Maori for the existence and protection of their customary rights; private property owners for their coastal property interests; and business people for investment activities such as aquaculture. Maori, too, were concerned to secure a footing in aquaculture. Despite such fundamental conflicts, the submissions taken together expressed a need to arrive at 'practical, acceptable and durable solutions' that reflect New Zealanders' desire to protect public access to the foreshore and seabed, and, at the same time, recognise the unique values and customary rights of Maori. This is a challenge that few governments would care to face.

This book has been about the relationship between the Crown and Maori, established by the Treaty of Waitangi in 1840. Although this relationship is central to government policy and practice relating to Maori, the Treaty relationship in the nation state of the twenty-first century is also one between the peoples living in New Zealand – Maori and non-Maori. As the country's founding document, the Treaty has significance for both.

The claims, investigations, hearings and settlements of recent decades follow a century and a half of patient argument, documentation and protest from Maori, to explain their position in relation to the 1840 Treaty. The last fifteen to twenty years have brought significant settlements,

The Nga Puhi waka taua (war canoe) *Ngatokimatawhaorua*, built for the 1940 centenary of the Treaty signing, was the largest of five waka in the Bay of Islands for Waitangi Day 2002. MICHAEL CUNNINGHAM, *NORTHERN ADVOCATE*, 7 FEBRUARY 2002

far-reaching policy changes, a wider acknowledgement of the Treaty, and greater empowerment for Maori in decision-making processes. From these experiences, a relationship 'akin to a partnership' has begun, and can become a real part of the country's future.

But such commitment requires a courageous political will to ensure that good processes are set in place, carefully followed and continually developed, in order to achieve just outcomes and equitable settlements. It is a responsibility of all governments, also, to work with Maori and Pakeha towards a vision for the future – one that expresses a full understanding of the nation's founding document, the Treaty of Waitangi, and one based on mutual respect for each other's culture.

APPENDIX ONE

Texts of the Treaty of Waitangi

[1] This English text was signed at Waikato Heads in March or April 1840 and at Manukau Harbour on 26 April. A total of thirty-nine chiefs signed. This text of the Treaty of Waitangi became the 'official' version. The handwritten original is in Archives New Zealand/Te Rua Mahara o te Kawanatanga, Wellington Office.

The Treaty of Waitangi

Her Majesty Victoria Queen of the United Kingdom of Great Britain and Ireland regarding with Her Royal Favor the Native Chiefs and Tribes of New Zealand and anxious to protect their just Rights and Property and to secure to them the enjoyment of Peace and Good Order has deemed it necessary in consequence of the great number of Her Majesty's Subjects who have already settled in New Zealand and the rapid extension of Emigration both from Europe and Australia which is still in progress to constitute and appoint a functionary properly authorized to treat with the Aborigines of New Zealand for the recognition of Her Majesty's sovereign authority over the whole or any part of those islands — Her Majesty therefore being desirous to establish a settled form of Civil Government with a view to avert the evil consequences which must result from the absence of the necessary Laws and Institutions alike to the native population and to Her subjects has been graciously pleased to empower and to authorize me William Hobson a Captain in Her Majesty's Royal Navy Consul and Lieutenant Governor of such parts of New Zealand as may be or hereafter shall be ceded to Her Majesty to invite the confederated and independent Chiefs of New Zealand to concur in the following Articles and Conditions.

Article the first

The Chiefs of the Confederation of the United Tribes of New Zealand and the separate and independent Chiefs who have not become members of the Confederation cede to Her Majesty the Queen of England absolutely and without reservation all the rights and powers of Sovereignty which the said Confederation or Individual Chiefs respectively exercise or possess, or may be supposed to exercise or to possess over their respective Territories as the sole sovereigns thereof.

Article the second

Her Majesty the Queen of England confirms and guarantees to the Chiefs and Tribes of New Zealand and to the respective families and individuals thereof the full exclusive and undisturbed possession of their Lands and Estates Forests Fisheries and other properties which they may collectively or individually possess so long as it is their wish and desire to retain the same in their possession; but the Chiefs of the United Tribes and the individual Chiefs yield to Her Majesty the exclusive right of Preemption over such lands as the proprietors thereof may be disposed to alienate at such prices as may be agreed upon between the respective Proprietors and persons appointed by Her Majesty to treat with them in that behalf.

Article the third

In consideration thereof Her Majesty the Queen of England extends to the Natives of New Zealand Her royal protection and imparts to them all the Rights and Privileges of British Subjects.

[signed] W. Hobson Lieutenant Governor

Now therefore We the Chiefs of the Confederation of the United Tribes of New Zealand being assembled in Congress at Victoria in Waitangi and We the Separate and Independent Chiefs of New Zealand claiming authority over the Tribes and Territories which are specified after our respective names, having been made fully to understand the Provisions of the foregoing Treaty, accept and enter into the same in the full spirit and meaning thereof in witness of which we have attached our signatures or marks at the places and the dates respectively specified.

Done at Waitangi this Sixth day of February in the year of Our Lord one thousand eight hundred and forty.

The Chiefs of the Confederation

[2] Most chiefs signed the Maori text of the Treaty. This text was signed at Waitangi on 6 February 1840, and thereafter in the north and at Auckland. The Maori is reproduced as it was written. The handwritten original is held by Archives New Zealand/Te Rua Mahara o te Kawanatanga, Wellington Office.

Te Tiriti o Waitangi

Ko Wikitoria te Kuini o Ingarani i tana mahara atawai ki nga Rangatira me nga Hapu o Nu Tirani i tana hiahia hoki kia tohungia ki a ratou o ratou rangatiratanga me to ratou wenua, a kia mau tonu hoki te Rongo ki a ratou me te Atanoho hoki kua wakaaro ia he mea tika kia tukua mai tetahi Rangatira – hei kai wakarite ki nga Tangata maori o Nu Tirani – kia wakaaetia e nga Rangatira maori te Kawanatanga o te Kuini ki nga wahikatoa o te wenua nei me nga motu – na te mea hoki he tokomaha ke nga tangata o tona Iwi Kua noho ki tenei wenua, a e haere mai nei.

Na ko te Kuini e hiahia ana kia wakaritea te Kawanatanga kia kaua ai nga kino e puta mai ki te tangata maori ki te Pakeha e noho ture kore ana.

Na kua pai te Kuini kia tukua a hau a Wiremu Hopihona he Kapitana i te Roiara Nawi hei Kawana mo nga wahi katoa o Nu Tirani e tukua aianei amua atu ki te Kuini, e mea atu ana ia ki nga Rangatira o te wakaminenga o nga hapu o Nu Tirani me era Rangatira atu enei ture ka korerotia nei.

Ko te tuatahi

Ko nga Rangatira o te wakaminenga me nga Rangatira katoa hoki ki hai i uru ki taua wakaminenga ka tuku rawa atu ki te Kuini o Ingarani ake tonu atu – te Kawanatanga katoa o o ratou wenua.

Ko te tuarua

Ko te Kuini o Ingarani ka wakarite ka wakaae ki nga Rangatira ki nga hapu – ki nga tangata katoa o Nu Tirani te tino rangatiratanga o o ratou wenua o ratou kainga me o ratou taonga katoa. Otiia ko nga Rangatira o te wakaminenga me nga Rangatira katoa atu ka tuku ki te Kuini te hokonga o era wahi wenua e pai ai te tangata nona te wenua – ki te ritenga o te utu e wakaritea ai e ratou ko te kai hoko e meatia nei e te Kuini hei kai hoko mona.

Ko te tuatoru

Hei wakaritenga mai hoki tenei mo te wakaaetanga ki te Kawanatanga o te Kuini – Ka tiakina e te Kuini o Ingarani nga tangata maori katoa o Nu Tirani ka tukua ki a ratou nga tikanga katoa rite tahi ki ana mea ki nga tangata o Ingarani.

[signed] W. Hobson Consul & Lieutenant Governor

Na ko matou ko nga Rangatira o te Wakaminenga o nga hapu o Nu Tirani ka huihui nei ki Waitangi ko matou hoki ko nga Rangatira o Nu Tirani ka kite nei i te ritenga o enei kupu. Ka tangohia ka wakaaetia katoatia e matou, koia ka tohungia ai o matou ingoa o matou tohu.

Ka meatia tenei ki Waitangi i te ono o nga ra o Pepueri i te tau kotahi mano, e waru rau e wa te kau o to tatou Ariki.

Ko nga Rangatira o te Wakaminenga

[3] This English translation of the Maori Treaty text, made by I. H. Kawharu, was printed in the *Report of the Royal Commission on Social Policy*, Wellington, 1988, pp.87–88. A comparison of this text with the English text of the 'official' version shows the differences of meaning, especially in the first and second articles.

The Treaty of Waitangi

Victoria, The Queen of England, in her concern to protect the chiefs and subtribes of New Zealand and in her desire to preserve their chieftainship and their lands to them and to maintain peace and good order considers it just to appoint an administrator one who will negotiate with the people of New Zealand to the end that their chiefs will agree to the Queen's Government being established over all parts of this land and (adjoining) islands and also because there are many of her subjects already living on this land and others yet to come.

So the Queen desires to establish a government so that no evil will come to Maori and European living in a state of lawlessness.

So the Queen has appointed me, William Hobson, a captain in the Royal Navy to be Governor for all parts of New Zealand (both those) shortly to be received by the Queen and (those) to be received hereafter and presents to the chiefs of the Confederation chiefs of the subtribes of New Zealand and other chiefs these laws set out here.

The First

The chiefs of the Confederation and all the chiefs who have not joined that Confederation give absolutely to the Queen of England for ever the complete government over their land.

The Second

The Queen of England agrees to protect the Chiefs, the subtribes and all the people of New Zealand in the unqualified exercise of their chieftainship over their lands, villages and all their treasures. But on the other hand the Chiefs of the Confederation and all the chiefs will sell land to the Queen at a price agreed to by the person owning it and by the person buying it (the latter being) appointed by the Queen as her purchase agent.

The Third

For this agreed arrangement therefore concerning the Government of the Queen, the Queen of England will protect all the ordinary people of New Zealand and will give them the same rights and duties of citizenship as the people of England.

(signed) William Hobson
Consul and Lieutenant-Governor

So we, the Chiefs of the Confederation and the subtribes of New Zealand meeting here at Waitangi having seen the shape of these words which we accept and agree to record our names and marks thus.

Was done at Waitangi on the sixth of February in the year of our Lord 1840.

The Chiefs of the Confederation

APPENDIX TWO

Treaty Signatories

A good deal of information is available on many of the people, both Maori and non-Maori, involved in the treaty-making of 1840, but research continues to yield more identifications and names. The lists that follow thus represent 'work in progress', and they are offered with a view to furthering knowledge of the Treaty and its participants.

The original Treaty of Waitangi was signed at the meeting of 5–6 February 1840 at Waitangi. This was the text hastily translated into Maori by the missionary Henry Williams and his son Edward. Subsequently, this original Treaty document was taken for meetings elsewhere in the north and at Auckland; it was then copied several times for additional signing meetings around the country. With the exception of one copy in English, chiefs signed the Treaty in the Maori language.

Responsibility for the Treaty, on the British side, fell on Lieutenant Governor William Hobson, whose signature appears on the Waitangi document. In drafting the English text, Hobson was assisted by his secretary, James Freeman, and by James Busby, the British Resident. Local missionaries also provided support. Over a six-month period in 1840, additional signatures of chiefs in various places around New Zealand were obtained. In addition to Hobson, negotiators included some of his officials, Church Missionary Society (CMS) and Wesleyan Missionary Society (WMS) missionaries, military men and a trader.

Copies of the Treaty

Hobson sent four copies of the Treaty to his superiors in New South Wales and London. Duplicates were usually sent too. Some of Hobson's dispatches, which included reports of Treaty meetings, were later printed in the *British Parliamentary Papers: Colonies New Zealand* (*BPP*). Copies of dispatches were kept in New Zealand and are now in Archives New Zealand files. The Colonial Office records relevant to New Zealand (CO 209) are held on microfilm at several repositories.

The copies sent by Hobson are:

1. An English-language copy in Hobson to Gipps (NSW), 5–6 February 1840, CO 209/6, 46–54.
2. An English-language copy in Hobson to Gipps (NSW), 16 February 1840, CO 209/7, 13–15.
3. English and Maori copies enclosed in Hobson to Russell, 15 October 1840, CO 209/7, 1/8. The Treaty spans two pages with the Maori on the left and the English on the right. A title at the top simply reads 'Treaty' and seems to apply to both. At the foot on the left, it says 'signatures taken off' and, on the right, notes that there were 512 signatures. It is not clear how the figure of 512 Treaty adherents was arrived at; it is now certain that the total signing was close to 540. The dispatch says that it was a 'certified' copy. When it was printed in *BPP*, 1841 (311), 98–99, the word 'Treaty' was placed over the Maori text and '(Translation)' over the English.
4. Hobson to the Secretary of State for Colonies, 26 May 1841, enclosed the Treaty in Maori and signatures of the Manukau-Kawhia Treaty copy. This was printed in *BPP*, 1841 (569), 110–11.

The original Treaty copies

The original Treaty signed first at Waitangi and another eight signed copies are held at Archives New Zealand, Wellington. All are in the Maori language except for the copy that went to Manukau Harbour and Waikato Heads. With one exception – a printed copy – all sheets are in long-hand. All contain the names of

APPENDIX TWO: TREATY SIGNATORIES   283

chiefs (together with their signatures, moko or marks) who wished to signify their agreement to the Treaty.

The original in Maori and the copies differ from each other in various ways: some have slight variations in the text; one was signed by Willoughby Shortland and not by William Hobson; some have the government seal and others have no seal.

Some Treaty negotiators took care to collect signatures and moko in an orderly fashion; their copies are fairly readily decipherable. Other copies are not so easy to read. In some cases, the names of chiefs appear on a copy but do not have a mark of any kind beside them. In many instances, names of chiefs are interspersed with names of hapu, but the distinction is not always clear.

The Treaty copies and the lists of names

Facsimile copies of each of the nine Treaty sheets were made in 1877 and were printed by the Government Printer. These facsimiles have been used in compiling the lists of names that appear on each Treaty copy. All Treaty copies had the text in full, as the small reproductions of each copy indicate. However, only the sections showing names are reproduced here at a legible size.

The Treaty copies are here arranged roughly in the order in which they were dispatched from the Bay of Islands in 1840. The signings at various locations, however, were often taking place at more or less the same time over the six-month period from February to September 1840. Around fifty meetings were held to discuss and/or sign a copy of the Treaty. Each Treaty copy has a brief introduction that identifies key facts about the copy.

For easy reference, the name of each chief has been given a number on the facsimile reproduction. This number is repeated with the chief's name on the relevant list. The number does not always indicate the sequence in which a chief signed. Kawiti, for example, appears as the first name at the top left of the Waitangi sheet and is listed as number 1, although he did not sign until May 1840. A few chiefs appear to have signed twice.

Many names on the sheets – chiefs, iwi and/or hapu – can be deciphered with confidence; others cannot. Tribal and hapu names have sometimes been found on the relevant Treaty copy, presumably given by the chiefs who signed. Information from tribal sources has often identified a name or hapu affiliation, or corrected a spelling; in many instances, identification has been made through research in documentary sources such as reports, letters, diaries and land court records.

Where identification of any name is not clear or is uncertain, this has been indicated with a query – ?.

In many cases, it has been possible to add the full name or other names by which a signatory was known. These additional names are usually enclosed in square brackets – [ ].

1. Waitangi Treaty Copy

This is the most confusing of all the Treaty sheets. It bears two hundred and forty names of chiefs, most of them from tribes north of Whangarei, and from Tamaki-makau-rau (Auckland), the Waitemata Harbour and the Hauraki Gulf. But there are many uncertainties regarding names, dates of signings and numbers signing at different locations. There are, for example, conflicting reports of the number who signed at Waitangi on 6 February and immediately after; there may have been forty-three, forty-five or fifty-two (although the first is most likely). Hokianga presents similar problems, as does Waimate North, where there was probably only one signing and not two as sometimes thought. This makes it virtually impossible to state figures precisely. The identification of place and date must remain tentative in many instances.

The first four columns across the sheet contain chiefs from various northern locations who may have signed at any one of three or more locations; a number of names were added to the top of the sheet after the 6 February signing at Waitangi.

Two separate signings – on 4 March and on 9 July – took place at Karaka Bay on the Tamaki River. A major signing was held at Kaitaia on 28 April involving Te Rarawa, Te Aupouri and Ngati Kahu; and from February through to August signatures were added at the Bay of Islands, sometimes by chiefs visiting the area.

The original draft in English, on which Henry Williams based this Maori translation, has not been found. His original translation, presented to the Waitangi meeting of 5 February, has also disappeared. Because it had corrections on it, the CMS missionary Richard Taylor offered to write it out on parchment for the 6 February meeting, which he did, saying that he was keeping the original paper copy for his pains.

Two women are known to have signed this Treaty copy: Ana Hamu (61), the widow of Te Koki who had been patron of the Paihia mission station; and Ereonora (207), the wife of Te Rarawa chief Nopera Panakareao. Koroniria Nuau (211) may also be a woman.

The names are presented on the copy in several ways: 'Te tohu o' (The sign of), or 'Ko tona tohu' and 'tona tohu', which are alternatives to the first; sometimes just the name is given. In a few instances, tribe/hapu identification has been added, but most have no identification. The odd phrase sometimes gives a clue to the location of a small group, but where identification is given on the list it is usually the result of research.

No.	Signed as	Probable name	Tribe	Hapu
Signed on 13 (?) May 1840, at the Bay of Islands				
1	Kawiti	Kawiti	Nga Puhi	Ngati Hine
2	Te Tirarau	Te Tirarau	Nga Puhi	Te Parawhau Te Uri-o-Hau?

No.	Signed as	Probable name	Tribe	Hapu
Signed on 17 February 1840, probably at Paihia or Waitangi, witnessed by J. R. Clendon				
3	Pomare	Pomare II [Whetoi]	Nga Puhi	Ngati Manu

Signed on 6 February 1840, at Waitangi, witnessed by James Busby, Henry Williams, Richard Taylor, John Mason, Samuel Ironside and James Stuart Freeman

No.	Signed as	Probable name	Tribe	Hapu
4	Hone Heke	Hone [Wiremu] Heke [Pokai]	Nga Puhi	Te Matarahurahu, Ngati Rahiri, Ngai Tawake, Ngati Tautahi
5	Hori Kingi Warerahi	Hori Kingi Wharerahi	Nga Puhi	Ngai Tawake, Ngati Tautahi, Te Patukeha, Te Uri-o-Ngongo
6	Tamati Pukututu	Tamati Pukututu	Nga Puhi	Te Uri-o-Te-Hawato, Te Uri-o-Ngongo
7	Hakero	Hakiro	Nga Puhi	Ngai Tawake, Ngati Rehia
8	Wikitene	Wikitene/Hikitene?	Ngati Wai?	Te Kapotai?
9	Pumuka	Pumuka	Nga Puhi/Te Roroa	Ngati Rangi, Ngati Pou

No.	Signed as	Probable name	Tribe	Hapu
10	Marupo	Marupo	Nga Puhi	Te Whanau Rara, Te Whanau Rongo, Matarahurahu, Ngati Rahiri, Ngati Pou
11	Te Tao	Te Tao	Nga Puhi	Te Kai Mata, Te Mahurehure?
12	Reweti Atuahaere	Te Reweti Atuahaere	Nga Puhi	Ngati Tautahi
13	Wiremu Hau	Wiremu Hau	Nga Puhi	Ngati Te Whiu, Ngati Pou, Ngati Miru
14	Te Kaua	Te Kaua	Nga Puhi?	Te Herepaka
15	Toua	Toua	Nga Puhi?	Ngati Rehia? Te Hikutu?
16	Mene	Mene	Nga Puhi?	Ngati Rehia, Ngai Tawake from Kororareka
17	Tamati Waka Nene	Tamati Waka Nene	Nga Puhi	Ngati Hao (Ngati Miru), Ngati Pou, Te Roroa
18	Matiu Huka?	Matiu Huka	Nga Puhi	Te Uri-o-Ngongo
19	Te Kamera	Te Kamera [Kaitieke]	Nga Puhi	Ngati Kawa, Ngare Hauata
20	Warau	Wharau?	Nga Puhi	Ngati Wai, Ngati Tokawero
21	Ngere	Te Ngere	Nga Puhi	Te Urikapana, Ngati Wai, Te Uri Taniwha?
22	Patuone	[Eruera Maihi] Patuone	Nga Puhi	Te Roroa, Ngati Hao, Ngati Pou
23	Paora Nohimatangi	Paora Nohi Matangi	Nga Puhi?	Te Popoto ki Utakura?
24	Ruhe	Ruhe	Nga Puhi from Kaikohe	Ngati Rangi, Ngati Pou, Te Uritaniwha

Signed at the Bay of Islands, date unknown

No.	Signed as	Probable name	Tribe	Hapu
25	Kaitara Wiremu Kingi	Kaitara Wiremu Kingi	Nga Puhi	Ngati Hineira, Te Urikapana, Ngati Rangi, Ngati Pou, Te Uri Taniwha
26	Taura	Taura	Nga Puhi?	Ngati Hine

Signed on 13 (?) May 1840, at the Bay of Islands

No.	Signed as	Probable name	Tribe	Hapu
27	Taurau	Taurau	Nga Puhi	Te Parawhau
28	Teroha	Te Roha/Tiroha?	Nga Puhi	Te Parawhau

Signed on 6 February 1840, at Waitangi

No.	Signed as	Probable name	Tribe	Hapu
29	Rewa	Rewa [Manu]	Nga Puhi	Ngai Tawake, Te Patukeha, Ngati Tautahi, Ngai Tawake, Te Uri-o-Ngongo
30	Moka	Moka [Te Kaingamata]	Nga Puhi	Te Patu Keha, Ngai Tawake, Ngati Tautahi, Te Uri-o-Ngongo

Signed on an unknown date, probably at the Bay of Islands

No.	Signed as	Probable name	Tribe	Hapu
31	Papahia	Papahia	Te Rarawa	Te Horokuhare, Ngati Haua
32	Takiri	Takiri	Te Rarawa?	Ngati Nanenane
33	Te Toko	Te Toko [Herewini?]	Te Rarawa	Te Patutoka
34	Wiremu Tana	Wiremu Tana	[Papahia?] Te Rarawa	Te Horohukare, Ngati Haua
35	Tangata Kotahi	Tangata Kotahi (This could be part of Wiremu Tana signature – 'for himself alone')	Te Rarawa?	
36	Te Tai	Te Tai	Te Rarawa	Ngati Te Reinga, Te Kaitutae
37	Te Toroihua	Te Toroihua	Nga Puhi?	
38	Kokeha	Te Keha	Nga Puhi?	Ngati Toki? or Te Hikutu?
39	Kowao/Howao?	Whao? Wao?	Nga Puhi?	Ngati Te Ra
40	Takurua	Takurua	Nga Puhi	Ngati Korokoro, Ngati Rangi
41	Te Hinake	Te Hinaki [Samuel?]	Nga Puhi	Ngati Hau or Matahuruhuru

Ko nga Rangatira o te Wakaminenga

1. Te Tohu o Kawiti
2. Te Tohu o Te Tirarau
3. Te Tohu o Pomare
4.
5. Te tohu o Hori Kingi Warerahi
6. Te Tohu o Tamati Pukututu
7. Te tohu o Hakero
8. Te tohu o W. Mukere
9. Te tohu o Pumuka
10. Te tohu o Marupo
11. Te tohu o Te Tao
12. Te tohu o Reweti Atuahaere
13. Wiremu Hau
14. Te tohu o te Kana
15. Te tohu o Tona
16. o Tareha, mo tona matua
17. Tawati Waka
18. Matiu Heuhea
19. Te tohu o te Kamira
20. Te tohu o Waraua
21. Te tohu o Ngere
22. Te tohu o Patuone
23. Paora Tohi matua
24. Te tohu o Ruke
    te tamaiti o Kopiri

25. Kaitara
26. Te Tohu o Taura
27.
28.
29. te totoru o Rewa
30.
31.
32.
33. Te Tohu totona tohu
34. Wiremu Tana
35. Tangata Wakahi
36. To Ihi totona tohu
37.
38.
39.
40.
41.
42. Te Tohu totona tohu
43.
44.
45. Ko Hiro totona tohu
46. Ko te Marama totona tohu
47. Ko Mue Ngwherehere tona tohu
48. Ko Mahu ai tona tohu
49. Wiremu Waina tona tohu

Ka meatia ki Waitemata i te ra tuawa o Maha

4th March 1840.

151. Wiremu Hoete
152. Te tohu o Hokopa
153. Te tohu o Te Awa
154. Te tohu o Te Tapuru
155. Te tohu o Te Titaha
156. Te tohu o Haku Kote
157. Te tohu o Riuinga
158. Hohepa
159. Paurote
160. Inoka
161. Henaki
162. Te tohu o Reka
163. Paora
164. Moki
165. Anaru
166. Te tohu o Waitangi
167. William

50. Te Tohu o te Tawaeroa
51. Te Tohu o te Wareumu
52. Te Tohu o te Mokowaro
53. Te ahu
54. Te Kupunga
55. Te Tohu o Hara no te urio to Hawato
56. Te tohu o Hakitara no te rawara
57. Te tohu o Hauwaitu (Tamati no te uri o Rua
58. Te tohu o te Mutatoriki no te Kapotai
59. Ko Rawiri Taiwanga
60. Te tohu o Paraara
61. Te totu o Ana Hamua
62. Te tohu o Hira Pure no te uri o Rua
63. Te tohu o Irai no ngati Tangi
64. Te tohu Wiremu na te Wanau roa
65. Te tohu o Wiremu Watitiu no nga te Wakahehe
66. Maure Hauraiga no te Uritanewa
67. Pokai no nga te Rahiri
68. tohu o te Kaumatu na nga te Wai
69. Te tohu o Tuirangi o te Matarahurahu
70. Hohepa o Tene pura no te Urimakoe
71. Hori Kingi Raumati no Ngati Toro
72. Te tohu o Tukakawaka no ngaite Woke

105. Manahi tona tohu
106. Paratene tona tohu
107. Hore Te Hira tona tohu
108. Ko te Keti tona tohu
109. Ko Kenana tona tohu
110. Ko Hero tona tohu
111. Te Uruti tona tohu
112. Wikama Hewa tona tohu
113. Ko Hiro tona tohu
114. Ko Tihame Toro tona
115. Ko Matiu tona tohu
116.
117. Ko Raihu tona tohu
118. Ko Katiki tona tohu
119. Hua tona tohu
120. Kiwi tona tohu no te Wakatu

No.	Signed as	Probable name	Tribe	Hapu
42	Te Totohu	Te Totohu/Te Tohu?	Nga Puhi	Ngati Hau, Ngai Tupoto
43	Omanu Te Wunu	Omanu Te Wunu, Omaia te whenua? (possibly not a name)	Nga Puhi	
44	Nga Manu	Nga Manu	Nga Puhi	Ngati Hau, Te Uri o Rorokai or Ngati Kaharau
45	Hiro	Hiro/Whiro?	Nga Puhi?	Ngati Tautahi?
46	Te Marama	Te Marama	Nga Puhi?	Ngati Tautahi?
47	Moe Ngaherehere	Moe Ngaherehere/ Moenga-herehere	Te Rarawa?	
48	Mahu	Mahu	Nga Puhi?	Te Hikutu? Ngai Tupoto?
49	Wiremu Wuna	Wiremu Wuna [Kaweka?]	Nga Puhi	Ngati Tama, Te Uri Mahoe
50	Te Tawaewae	Te Tawaewae	Ngati Wai	Ngati Manu
51	Wareumu	Te Whareumu [son of Te Whareumu King George?]	Ngati Wai from Kororareka	Ngati Manu, Te Uri Karaka
52	Makoware	Makoware	Nga Puhi	Te Parawhau, Ngati Rua-Ngaio
53	Te Ahu	[Parore] Te Ahu [Waata?]	Nga Puhi	Te Parawhau, Ngati Rua-Ngaio
54	Tukupunga	Tukupunga	Nga Puhi?	Te Parawhau? Te Uriroroi? Ngai Tahuhu?

Signed on 6 February 1840, at Waitangi (?)

No.	Signed as	Probable name	Tribe	Hapu
55	Hara	Hara	Nga Puhi	Te Uri-o-Te-Hawato, Ngati Rangi
56	Hakitara	Hakitara	Te Rarawa	
57	Hawaitu	Hawaitu [Hawaito?] [Tamati?]	Nga Puhi	Te Uri-o-Hua
58	Te Matatahi	Te Matatahi [Te Manataki?]	Nga Puhi	Te Kapotai
59	Rawiri Taiwanga	Rawiri Taiwhanga	Nga Puhi	Ngati Tautahi, Te Uri-o-Hua, Te Uri Taniwha, Ngati Kura, Te Uri-o-Ngongo
60	Paraara	Paraara	Nga Puhi?	
61	Ana Hamu	Ana Hamu	Nga Puhi?	Te Uri-o-Ngongo?
62	Hira Pure	Te Hira Pure	Nga Puhi	Te Uri-o-Hua, Te Uri Taniwha
63	Iwi	Iwi	Nga Puhi?	Ngati Rangi, Te Urikapana
64	Wiorau	Whiorau	Nga Puhi	Te Whanau Rara
65	Wiremu Watipu	Wiremu Watipu [Whatipu?]	Nga Puhi	Ngati Wakaheke (Whakaheke?)
66	Piripi Haurangi	Piripi Haurangi	Nga Puhi	Te Uri Taniwha
67	Pokai	Pokai Te Ika or Rawhiti	Nga Puhi	Ngati Rahiri
68	Te Kauwata	Te Kauwhata	Ngati Wai	Ngati Wai
69	Tuirangi	Tuirangi/Tuhirangi	Nga Puhi	Te Matarahurahu, Ngati Rahiri, Ngai Tawake
70	Hohepa Otene	Hohepa Otene [Pura]	Nga Puhi	Te Urimahoe, Te Uri-kopura, Ngati Tama, Te Kohatutaka
71	Hone Kingi Raumati	Hone Kingi Raumati	Nga Puhi	Ngati Toro, Ngahengahe, Te Popoto
72	Tuhakuaha	Tuhakuaha [Tukakawaha?]	Nga Puhi	Ngai Tawake

Signed on an unknown date, at the Bay of Islands

No.	Signed as	Probable name	Tribe	Hapu
73	Tawatanui	Tawatanui [Tawatawa]	Ngati Wai Nga Puhi?	Te Kapotai? Ngati Tautahi? Te Uri Taniwha?
74	Te Rawiti	Te Rawiti [Te Rawhiti]	Nga Puhi?	Te Uri-o-Hua
75	Kuhanga	Te Kuhanga [Maihi Paraone Kawiti?]	Nga Puhi	Ngati Hine
76	Paraha	Paraha [Pararaha?]	Nga Puhi	Ngati Hine? Ngati Wai?
77	Tahua	[Hori Kingi] Tahua	Ngati Wai?	Ngati Manu, Te Uri Karaka
78	Te Puka	Te Puka	Nga Puhi?	

288   AN ILLUSTRATED HISTORY OF THE TREATY OF WAITANGI

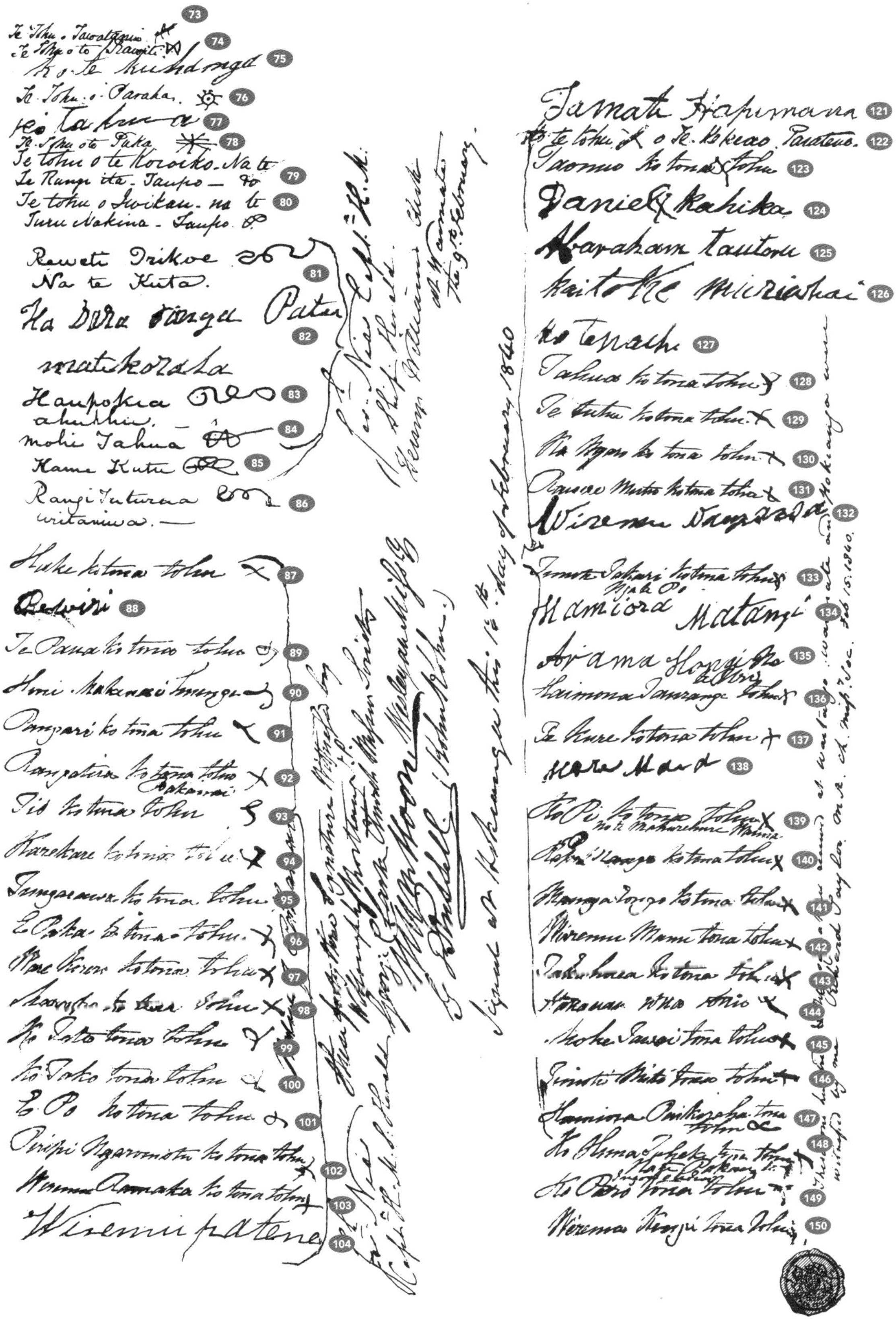

Te Tohu. Tawateaui ✗ [73]
Te Tohu o te Rauiti ✗ [74]
Ko te Huikaonga [75]
Te Tohu i Paraka. ☼ [76]
Ko Takaru a [77]
Te Tohu o te Puka ✳ [78]
Te tohu o te Koroiko. Na to [79]
Te Rangi ita. Taupo — ✗ [80]
Te tohu o Iwikau. na te [80]
Turu Nakina - Taupo ☉.

Reweti Trikoe ✗ [81]
Na te Kuta.

Na Dora Janga Pater [82]

matikonaha

Haupokia ✗ [83]
ahuihiu.
mohi Tahua ✗ [84]
Kame Kutu ✗ [85]
Rangi Tuturua ✗ [86]
uritaniwa. —

Huke ki tona tohu ✗ [87]

Rewiri [88]

Te Pana ki tona tohu ✗ [89]

Hini Makanui Imenge [90]

Ompari ko tona tohu ✗ [91]

Rangatira ki tona tohu ✗ [92]
Aokawai
Tio ki tona tohu ✗ [93]

Karekare ki tona tohu ✗ [94]

Tangaroawa ki tona tohu ✗ [95]

E Paika ki tona tohu ✗ [96]

Hare Kiron ki tona tohu ✗ [97]

Kaoniho ki tona tohu ✗ [98]

Ko Tato tona tohu ✗ [99]

Ko Toko tona tohu ✗ [100]

E Po ko tona tohu ✗ [101]

Piripi Ngaromota ki tona tohu ✗ [102]

Wiremu Annaka ki tona tohu ✗ [103]

Wiremu Patene [104]

Tamati Hapimana [121]
Ko te tohu ✗ o te Hokiao Pautene. [122]
Tiromo ki tona tohu [123]
Daniel Kahika [124]
Abaraham tautoru [125]
kaitoke muriwhai [126]
Ko te Nahi [127]
Tahua ki tona tohu ✗ [128]
Te tutu ki tona tohu ✗ [129]
Na Ngaru ko tona tohu ✗ [130]
Amoa Muito ki tona tohu ✗ [131]
Wiremu Nanawao [132]
Tamati Pakari ki tona tohu ✗ [133]
Ngati Po
Hamiona Matangi [134]
Arama Hongi te [135]
Hirini
Haimona Tauranga tohu ✗ [136]
Te Kure ki tona tohu ✗ [137]
Hare Hau ✗ [138]
Ko Pi ki tona tohu ✗ [139]
Ko te Maharehu Wania
Ko te Mango ki tona tohu ✗ [140]
Manga Tongo ki tona tohu ✗ [141]
Wiremu Manu tona tohu ✗ [142]
Takuhuca ki tona tohu ✗ [143]
Ahuau wha Hiio ✗ [144]
Mohi Tauai tona tohu ✗ [145]
Hirini Muito tona tohu ✗ [146]
Hamiona Oniki tona tohu ✗ [147]
Ko Huna Pokai tona tohu ✗ [148]
Ko Pora
Ko Pari tona tohu ✗ [149]
Wiremu Rangi tona tohu ✗ [150]

No.	Signed as	Probable name	Tribe	Hapu

Signed on 6 February 1840, at Waitangi (?)

No.	Signed as	Probable name	Tribe	Hapu
79	Te Koroiko	Te Koroiko/Korohiko	Ngati Tuwharetoa	Te Rangi-ita
80	Iwikau	Iwikau [Te Heuheu]	Ngati Tuwharetoa	Ngati Turamakina

Signed on 9–10 February 1840, at Waimate North, witnessed by Joseph Nias, Henry Williams and Richard Taylor

No.	Signed as	Probable name	Tribe	Hapu
81	Reweti Irikoe	Reweti Irikoe	Nga Puhi	Ngati Kuta
82	Ha Oara Ringa Patu?	Paora Ringa Patu/Pararinga	Nga Puhi?	Te Patukoraha?
83	Haupokia	Haupokia from Te Ahuahu	Nga Puhi	Ngati Toro? Ngati Rangi?
84	Mohi Tahua	Mohi Tahua	Nga Puhi	
85	Kame Kutu	Kame Kutu	Nga Puhi	
86	Rangi Tuturua	Rangi Tuturua	Nga Puhi	Te Uri Taniwha

Signed on 12 February 1840, at Hokianga, witnessed by Joseph Nias, Willoughby Shortland, George Clarke Snr, William Woon and G. F. Russell

No.	Signed as	Probable name	Tribe	Hapu
87	Hake	Hake [Huke?]	Nga Puhi?	Te Urikapana, Te Roroa, Ngati Pou?
88	Rewiri	Rawiri [Tukiata?]	Nga Puhi	Ngati Korokoro?
89	Te Pana	Te Pana [Ruka?]	Nga Puhi	Te Roroa
90	Hone Makinaihunga	Hone Makinaihunga [Makihuna?]	Nga Puhi	Te Pokare, Ngati Rauawa
91	Pangari	Pangari	Nga Puhi	Ngati Hua, Ngati Whiu, Te Waiariki
92	Rangatira (Pakanae)	Rangatira [Moetara]	Nga Puhi	Ngati Korokoro, Te Hikutu, Ngati Hau, Ngai Tu
93	Tio	Tio [Te Tukuaka?]	Nga Puhi	Te Pouka, Ngati Hau?
94	Karekare	Karekare	Nga Puhi	Te Uri-o-Hau? Ngati Hau?
95	Tungarawa	Tungarawa	Nga Puhi?	
96	E Paka	Paka	Nga Puhi?	Ngati Korokoro?
97	Ware Korero	Whare Korero [Paka?]	Nga Puhi?	
98	Marupo	Marupo	Nga Puhi	Ngati Hau
99	Toto	Toto [Tete Whatarau?]	Nga Puhi	Ngati Korokoro
100	Toko	Toko [Tako?]	Nga Puhi	Ngati Korokoro
101	E Po	Pou [Po]	Nga Puhi?	Te Hikutu, Ngati Kerewhati?
102	Piripi Ngaromotu	Piripi Ngaromotu	Nga Puhi	Ngati Pakau, Ngati Wharekawa
103	Wiremu Ramaka	Wiremu Ramaka	Nga Puhi	Ngati Pakau, Ngati Wharekawa
104	Wiremu Patene	Wiremu Patene	Nga Puhi, Te Rarawa	Te Uri-kopura, Te Uri Mahoe, Ngati Tama, Te Kohatutaka?
105	Manaihi	Manaihi	Nga Puhi?	
106	Paratene	Paratene	Nga Puhi?	Te Uri-o-Hua?
107	Te Hira	Te Hira	Te Rarawa?	from Motu Kiore?
108	Turau	[Wiremu Waka] Turau	Nga Puhi, Te Roroa?	Ngati Hao
109	Te Reti	Te Reti [Whatiia?]	Nga Puhi?	Ngai Tupoto?
110	Kenana	Kenana	Nga Puhi?	
111	Pero	Pero	Nga Puhi	Ngai Tupoto, Ngati Pakau?
112	Te Uruti	Te Uruti	Nga Puhi	Ngai Tupoto
113	Witikama Rewa	Witikama Rewa	Nga Puhi?	
114	Tira	Tiro	Nga Puhi	Ngati Tama, Te Whanau Puku, Te Pokare
115	Tipane Toro	Tipane/Tipene Te Toro	Nga Puhi	Te Kapotai? Ngati Toro?
116	Matiu	Matiu	Nga Puhi	Ngati Tama, Te Uri-o-Rorokai, Te Uri-o-Ngongo?
117	Kaihu	Kaihu	Nga Puhi?	Te Hikutu, Ngati Kerewhati
118	Kaitoke	Kaitoke	Nga Puhi	Te Hikutu

290   AN ILLUSTRATED HISTORY OF THE TREATY OF WAITANGI

We do hereby certify that this Sheet of Parchment unsigned was appended in our presence to the Treaty of Waitangi, which bears date the 5 February 1840, on board H.M.S. Herald in the Waitemata on the 29th day of February 1840. —

Jos. Nias Capt. R. N.
Ship Herald's —

Geo. Cooper Colonial Treasurer

We the undersigned have witnessed the signatures of the sixty Chiefs of Kaitaia & the neighbouring tribe the 28th day of April 1840

William Gilbert Puckey of the Ch. mission
John Johnson M.D.
R. D. Mair, Lt. R.N. Kyle —
Wm. M. Phier.

Richard Taylor M.A. of ye Ch. mission

Willoughby Shortland
Colonial Secretary

168 Nopere Panakaraas
Chief of the Rarawa
169 Paora Ngarure
170 Wiremu Wenhana
171 Uimu
172 Kiroi on a Tangata
173 Matenga Paerata
174 Rapata Wakahoha
175 Hare Popata Waka
176 Tana
177 (Tactumu) Chief of the Aupouri
178 Matiu Waku
179 Tokitehi
180 Paratene Wauora
181 Rapuli Kehurehu
182 Koroneho Pupu
183 Piripi Raoraa
184 Kopa
185 Minata Horgi
186 Otopi
187 Paeta
188 Marapia
189 Paratene Karuhun
190 Tamati Pawau

206 Puhipe   Puk. goh + Ahipara
207 Ereonora
208 Pbau chief of Pakapoto
209 Rawiri + Ahipara
210 Kepa Waka
211 Koonuna Iuau
211 Ngare
213 Tamona Iavau
214 Wele chief of Awanui
215 Ruanu
216 Hauuu
217 Huu
218 Rawaraka
219 Romni Awaraa
220 Ree
221 Papanu
222 Takaraca Kohaya
223 Rawa Keetike
224 Tera Tamakamu
224 Karaka Kawau
226 Paora Kou
227 Tamona Wauora
228 Paahama auu

No.	Signed as	Probable name	Tribe	Hapu
119	Hira	Hira	Nga Puhi?	Ngati Poto?
120	Kiri Kotiria	Kiri Kotiria	Nga Puhi	Te Hikutu
121	Tamati Hapimana	Tamati Hapimana	Nga Puhi	Ngati Matakiri?
122	Te Kekeao Paratene	Te Kekeao Paratene	Nga Puhi	Ngati Matakiri, Te Uri Taniwha
123	Taonui	[Makoare] Taonui	Nga Puhi	Te Popoto
124	Daniel Kahika	Raniera Kahika	Nga Puhi	
125	Abraham Tautoru	Aperahama Tautoru [Taonui?]	Nga Puhi	Te Popoto?
126	Kaitoke Muriwhai	Kaitoke Muriwai	Nga Puhi	Te Popoto? Te Hikutu, Ngati Pare, Ngati Kawhare?
127	Te Naihi	Te Naihi/Te Maihi? [Rotohiko?]	Nga Puhi	Ngati Uru? Te Popoto?
128	Tahua	Tahua [Wiremu Hopihona?]	Nga Puhi?	Te Popoto?
129	Te Tuhu	Te Tuhu/Te Tohu?	Nga Puhi	Te Ihu Tai?
130	Ngaro	Ngaro	Nga Puhi?	Patupo, Ngati Toro
131	Rawiri Mutu	Rawiri Mutu	Nga Puhi?	Te Ihu Tai, Ngati Whiu, Te Uri Taniwha? Ngati Hua
132	Wiremu Whangaroa	Wiremu Whangaroa	Nga Puhi, Te Roroa	Ngati Pou
133	Timoti Takari	Timoti Takari [Takiri?]	Te Roroa	Ngati Pou
134	Hamiora Matangi	Hamiora Matangi	Nga Puhi	Te Popoto?
135	Arama Hongi	Arama Hongi	Nga Puhi	Ngati Uru
136	Haimona Tauranga	Haimona Tauranga	Nga Puhi	Ngati Tama
137	Te Kure Kotoria?	Te Kure Kotiria?/Te Kuri?	Nga Puhi?	Ngai Tu?
138	Heremaia?	Heremaia Te Kuri?	Nga Puhi?	Ngai Tu?
139	Pi	[Arama Karaka] Pi	Nga Puhi	Te Mahurehure
140	Repa Mango	Repa Mango	Nga Puhi?	Matapungarehu?
141	Maunga Rongo	Maunga Rongo	Nga Puhi?	Ngati Uru?
142	Wiremu Manu	Wiremu Manu	Nga Puhi?	
143	Takahorea	Takahorea	Nga Puhi	Ngahengahe
144	Wakanau	Wakanau/Whakanau/ Hokamau?	Nga Puhi?/ Te Rarawa?	Ngati Hine?
145	Mohi Tawai	Mohi Tawhai	Nga Puhi from Waima	Mahurehure, Te Uri Kaiwhare, Te Uri-o-te-Aho, Ngai Tupoto, Ngati Hau
146	Timoti Mito	Timoti Mito	Nga Puhi	Te Kohatutaka
147	Hamiora Paikoraha	Hamiora Paikoraha/ Hamiora Paekoraha	Te Roroa	Ngati Pakau
148	Huna Tuheki	Huna Tuheke/Huna Taheke	Nga Puhi	Ngati Pakau, at Te Taheke
149	Pero	Pero/Paro?	Nga Puhi?	
150	Wiremu Kingi	Wiremu Kingi	Nga Puhi?/ Te Rarawa?	Ngati Rehia? Ngati Korokoro?

Signed on 4 March 1840, at Karaka Bay, Tamaki, witnessed by Joseph Nias, Henry Williams and William Thomas Fairburn

No.	Signed as	Probable name	Tribe	Hapu
151	Wiremu Hoete	Wiremu Hoete	Ngati Paoa?	
152	Hokopa	Hakopa	Ngati Paoa?	
153	Te Awa	Te Awa/Awha?	Ngati Paoa?	
154	Te Tapuru	Te Tapuru	Ngati Paoa?	
155	Te Titaha	Te Titaha	Ngati Paoa?	
156	Kahu Kote	Kahukoti [Te Karamu?]	Ngati Paoa	
157	Ruinga	Ruinga	Ngati Paoa	
158	Hohepa	Hohepa	Ngati Paoa?	
159	Pouroto	[Patara?] Pouroto	Ngati Paoa	
160	Inoha	Inoha	Ngati Paoa?	

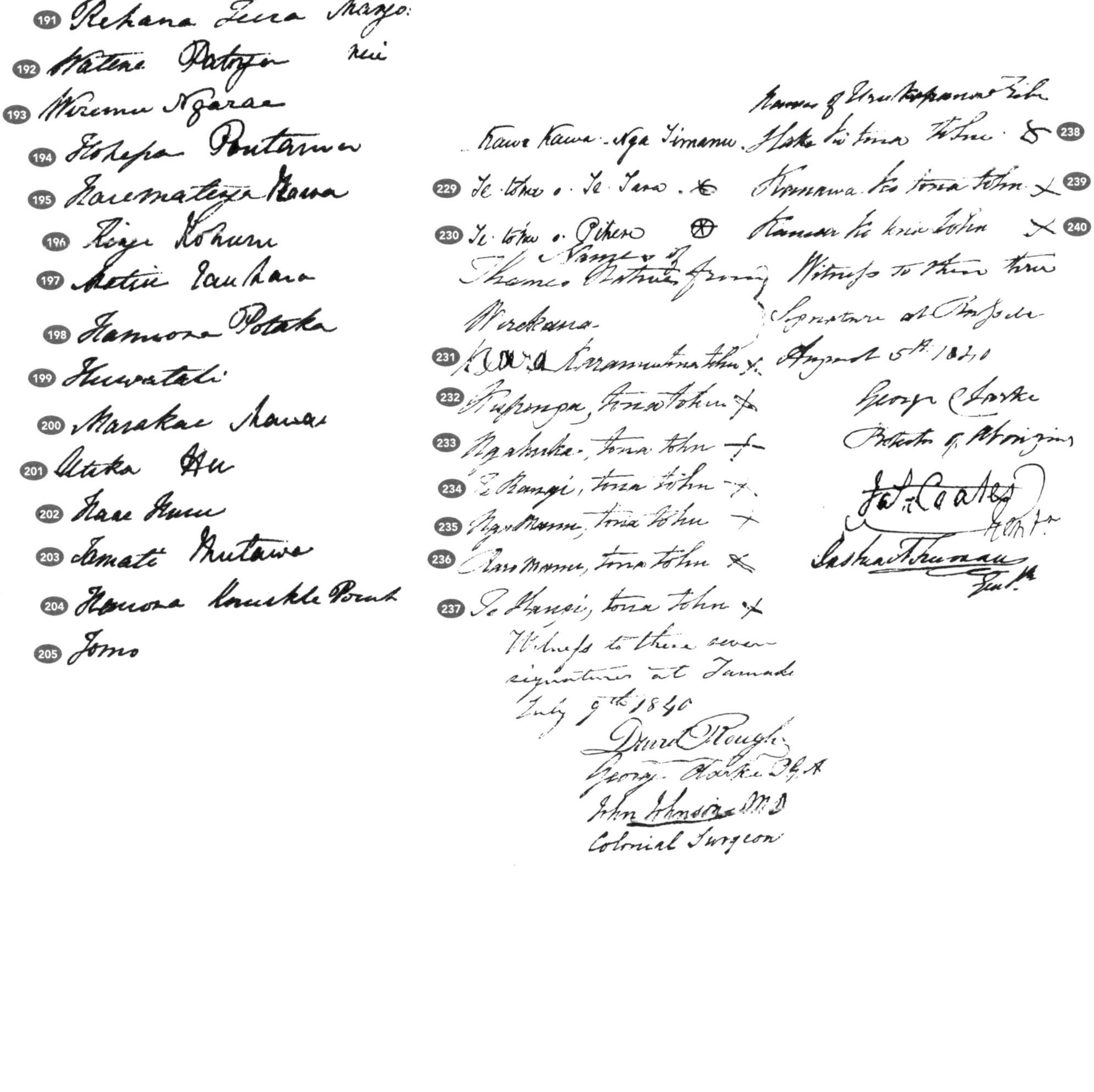

191. *Rehana Tewa Mango*
192. *Watene Patoja* *rui*
193. *Wiremu Ngarae*
194. *Etehepa Poutaewa*
195. *Karumateya Kawa*
196. *Rire Kohuru*
197. *Metiu Eaukaua*
198. *Hamiora Potaka*
199. *Huewataki*
200. *Marakae Mawai*
201. *Utuka Au*
202. *Hare Huru*
203. *Lematu Mutawa*
204. *Hamora Leuekle Point*
205. *Tomo*

Kawa Kawa - Nga Timanu

229. *Te tohu o Te Tara.* ✗
230. *Te tohu o Pehere* ✗
Names of Thames Natives being
Wirekana.
231. *Kawa Raramutma tohu* ✗
232. *Pupempa, tona tohu* ✗
233. *Ngataika, tona tohu* ✗
234. *Te Rangi, tona tohu* ✗
235. *Nga Manu, tona tohu* ✗
236. *Ran Manu, tona tohu* ✗
237. *Te Hanui, tona tohu* ✗
Witness to these seven
signatures at Tamaki
July 9th 1840
David Rough
George Clarke DGA
John Johnson MD
Colonial Surgeon

Names of Wirekapanne Iwi

238. *Hoke ki tona tohu* ✗
239. *Kimawa ki tona tohu* ✗
240. *Kamua ki kui tohu* ✗
Witness to these three
Signature at Omapere
August 5th 1840

George Clarke
Protector of Aborigines

Jas. Coates

Sasha Truman

No.	Signed as	Probable name	Tribe	Hapu
161	Hinaki	Hinaki	Ngati Paoa?	
162	Keka?	Keka/Keha?	Ngati Paoa?	
163	Paora	Paora [Tuhaere?]	Ngati Whatua?	Te Taou?
164	Mohi	Mohi	Ngati Paoa?	
165	Anaru	Anaru	Ngati Paoa?	
166	Waitangi	Waitangi	Ngati Paoa?	
167	William Korokoro	William Korokoro	Nga Puhi	Ngati Wai, Ngare Raumati, Ngai Tawake Parapuwha, Te Kapotai

Signed on 28 April 1840, at Kaitaia, witnessed by William G. Puckey, John Johnson, H. D. Smart, Richard Taylor and Willoughby Shortland

No.	Signed as	Probable name	Tribe	Hapu
168	Nopera Panakarao	Nopera Panakareao	Te Rarawa	Te Patu
169	Paora Ngaruwe	Paraone Ngaruhe	Te Aupouri	
170	Wiremu Wirehana	Wiremu Wirehana	Te Rarawa?	
171	Rimu	Rimu	Te Rarawa?	
172	Himona Tangata	Himona Tangata	Te Rarawa?	
173	Matenga Paerata	Matenga Paerata	Te Rarawa	Te Patukoraha
174	Rapata Wakahoho	Rapata Wakahoho/ Rapata Whakahoki?	Te Rarawa?	
175	Hare Popata Waha	Hare Popata Waha	Te Rarawa, Ngati Kahu	Kaitote, Te Patukoraha, Ngai Taranga
176	Tana	Tana/Taua [Te Wheinga?]	Te Rarawa?	Te Patukoraha
177	Taitimu	Wiki Taitimu	Te Aupouri	
178	Matiu Huhu	Matiu Huhu	Te Aupouri, Te Rarawa	
179	Tokitahi	Tokitahi		
180	Paratene Waiora	Paratene Waiora	Te Aupouri	
181	Rapiti Rehurehu	Rapiti Rehurehu/Raharuhi		
182	Koroneho Pupu	Koroneho Pupu		
183	Piripi Raorao	Piripi Raorao		
184	Kopa	Kopa/Kapa	Te Aupouri	
185	Meinata Hongi	Meinata Hongi		
186	Otopi	Otopi		
187	Paetai	Paetai		
188	Marama/Maiapia	Marama?	Te Rarawa?	Ngai Takoto?
189	Paratene Karuhuri	Paratene Karuhuri		
190	Tamati Pawau	Tamati Pawau		
191	Rehana Teira	Reihana Teira	Te Rarawa? from Mangonui	Te Patukoraha
192	Watene Patonga	Watene Patonga		
193	Wiremu Ngarae	Wiremu Ngarae		
194	Hohepa Poutama	Hohepa Poutama		
195	Harematenga Kawa	Hare Matenga Kawa	Te Rarawa?	Te Patukoraha?
196	Kingi Kohuru	Kingi Kohuru		
197	Matiu Tauhara	Matiu Tauhara	Te Rarawa, Ngati Kahu, Te Roroa	
198	Hamiona Potaka	Hamiona/Hamiora Potaka		
199	Huwatahi	Huwatahi/Huatahi [Heteraka?]	Ngati Kuri?	
200	Marakae Mawae	Marakae Mawae/ Marakai Mawai		
201	Utika Hu	Utika Hu/Uti Kahu		

No.	Signed as	Probable name	Tribe	Hapu
202	Hare Huru	Hare Huru/Huhu	Ngati Kahu? Te Aupouri? Nga Puhi?	Parapuwha?
203	Tamati Mutawa	Tamati Mutawa		
204	Hauona	Hauona/Hauora from Knuckle Point		
205	Tomo	Tomo		
206	Puhipi	Puhipi [Te Ripi]	Te Rarawa	Te Pukepoto, Ahipara
207	Ereonora	Ereonora	Te Rarawa	
208	Poau	Poau/Poari [Te Mahanga]	Te Rarawa	Te Pukepoto, Ahipara
209	Rawiri	Rawiri	Te Rarawa	
210	Kepa Waha	Kepa Waha		
211	Koroniria Nuau	Koroniria Nuau [Haunui]		
212	Ngare	Ngare		
213	Hamiora Tawari	Hamiora Tawari		
214	Witi	Whiti	Te Rarawa at Awanui	
215	Ruanui	Ruanui		
216	Haunui	Haunui		
217	Kuri	Kuri	Te Aupouri, Te Rarawa	
218	Kawaraki	Kawaraki		
219	Rawiri Awarau	Rawiri Awarau	Te Rarawa	Te Patukoraha, Ngai Takoto
220	Ru	Ru		
221	Papanui	Papanui		
222	Hakaraia Kohanga	Hakaraia Kohanga		
223	Kawaheitiki	Kawaheitiki/Kawahutiki		
224	Pera Kamukamu	Pera Kamukamu		
225	Karaka Kawau	Karaka Kawau		
226	Paora Hoi	Paora Hoi		
227	Himiona Waiuora	Himiona Waiuora/ Himiona Whareora		
228	Aperahama	Aperahama	from Oruru	

Signed at the Bay of Islands (?), date unknown

No.	Signed as	Probable name	Tribe	Hapu
229	Te Tara	Te Tara	Ngati Wai?	Ngati Manu from Kawakawa
230	Pihere	Pihere	Ngati Wai?	Ngati Manu from Kawakawa

Signed on 9 July 1840, at [Karaka Bay?] Tamaki, witnessed by David Rough, George Clarke Snr and John Johnson; signatories said to be 'Thames natives from Wharekawa'

No.	Signed as	Probable name	Tribe	Hapu
231	Karamu?	Karamu? Kahukoti?	Ngati Paoa?	
232	Kupenga	Te Kupenga	Ngati Paoa	
233	Ngahuka	Ngahuka	Ngati Paoa	
234	Te Rangi	Te Rangi	Nga Puhi?	Parapuwha?
235	Nga Manu	Nga Manu	Ngati Paoa?	
236	Raro Maru	Raro Maru	Ngati Paoa?	
237	Te Hangi	Te Hangi	Ngati Paoa?	

Signed on 5 August 1840, at Russell, witnessed by George Clarke Snr, James Coates and James S. Freeman

No.	Signed as	Probable name	Tribe	Hapu
238	Hake	Hake	Nga Puhi	Te Urikapana
239	Kanawa	Te Kanawa	Nga Puhi?	Te Urikapana, Ngati Hauata
240	Kaniwa?	Te Kaniwa/Kauwa		

2. Manukau-Kawhia Treaty Copy

Hobson suffered a stroke on 1 March while on a trip to the Waitemata Harbour and returned to the Bay of Islands, where he made a gradual recovery. Responsibility for furthering Treaty business was taken up by Willoughby Shortland. Copies of the Treaty were made and were dispatched from the Bay of Islands. There is no record of the number of copies made. On 13 March, Shortland sent this copy, under his own signature, to Captain W. C. Symonds to obtain signatures in the Manukau Harbour area and in districts south of it on the west coast. Symonds was an unattached British army officer who was working in the area on behalf of a proposed Scottish land company settlement. With James Hamlin, a CMS catechist on the southern shores of the Manukau Harbour, he assembled a number of chiefs (probably at Awhitu), but failed to get their agreement. On 20 March, a second meeting was held. Many Waikato chiefs were present, including the great chief Te Wherowhero; none of them would sign, but three Ngati Whatua chiefs did. Symonds then sent the Treaty copy to the Wesleyan missionary John Whiteley at Kawhia who, with his assistant James Wallis, obtained further signatories. The last name was added on 3 September 1840.

Each name has the prefix 'Ko', which is not part of the name, and has 'his mark' following the moko or mark.

No.	Signed as	Probable name	Tribe	Hapu

Signed on 20 March 1840, at Manukau Harbour, witnessed by W. C. Symonds and James Hamlin

No.	Signed as	Probable name	Tribe	Hapu
1	Te Kawau	[Apihai] Te Kawau	Ngati Whatua	Te Taou, Nga Oho
2	Te Tinana	[Ihikiera?] Te Tinana	Ngati Whatua	Te Taou
3	Te Reweti	Te Reweti [Tamaki]	Ngati Whatua	Te Taou

Signed on 28 April 1840, at Kawhia, witnessed by James Wallis

4	Rawiri	Rawiri	Nga Puhi?	

Signed on 21 May 1840 [at Kawhia?], witnessed by John Whiteley

5	Te Kanawa	Te Kanawa	Waikato	Ngati Mahuta
6	Tariki	Tariki	Waikato? Ngati Maniapoto?	from Patupatu pa
7	Haupokia	Haupokia [Te Pakaru]	Ngati Maniapoto?	

Signed on 25 May 1840, witnessed by John Whiteley

8	Te Waru	[Hori] Te Waru [Haunui]	Waikato	Ngati Te Apakura

Signed on 15 June 1840, witnessed by John Whiteley

9	Taunui	Te Taonui	Waikato? Ngati Maniapoto?	from Patupatu pa
10	Hone Waitere, Te Aotearoa	Hone Waitere	Ngati Maniapoto?	from Aotea?
11	Te Matenga, Te Wahapu	Te Matenga		from Te Wahapu?

Signed on 27 August 1840, at Kawhia

12	Ngamotu	[Wiremu Hopihana?] Ngamotu	Ngati Maniapoto?	

Signed on 3 September 1840 [at Kawhia?]

13	Warekaua	Wharekaua/Wharekawa?	Waikato?	from Whakatiwai?

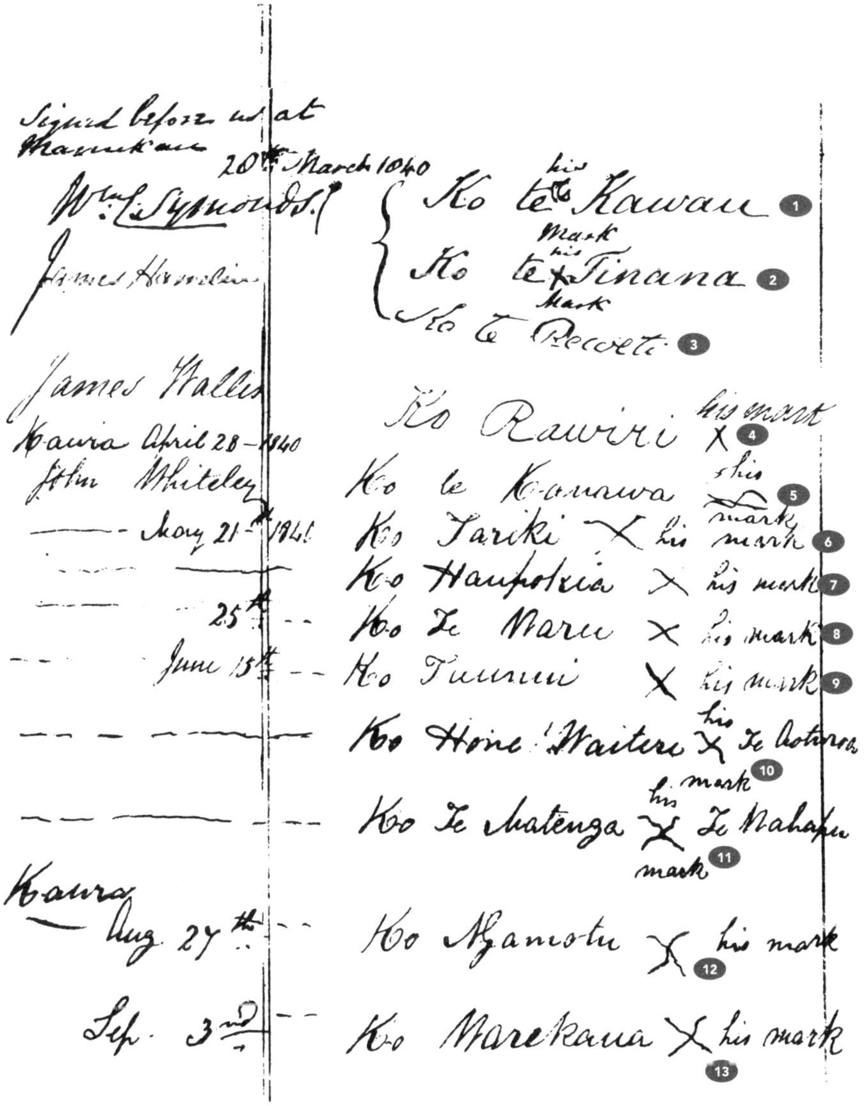

Signed before us at
Manukau 20th March 1840

Wm. C. Symonds?

James Hamlin

James Wallis
Kawia April 28 - 1840
John Whiteley
— May 21st 1840
— 25th
— June 15th

Kawia
— Aug 27th
Sep. 3rd

Ko te Kawau   ①
his Mark

Ko te ✗ Tinana   ②
his Mark

Ko te Reweti   ③

Ko Rawiri   his mark ✗ ④

Ko te Kanawa   his mark ⑤

Ko Tariki ✗ his mark ⑥

Ko Haupokia ✗ his mark ⑦

Ko Te Maru ✗ his mark ⑧

Ko Tuumu ✗ his mark ⑨

Ko Hone 'Waitere ✗ his Te Aotaroa ⑩

Ko Te Matenga ✗ his mark Te Wahapu ⑪

Ko Ngamotu ✗ his mark ⑫

Ko Marekawa ✗ his mark ⑬

APPENDIX TWO: TREATY SIGNATORIES   297

3. Waikato-Manukau Treaty Copy

This was the only Treaty copy (as far as we know) sent out in English. Robert Maunsell, a CMS missionary stationed near the mouth of the Waikato River, received it in late March or early April, just as a large mission meeting of some fifteen hundred Maori was assembling. Maunsell believed that the thirty-two chiefs who first signed his copy comprised most of the leading men of the area. The names show that they were mainly from the lower Waikato region, while some came from Ngaruawahia and further upstream.

In mid April 1840, William Symonds carried this Treaty copy back to Manukau Harbour, where seven more Waikato chiefs signed (at Awhitu?) on 26 April. Te Wherowhero and several others at this meeting would not sign. Maunsell took care to record the tribe or hapu for most of the chiefs. Sometimes he noted their location, although this was seldom fixed: political and seasonal pressures meant that chiefs and their people moved about a good deal.

Each name is prefixed by 'Ko te tohu o' – The sign of. Number 15, Hoana (Joanna?) Riutoto, is a woman of rank.

No.	Signed as	Probable name	Tribe	Hapu

Signed in late March or early April 1840, at Waikato Heads, witnessed by Robert Maunsell and Benjamin Ashwell, dated 11 April 1840

No.	Signed as	Probable name	Tribe	Hapu
1	Paengahuru	Paengahuru	Waikato	Ngati Tipa
2	Kiwi Ngarau	Kiwi Ngarau	Waikato	Ngati Tahinga
3	Te Paki	[Hone Wetere] Te Paki	Waikato	Te Ngaungau
4	Ngapaka	Ngapaka	Waikato	Ngati Tipa
5	Kukutai	[Waata?] Kukutai	Waikato	Ngati Tipa
6	Te Ngoki	Te Ngoki?/Te Ngohi?	Ngati Maniapoto	from Kawhia
7	Muriwenua	Muriwhenua	Ngati Haua	from Aotea
8	Te Pakaru	Te Pakaru	Ngati Maniapoto	from Kawhia
9	Waraki	Te Waraki	Ngati Maniapoto	from Kawhia
10	Kiwi (Te Roto)	Kiwi Te Roto	Waikato	Ngati Mahuta from Kawhia
11	Te Paerata	Te Paerata	Waikato	Ngati Pou
12	Te Katipa	Te Katipa	Waikato	Ngati Pou
13	Maikuku	Maikuku	Waikato	Ngati Te Ata
14	Aperahama Ngakainga	Aperahama Ngakainga	Waikato	Ngati Te Ata
15	Hoana Riutoto	Hoana Riutoto	Waikato	Ngati Mahuta
16	Te Wairakau	Te Wairakau	Waikato	Ngati Te Ata
17	Hako	Hako	Waikato?	Ngati Te Wehi from Aotea
18	Wiremu Te Awa-i-taia	Wiremu Nera Te Awa-i-taia	Waikato	Ngati Mahanga from Whaingaroa (Raglan)
19	Tuneu Ngawaka	Tuneu Ngawaka	Waikato	Ngati Tahinga?
20	Kemura Wareroa	Kemura Whareroa	Waikato	Ngati Tahinga
21	Pohepohe	Pohepohe	Ngati Haua	from Matamata
22	Pokawa Rawhirawhi	Pokawa Rawhirawhi	Ngati Haua	from Matamata
23	Te Puata	Te Puata	Waikato	Ngati Ruru at Otawhao
24	Te Mokorau	Te Mokorau	Waikato	Ngati Ruru at Otawhao
25	Pungarehu	Pungarehu	Waikato	Ngati Apakura at Parawera
26	Pokotukia	Pokotukia/Pohotukia?	Ngai Te Rangi?	from Tauranga?
27	Tekeha	Te Keha?	Waikato	Ngati Naho at Te Horo
28	Te Warepu	Te Wharepu	Waikato	Ngati Hine at Taupiri

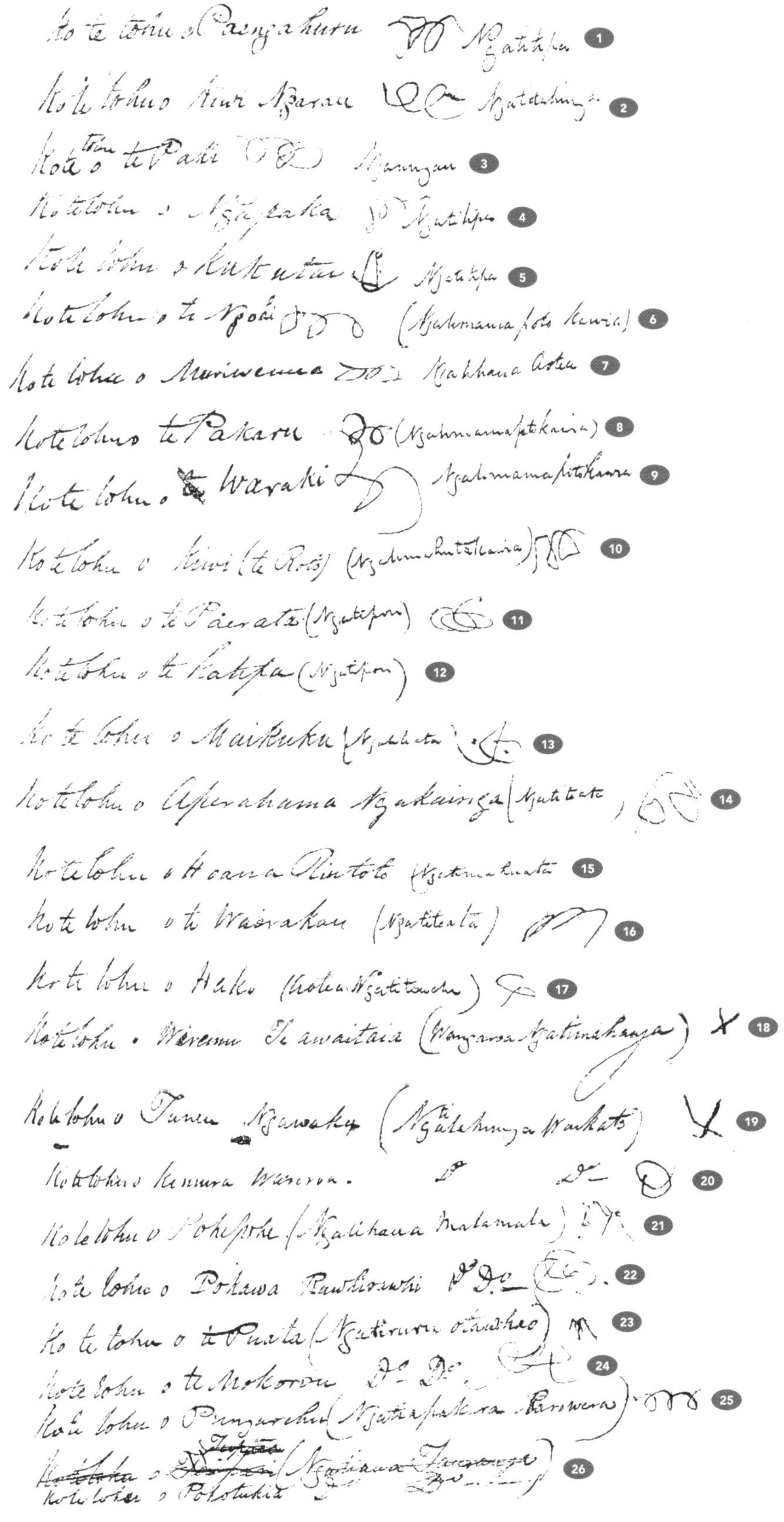

Ko te tohu o Paengahuru — Ngatihau [1]

Ko te tohu o Kiwi Ngarau — Ngatitahinga [2]

Ko te tohu o te Paki — Ngaungau [3]

Ko te tohu o Ngapeaka — Ngatihau [4]

Ko te tohu o Kukutau — Ngatahu [5]

Ko te tohu o te Ngohi — (Ngahinama foto kiwia) [6]

Ko te tohu o Muriwenua — Ngahhaua Aotea [7]

Ko te tohu o te Pakaru — (Ngahinamapitikaina) [8]

Ko te tohu o Waraki — Ngahinamapitikawa [9]

Ko te tohu o Kiwi (te Roto) — (Ngahinahutikaira) [10]

Ko te tohu o te Paerata (Ngatipou) [11]

Ko te tohu o te Kahepa (Ngatipou) [12]

Ko te tohu o Maikuku (Ngatihau) [13]

Ko te tohu o Aperahama Ngakainga (Ngatitata) [14]

Ko te tohu o Hoana Riototo (Ngatimahuta) [15]

Ko te tohu o te Waerakau (Ngatitata) [16]

Ko te tohu o Hako (Ngatea Ngatitawha) [17]

Ko te tohu o Wiremu Te Awaitaia (Wangaroa Ngatimahanga) [18]

Ko te tohu o Tunui Ngawake (Ngatihinga o Waikato) [19]

Ko te tohu o Kimura Wareroa [20]

Ko te tohu o Pohepohe (Ngatihaua Matamata) [21]

Ko te tohu o Pohawa Rawhirawhi [22]

Ko te tohu o te Puata (Ngatiruru otiwaheo) [23]

Ko te tohu o te Mokoroa [24]

Ko te tohu o Punganehu (Ngatipakoa Rorowera) [25]

Ko te tohu o Turau (Ngatihaua Tauranga) [26]

Ko te tohu o Pototukia

[Handwritten signatures, treaty sheet:]

Ko te tohu o te keha (Ngatinaho te Hoho) — 27

Ko te tohu te Wanipu (Ngatihine Taupiri) — 28

Ko te tohu te Kanawa (Do Do) — 29

Ko te tohu o te Whata Ngatitipa Waingaroa — 30

Ko te tohu o Ngawaka (te Ao) (Ngatinhauroa Putataka) — 31

Ko te tohu o Peehi (Otawao Ngatiruru) — 32

The preceding names have been obtained by us at this station & embrace as we conceive with the exception of two the names of the principal men of Waikato

Apr.l 11. 1840 Waikato Heads

R. Maunsell

B. Ashwell

Ko te tohu o Wiremu, Ngawaro — 33

Ko te tohu o Hone Kingi o — 34 } (Ngatetiati)

Ko te ta Wha Do — 35

Ko te tohu o Tamati — 36

Ko te tohu o Rabata Waiti — 37

Ko te tohu o Te Awarahi — 38 — signed before me April 26th 1840

Ko te tohu o Rehurehu — 39

W. C. Symonds.

No.	Signed as	Probable name	Tribe	Hapu
29	Te Kanawa	Te Kanawa	Waikato	Ngati Hine at Taupiri
30	Te Whata	Te Whata	Waikato	Ngati Tipa at Whaingaroa (Raglan)
31	Ngawaka (Te Ao)	Ngawaka Te Ao	Waikato	Ngati Whauroa at Putataka
32	Peehi	Peehi	Waikato	Ngati Ruru at Otawhao

Signed on 26 April 1840, at Manukau Harbour, witnessed by W. C. Symonds

No.	Signed as	Probable name	Tribe	Hapu
33	Wiremu Ngawaro	Wiremu Ngawaro	Waikato	Ngati Te Ata
34	Hone Kingi	Hone Kingi	Waikato	Ngati Te Ata
35	Ko te ta Wha	Te Tawa?/Te Tawha?	Waikato	Ngati Te Ata
36	Tamati	Tamati	Waikato?	
37	Rabata Waiti	Rapata Waiti	Waikato?	
38	Te Awarahi	Te Awarahi	Waikato	Ngati Te Ata
39	Rehurehu	Rehurehu	Waikato?	

4. Printed Treaty Copy

The names of the Waikato chiefs on this sheet were witnessed by Robert Maunsell, but there is no indication of the date or place of signing. The chiefs were possibly visiting Maunsell's mission at the Waikato River mouth. Ngati Pou lived on the east and west banks of the river further upstream; Ngati Te Wehi were at Raglan.

This printed copy was one of two hundred printed on 17 February at Paihia. It seems likely that it was dispatched with the English Treaty copy sent to Maunsell (copy 3) to assist him in explaining the terms of the Treaty in Maori.

No.	Signed as	Probable name	Tribe	Hapu

Signed in the Waikato, date unknown, witnessed by R. Maunsell

No.	Signed as	Probable name	Tribe	Hapu
1	Te Uira	Te Uira	Waikato	Ngati Pou
2	Ngahu	Ngahu	Waikato	Ngati Pou
3	Rahiri	Rahiri	Waikato	Ngati Mariu?
4	Te Noke	Te Noke	Waikato	Ngati Te Wehi
5	Te Wera	Te Wera	Waikato	Ngati Mariu?

Ka meatia tenei ki Waitangi, i te ono o nga ra o Pepuere, i te tau kotahi mano, ewaru rau, ewa tekau, o to tatou Ariki.

PAIHIA: Printed at the Press of the Church Missionary Society.

APPENDIX TWO: TREATY SIGNATORIES   301

5. Tauranga Treaty Copy

A Treaty copy had been received by the CMS missionary Alfred Nesbit Brown at Tauranga by 1 April 1840. The area was troubled by inter-tribal fighting and Brown hesitated to raise the matter with local chiefs. On 10 April, however, several missionaries gathered for a meeting and that day, or in the weeks following, twenty-one Tauranga chiefs signed. Tupaea and some other Otumoetai chiefs would not sign, and Brown put the copy aside, possibly hoping that they might do so later. The copy was finally sent back to Hobson on 23 May.

Most of the Treaty signings were witnessed by Europeans. This one, however, was witnessed by Hoani Aneta, Brown's mission assistant, who also signed the copy.

With each name are the words 'tana tohu' – his mark (or sign).

No.	Signed as	Probable name	Tribe	Hapu
Signed on 10 April 1840 or later, at Tauranga, witnessed by Hoani Aneta, Henry Taylor and James Stack				
1	Te Wanake	Te Whanake	Ngai Te Rangi	
2	Huitao	Huitao	Ngai Te Rangi	from Otumoetai
3	Tamaiwhahia	Tamaiwhahia	Ngai Te Rangi	
4	Te hui	[Tipene?] Te Hui	Ngai Te Rangi	from Otumoetai
5	Te paetui	Te Paetui/Te Paetai	Ngai Te Rangi	
6	Te Kou	Te Kou-o-Rehua	Ngati Pukenga	
7	Reko	Reko	Ngai Te Rangi	
8	Tari	Tari/Tare	Ngai Te Rangi	Ngai Tukairangi?
9	Te Matatahuna	Te Matatahuna	Ngai Te Rangi	
10	Te Konikoni	Te Konikoni	Ngai Te Rangi	
11	Tanarumia	Tanarumia	Ngai Te Rangi	
12	Nuka	Nuka [Taipari]	Ngai Te Rangi	Ngati He
13	Te Tutahi	Te Tutahi	Ngai Te Rangi	
14	Te Pohoi	Te Pohoi	Ngai Te Rangi	
15	Putarahi	Putarahi	Ngai Te Rangi	
16	Pikitia	Pikitia	Ngai Te Rangi	
17	Te Mako	Te Mako	Ngai Te Rangi	
Signed in April (?) 1840, at Tauranga, witnessed by James Stack				
18	Te Peika	Te Peika	Ngai Te Rangi	
19	Kapa	Kapa	Ngai Te Rangi	
20	Te Haere Roa	Te Haereroa	Ngai Te Rangi	
21	Hoani Aneta	[Ahikaiata] Hoani Aneta	Ngai Te Rangi	

1. Ko te Wanake tana [mark] tohu - Tauranga
   2. Hui tao tana [mark] tohu
   3. Tamaiwhahia tana [mark] tohu
   4. Te hui tana [mark] tohu
   5. Te paetu tana [mark] tohu
   6. Te kou tana [mark] tohu
   7. Reko tana [mark] tohu
   8. Tari tana [mark] tohu
   9. Te matatahuna [mark] tana [mark] tohu
   10. Te konikoni tana [mark] tohu
   11. Tanarumia tana [mark] tohu
   12. Naka tana [mark] tohu
   13. Te Tutahi tana [mark] tohu

Witness: Native European 14. Hoani Aneta Te Pohoi tana [mark] tohu

Henry Taylor

James Stack
   15. Puta rahi tana [mark] tohu
   16. Pikitia tana [mark] tohu
   17. Te mako tana [mark] tohu

Witness James Stack
   18. Te Peika tana [mark] tohu Tauranga
   19. Kapea
   20. Te haere roa tana [mark] tohu
   21. Hoani Aneta

APPENDIX TWO: TREATY SIGNATORIES 303

6. Bay of Plenty (Fedarb) Treaty Copy

Before the Tauranga Treaty copy was returned to Hobson, a local missionary, James Stack, was authorised by Major Thomas Bunbury to make two copies. One was sent inland to Rotorua and Taupo, where CMS missionaries were working, but Te Arawa and Ngati Tuwharetoa of those regions refused to sign, and the copy has disappeared. A second copy was made and entrusted to James Fedarb, trading-master of the Bay of Islands schooner *Mercury*, which was sailing down the Bay of Plenty coast.

Fedarb left Tauranga on 22 May. Over the next three to four weeks, he secured agreement at Whakatane, Opotiki, Torere and Te Kaha. Returning to the Bay of Islands on 19 June, he entrusted his copy to William Colenso, the missionary printer, to pass on to Hobson. No one commented on the fact that the signature – William Hobson – on the copy was, strictly speaking, forged since the copier had written the name in his own hand.

The Fedarb copy has other interesting features. At the request of chiefs affiliated to the Church Missionary Society, Fedarb identified the Opotiki chiefs who were Roman Catholic by placing a cross beside each name. This is the only other Treaty copy signed by Maori witnesses, Papahia and Wiremu Maihi, both possibly from the north.

No.	Signed as	Probable name	Tribe	Hapu
Signed on 27–28 May 1840, at Opotiki, witnessed by James W. Fedarb, Papahia and Wiremu Maihi				
1	Tautoru	Tauatoro	Te Whakatohea	Ngai Tamahaua, Ngati Ngahere
2	Takahi	Takahi	Te Whakatohea	Te Upokorehe
3	Aporotanga	[Te Awanui] Aporotanga	Te Whakatohea	Ngati Rua
4	Rangimatanuku	Rangimatanuku	Te Whakatohea	Ngati Rua
5	Rangihaerepo	Rangihaerepo	Te Whakatohea	Te Upokorehe, Ngai Tamahaua
6	Ake	Ake	Te Whakatohea	Te Upokorehe
7	Wakiia	Te Whakia	Te Whakatohea	
Signed on 11 June 1840, at Torere				
8	Putiki	Putiki	Ngai Tai	
9	Rangihuataki	Rangihuataki	Ngai Tai	
Signed on 14 June 1840, at Te Kaha				
10	Haupururangi	Te Aopururangi	Te Whanau-a-Apanui	Te Whanau-a-Te Ehutu
11	Hahiwaru	Te Ahiiwaru [Tamatama-a-rangi]	Te Whanau-a-Apanui	Te Whanau-a-Te Ehutu
12	Haomarama	Te Aomarama	Te Whanau-a-Apanui	Te Whanau-a-Te Ehutu
13	Warau	Te Wharau	Te Whanau-a-Apanui	Te Whanau-a-Te Ehutu
Signed on 14 June 1840, at Torere				
14	Na Taku	Nataku	Ngai Tai?	

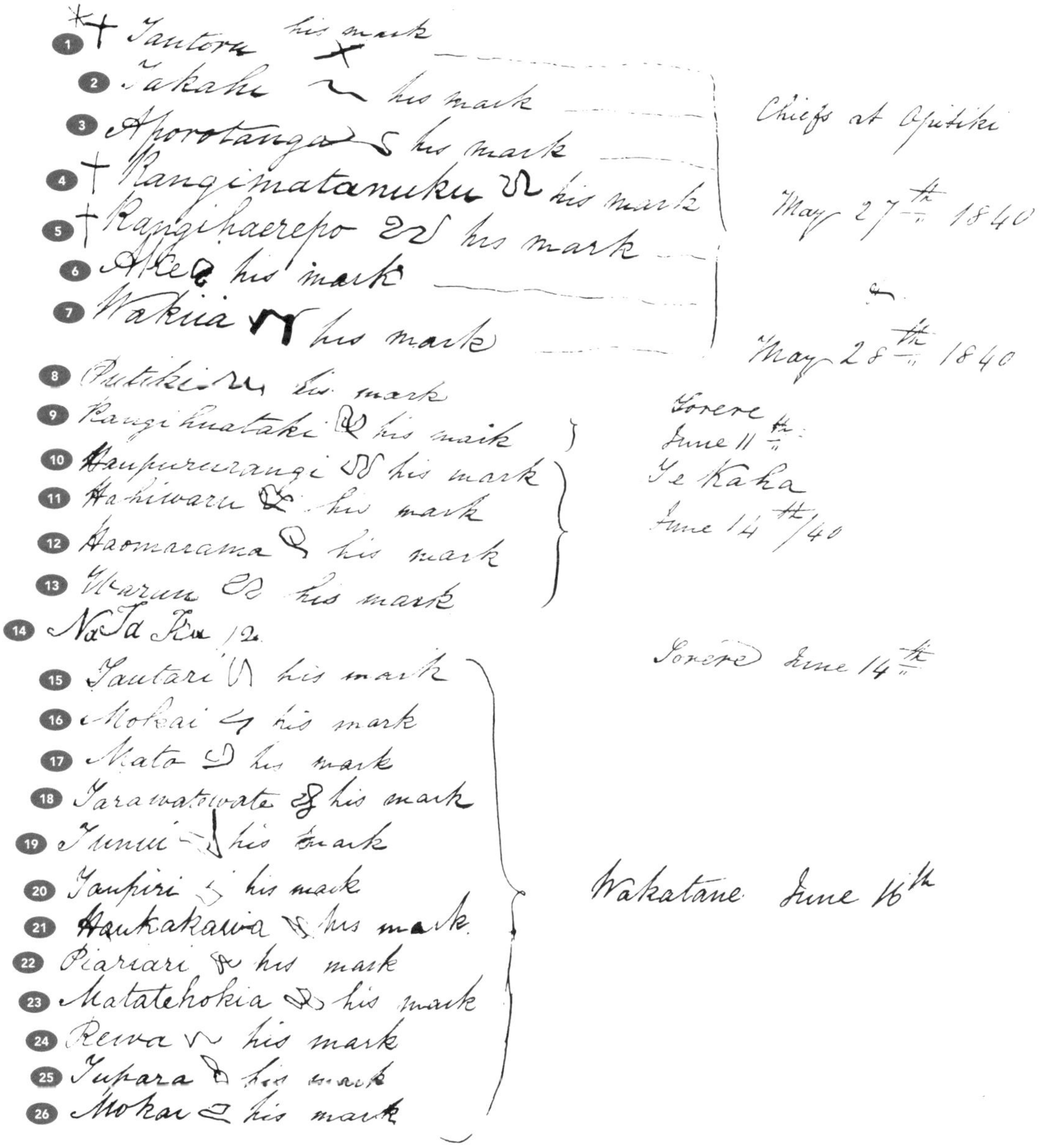

Handwritten signatory list (numbered 1–26):

1. † Tautoru his mark X
2. Takahi ~ his mark
3. Aporotanga ∫ his mark
4. † Rangimatanuku 𝒱 his mark
5. † Rangihaerepo 𝒱 his mark
6. Ake his mark
7. Wakiia 𝒱 his mark
8. Pwtiki ~ his mark
9. Rangihuataki his mark
10. Haupururangi his mark
11. Hahiwaru his mark
12. Haomarama his mark
13. Waruu his mark
14. Na Ta Ku 12.
15. Tautari his mark
16. Mokai his mark
17. Mato his mark
18. Tarawatewate his mark
19. Tunui his mark
20. Taupiri his mark
21. Haukakawa his mark
22. Piariari his mark
23. Matatehokia his mark
24. Rewa ~ his mark
25. Tupara his mark
26. Mokai his mark

Annotations (right side):

Chiefs at Opotiki
May 27th 1840

May 28th 1840

Torere June 11th
Te Kaha June 14th/40

Torere June 14th

Wakatane June 16th

No.	Signed as	Probable name	Tribe	Hapu

Signed on 16 June 1840, at Whakatane

No.	Signed as	Probable name	Tribe	Hapu
15	Tautari	Tautari	Ngati Awa	Ngati Pukeko
16	Mokai	Mokai	Ngati Awa	Ngati Pukeko
17	Mato	Mato	Ngati Awa	Ngati Pukeko
18	Tarawatewate	Tarawhatiwhati?	Ngati Awa	Ngati Pukeko
19	Tunui	Tunui	Ngati Awa	Ngati Pukeko
20	Taupiri	Taupiri	Ngati Awa	Ngati Pukeko
21	Haukakawa	Haukakawa	Ngati Awa	Ngati Pukeko
22	Piariari	Piariari	Ngati Awa	Ngati Pukeko
23	Matatehokia	Matatehokia	Ngati Awa	Ngati Pukeko
24	Rewa	Rewa	Ngati Awa	Ngati Pukeko
25	Tupara	Tupara	Ngati Awa	Ngati Pukeko
26	Mokai	Mokai	Ngati Awa	Ngati Pukeko

7. Herald-Bunbury Treaty Copy

On 28 April, Major Thomas Bunbury sailed from the Bay of Islands on HMS *Herald*; his directions were to complete negotiations in North Island areas that had not been covered and to secure Treaty agreement in the South Island. The interpreter for the trip was Henry Williams's son Edward, who had assisted with the translation of the Waitangi draft treaty into Maori on 4 February.

On 4–5 May, Bunbury met with chiefs at Coromandel Harbour. Some signed, but others felt that more time should be allowed for consultation and refused to sign. Off the Mercury Islands, the *Herald* anchored and was boarded by two chiefs who signed without hesitation. Bunbury now left the *Herald* and boarded the *Trent* to go in to Tauranga.

He arrived at Tauranga on 11 May, and the following day held a meeting at Te Papa, but failed to get any further Tauranga signatures. He authorised the Fedarb Treaty copy and the one that went in to Rotorua-Taupo; and then, anxious to get away to the South Island, he returned to the *Herald*.

Landing on Banks Peninsula on 28 May, Bunbury held a meeting at Akaroa that day and on 30 May, when two chiefs signed. As the ship headed further south, bad weather forced it to bypass Otago and run for Stewart Island (where Bunbury proclaimed sovereignty over the island on 5 June). The next signing, at Ruapuke, was held on 10 June. Returning up the east coast, one of the *Herald*'s boats put in to Otago Harbour where two chiefs signed at the heads. The ship moved on to Cook Strait, and at Guard's Bay in Cloudy Bay another signing took place on 17 June. The Ngati Toa chief Nohorua insisted that his signature be witnessed by his son-in-law, the whaler Joseph Thoms. Nohorua argued that should his grandchildren lose their land, their father might share the blame.

Having proclaimed sovereignty over the South Island on Horahorakakahu Island, Bunbury sailed for Kapiti. Off Mana Island, he found Te Rauparaha and insisted that he sign Bunbury's Treaty copy, although the chief assured him that he had already given his agreement to Henry Williams. After a brief call at the Tukituki River in Hawke's Bay, where Te Hapuku signed, Bunbury arrived back at the Bay of Islands on 2 July.

Like some of the other Treaty copies, this copy prefixed the chiefs' names with 'Ko te tohu o' – The sign of.

No.	Signed as	Probable name	Tribe	Hapu

Signed on 4 May 1840, at Coromandel Harbour, witnessed by Joseph Nias and Thomas Bunbury

1	Te Horeta Te Taniwa	Te Horeta Te Taniwha	Ngati Whanaunga	Te Mateawa?
2	Kitahi	Kitahi [Te Taniwha]	Ngati Whanaunga	Te Mateawa?
3	Puakanga	Puakanga	Ngati Whanaunga?	
4	Hauauru	Hauauru	Ngati Paoa, Ngati Whanaunga	

Signed on 7 May 1840, on HMS Herald *off Mercury Islands, witnessed by Joseph Nias*

5	Purahi	Purahi	Ngati Maru	from Mercury Bay?
6	Ngataiaepa	Nga Taiepa	Ngati Paoa	Te Rapupo

Signed on 30 May 1840, at Akaroa, witnessed by Thomas Bunbury and Edward M. Williams

7	Iwikau	Iwikau	Ngai Tahu	Ngati Rangiamoa
8	John Love	John Love [Tikao]	Ngai Tahu	Ngai Te Kahukura, Ngai Tuahuriri

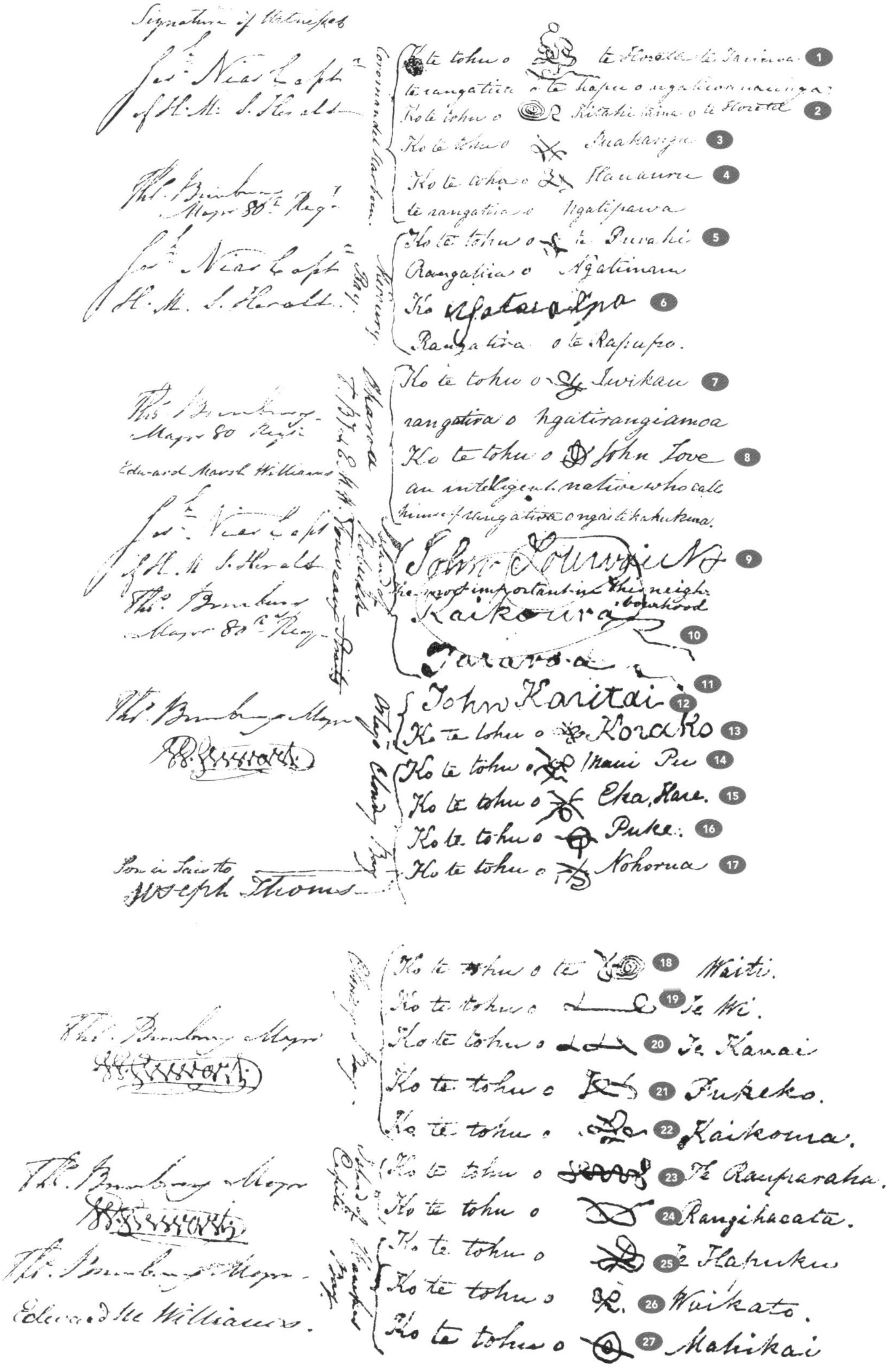

Signature of Witnesses

Jas. Nias Capt.
of H.M.S. Herald

Ths. Bunbury
Major 80th Regt.

Jas. Nias Capt.
H.M.S. Herald

Ths. Bunbury
Major 80 Regt.

Edward Marsh Williams

Jas. Nias Capt.
of H.M.S. Herald

Ths. Bunbury
Major 80th Regt.

Ths. Bunbury Major
R.B. Everard

Son in law to
Joseph Thoms

Ths. Bunbury Major
R.B. Everard

Ths. Bunbury Major
R.B. Everard

Ths. Bunbury Major
Edward M. Williams.

Ko te tohu o te Hiwoka te Iwikau [1]
te rangatira o te hapu o ngatiwanaunga.

Ko te tohu o Kitahi aina o te Hiwoka [2]

Ko te tohu o Inakarope [3]

Ko te wha o Hanauru [4]
te rangatira o Ngatipawa

Ko te tohu o te Purahi [5]
Rangatira o Ngatinaira

Ko Ngatarawapo [6]
Rangatira o te Rapupo.

Ko te tohu o Iwikau [7]
rangatira o Ngatirangiamoa

Ko te tohu o John Love [8]
an intelligent native who calls
himself rangatira ongaitikahukina.

John Louwie No [9]
The most important in the neighbourhood

Kaikoura [10]

Tararaa [11]

John Karitai [12]

Ko te tohu o Korako [13]

Ko te tohu o Maui Pu [14]

Ko te tohu o Eka Hare. [15]

Ko te tohu o Puke. [16]

Ko te tohu o Nohorua [17]

Ko te tohu o te Waiti. [18]

Ko te tohu o Te Wi. [19]

Ko te tohu o Te Kanai [20]

Ko te tohu o Pukeko. [21]

Ko te tohu o Kaikoura. [22]

Ko te tohu o Te Rauparaha. [23]

Ko te tohu o Rangihaeata. [24]

Ko te tohu o Te Hapuku [25]

Ko te tohu o Waikato. [26]

Ko te tohu o Mahikai [27]

No.	Signed as	Probable name	Tribe	Hapu

Signed on 10 June 1840, on HMS Herald *at Ruapuke, witnessed by Joseph Nias and Thomas Bunbury*

No.	Signed as	Probable name	Tribe	Hapu
9	John Touwaick	Hone Tuhawaiki	Ngai Tahu, Ngati Mamoe	Ngati Ruahikihiki
10	Kaikoura	Kaikoura	Ngai Tahu	
11	Taiaroa/Tararoa	Tararoa?	Ngai Tahu?	

Signed on 13 June 1840, at Otago Heads, witnessed by Thomas Bunbury and William Stewart

No.	Signed as	Probable name	Tribe	Hapu
12	John Karitai	Hone Karetai	Ngai Tahu	Ngati Ruahikihiki, Ngati Moki, Ngai Te Kahukura, Ngai Tuahuriri, Ngati Hinekura
13	Korako	Korako	Ngai Tahu	Ngai Tuahuriri, Ngati Huirapa

Signed on 17 June 1840, at Guard's Bay, Cloudy Bay, witnessed by Thomas Bunbury, William Stewart and (for Nohorua) Joseph Thoms

No.	Signed as	Probable name	Tribe	Hapu
14	Maui Pu	Maui Pu	Ngati Toa?	
15	Eka Hare	Kahare/Hari? [Charley?]	Ngati Toa?	
16	Puke	Puke	Ngati Toa?	
17	Nohorua	Nohorua [Tom Street]	Ngati Toa	Ngati Kimihia?
18	Waiti	Waiti/Whaiti?	Ngati Toa?	
19	Te Wi	Te Whi	Ngati Toa?	
20	Te Kanai	Te Kanae	Ngati Toa?	Ngati Awhai-a-Te-Hau?
21	Pukeko	Pukeko	Ngati Toa?	from Porirua?
22	Kaikoura	Kaikoura	Ngati Toa?	

Signed on 19 June 1840, off Mana Island, witnessed by Thomas Bunbury and William Stewart

No.	Signed as	Probable name	Tribe	Hapu
23	Te Rauparaha	Te Rauparaha	Ngati Toa	Ngati Koata, Ngati Rarua, Ngati Rakau, Ngati Kimihia
24	Rangihaeata	Te Rangihaeata	Ngati Toa	Ngati Kimihia, Ngati Te Maunu, Ngati Koata, Ngati Rarua, Ngati Rakau

Signed on 24 June 1840, in Hawke's Bay, witnessed by Thomas Bunbury and Edward M. Williams

No.	Signed as	Probable name	Tribe	Hapu
25	Te Hapuku	Te Hapuku [Te Ikanui-o-te-moana]	Ngati Te Whatu-i-apiti, Ngati Kahungunu	Ngati Te Rangi-ko-ia-anake
26	Waikato	[Hoani] Waikato	Ngati Te Whatu-i-apiti, Ngati Kahungunu	
27	Mahikai	Mahikai [Harawira]	Ngati Kahungunu	

8. Henry Williams Treaty Copy

At the beginning of April, Henry Williams left the Bay of Islands on the schooner *Ariel* to carry out Treaty negotiations in the south. Having left a Treaty copy with William Williams at Turanga (Gisborne) on 8 April, he arrived at Port Nicholson (Wellington) in mid April. For ten days, he could not persuade chiefs to sign, but a meeting was finally arranged on the *Ariel*, where many gave their assent. A number of chiefs in the Queen Charlotte Sound vicinity and at Rangitoto (d'Urville Island) also signed.

In May, Williams received chiefs' agreement at Otaki, Waikanae, in the Manawatu, at Wanganui, and at Motu Ngarara, a small island off the southern tip of Kapiti. He had intended to take his Treaty copy to Otago, but when he returned to Kapiti in early June he found that Major Bunbury had been deputed to promote the Treaty in the south. Williams then returned with his copy to the Bay of Islands.

Williams's copy has the names of several women – Kahe Te Rau-o-te-rangi (4), Rangi Topeora (78) and Rere-o-maki (120). It is possible that other women may have signed – for example, Pakewa (33), and Kehu (86), by which name the mother of Wiremu Kingi Te Rangitake was known.

All names are prefixed by 'Te tohu o' – The sign of.

No.	Signed as	Probable name	Tribe	Hapu

Signed on 29 April, on the Ariel *at Port Nicholson (Wellington), witnessed by Henry Williams and George Thomas Clayton*

No.	Signed as	Probable name	Tribe	Hapu
1	Tuarau	Tuarau	Te Ati Awa	Ngati Tawhirikura
2	Te Hiko-o-te-rangi	Te Hiko-o-te-rangi	Ngati Toa	Ngati Rarua, Ngati Te Manu
3	Tungia	Tungia	Ngati Toa	Ngati Te Maunu
4	Kahe	Kahe [Te Rau-o-te-rangi]	Ngati Toa	
5	Te Ware Pouri	Te Wharepouri [Te Kakapi-o-te-rangi]	Te Ati Awa	Ngati Tawhirikura, Ngati Te Whiti
6	Matangi	Matangi	Te Ati Awa	Ngati Te Whiti
7	Te Tarenga Kuri	Te Taringa Kuri [Te Kaeaea]	Ngati Tama	
8	Te Wakakeko	[Noa] Te Whakakeko	Ngati Tama	from Kaiwharawhara
9	Porutu	[Ihaia] Porutu	Te Ati Awa	Te Matehou?
10	Ngatata	[Wi Tako] Ngatata-i-te-rangi	Te Ati Awa, Taranaki	Ngati Te Whiti
11	Te Puakawe	Te Puakawe	Te Ati Awa?	Te Matehou?
12	Napuna	1. Ngapuna 2. [Mohi] Ngaponga	1. Te Ati Awa 2. Taranaki	1. Te Matehou 2. Ngati Haumia
13	Wairarapa	[Wiremu Kingi] Wairarapa	Te Ati Awa	Te Matehou
14	Mohiroa	[Te Ropiha] Moturoa	Te Ati Awa	Te Matehou
15	Te Tute	Te Tute [Hone Tutenuku?]	Te Ati Awa?	Ngati Tawhirikura?
16	Ingo	Ingo [Takutu]	Te Ati Awa	Te Matehou
17	Paka	[Pamarihi?] Paka	Te Ati Awa?	Ngati Tawhirikura?
18	Te Wakatauranga	Te Wakatauranga/ Whakatauranga?	Ngati Tama	from Kaiwharawhara
19	Hore	Hori [Pakihi?]	Ngati Tama?	Ngati Rangi?
20	Pani	Pani [Wharetiti?]	Ngati Tama	Ngati Rongonui
21	Rawi	Rawi		
22	Kopiri	[Hohepa?] Kopiri	Te Ati Awa	Te Matehou
23	Wanga	[Rota?] Wanganga?	Ngati Tama	
24	Ngapapa	[Te Keepa] Ngapapa	Ngati Tama	
25	Reihana Reweti	Reihana Reweti	Nga Puhi?	
26	Patuhiki	Patuhiki	Te Ati Awa?	
27	Te Huka	Te Huka		

No.	Signed as	Probable name	Tribe	Hapu
28	Te Kahu	[Hoani] Te Iwi-Kahu	Te Ati Awa	Te Matehou
29	Kopeka	[Harawira] Kopeka	Te Ati Awa	Ngati Tawhirikura
30	Rerewa	Rerewha	Te Ati Awa	Ngati Tawhirikura
31	Te Puni	[Honiana] Te Puni-kokopu	Te Ati Awa	Ngati Te Whiti, Ngati Tawhirikura
32	Tuhoto	Tuhatu [Moengarangatira]	Te Ati Awa	Ngati Tawhirikura
33	Pakewa	Pakewa	Te Ati Awa?	Puketapu?
34	Popuka	Popuka [Makere]	Te Ati Awa	Ngati Te Whiti, Ngati Tawhirikura

Signed on 4 May 1840, in Queen Charlotte Sound, witnessed by Henry Williams and George Thomas Clayton

No.	Signed as	Probable name	Tribe	Hapu
35	Toheroa	[Te Manu?] Toheroa	Te Ati Awa	Ngati Komako of Puketapu
36	Rewa	Rewa/Rewha?	Ngati Toa	
37	Watino	[Rawiri] Watino	Te Ati Awa	
38	Te Tupe	[Ihaia?] Te Tupe	Te Ati Awa	
39	Tiaho	Tiaho	Te Ati Awa	
40	Tikaukau	Tikaokao?	Ngati Tama?	
41	Te Orakaka	Te Orakaka		
42	Tuterapouri	Tuterapouri?		
43	Te Tirarau	Te Tirarau	Ngati Mutunga	Ngati Hinetuhi
44	Ngaoranga	Nga-oranga?		
45	Hone	Hone		
46	Inana	Inana		
47	Kaparangi	Kaparangi/Kapurangi?	Ngati Rarua?	
48	Tapotuku	Tapotuku		

Signed on 5 May 1840, in Queen Charlotte Sound, witnessed by Henry Williams and George Thomas Clayton

No.	Signed as	Probable name	Tribe	Hapu
49	Huriwenua	Huriwhenua	Te Ati Awa	Ngati Rahiri
50	Taukina	[Paora] Taukina	Te Ati Awa	Ngati Rahiri
51	Iwikau	[Pitama?] Te Iwikau	Te Ati Awa?	
52	Punga	Punga		
53	Te Rangowaka	Te Rangowaka		
54	Nga Kirikiri	Nga Kirikiri		
55	Potiki	Potiki		
56	Nga Taraheke	Nga Taraheke		
57	Anara	Anara		
58	Pikau	Pikau		
59	Te Uapiki	Te Uapiki		
60	Maru	Maru		
61	Karaka	Karaka		

Signed on 11 May 1840, at Rangitoto (d'Urville Island), witnessed by Henry Williams and George Thomas Clayton

No.	Signed as	Probable name	Tribe	Hapu
62	Te Wetu	Te Whetu		
63	Pari	Pari		
64	Taropiko	Taropiko		
65	Te Putete	[Turi] Te Patete	Ngati Koata	
66	Te Rangiahua	Te Rangiahua		
67	Tahanui	Tahanui		
68	Orokaka	Orokaka		
69	Toitoi	Toitoi		
70	Te Muho	Te Muho		
71	Te Ipukohu	Te Ipukohu		
72	Te Tihi	Te Tihi Tawhirikura		
73	Huia	Huia		
74	Nukumai	Nukumai		

Names of Chiefs in Port Nicholson and the Neighbourhood

#	Name
1	Tuarau
2	Te Hiko o te Rangi
3	Tungia
4	Kahe
5	Te Ware Pouri
6	Matangi
7	Te Tarengakuri
8	Te Wakakeko
9	Porutu
10	Ngatata
11	Te Puakawe
12	Napuna
13	Wairarapa
14	Mohiroa
15	Te Tute
16	Inngo
17	Taka
18	Te Wakataunga
19	Hore
20	Pani
21	Kawi
22	Kopiri
23	Wanga
24	Ngapaka
25	Reihana Rewete
26	Patukiki
27	Te Huka
28	Te Kahu
29	Kopeka
30	Rerewa
31	Te Puni
32	Tuhoto
33	Pakewa
34	Popuka

Chiefs of Queen Charlotte's Sound

35	Toherama
36	Kewa
37	Watine
38	Te Tupe
39	Tiako
40	Te Raukawa
41	Te Orakaka
42	Tuterapouri
43	Te Tirarau
44	Ngaoranga
45	Hone
46	Inana
47	Kaparangi
48	Tapotuku

Names of Chiefs of Queen Charlotte's Sound

49	Huriwenua
50	Taukina
51	Twikau
52	Tunga
53	Te Rangowaka
54	Nga Kirikiri
55	Potiki
56	Nga Taraheke
57	Amara
58	Pikau
59	Te Uabiki
60	Maru
61	Karaki

Names of Chiefs at Rangitoto

62	Te Wetu
63	Pari
64	Taropiko
65	Te Putete
66	Te Rangiahua
67	Tahanui
68	Orokaka
69	Toitoi
70	Te Muiho
71	Te Tpukohu
72	Te Tihi
73	Huia
74	Nukumai

Chiefs of Kapiti

75	Oko he Manawatu &c Te Rauparaha
76	Katu
77	Te Wiwi
78	Topeora
79	Te Ruru
80	Malta
81	Kiharoa
82	Te Ruke
83	Toremi
84	Te Ahoaho
85	Taurangi
86	Kehu
87	Te Rakeke
88	Taumaru
89	Mahu
90	Te Ota
91	Paturoa
92	Te Tohe
93	Te Wetu
94	Tauheke
95	Pakau
96	Witiopai

Names of Chiefs at Waikanae and Neighbourhood

97	Reretauwangawanga
98	Witi
99	Te Patukikeu
100	Ngaurukau
101	Te Hike
102	Tuarname
103	Ngapuke
104	Te Patukakariki
105	Ngakaue
106	Pukerangiora
107	Kukutai
108	Koinaki
109	Karanga
110	Hohepa Matahau
111	Kiha
112	Wangarue
113	Hurenui
114	Te Uchi
115	Pehi
116	Keletakere

Chiefs of Wanganui

117	Te Anana
118	Tawito
119	Te Mawae
120	Rere
121	Te Tauri
122	Kore
123	Turoa
124	Taka
125	Kurawatira
126	Te Rangiwakaruru
127	Uripo
128	Te Hiko
129	Wakaterangi
130	Pakoro

Chiefs of Motu Ngarara

#	Name
131	Te Rangihuroa
132	Te Ohu

* Te Hiko o Te Range is a Chief of the Island of Mana (Cloudy Bay)

o Te Rauparaha is Principal chief of Kapiti and Cooks Straits

x Huriwenua Principal Chief of Queen Charlotte Sound

!! These Chiefs are the Principals of their tribes.

Henry Williams clerk

Geo. Tho. Clayton   Merchant

No.	Signed as	Probable name	Tribe	Hapu

Signed on 14 May 1840 [at Kapiti?], witnessed by Henry Williams and Octavius Hadfield

No.	Signed as	Probable name	Tribe	Hapu
75	Te Rauparaha	Te Rauparaha	Ngati Toa	Ngati Kimihia
76	Katu	Katu [Tamehana Te Rauparaha]	Ngati Toa	Ngati Kimihia
77	Te Wiwi	[Henare Matene] Te Whiwhi	Ngati Raukawa	Ngati Huia, Ngati Kikopiri
78	Topeora	Rangi Topeora [Kuini Wikitoria]	Ngati Toa	Ngati Kimihia, Ngati Te Maunu

Signed on 19 May 1840 [at Otaki?], witnessed by Henry Williams and Octavius Hadfield

No.	Signed as	Probable name	Tribe	Hapu
79	Te Ruru	[Aperahama?] Te Ruru	Ngati Raukawa	Ngati Huia
80	Matia	Matia	Ngati Raukawa	
81	Kiharoa	Kiharoa [Kihaoro]	Ngati Raukawa	Ngati Pane, Ngati Turanga
82	Te Puke	[Hori Kingi?] Te Puke	Ngati Raukawa	Ngati Waihurehia?
83	Toremi	[Horomona] Toremi	Ngati Raukawa, Rangitane	
84	Te Ahoaho	Te Ahoaho	Ngati Raukawa?	
85	Tahurangi	Tahurangi		
86	Kehu	Te Kehu [Te Whetu-o-te-ao?]	Te Ati Awa?	

Signed on 21 May 1840, at Tawhirihoe pa, between the Rangitikei and Manawatu Rivers, witnessed by Henry Williams and Octavius Hadfield

No.	Signed as	Probable name	Tribe	Hapu
87	Te Hakeke	Te Hakeke	Ngati Apa	
88	Taumaru	Taumaru	Ngati Apa	
89	Mahi	[Mohi] Mahi	Ngati Apa	

Signed on 26 May 1840, in the Manawatu district, witnessed by Henry Williams and Octavius Hadfield

No.	Signed as	Probable name	Tribe	Hapu
90	Te Ota	[Wi] Te Otaota?	Ngati Te Upokoiri	
91	Paturoa	[Rawiri?] Pateroa	Ngati Te Upokoiri	
92	Te Tohe	Te Tohi/Te Tohu?	Ngati Te Upokoiri?	
93	Te Wetu	Te Whetu	Ngati Raukawa?	Ngati Te lhiihi?
94	Tauheke	Taueki/Tauheke	Muaupoko, Ngati Apa	
95	Pakau	[Wi Hape] Pakau/Pakao?	Te Ati Awa	Ngati Te Whiti, Ngati Tawhirikura, Ngati Te Waiponga
96	Witiopai	Whitiopai		

Signed on 16 May 1840, at Waikanae, witnessed by Henry Williams and Octavius Hadfield

No.	Signed as	Probable name	Tribe	Hapu
97	Reretauwangawanga	Te Rere-ta-whangawhanga	Te Ati Awa	Manukorihi
98	Witi	Whiti [Wiremu Kingi Te Rangitake]	Te Ati Awa	Ngati Kura, Ngati Mutunga
99	Te Patukekeno	Te Patukekino/ Te Patukaikino?	Te Ati Awa?	
100	Ngaraurekau	Ngaraurekau	Te Ati Awa?	
101	Te Heke	Te Heke	Te Ati Awa?	
102	Tuamane	Tuamane		
103	Ngapuke	1. Ngapuke 2. Ngapaki?	1. Te Ati Awa? 2. Ngati Raukawa?	
104	Te Patukakariki	[Wiremu?] Te Patukakariki	Te Ati Awa, Ngati Toa?	Ngati Tuaho, Ngati Tihina?
105	Ngakaue	Ngakaue/Ngakawe?		
106	Pukerangiora	Pukerangiora		
107	Kukutai	Kukutai	Te Ati Awa?	
108	Koinaki	Koinaki	Te Ati Awa?	

No.	Signed as	Probable name	Tribe	Hapu
109	Raranga	Raranga	Te Ati Awa?	
110	Hohepa Matahau	Hohepa [Ripahau] Matahau	Ngati Raukawa?	
111	Kiha	Kiha	Te Ati Awa?	
112	Hiangarere	Hiangarere	Te Ati Awa?	
113	Hurerua	Hurerua	Te Ati Awa?	
114	Te Wehi	Te Wehi	Te Ati Awa?	
115	Pehi	Pehi	Te Ati Awa?	
116	Ketetakere	Ketetakere	Te Ati Awa?	

Signed on 23 May 1840, at Wanganui, witnessed by Henry Williams and Octavius Hadfield

No.	Signed as	Probable name	Tribe	Hapu
117	Te Anaua	[Hori Kingi] Te Anaua	Te Ati Haunui-a-Paparangi	Ngati Ruaka
118	Tawito	Tawhito [-o-te-rangi]	Te Ati	Ngati Ruaka
119	Te Mawae	Te Mawae	Te Ati Haunui-a-Paparangi	Ngati Ruaka
120	Rere	Rere-o-maki	1. Te Ati Haunui-a-Paparangi 2. Te Arawa	1. Ngati Ruaka
121	Te Tauri	[Wiremu?] Te Tauri	Ngati Tuwharetoa?	Ngati Te Rangi-ita?
122	Rore	Rore	Te Ati Haunui-a-Paparangi	
123	Turoa	[Te Peehi?] Turoa	Te Ati Haunui-a-Paparangi?	
124	Taka	Taka	Te Ati Haunui-a-Paparangi?	
125	Kurawatiia	Kurawatiia/Kurawhatiia?	Te Ati Haunui-a-Paparangi?	
126	Te Rangiwakarurua	Te Rangawakarurua/ Te Rangiwhakarurua?	Te Ati Haunui-a-Paparangi?	

Signed on 31 May 1840, at Wanganui, witnessed by Henry Williams and Octavius Hadfield

No.	Signed as	Probable name	Tribe	Hapu
127	Uripo	Uripo	Te Ati Haunui-a-Paparangi?	
128	Te Hiko	Te Hiko	Te Ati Haunui-a-Paparangi?	
129	Takaterangi	Taka Te Rangi/Takarangi	Te Ati Haunui-a-Paparangi?	
130	Pakoro	Pakoro [Turoa?]	Te Ati Haunui-a-Paparangi	

Signed on 4 June 1840, at Motungarara, witnessed by Henry Williams and George Thomas Clayton

No.	Signed as	Probable name	Tribe	Hapu
131	Te Rangihiroa	Te Rangihiroa	Ngati Toa	Ngati Te Maunu
132	Te Ohu	Te Ohu	Te Ati Awa?	

9. East Coast Treaty Copy

On 8 April 1840, Henry Williams delivered this copy to his brother William Williams at Turanga (Gisborne), where a CMS station had been established earlier in the year. William Williams was asked to get the agreement of chiefs from East Cape to Ahuriri (Napier). From 5 May on, the signatures of twenty-four chiefs from the Turanga district were put on this Treaty copy. According to the missionary, this represented almost the whole leadership of the district.

In the latter half of May, William Williams travelled up to East Cape, gathering further signatures. He had intended to visit tribal groups south of Turanga at the end of July or in August, but this plan was shelved. He had anticipated obtaining seventy to eighty signatures, but the final number was forty-one. He also failed to receive the agreement of the great chief Te Kani-a-Takirau, although he used the chief's house at Tolaga Bay as a place of assembly.

The names on this sheet were written across the sheet in groups of three.

No.	Signed as	Probable name	Tribe	Hapu

Signed from 5 to 12 May 1840, at Turanga, witnessed by William Williams, Henry Williams Jnr and George Clarke Jnr

1	Manutahi	[Kemara?] Manutahi	Rongowhakaata	Ngati Maru
2	Mangere	[Te Waaka] Mangere	Rongowhakaata	Ngati Kaipoho
3	Turangi Pototi	Paratene Turangi [Paratene Pototi]	Rongowhakaata	Ngai Tawhiri, Ngai Te Kete
4	Turuki	Te Turuki	Rongowhakaata	Ngati Maru
5	Maronui	Maronui	Rongowhakaata	Ngati Kaipoho
6	Te Urimaitai	Te Urimaitai	Ngati Porou	Te Aitanga-a-Hauiti
7	Te Kaingakiore	[Tamati?] Te Kaingakiore	Rongowhakaata	Ngai Tahupo, Ngati Kaipoho
8	Tauamanaia	Tauamanaia	Rongowhakaata	
9	Tuwarakihi	Tuwarakihi	Rongowhakaata?	
10	Eruera Wna	Eruera Wananga/Wuna?	Nga Puhi?	
11	Ma te nga Tukareaho	Matenga Tukareaho	Ngati Rakai-paka	from Nuhaka/Wairoa
12	Turoa	[Raniera?] Turoa	Rongowhakaata?	
13	Ko Paia te Rangi	[Wiremu Kingi] Paia Te Rangi	Rongowhakaata	Ngati Maru
14	Tuhura	Tuhura	Rongowhakaata	Ngati Maru
15	Mahuika	[Wi?] Mahuika	Te Aitanga-a-Mahaki	Nga Potiki
16	Tutapaturangi	Tutapaturangi/ Tu-te-pakihi-rangi?	Ngati Kahungunu?	Te Aitanga-a-whare, from Mahia?
17	Te Hore	Te Hore	Te Aitanga-a-Mahaki/ Rongowhakaata	
18	Te Panepane	Te Panepane	Te Aitanga-a-Mahaki/ Rongowhakaata	
19	Titirangi [Rawiri]	Titirangi	Te Aitanga-a-Mahaki	Ngati Wahia, Ngati Matepu
20	Te Pakaru [Enoka]	Te Pakaru	Te Aitanga-a-Mahaki	Te Whanau-a-Taupara
21	Te Wareana	[Te Poihipi?] Te Wareana	Te Aitanga-a- Mahaki/ Rongowhakaata?	
22	Tawarau	Tawarau	Te Aitanga-a-Mahaki, Te Whanau-a-Kai	Te Whanau-a-Taupara,
23	Wakahingatu	Wakahingatu	Rongowhakaata	
24	A e ra Te Eke	Rawiri Te Eke	Te Aitanga-a-Hauiti	Ngati Oneone

314   AN ILLUSTRATED HISTORY OF THE TREATY OF WAITANGI

Mark of — [1] Manutahi / Turanga	Mark of — [2] Mangere / Turanga	Mark of — [3] Pototi / Turanga
Mark of — [4] Turuki / Turanga	Mark of — [5] Maronui / Turanga	Mark of — [6] Te Urimaitai / Turanga
Mark of — [7] Te Kaingakiore / Turanga	Mark of toua [8] Tauamanaia / Turanga	Mark of — [9] Tuwarakihi / Turanga
E ... Wina [10] Turanga	Ma te nga te Kaiwaho [11] Wairoa	Turoa [12] Turanga
Ko Pai a te rangi [13] Turanga	Mark of — [14] Tuhura / Turanga	Mark of — [15] Mahuika / Turanga
Mark of — [16] Tutapaturangi / Teitangaware / Turanga	Mark of — [17] Te Hore / Turanga	Mark of — [18] Te Panepane / Turanga
Mark of — [19] Titirangi / Turanga	Mark of — [20] Te Pakaru / Turanga	Mark of — [21] Te Wareana / Turanga
Mark of — [22] Tawarau / Turanga	Mark of — [23] Wakahingatu / Turanga	Mark of — [24] Te Eke / Turanga
Mark of — [25] Rangiuia / Uawa	Mark of — [26] Parekahika / Uawa	Mark of — [27] Te Tore / Ahuriri
Mark of — [28] Te Mimiopaoa / Waiapu	Mark of — [29] Rangiwakatataua / Waiapu	Mark of — [30] Tutaefa / Waiapu
Mark of — [31] Rangiwai / Waiapu	Mark of — [32] Takatua / Waiapu	Mark of — [33] Te Kaumoterangi / Waiapu
Mark of — [34] Kakatarau / Waiapu	Mark of — [35] David Rangikatia / Waiapu	Mark of — [36] Korauruterangi / Waiapu
Mark of — [37] Awarau / Waiapu	Mark — [38] Tamauwakanehua / Tokomaru	Mark of — [39] Te Potae / Tokomaru
Mark of — [40] Tamitere / Tokomaru	Mark of — [41] Te Mokonoronga / Tokomaru	

No.	Signed as	Probable name	Tribe	Hapu

Signed on 16–17 May 1840, at Uawa (Tolaga Bay), witnessed by William Williams and George Clarke Jnr

No.	Signed as	Probable name	Tribe	Hapu
25	Rangiuia	[Nopera] Te Rangiuia	Ngati Porou	Te Aitanga-a-Hauiti
26	Parekahika	[Hori?] Parekahika	Ngati Porou	Te Aitanga-a-Hauiti

Signed at Uawa or Waiapu, witnessed by William Williams and George Clarke Jnr

No.	Signed as	Probable name	Tribe	Hapu
27	Te Tore	Te Tore	Ngati Matepu?	from Ahuriri

Signed from 25 to 31 May 1840, at Whakawhitira Waiapu, witnessed by William Williams and George Clarke Jnr

No.	Signed as	Probable name	Tribe
28	Te Mimiopaoa	Te Mimi-o-Paoa	Ngati Porou, Rongowhakaata
29	Rangiwakatatae	Rangiwakataetae	Ngati Porou
30	Tutaepa	Tutaepa	Ngati Porou
31	Rangiwai	Rangiwai	Ngati Porou
32	Takatua/Pakatua	Takatua/Pakatua?	Ngati Porou
33	Te Kauruoterangi	Te Kauru-o-te-rangi	Ngati Porou
34	Kakatarau	Kakatarau	Ngati Porou

Signed about 1 June 1840, at Rangitukia Waiapu, witnessed by William Williams and George Clarke Jnr

No.	Signed as	Probable name	Tribe
35	David Rangikatia	Rawiri Rangikatia	Ngati Porou
36	Koiauruterangi	Koiauru-te-rangi?	Ngati Porou
37	Awarau	Awarau	Ngati Porou

Signed on 9 June 1840, at Tokomaru, witnessed by William Williams and George Clarke Jnr

No.	Signed as	Probable name	Tribe	Hapu
38	Tamaiwakanehu	[Tamati Waaka] Tama-i-whakanehua-i-te-rangi	Ngati Porou	Te Whanau-a-Ruataupare, Te Whanau-a-Te-Ao
39	Te Potae	[Enoka] Te Potae-aute	Ngati Porou	Te Whanau-a-Ruataupare, Te Whanau-a-Te-Poriro
40	Tamitere	[Te Keepa?] Tamitere	Ngati Porou	Te Whanau-a-Ruataupare
41	Te Mokopuorongo	[Paratene?] Te Mokopuorongo	Ngati Porou	Te Whanau-a-Ruataupare

APPENDIX THREE

Iwi Locations, 2001

The map provides an approximate indication of where iwi are located. Iwi include those who have 1,000 or more affiliate responses, based on the 2001 Census of Population and Dwellings. Responses may include identification with more than one iwi.

SOURCE: STATISTICS NEW ZEALAND, *NEW ZEALAND OFFICIAL YEARBOOK 2002*, AUCKLAND, 2002

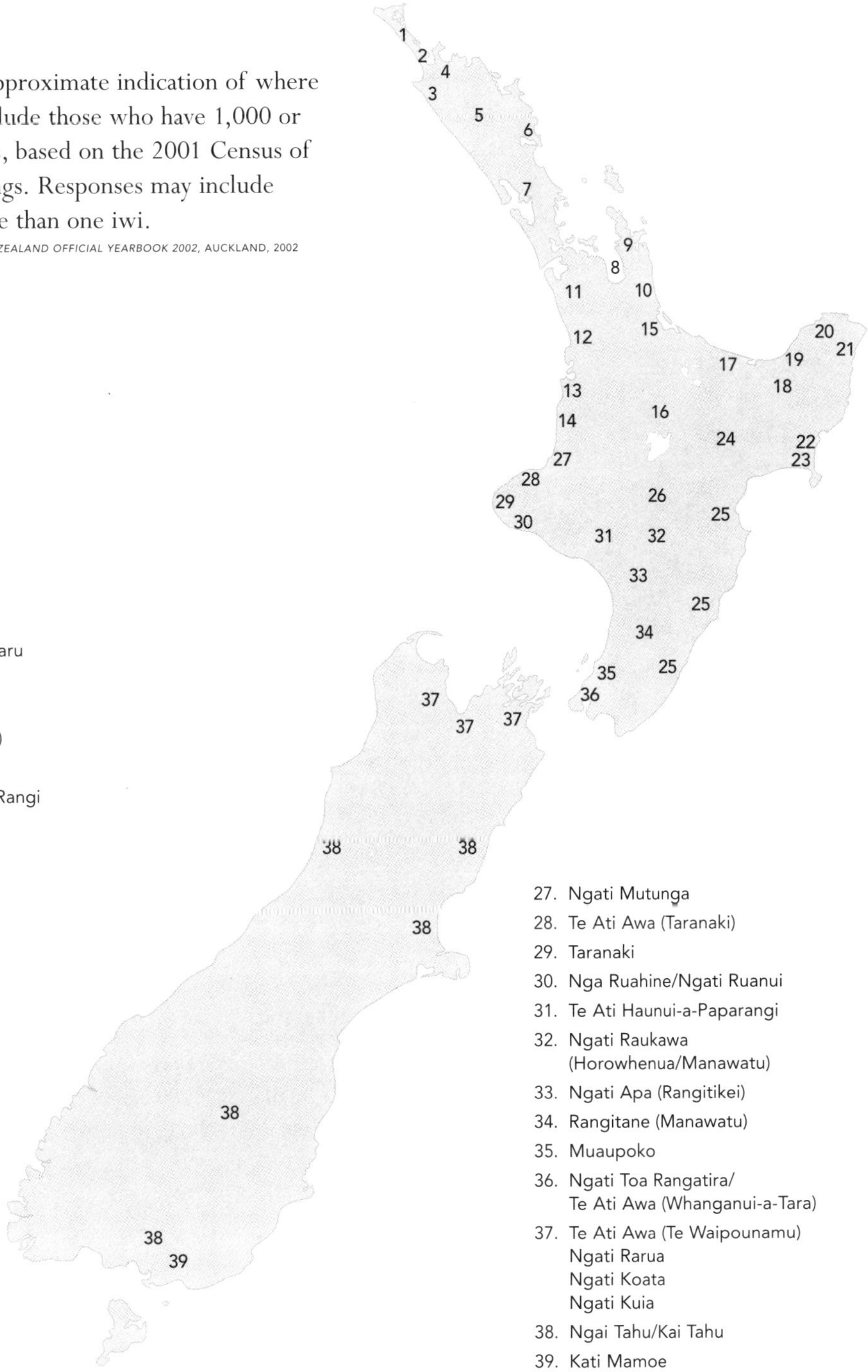

1. Ngati Kuri
2. Te Aupouri
3. Te Rarawa
4. Ngati Kahu
5. Nga Puhi
6. Ngati Wai
7. Ngati Whatua
8. Ngati Paoa
9. Ngati Whanaunga
10. Ngati Tamatera/Ngati Maru
11. Ngati Haua (Waikato)
12. Waikato
13. Ngati Raukawa (Waikato)
14. Ngati Maniapoto
15. Ngati Ranginui/Ngai Te Rangi
16. Te Arawa
17. Ngati Awa
18. Whakatohea
19. Ngai Tai
20. Whanau-a-Apanui
21. Ngati Porou
22. Rongowhakaata/
    Te Aitanga-a-Mahaki/
    Ngai Tamanuhiri
23. Rongomaiwahine
24. Tuhoe
25. Ngati Kahungunu
26. Ngati Tuwharetoa

27. Ngati Mutunga
28. Te Ati Awa (Taranaki)
29. Taranaki
30. Nga Ruahine/Ngati Ruanui
31. Te Ati Haunui-a-Paparangi
32. Ngati Raukawa
    (Horowhenua/Manawatu)
33. Ngati Apa (Rangitikei)
34. Rangitane (Manawatu)
35. Muaupoko
36. Ngati Toa Rangatira/
    Te Ati Awa (Whanganui-a-Tara)
37. Te Ati Awa (Te Waipounamu)
    Ngati Rarua
    Ngati Koata
    Ngati Kuia
38. Ngai Tahu/Kai Tahu
39. Kati Mamoe

APPENDIX THREE: IWI LOCATIONS, 2001   317

APPENDIX FOUR

Maori Land, 1860–1939

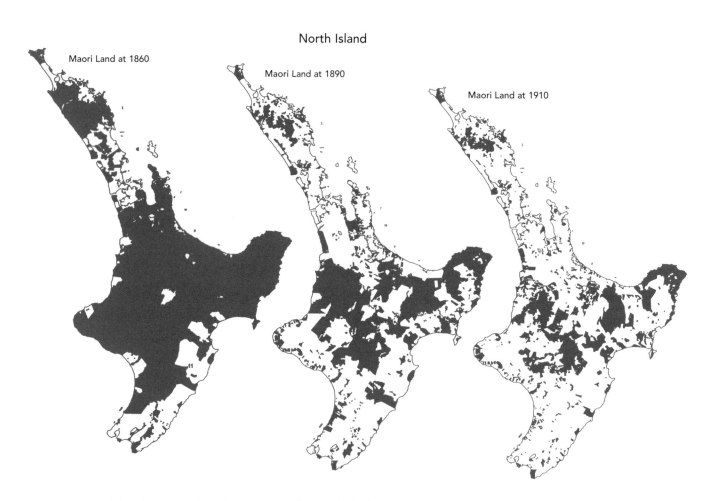

These five maps chart the alienation of Maori land (shown in black) from 1860 to 1939.

Maori Land at 1860: 1840–65 was the main period of Crown pre-emption purchases. In addition to the areas shown here in white, the Crown purchased a further 380,000 acres (152,000 hectares) between 1860 and 1865, mainly in Northland and Lower Waikato, and the Wellington provincial government purchased the Rangitikei-Manawatu block. Confiscations were proclaimed in Waikato, Taranaki, Bay of Plenty and the East Coast in 1864–65.

Maori Land at 1890: 1865–90 was the main period of Crown and private purchase of Maori land under the Native Land Acts.

Maori Land at 1910: 1891–99 was the main period of alienation under the Liberal governments, with Crown pre-emption largely restored. Relatively small areas were sold under the Maori Land Councils (Boards) between 1900 and 1909.

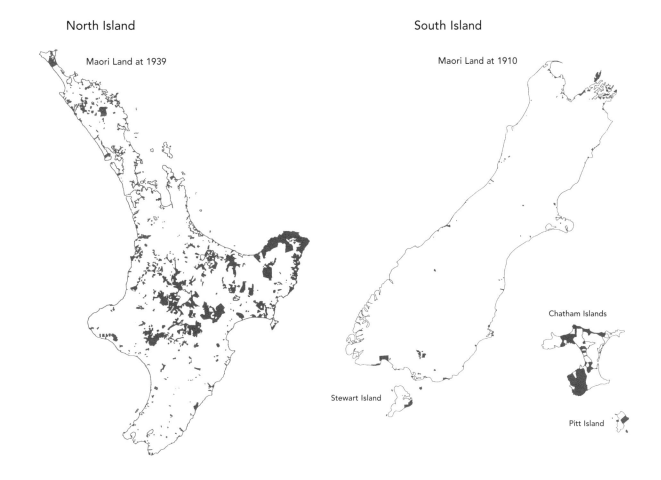

Maori Land at 1939 (North Island): About 3.5 million acres (1.4 million hectares) were sold between 1910 and 1939, some 2.3 million acres (920,000 hectares) through the Maori Land Boards in the period 1910–30 and other portions by the Maori Trustee and other agencies. The map does not appear to show perpetual leases as Maori Land.

Maori Land at 1910 (South Island):
1. The entire South Island and Stewart Island had been purchased by 1865, except for 175,000 acres (70,000 hectares) of reserves and land excluded from sale.
2. This remnant was diminished by the purchase of Taitapu (44,000 acres or 17,600 hectares) in north-west Nelson before 1910.
3. The large reserves in Southland and Stewart Island shown here, and other small reserves, were created under the South Island Landless Natives Act 1906, which added 112,000 acres (44,800 hectares) to the total, but most of it was of poor quality and difficult to access.
4. 45,000 acres (18,000 hectares) of South Island reserves were sold between 1910 and 1939.

SOURCE: BASED ON *NATIONAL OVERVIEW*, RANGAHAUA WHANUI SERIES, WAITANGI TRIBUNAL, WELLINGTON, 1997, VOL.II, PP.X–XIV

APPENDIX FIVE

Waitangi Tribunal Timeline

Year	Tribunal History and Claims		Legislation
1974			14 March 1974 – draft Bill entitled *Treaty of Waitangi Bill* introduced into Parliment by Matiu Rata, Minister of Maori Affairs – deferred several times, then languished.
1975	First Chairperson – Chief Judge Kenneth Gillanders Scott		***Treaty of Waitangi Act 1975*** establishes the Waitangi Tribunal, and enables claims to be brought in respect of actions of the Crown in breach of the Treaty since 1975. Provides that the Chief Judge of the Maori Land Court is also the Chairperson of the Waitangi Tribunal.
1976	Founding members of the first Waitangi Tribunal – Laurence Henry Southwick and Graham Latimer		12 July 1976 – Cabinet deferred a decision on the recommendation that it should approve the implementation of the *Treaty of Waitangi Act 1975* through the establishment of the Waitangi Tribunal. 8 November 1976 – As an application had been lodged under the Treaty of Waitangi Act 1975 to have a matter relating to fishing regulations considered by the Tribunal, Cabinet decided that the Tribunal should be constituted. 13 December 1976 – Cabinet approved for reference to Caucus that the Governor General appoint two members on the recommendation of the Minister of Maori Affairs and the Minister of Justice in order to constitute the first Waitangi Tribunal.
1978	WAI 1	Claim by J. P. Hawke and others of Ngati Whatua concerning the Fisheries Regulations Report	
	WAI 2	Waiau Pa Power Station Claim Report	
1980	Second Chairperson – Chief Judge Edward Taihakurei Durie		
1983	WAI 6	Motunui-Waitara Claim Report *Outcome: Motunui-Waitara Sewerage Treatment plant and long outfall completed.*	
1984	WAI 4	Kaituna River Claim Report *Outcome: Rotorua Sewerage Scheme completed.*	

320   AN ILLUSTRATED HISTORY OF THE TREATY OF WAITANGI

1985	WAI 8	Manukau Claim Report	***The Treaty of Waitangi Amendment Act 1985***
	Outcome:	*Implementation of the Manukau Report recommendations completed.*	empowers the Waitangi Tribunal to hear claims relating to actions of the Crown since 6 February 1840 when the Treaty of Waitangi was signed.
	Outcome:	*Recommendations influence the Resource Management Act 1991.*	
			Claims start flooding in.
	WAI 12	Motiti Island Claim Report	
	WAI 19	Claim Relating to Maori 'Privilege' Report	
		Waitangi Tribunal membership increased to six including the Chairperson.	

1986	WAI 11	Te Reo Maori Claim Report	***State-Owned Enterprise Act 1986***
	Outcome:	*The Maori Language Act 1987.*	Section 9 states: 'Nothing in this Act shall permit the Crown to act in any manner that is inconsistent with the principles of the Treaty of Waitangi.'
	Outcome:	*Te Taura Whiri i te Reo Maori — the Maori Language Commission established 1987.*	
	Outcome:	*Maori recognised as an official language of Aotearoa / New Zealand.*	The Court of Appeal hears the 'SOE Lands case', and enunciates Treaty principles.
	Outcome:	*Te Upoko o te Ika — the birth of iwi radio-granted licences by the Ministry of Commerce 1987 after broadcasting on a trial basis since 1983.*	
	WAI 18	Lake Taupo Fishing Rights Report	

1987	WAI 9	Orakei Claim Report	***The Maori Language Act 1987***
	Outcome:	*Orakei Act 1991 — housing and $3 million cash.*	establishes Te Taura Whiri i te Reo Maori, the Maori Language Commission, and recognises Maori as an official language of New Zealand.
	WAI 10	Waiheke Island Claim Report	
	Outcome:	*1990 transfer of land, stock and finance, at an overall cost of $1.03 million, to Ngati Paoa Development Trust Board.*	
	WAI 15	Te Weehi Claim to Customary Fishing Rights Report	
	WAI 25	Claim Relating to Maori Representation on Auckland Regional Authority Report	
		First Deputy Chairperson — Deputy Chief Judge Ashley McHugh	

1988	WAI 22	Muriwhenua Fishing Claim Report	***The Treaty of Waitangi (State Enterprises) Act 1988***
	Outcome:	*The Maori Fisheries Act 1989 establishes Te Ohu Kai Moana — Maori Fisheries Commission (later Treaty of Waitangi Fisheries Commission) to distribute $170 million in assets.*	provides that where former SOE land sold to private parties is subsequently found to have been acquired by the Crown in breach of the Treaty principles, the Tribunal is empowered to order the repurchase of the land for return to Maori claimants.
	Outcome:	*Maori control over 50 per cent of New Zealand's total fisheries.*	
	WAI 17	Mangonui Sewerage Claim Report.	
		Waitangi Tribunal membership increased to sixteen plus the Chairperson.	

1989	WAI 83	Report on the Waikawa Block	***The Crown Forest Assets Act 1989***
		Waitangi Tribunal research funding assisted Tainui to progress their claim to a settlement of $170 million through direct negotiations with the Crown.	provides that rentals from forested lands licensed to forest companies are held by the Crown Forestry Rental Trust. Income from the invested funds is used to research Treaty claims. If the land is found to have been acquired in breach of the Treaty principles, the Tribunal may order the return of the land, the accumulated rentals and interests in the forestry.

1989 cont'd

Crown Forestry Rental Trust (CFRT) formed and becomes a major research funds provider for Treaty claims.

The Maori Fisheries Act 1989
provides the first fisheries settlement of $170 million.

1990

WAI 3   Report on Proposed Discharge of Sewerage at Welcome Bay

WAI 5   Report on Imposition of Land Tax

WAI 13   Report on Fisheries Regulations

WAI 14   Report on Tokaanu Building Sections

WAI 34   Report on Proposed Sewerage Scheme at Kakanui

WAI 103   Report on Roadman's Cottage, Mahia

WAI 26, 150   Claims Concerning the Allocation of Radio Frequencies
Outcome: Te Mango Paho – the Maori Language Broadcasting Funding Agency – established 1990.

WAI 32   Ngati Rangiteaorere Claim
Outcome: Te Ngae Farm returned 1993/4 and $0.76 million.

Education Amendment Act 1990
empowers the Waitangi Tribunal to make binding recommendations for the return of certain education lands to Maori.

NZ Railways Corporation Restructuring Act 1990
empowers the Waitangi Tribunal to make binding recommendations for the return of certain railway lands to Maori.

1991

WAI 27   The Ngai Tahu Report, Vols 1–3
Outcome: Te Runanga o Ngai Tahu established 1996/7 to receive the Ngai Tahu settlement.
Outcome: Ngai Tahu Claims Settlement Act 1998.

WAI 27   Supplementary Report on Ngai Tahu Legal Personality

WAI 45   Kaimaumau Interim Report

WAI 202   Report on the Tamaki Maori Development Authority Claim

WAI 261   Interim Report on the Auckland Hospital Endowments Claim

Orakei Act 1991
provides housing and $3 million cash, constituting full and final settlement in relation to the Orakei block.

Resource Management Act 1991
Section 6(e): a requirement to recognise and provide for the relationship of Maori and their culture and traditions with their ancestral lands, water, sites, waahi tapu and other taonga.
Section 7: a requirement to have particular regard to Kaitiakitanga.
Section 8: a requirement to take into account the principles of the Treaty of Waitangi.

1992

WAI 264   Report on Auckland Railway Lands
WAI 264   Report on Wellington Railway Lands
Outcome: Interim settlements.

WAI 119   Mohaka River Report

WAI 67   Report on Oriwa 1B3 Block

WAI 264   Report on Railway Land at Waikanae

WAI 276, 72, 121   Interim Report on Sylvia Park and Auckland Crown Asset Disposals

WAI 321   Appointments to the Treaty of Waitangi Fisheries Commission Report

WAI 307   The Fisheries Settlement Report
Outcome: Tribunal scrutiny of the Fisheries Claims Act 1992.

The Treaty of Waitangi (Fisheries Claims) Settlement Act 1992
confirms the 'Sealord' deal, and other aspects of the settlement of commercial fisheries claims. The Tribunal is prevented from hearing any further Maori claims in respect of commercial fisheries.

The Treaty of Waitangi Amendment Act 1992
prevents the Tribunal from making recommendations over private land (other than former SOE land regulated by the 1988 Act). Remedies for breaches of Treaty principles are to be derived only from Crown property and public revenue.

---

322   AN ILLUSTRATED HISTORY OF THE TREATY OF WAITANGI

1992 cont'd	WAI 27	The Ngai Tahu Sea Fisheries Report	The Office of Treaty Settlements (OTS) formed from the previous Treaty of Waitangi Policy Unit (TOWPU). OTS conducts negotiations with Maori claimants on levels of remedy. Treaty breaches need to be demonstrated but not necessarily via a Waitangi Tribunal hearing.
	Outcome:	*Maori receive 50 per cent share in the Sealords Fishing Company and 20 per cent of new quota species.*	
	WAI 38	Te Roroa Report	
	Outcome:	*Treaty of Waitangi Amendment Act 1992.*	
	Outcome:	*Te Roroa in negotiation with the Crown after lengthy delay.*	

1993	WAI 33	Pouakani Report	
	Outcome:	*Pouakani settlement 1999/2000 of $2.65 million.*	
	WAI 35	Maori Development Corporation Report	
	Outcome:	*Transfer of Crown shares in the Maori Development Corporation to the Poutama Trust completed 1999.*	
	WAI 212	Te Ika Whenua – Energy Assets Report	
	WAI 212	Interim Report on the Rangitaiki and Wheao Rivers Claim	
	WAI 304	Ngawha Geothermal Resource Report	
	WAI 153	Preliminary Report on the Te Arawa Representative Geothermal Resource Claims	
	WAI 167	Interim Report and Recommendation in Respect of the Whanganui River Claim	
	WAI 264	Report on South Auckland Railway Lands	
	WAI 273	Report on Tapuwae 1B and 4 Incorporation	
	WAI 322	Report on the Tuhuru Claim	
		Second Deputy Chairperson – Deputy Chief Judge Norman Smith	

1994	WAI 315	Te Maunga Railways Land Report	The Crown's 'Proposals for Settlement of Treaty of Waitangi Claims' (commonly known as the 'fiscal envelope'). The Crown acknowledges that historical grievances arising from Treaty breaches need to be remedied, but proposes to remedy them for a total of $1 billion spread over ten years.
	Outcome:	*Te Maunga Railway Land settlement 1996/7.*	
	WAI 413	Maori Electoral Option Report	
	Outcome:	*Increased Crown funding to increase the number of Maori registered on the electoral rolls.*	
	WAI 176	Report on Broadcasting Claim	

1995	WAI 84	The Turangi Township Report	***Waikato-Raupatu Claims Settlement Act 1995*** prevents the Waitangi Tribunal from hearing Waikato-Raupatu Claims.
	WAI 84	The Turangi Remedies Report	
	Outcome:	*Ngati Turangitukia Claims Settlement Act 1999.*	
	Outcome:	*Settlement of $5 million.*	
		The Waitangi Tribunal was prepared to use its binding powers for the first time to order the return of State-Owned Enterprise land after the failure of the Crown and claimants to agree on a level of settlement for the established breaches. Subsequently, the matter was settled.	
	WAI 143	The Taranaki Report: Kaupapa Tuatahi	
	Outcome:	*Heads of Agreement – Ngati Tama $14.5 million.*	
		Heads of Agreement – Ngati Ruanui $41 million.	

APPENDIX FIVE: WAITANGI TRIBUNAL TIMELINE   323

1995 cont'd	*Heads of Agreement – Ngati Mutunga*	
	$14.5 million.	
	Heads of Agreement – Te Atiawa $34 million.	
	WAI 27 The Ngai Tahu Ancillary Claims Report	
	Outcome: The Ngai Tahu settlement in 1998 of	
	$170 million.	
	WAI 55 Te Whanganui-a-Orotu Report	
	WAI 55 The Whanganui-a-Orotu Report on	
	Remedies	
	WAI 449 Kiwifruit Marketing Report	
	Outcome: The Waitangi Tribunal did not uphold the	
	claimants' case.	
1997	Rangahaua Whanui Series – National Overview	
	(3 Volumes) Report commissioned by Waitangi	
	Tribunal, written by Dr Alan Ward	
	Outcome: 15 casebook inquiry districts established.	
	Outcome: Criteria for prioritising claims established.	
	WAI 45 Muriwhenua Land Report	
	Outcome: Muriwhenua in negotiation with the Crown.	
	Outcome: Ngati Kahu o Whangaroa in negotiation with	
	the Crown.	
1998	WAI 414 Te Whanau o Waipareira Report	**The Ngai Tahu Claims Settlement Act 1998** provides for a settlement package valued at $170 million, plus a relativity clause.
	Outcome: Social Welfare funding policy to include non-iwi	
	groups.	
	WAI 212 Te Ika Whenua Rivers Report	**The Treaty of Waitangi Amendment Act 1998** provides that a Judge or retired Judge of the High Court or the Chief Judge of the Maori Land Court can preside as Chairperson of the Waitangi Tribunal.
1999	WAI 46 The Ngati Awa Raupatu Report	**Ngati Turangitukia Claims Settlement Act 1999** provides full and final settlement to the value of $5 million.
	Outcome: Heads of Agreement – Ngati Awa $42.39 million.	
	WAI 167 The Whanganui River Report	
	WAI 718 The Wananga Capital Establishment Report	
	WAI 776 Radio Spectrum Management and	
	Development Interim Report	
	WAI 776 The Radio Spectrum Management and	
	Development Final Report	
	3rd Deputy Chairperson – Chief Judge Joseph Victor	
	Williams	
2000	WAI 674 Kaipara:	869 Claims registered with the Waitangi Tribunal to 1 September 2000.
	Outcome: Te Uri o Hau Settlement.	
	WAI 789 The Mokai School Report	The Minister in Charge of Treaty Negotiations enunciates Treaty claim settlement principles.
	Justice Durie recognised for 20 years of service to the	
	Waitangi Tribunal as Chairperson.	

SOURCE: WAITANGI TRIBUNAL/TE ROOPU WHAKAMANA I TE TIRITI O WAITANGI, TWENTY-FIVE YEARS OF SERVICE, 1975–2000, WELLINGTON, 2000.
REPRODUCED WITH THE PERMISSION OF THE WAITANGI TRIBUNAL.

A Note on Text, Illustrations and Sources

Text

This book is written for the general reader, and accessibility has been the priority. Maori words in common use are assumed to be understood; for less common words, explanations or translations are given. Honorifics and titles are generally avoided. Footnotes and references have not been included; the research base for this book is outlined below, and in the bibliography. A list of quotation sources follows. Maps and tables can be accessed through the index, where abbreviations used in the text are also identified.

Illustrations

The contribution of organisations and individuals who supplied illustrations is gratefully acknowledged. Copyright-holders and owners are identified alongside the illustrations. Every attempt has been made to contact copyright-holders; the publishers would be glad to hear from anyone with further information.

Captions have been based on information supplied with the illustration, and from supplementary research. For contemporary images, in particular, full information is not always available. Further details would again be welcome.

Photographs obtained from newspaper files and archives are not always dated; such photographs are placed in period, but no speculative date has been added. It should be noted that the *Dominion Post* is sometimes credited with photographs that appeared in either the *Dominion* or the *Evening Post*. This acknowledgement refers to the current supplier and copyright-holder of these photographs, not the place of first publication.

Sources

This book is based on research over thirty years. The key sources for the nine chapters are outlined below.

Chapters One to Four cover the nineteenth century. The basis for these is Claudia Orange, *The Treaty of Waitangi*, 1987. This publication derives from a longer study: 'The Treaty of Waitangi: A Study of its Making, Interpretation and Role in New Zealand History', PhD thesis, University of Auckland, 1984.

The main sources used are the government records at Archives New Zealand, and a multitude of private papers and journals held by the Alexander Turnbull Library and other libraries. Contemporary publications, including newspapers, provided additional insights. In the last twenty to thirty years, modern historical research has added valuable new information. This has been particularly helpful in providing profiles of historical figures (as in *The Dictionary of New Zealand Biography*, 1990–2000), in giving reliable historical background or detail (as in James Belich, *Making Peoples*, 1996, and *The New Zealand Wars*, 1986), and in contributing to scholarly assessments of the Treaty itself (as in Peter Adams, *Fatal Necessity*, 1977, and Paul McHugh, *The Maori Magna Carta*, 1991).

Chapters Five to Eight deal with the twentieth century, and **Chapter Nine** with the twenty-first century. Sources such as parliamentary records (*New Zealand Parliamentary Debates, Appendices to the Journals of the House of Representatives*) have continued to be useful. These chapters have greatly benefited from the research stimulated by, or associated with, the Waitangi Tribunal's work. The three-volume *National Overview*, Rangahaua Whanui Series (1997), overseen by Alan Ward, has provided essential information for all chapters. The Tribunal's reports and its regular publication, *Te Manutukutuku*, have been a major source.

Government reports and papers, many not in published form, have been valuable. A flood of publications has revealed the country's history in greater detail; this study draws particularly on I. H. Kawharu (ed.), *Waitangi* (1989), Jane Kelsey, *A Question of Honour?* (1990), W. L. Renwick, *The Treaty Now* (1990), F. M. Brookfield, *Waitangi and Indigenous Rights* (1999), Alan Ward, *An Unsettled History* (1999), Andrew Sharp and Paul McHugh (eds), *Histories, Power and Loss* (2001), and Janine Hayward, *Local Government and the Treaty of Waitangi* (2003). The media, especially the daily press throughout the country, have been a significant source for revealing the impact of events as they have occurred.

For all the chapters, research has widened to take in the wealth of legal material now available, including the *Maori Law Review*, and numerous articles, monographs and published papers. These have informed the book's account of the ongoing development of Treaty policy and related issues. Websites such as www.waitangi-tribunal.govt.nz and www.ots.govt.nz have expanded the information base; interviews with key players have clarified essential points.

Quotation sources

P.10. 'The natives of New Zealand ...': P. Harvard-Williams (ed.), *Marsden and the New Zealand Mission: Sixteen Letters*, Dunedin, 1961, pp.36, 41. **P.12. 'As far as has been ascertained ...':** Busby to Colonial Secretary New South Wales, 31 October 1835, Busby dispatches, qMS, Alexander Turnbull Library. **P.24. 'In this translation ...':** Hugh Carleton, *The Life of Henry Williams, Archdeacon of Waimate*, 2 vols, Auckland, 1874; Vol.2, p.12. **P.28. 'In front of the platform':** William Colenso, *The Authentic and Genuine History of the Signing of the Treaty of Waitangi*, Wellington, 1890; reprint 1971, pp.15–16. **'their ears adorned ...':** Felton Mathew, Journal, 5 February 1840, Papers 1840–48, NZ MS 78–79, Auckland City Library. **'Her Majesty the Queen ...':** this account in Colenso's *History*, pp.16–17, is taken almost verbatim from pencil notes made during the meeting, in 'Notebook', Colenso Papers, X, Hawke's Bay Museum. **PP.29–30. 'Rewa said ...':** This account of the Waitangi signing is summarised from Colenso, *History*, pp.17–28. **P.31. 'There was considerable excitement ...':** Carleton, *Williams*, Vol.2, p.14. **PP.32–34. 'The Governor says ...':** This account of the Waitangi signing is from Colenso, *History*, pp.32–35. **P.34. 'I assured them [the Maori] ...':** Hobson to Gipps, 5–6 February 1840, *British Parliamentary Papers: Colonies New Zealand*, Vol.3, 1835–42, (311), pp.8–9. **PP.36–37. 'We are glad to see the ...':** This account of the Hokianga signing is based on Enclosure 2 in Shortland to Stanley, 18 January 1845, *British Parliamentary Papers: Colonies New Zealand*, Vol.4, 1843–45, (108), pp.9–11, and Richard Taylor Journal, 12 February 1840, MS 302, Auckland Museum. **'repeated assurances ...':** J. Hobbs to William Martin, 22 October 1847, in William Martin, *England and the New Zealanders*, Auckland, 1847, pp. 73–74. **P.38. 'The shadow of the land ...':** This account of the Kaitaia signing is based on Enclosure 1 in Shortland to Stanley, 18 January 1845, *British Parliamentary Papers: Colonies New Zealand*, Vol.4, 1843–45, (108), pp.9–11. No source has been found for Nopera's words as he spoke them in Maori. Various words have been suggested for the word 'shadow': wairua, atarangi and atakau. **P.43. 'came on board ...':** Bunbury to Hobson, 28 June 1840, Enclosure 10 in Hobson to Secretary of State for Colonies, 15 October 1840, *British Parliamentary Papers: Colonies New Zealand*, Vol.3, 1835–42, (311), pp.108–9. **P.49. 'From a distance ...':** William Swainson, *Auckland, the Capital of New Zealand, and the Country Adjacent*, London/Auckland, 1853, p.142. **P.53. 'I ask you pakehas ...':** *Wellington Spectator*, 10 July 1844. **P.59. 'damp the ardour ...'** J. C. Richmond to J. M. Richmond, 13 August 1851 in G. H. Scholefield (ed.), *The Richmond-Atkinson Papers*, Wellington, 1960, Vol.1, p.103. **P.61. 'This is the commencement ...':** 'A Compendium of Official Documents Relative to Native Affairs in the South Island Compiled by Alexander Mackay', Wellington, 1872–73, Vol.1, p.228. **P.62.** Lady [Mary] Martin, *Our Maoris*, London, 1884. **P.63.** William Martin, *The Taranaki Question*, Auckland, 1860, p.82. **PP.64–67.** The account of the Kohimarama conference is based on: *The Maori Messenger. Te Karere Maori*, 14 July 1860; Register of Proceedings of Native Chiefs at Kohimarama, MA 23/10, Archives New Zealand; Claudia Orange, 'The Covenant of Kohimarama: A Ratification of the Treaty of Waitangi', *New Zealand Journal of History*, Vol.14, no.1 (1980). **P.67. 'submission without reserve ...':** *AJHR*, 1891, G-1, pp.xi–xii. **P.82. 'the abandonment of the system ...':** *NZPD*, 1864–66, p.205. **P.83. 'Numerous witnesses bear ...':** *AJHR*, 1891, G-1, pp.xi–xii.

P.85. 'The seas around their coasts ...': William Colenso, 'On the Maori Races of New Zealand', *Transactions and Proceedings of the New Zealand Institute*, Vol.1 1868 (2nd ed. 1875), p.345. **P.86.** Edward Shortland, *Traditions and Superstitions of the New Zealanders*, London, 1856, reprinted 1980, p.214, in *The Treaty of Waitangi and Maori Fisheries/Mataitai: Nga Tikanga Maori me te Tiriti o Waitangi*, Law Commission, Wellington, 1989, p.33. **P.87. 'On the West Coast ...':** Resident Magistrate Kaipara to Attorney-General, William Swainson, Archives New Zealand IA 1855/202, in *The Treaty of Waitangi and Maori Fisheries*, p.145. **P.88. 'evil consequences ...':** Judge Fenton in the Hauraki Native Land Court minute book 4, folio 236 (printed judgement: p.11), cited in R.P. Boast, *The Foreshore*, Rangahaua Whanui National theme Q, Waitangi Tribunal, Wellington, 1996. **'Nothing in this Act ...':** Fish Protection Act 1877, *New Zealand Statutes*, 1877, p.354. **P.89. 'The Natives occasionally ...',** *AJHR*,1869, F-7, p.7. **'plundering all the oysters ...':** *NZPD*, Vol.27,1877, p.65. **P.90. 'Now, with regard to the land ...':** *AJHR*, 1885 G-1. In *The Treaty of Waitangi and Maori Fisheries*, pp. 47, 146, 147. **P.91. 'The Natives at Waitaki ...':** *AJHR*, 1891, G-7a, pp.6–7. **'... along the coast of Otago ...':** *NZPD*, Vol.65, 1903, p.17. In *The Treaty of Waitangi and Maori Fisheries*, pp.165,163. **P.94. 'indiscriminately ... destroyed ...':** *AJHR*, 1950, G-2, p.7. **P.96. 'They have been taken away ...':** *AJHR*, 1879, Sess. II, G-8, p.13. **P.110. 'For the first time ...':** Alan Ward, *An Unsettled History*, Wellington, 1999, p.152. **P.123. 'arising out of ...':** cited by Claudia Orange, 'A Kind of Equality: Labour and the Maori People, 1935–1949', MA thesis, Auckland, 1977, p.31; see also p.230. **P.138. 'There is no doubt ...':** Koro Dewes, 'Waitangi Day 1968; some food for thought', *Comment*, XXXV (June 1968), pp.12–14. **P.153.** Jane Kelsey, *A Question of Honour?*, Wellington, 1990, p.60. **P.162. 'all future legislation ...':** Geoffrey Palmer, *New Zealand's Constitution in Crisis*, Dunedin, 1992, pp.82–83. **P.163. 'Nothing in this Act ...':** State-Owned Enterprises Act 1986, *New Zealand Statutes, 1986,* p.1310. **PP.165–66. 'the principles of the Treaty of Waitangi ...'; 'any other acts ...':** *The Treaty of Waitangi in the Court of Appeal: The Full Judgments of the Court in the New Zealand Maori Council's Case*, Court of Appeal, Wellington, 1987, p.44. **P.174. 'to make better provision ...':** Maori Fisheries Act 1989, *New Zealand Statutes 1989*, p.2649. **PP.180, 182.** W. H. Oliver, *Claims to the Waitangi Tribunal*, Wellington, 1991, pp.38, 45. **PP.195, 196. 'They are not an attempt ...'; 'strong statements ...':** *Principles for Crown Action on the Treaty of Waitangi*, Department of Justice, Wellington, July 1989. **P.198.** Geoffrey Palmer, *New Zealand Herald*, 2 January 1990. **P.200.** Queen Elizabeth II, *New Zealand Herald*, 7 February 1990. **P.201.** Whakahuihui Vercoe, *New Zealand Herald*, 7 February 1990. **P.202.** Geoffrey Palmer, *New Zealand Herald*, 7 February 1990. **P.208.** Douglas Graham, *Dominion*, 8 September 1999. **PP. 217, 221.** Douglas Graham, *Trick or Treaty?* Wellington, 1997, pp.58, 50. **P.233. 'The processes and functions ...':** *The Settlement of Claims under the Treaty of Waitangi: Report of the Controller and Auditor General*, Second Report for 1995, 12 September 1995, Office of the Controller and Auditor-General/Tumuaki o te Mana Arotake, Wellington. **P.240.** Keith Jackson and Alan McRobie, *New Zealand Adopts Proportional Representation: Accident? Design? Evolution?*, Christchurch, 1998, p.229. **P.247. 'fair, durable and final ...':** *Healing the Past, Building a Future. A Guide to Treaty of Waitangi Claims and Negotiations with the Crown*, Office of Treaty Settlements, Wellington, 2002, p.30. **P.248–49.** Alan Ward, *An Unsettled History*, p.171.

Bibliography

This bibliography is a selective list of works that have been used for this publication. In the text, the following abbreviations are used for official publications: *AJHR – Appendices to the Journals of the House of Representatives*; *BPP – British Parliamentary Papers: Colonies New Zealand*; *NZPD – New Zealand Parliamentary Debates*.

Private and official papers

Alexander Turnbull Library, National Library of New Zealand / Te Puna Matauranga o Aotearoa, Wellington

Ashworth, Edward, Journals, 1841–45, MS 1841–45P
Best, Elsdon, Papers, 1869–1930, MS Papers 72
Buick, Thomas Lindsay, Papers, 1900–30, MS Papers 58
Busby, James, Dispatches from the British Resident in New Zealand, 1833–39, qMS 1833–39
Colenso, William, 'Memoranda of the Arrival of Lieut. Govr. Hobson in New Zealand 1840', MS Papers 1611
Colenso, William, Papers, MS Col 1833–63
FitzGerald, James Edward, Papers, 1839–95, MS Papers 64
Hadfield, Octavius, Papers, 1833–1902, qMS 1833–1902
Hamlin, James, Journal, 1826–37, qMS Ham 1826–37
Hobson, William, Letters, 1841–42, MS Papers 813
Hobson, William, Papers, 1833–46, MS Papers 46
Hobson, William, Records, 1840, MS Papers 2227
Ironside, Samuel, Diary, 1839–43, Micro MS 474
McDonnell, Alexander Francis, Papers, 1845–1938, MS Papers 151
McLean, Donald, Papers, 1832–1927, MS Papers 32
Mair Family, Papers, 1839–1940, MS Papers 93
Mantell, Walter Baldock Durrant, Papers, 1842–95, MS Papers 83
Marsden Family, Papers, 1802–94, MS Papers 453
Official Correspondence Relating to the Signing of the Treaty of Waitangi, 1840, qMS 1840
Orton, Joseph, Journal, 1840, Micro MS 758
Stafford, Edward, Papers, MS Papers 28
Weld, Frederick Aloysius, Correspondence, 1846–91, qMS 1846–99
Williams, Edward Marsh, Journal of a Voyage to the Northern and Southern Islands of New Zealand in HMS *Herald*, 1840, MS 1840
Woon, William, Journal, 1830–59, qMS 1830–59

Archives New Zealand / Te Rua Mahara o te Kawanatanga

British Resident Papers, 1832–40
Governor New Zealand, 1840–50
Internal Affairs Department (previously Colonial Secretary's Department)
Maori Affairs Department (previously Native Department)

Auckland City Library / Tamaki Pataka Korero

Clendon, James Reddy, Journal and Papers, 1839–72, MS 476
Declaration of Independence, 28 October 1835 (Maori text) G NZM
Fedarb, James, Diary, 1839–52, NZ MS 375
Johnson, John, Journal, 1840, NZ MS 27
Ko ta te Kawana Korero ki nga Rangatira Maori i Huihui ki Waitemata i te 10 o nga ra o Hurae, 1860, NZM
Ko te Pitihana a nga Iwi o Niu Tireni ki Ingarani (7 April 1883), G NZM
Mathew, Felton, Papers, 1840–48, NZ MS 78–89

328　AN ILLUSTRATED HISTORY OF THE TREATY OF WAITANGI

Auckland Museum / Tamaki Paenga Hira

Busby, James, Letters and Papers, MS 46
Colenso, William, Day and Waste Book, MS 76
Hobbs, John, Diaries, 1823–60, MS 144
Hobson, William, Letters, MS 802
Sewell, Henry, Journal, MS 459
Taylor, Richard, Journal, 1833–73, MS 302
Whiteley, John, Journal, 1832–63, MS 331
Williams, Henry, Letters, 1822–50, MS 72c

Hawke's Bay Museum / Ruawharo ta-u-Rangi, Napier

Colenso, William, Journal, 1839–40
Colenso, William, Notebook, 1840

Museum of New Zealand / Te Papa Tongarewa

Mathew, Felton, Journal

Public Record Office, London

Colonial Office, Original Correspondence of the Secretary of State for Colonies, and Governors' Dispatches, 1837–51, and various years thereafter

Rhodes House Library, Oxford

Aborigines' Protection Society, Papers, G98, 99

University of Auckland Library / Te Tumu Herenga

Ashwell, Benjamin Y., Letters and Journals, 1834–69
Brown, Alfred N., Journal, 1835–50
Chapman, Thomas, Letters and Journals, 1830–69
Kemp, James, Journal, 1832–52
Morgan, John, Letters and Journals, 1833–65
Puckey, William G., Letters and Journals, 1831–68

Reports, government/official publications, and published documents

Appendices to the Journals of the House of Representatives, New Zealand, 1858–1980, and various years thereafter
Appendices to the Journals of the Legislative Council, New Zealand, 1858–1900, and various years thereafter
British Parliamentary Papers: Colonies New Zealand, 1836–86, Irish University Press, Shannon, c.1968–
Court of Appeal, *Ngati Apa et al v the Attorney-General*, CA173/01 [19 June 2003]
— *The Treaty of Waitangi in the Court of Appeal: The Full Judgments of the Court in the New Zealand Maori Council's Case*, Wellington, 1987
Crown Forestry Rental Trust/Nga Kaitiaki Reti Ngahere Karauna, *Business Plan 2002–2003*, Wellington, 2002
— *Maori Experiences of the Direct Negotiations Process*, Wellington, 2003
— *Reports to Appointors*, 1995–2002, Wellington, 1995–2002
Department of Justice, *Crown Proposals for the Settlement of Treaty of Waitangi Claims*, Wellington, 8 December 1994
— *Interdepartmental Committee on Maori Fishing Rights: First Report*, November 1985
— *Principles for Crown Action on the Treaty of Waitangi*, Wellington, July 1989
— *Report on Submissions on Crown Proposals for the Treaty of Waitangi Claims*, Wellington, December 1995
— *The Crown and the Treaty of Waitangi: A Short Statement of the Principles on which the Crown Proposes to Act*, Wellington, July 1989
Hunn, J. K., *Report on Department of Maori Affairs; With Statistical Supplement, 24 August 1960*, Government Printer, Wellington, 1961
Law Commission/Te Aka Matua o Te Ture, *The Treaty of Waitangi and Maori Fisheries/Mataitai: Nga Tikanga Maori me te Tiriti o Waitangi*, Wellington, March 1989
— *Treaty of Waitangi Claims: Addressing the Post-settlement Phase: An Advisory Report for Te Puni Kokiri, the Office of Treaty Settlements and the Chief Judge of the Maori Land Court*, Wellington, 2002
Local Government New Zealand/Te Putahi Matakokiri, *He Waka Taurua – Local Government and the Treaty of Waitangi*, March 1999
— *Liaison and Consultation with Tangata Whenua: A Survey of Local Government Practice*, December 1997
Minister in Charge of Treaty of Waitangi Negotiations, *Report of Submissions on the Crown's Policy Proposals on Treaty Claims Involving Public Works Acquisitions*, Wellington, June 1996

Minister of Maori Affairs, *Partnership Perspectives: A Discussion Paper on Proposals for a New Partnership*, Wellington, April 1988

Ministerial Advisory Committee on a Maori Perspective for the Department of Social Welfare, *Puao-te-ata-tu = Day break: The Report of the Ministerial Advisory Committee on a Maori Perspective for the Department of Social Welfare*, The Committee, Wellington, 1986

Ministerial Planning Group, *Ka Awatea: A Report of the Ministerial Planning Group*, Wellington, March 1991

Ministry for the Environment/Manatu Mo Te Taiao [Diane Crengle], *Taking into Account the Principles of the Treaty of Waitangi: Ideas for the Implementation of section 8 Resource Management Act 1991*, Wellington, January 1993

Ministry of Fisheries/Te Tautiaki i nga Tini a Tangaroa, *A Guide to the Kaimoana Customary Fishing Regulations 1998*, Wellington, 1998

— *Fisheries (Kaimoana Customary Fishing) Regulations,* Wellington, 1998

— *Fisheries (South Island Customary Fishing) Regulations,* Wellington, 1998

New Zealand Parliamentary Debates, 1854–1970, and various years thereafter

Office of the Controller and Auditor-General/Tumuaki o te Mana Arotake [D. J. D. McDonald], *The Settlement of Claims under the Treaty of Waitangi: Report of the Controller and Auditor General*, Second Report for 1995, 12 September 1995

Office of the Parliamentary Commissioner for the Environment/Te Kaitiaki Taiao a Te Whare Paremata Aotearoa, *Environmental Information and the Adequacy of Treaty Settlement Procedures*, Wellington, September 1994

— *Exploring the Concept of a Treaty Based Environmental Audit Framework*, Wellington, May 2002

— *Indigenous Claims and the Process of Negotiation on Settlement in Countries with Jurisdictions and Populations Comparable to New Zealand's*, Wellington, 1994

— *Kaitiakitanga and Local Government: Tangata Whenua Participation in Environmental Management [and Summary]*, Wellington, June 1998

Office of Treaty Settlements/Te Tari Whakatau Take e pa ana ki te Tiriti o Waitangi, *Ka Tika a Muri, Ka Tika a Mua: Healing the Past, Building a Future: A Guide to Treaty of Waitangi Claims and Negotiations with the Crown*, Wellington, 2002

Officials Co-ordinating Committee on Local Government, *Reform of Local and Regional Government*, Wellington, October 1989

Parliamentary Debates, Great Britain, 1840–70, 1885

State Services Commission/Te Komihana O Nga Tari Kawanatanga, *The Public Service and the Treaty of Waitangi*, Wellington, 1995

Te Puni Kokiri/Ministry of Maori Development, *He Tirohanga o Kawa ki te Tiriti o Waitangi: A Guide to the Principles of the Treaty of Waitangi as Expressed by the Courts and the Waitangi Tribunal*, Wellington, 2001

— *Maori in the New Zealand Economy*, 3rd edn, Wellington, 2002

— *Nga Kai o te Moana, Kaupapa Takina: Customary Fisheries, Philosophy and Practices, Legislation and Change*, Wellington, 1993

Waitangi Tribunal Reports (selected)

WAI 4	The Kaituna River Report 1984
WAI 6	The Motunui-Waitara Report 1983
WAI 8	The Manukau Report 1985
WAI 9	The Orakei Report 1987
WAI 10	The Waiheke Island Report 1987
WAI 11	Te Reo Maori Report 1986
WAI 17	The Mangonui Sewerage Report 1988
WAI 22	The Muriwhenua Fishing Report 1988
WAI 26, 150	The Allocation of Radio Frequencies Report 1990
WAI 27	The Ngai Tahu Report 1991 (3 Vols)
WAI 27	The Ngai Tahu Sea Fisheries Report 1992
WAI 27	The Ngai Tahu Ancillary Claims Report 1995
WAI 38	Te Roroa Report 1992
WAI 45	The Muriwhenua Land Report 1997
WAI 46	The Ngati Awa Raupatu Report 1999
WAI 55	Te Whanganui-a-Orotu Report 1995
WAI 84	The Turangi Township Report 1995
WAI 84	The Turangi Township Remedies Report 1998
WAI 119	The Mohaka River Report 1992
WAI 143	The Taranaki Report: Kaupapa Tuatahi 1995
WAI 145	Te Whanganui a Tara me ona Takiwa: Report on the Wellington District 2003

WAI 167	The Whanganui River Report 1999
WAI 176	The Broadcasting Claim Report 1994
WAI 307	The Fisheries Settlement Report 1992
WAI 413	Maori Electoral Option Report 1994
WAI 414	Te Whanau o Waipareira Report 1998
WAI 674	The Kaipara Interim Report 2002
WAI 796	The Petroleum Report 2003
WAI 953	Ahu Moana: The Aquaculture and Marine Farming Report 2002
WAI 1071	Report on the Crown's Foreshore and Seabed Policy 2004

(For further reports, see www.waitangi-tribunal.govt.nz)

Newspapers and periodicals

Dominion, 1984–2002
Dominion Post, 2002–2004
Mana, 1993–2004
Maori Law Review, 1994–2003
New-Zealander, 1845–66
Southern Cross, 1843–45, 1847–60
Te Hokio, 1861–63
Te Karere Maori, 1842–63
Te Manutukutuku (Waitangi Tribunal), 1989–2004
Te Paki o te Matariki, 1891–1902
Te Wananga, 1874–76
The Times (London), 1840, 1843–48, 1860–67
Waka Maori, 1873–77

Books, chapters, occasional papers, pamphlets

Adams, P., *Fatal Necessity: British Intervention in New Zealand, 1830–47*, Auckland University Press/Oxford University Press, Auckland, 1977

Anglican Treaty of Waitangi Commission, *The Treaty of Waitangi: A Discussion Paper*, Anglican Treaty of Waitangi Commission, 1985

Atkinson, Neill, *Adventures in Democracy: A History of the Vote in New Zealand*, University of Otago Press, Dunedin, 2003

Awatere, Donna, *Maori Sovereignty,* Broadsheet, Auckland, 1984

Belgrave, Michael, 'Individualism, Collectivism, and the Recognition of Te Tino Rangatiratanga', in Christine Cheyne, Mike O'Brien and Michael Belgrave, *Social Policy in Aotearoa/New Zealand*, Oxford University Press, Auckland, 1997

—— 'Something Borrowed, Something New: History and the Waitangi Tribunal', in Bronwyn Dalley and Jock Phillips (eds), *Going Public: The Changing Face of New Zealand History*, Auckland University Press, Auckland, 2001

Belich, James, *Making Peoples: A History of the New Zealanders from Polynesian Settlement to the end of the Nineteenth Century*, Allen Lane [London]/Penguin Press, Auckland, 1996

—— *The New Zealand Wars, and the Victorian Interpretation of Racial Conflict*, Auckland University Press, Auckland, 1986

Bennett, F. A., *Te Keehi a te Arawa mo nga Moana, me te Whaiwhai mo te Mana o te Tiriti o Waitangi*, Rotorua, 1912

Binney, J., 'The Maori and the Signing of the Treaty of Waitangi', in David Green (ed.), *Towards 1990: Seven Leading Historians Examine Significant Aspects of New Zealand History,* GP Books, Wellington, 1989

Brookfield, F. M., *Waitangi and Indigenous Rights: Revolution, Law and Legitimation*, Auckland University Press, Auckland, 1999

Buddle, Thomas, *The Maori King Movement*, New Zealander Office, Auckland, 1860

Buick, T. Lindsay, *The Treaty of Waitangi, Or How New Zealand Became a British Colony*, 3rd edn, Thomas Avery & Sons Ltd, New Plymouth, 1936 (reprinted Capper, 1976)

—— *Waitangi: Ninety-four Years After*, Thomas Avery & Sons Ltd, New Plymouth, 1934

Bunbury, Thomas, *Reminiscences of a Veteran*, 3 vols, Charles J. Skeet, London, 1861

Butterworth, G. V., *Maori Affairs: A Department and the People Who Made It*, Iwi Transition Agency: GP Books, Wellington, 1990

Byrnes, Giselle, 'Jackals of the Crown? Historians and the Treaty Claims Process', in Bronwyn Dalley and Jock Phillips (eds), *Going Public: The Changing Face of New Zealand History*, Auckland University Press, Auckland, 2001

—— *The Waitangi Tribunal and New Zealand History*, Oxford University Press, Auckland, 2004

Carleton, Hugh, *The Life of Henry Williams, Archdeacon of Waimate*, 2 vols, Upton, Auckland, 1874

Clarke, George [Jun.], *Notes on Early Life in New Zealand*, J. Walch, Hobart, 1903

Coates, Ken S., and P. G. McHugh (eds), *Living Relationships: The Treaty of Waitangi in the New Millennium*, Victoria University Press, Wellington, 1998

Colenso, W., *The Authentic and Genuine History of the Signing of the Treaty of Waitangi*, Government Printer, Wellington, 1890 (reprinted Capper, 1971)

Consedine, Robert, and Joanna Consedine, *Healing our History: The Challenge of the Treaty of Waitangi*, Penguin, Auckland, 2001

Cooper, Ronda, *The Importance of Monsters: A Decade of RMA Debate*, Parliamentary Commissioner for the Environment, Wellington, 2002

— and Rachel Brooking, 'Ways through Complexities', in Merata Kawharu (ed.), *Whenua: Managing our Resources,* Reed Books, Auckland, 2002

Dalton, B. J., *War and Politics in New Zealand, 1855–1870*, Sydney University Press, Sydney, 1967

Diamond, Paul, *A Fire in Your Belly: Maori Leaders Speak*, Huia Publishers, Wellington, 2004

Durie, Mason, *Te Mana, te Kawanatanga: The Politics of Maori Self-determination*, Oxford University Press, Auckland, 1998

Elder, J. R. (ed.), *The Letters and Journals of Samuel Marsden, 1765–1838*, Coulls, Somerville, Wilkie Ltd/A. H. Reed, Dunedin, 1932

Facsimiles of the Declaration of Independence and the Treaty of Waitangi, Wellington, 1877 (reprinted Government Printer, 1976)

FitzRoy, Robert, *Remarks on New Zealand*, W. & H. White, London, 1846

Fox, W., *A Chapter in the History of New Zealand: The Treaty of Waitangi*, London, 1883

Gardiner, Wira, *Return to Sender: What Really Happened at the Fiscal Envelope Hui*, Reed, Auckland, 1996

— *Te Mura o te Ahi: The Story of the Maori Battalion*, Reed, Auckland, 1992

Gilling, Brian, and Vincent O'Malley, *The Treaty of Waitangi in New Zealand History*, Occasional Papers Series No. 3, Treaty of Waitangi Research Unit, Victoria University of Wellington, 2000

Gorst, J. E., *The Maori King*, Macmillan, London, 1864; ed. Keith Sinclair, Pauls Book Arcade, Hamilton, 1959

Graham, Douglas, *The Legal Reality of Customary Rights for Maori*, Occasional Papers Series No. 6, Treaty of Waitangi Research Unit, Victoria University of Wellington, 2000

— *Trick or Treaty?,* Institute of Policy Studies, Victoria University of Wellington, Wellington, 1997

Harrison, Noel, *Graham Latimer: A Biography*, Huia Publishers, Wellington, 2002

Hayward, Janine (ed.), *Local Government and the Treaty of Waitangi,* Oxford University Press, [Melbourne], 2003

— and Nicola R. Wheen (eds), *The Waitangi Tribunal: Te Roopu Whakamana i te Tiriti o Waitangi*, Bridget Williams Books, Wellington, 2004

Henderson, J. McLeod, *Ratana: The Man, the Church, the Political Movement*, A. H. & A. W. Reed, Wellington, 1963

Hill, Richard S., *The Treaty of Waitangi Today*, Occasional Papers Series No. 2, Treaty of Waitangi Research Unit, Victoria University of Wellington, 2000

— and Vincent O'Malley, *The Maori Quest for Rangatiratanga/Autonomy, 1840–2000*, Occasional Papers Series No. 4, Treaty of Waitangi Research Unit, Victoria University of Wellington, 2000

Hohepa, P. W., *Waitangi: A Promise or a Betrayal?*, Occasional Papers on Race Relations, No. 2, New Zealand Race Relations Council, Wellington, 1971

Jackson, Keith, and Alan McRobie, *New Zealand Adopts Proportional Representation: Accident? Design? Evolution?*, Hazard Press, Christchurch, 1998

Jackson, Moana, *He Whaipaanga Hou. The Maori and the Criminal Justice System: A New Perspective*, Policy and Research Division, Department of Justice, 1987–88

Kawharu, I. H. (ed.), *Waitangi: Maori and Pakeha Perspectives of the Treaty of Waitangi*, Oxford University Press, Auckland, 1989

Kelsey, Jane, *A Question of Honour? Labour and the Treaty 1984–1989*, Allen & Unwin, Wellington, 1990

Kernot, Bernard, and Alistair McBride (eds), *Te Reo o te Tiriti Mai Rano: The Treaty is Always Speaking*, Alistair McBride for Combined Chaplaincies at Victoria University of Wellington, Wellington, 1989

King, Michael, *The Penguin History of New Zealand*, Penguin, Auckland, 2003

Ko te Pukapuka o te Tiriti o Kohimarama, Auckland, 1889

Ko te Tiriti i Tuhia ki Waitangi 1840, Meeke Tanera, Auckland, 1922

McHugh, Paul, *The Maori Magna Carta*, Oxford University Press, Auckland, 1991

McKenzie, D. F., *Oral Culture, Literacy and Print in Early New Zealand: The Treaty of Waitangi*, Victoria University Press, Wellington, 1985

McLay, Geoff (ed.), *Treaty Settlements: The Unfinished Business*, New Zealand Institute of Advanced Legal Studies/ Victoria University of Wellington Law Review, Wellington, 1995

McLeay, Elizabeth, 'The New Parliament', in Jonathan Boston et al. (eds), *Left Turn: The New Zealand General Election of 1999*, Victoria University Press, Wellington, 2000

McLintock, A. H., *Crown Colony Government in New Zealand*, Government Printer, Wellington, 1958

Martin, William, *England and the New Zealanders*, Bishops' Auckland, Auckland, 1847

— *The Taranaki Question*, Melanesian Press, Auckland, 1860

Mathew, Felton, *The Founding of New Zealand: The Journals of Felton Mathew, First Surveyor-general of New Zealand, and his Wife, 1840–1847*, ed. J. Rutherford, A. H. & A. W. Reed, Auckland, 1940

Monin, Paul, *This is My Place: Hauraki Contested, 1769–1875*, Bridget Williams Books, Wellington, 2001

Mulgan, Richard, *Maori, Pakeha and Democracy*, Oxford University Press, Auckland, 1989

National Council of Churches, *The Pakeha and the Treaty: Signposts*, NCC, Auckland, 1986

— *Waitangi, 1984 – A Turning Point?*, NCC, Auckland, 1984

— *What Happened at Waitangi in 1983*, NCC, Auckland, 1983

Nga Korero o te Hui o te Whakakotahitanga i tu ki te Tiriti o Waitangi, Aperira 14 1892, Auckland, 1892

Ngata, Apirana, *The Treaty of Waitangi: An Explanation / Te Tiriti o Waitangi: He Whakamarama*, trans. M. R. Jones, Wellington, 1963

Oliver, W. H., *Claims to the Waitangi Tribunal*, Department of Justice, Wellington, 1991

— (ed.), *The Dictionary of New Zealand Biography*, Vol.1, Allen & Unwin / Department of Internal Affairs, Wellington, 1990

Orange, Claudia (ed.), *The Dictionary of New Zealand Biography*, Vol.2, Bridget Williams Books / Department of Internal Affairs, Wellington, 1993

— *The Dictionary of New Zealand Biography*, Vols 3–5, Auckland University Press / Department of Internal Affairs, Auckland / Wellington, 1996–2000

— 'An Exercise in Maori Autonomy: The Maori War Effort Organisation', in Judith Binney (ed.), *The Shaping of History: Essays from the New Zealand Journal of History*, Bridget Williams Books, Wellington, 2001

— *The Treaty of Waitangi*, Allen & Unwin / Port Nicholson Press, Wellington, 1987

Palmer, Geoffrey, *New Zealand's Constitution in Crisis*, John McIndoe, Dunedin, 1992

Paremata Maori o Nui Tireni, Auckland, 1895

Paremata Maori o Nui Tireni, Webb & Co., Otaki, 1892

Porter, Frances (ed.), *The Turanga Journal 1840–1850: Letters and Journals of William and Jane Williams, Missionaries to Poverty Bay*, Price Milburn for Victoria University Press, Wellington, 1974

Ramsden, Eric, *Busby of Waitangi: H.M.'s Resident at New Zealand 1833–1840*, A. H. & A. W. Reed, Wellington, 1942

Reed, Vernon H., *The Gift of Waitangi: A History of the Bledisloe Gift,* Reed, Wellington, 1957

Renwick, W. L., *The Treaty Now*, GP Books, Wellington, 1990

— (ed.), *Sovereignty and Indigenous Rights: The Treaty of Waitangi in International Contexts*, Victoria University Press, Wellington, 1991

Rogers, Lawrence (ed.), *The Early Journals of Henry Williams, Senior Missionary of the Church Missionary Society, 1826–40*, Pegasus, Christchurch, 1961

Runanga o Waitangi, Ngaruawahia, 1984

Rusden, G. W., *Aureretanga: Groans of the Maori*, London, 1888; reprinted Hakaprint, Cannons Creek, 1974

Sewell, Henry, *The Journal of Henry Sewell, 1853–57*, ed. W. David McIntyre, Whitcoulls, Christchurch, 1980

Sharp, Andrew, *Justice and the Maori: Maori Claims in New Zealand Political Argument in the 1980s*, Oxford University Press, Auckland, 1990

— 'The Problem of Maori Affairs', in Martin Holland and Jonathan Boston (eds), *The Fourth Labour Government: Politics and Policy in New Zealand*, 2nd edn, Oxford University Press, Auckland, 1990

— 'The Waitangi Tribunal 1984–1996', in Raymond Miller (ed.), *New Zealand Politics in Transition*, Oxford University Press, Auckland, 1997

— and Paul McHugh (eds), *Histories, Power and Loss: Uses of the Past – a New Zealand Commentary*, Bridget Williams Books, Wellington, 2001

Sinclair, Keith, *The Origins of the Maori Wars*, 2nd edn, New Zealand University Press, Wellington, 1961

Sullivan, Ann, and Jack Vowles, 'Realignment? Maori and the 1996 Election', in Jack Vowles et al. (eds), *Voters' Victory? New Zealand's First Election under Proportional Representation*, Auckland University Press, Auckland, 1998

Sweetman, Edward, *The Unsigned New Zealand Treaty*, Arrow Printery, Melbourne, 1939

Taiwhanga, Sydney David, *Proposals of Mr Sydney David Taiwhanga, M.H.R., for the Colonization and Settlement of Maori Lands*, Edwards & Co. Printers, Wellington, 1888

Te Hikoi ki Waitangi, 1984, Auckland, 1984

Te Huihuinga o Etahi o nga Rangatira o te Motu nei ki Kohimarama, [Auckland], 1889

Temm, P., *The Waitangi Tribunal: The Conscience of the Nation*, Random Century Press, Auckland, 1990

The Treaty of Waitangi: Its Origins and Significance: A Series of Papers Presented at a Seminar Held at Victoria University of Wellington, 19–20 February 1972, Victoria University of Wellington, Wellington, 1972

Treaty of Waitangi Hui, Whangarei, 1985

Waitangi Action Committee, *Remember Waitangi*, WAC, Auckland, 1982

Ward, Alan, *A Show of Justice: Racial 'Amalgamation' in Nineteenth Century New Zealand*, ANU Press, Canberra, 1974
— *An Unsettled History: Treaty Claims in New Zealand Today*, Bridget Williams Books, Wellington, 1999
— *National Overview*, 3 vols, Waitangi Tribunal Rangahaua Whanui Series, Waitangi Tribunal/GP Publications, Wellington, 1997
Wards, Ian, *The Shadow of the Land: A Study of British Policy and Racial Conflict in New Zealand 1832–1852,* Department of Internal Affairs/Government Printer, Wellington, 1968
Williams, Charlotte, *The Too-hard Basket: Maori and Criminal Justice since 1980*, Institute of Policy Studies, Wellington, 2001
Williams, Jeanine, *Frederick Weld: A Political Biography*, Auckland University Press/Oxford University Press, Auckland, 1983
Williams, John A., *Politics of the New Zealand Maori: Protest and Co-operation, 1891–1909*, Oxford University Press, Auckland, 1969
Wilson, Margaret, and Anna Yeatman (eds), *Justice and Identity: Antipodean Practices*, Bridget Williams Books, Wellington, 1995

Journal articles

Bennion, Tom (ed.), 'The Foreshore and Seabed Decision', *Maori Law Review*, Wellington, May 2004
Boast, R. P., 'The Treaty of Waitangi: A Framework for Resource Management Law', *Victoria University of Wellington Law Review*, Vol.19, No.4 (1989)
Brookfield, F. M., 'Maori Customary Title in Foreshore and Seabed', *New Zealand Law Journal*, 34, February 2004
Brooking, Tom, '"Busting Up" the Greatest Estate of All: Liberal Maori Policy 1891 to 1910', *New Zealand Journal of History*, Vol.26, No.1 (1992)
Dewes, Koro, 'Waitangi Day 1968: Some Food for Thought', *Comment*, No.35 (June 1968), pp.12–14
Durie, E. Taihakurei, and Gordon S. Orr, 'The Role of the Waitangi Tribunal and the Development of a Bicultural Jurisprudence', *New Zealand Universities Law Review*, Vol.14, No.1 (1990)
Frame, Alex, 'A State Servant Looks at the Treaty', *New Zealand Universities Law Review*, Vol.14, No.1 (1990)
Grinlinton, David, 'Private Property Rights versus Public Access: The Foreshore and Seabed Debate', *New Zealand Journal of Environmental Law*, Vol.7 (2003)
Hayward, Janine, 'Local Government and Maori: Talking Treaty', *Political Science*, Vol.50, No.2 (1999)
— 'The Treaty of Waitangi, Maori and the Evolving Crown', *Political Science*, Vol.49, No.2 (1998)
Keith, Kenneth, 'The Treaty of Waitangi in the Courts', *New Zealand Universities Law Review*, Vol.14, No.1 (1990)
Kenderdine, Shonagh, 'Legal Implications of Treaty Jurisprudence', *Victoria University of Wellington Law Review*, Vol.19, No.4 (1989)
McHugh, P. G., 'Sealords and Sharks: The Maori Fisheries Agreement (1992)', *New Zealand Law Journal* [1992], 354–58
Mikaere, A., and S. Milroy, 'Treaty of Waitangi and Maori Land Law', *New Zealand Law Review*, 2000, 2001
— 'Maori Issues', *New Zealand Law Review*, 1998, 1999
Mikaere, A.L., 'Maori Issues', *New Zealand Law Review*, 1995, 1996
— 'Maori Issues', *New Zealand Recent Law Review*, 1993, 1994
— and D. V. Williams, 'Maori Issues', *New Zealand Recent Law Review*, 1989, 1990, 1991, 1992
Milroy, S. T., 'Maori Issues', *New Zealand Law Review,* 1997
Orange, Claudia, 'The Covenant of Kohimarama: A Ratification of the Treaty of Waitangi', *New Zealand Journal of History*, Vol.14, No.1 (1980)
O'Sullivan, Dominic, 'The 1996 General Election and the Labour Vote in the Maori Electorates', *He Pukenga Korero*, Vol.5, No.1 (1999)
Palmer, Geoffrey, 'The Treaty of Waitangi – Principles for Crown Action', *Victoria University of Wellington Law Review*, Vol.19, No.4 (1989)
Ross, R. M., 'Te Tiriti o Waitangi: Texts and Translations', *New Zealand Journal of History*, Vol.6, No.2 (1972)
Sinclair, Fergus, 'Kauwaeranga in Context', *Victoria University of Wellington Law Review*, Vol.29, No.1 (1998)
Sorrenson, M. P. K., 'Giving Better Effect to the Treaty: Some Thoughts for 1990', *New Zealand Journal of History*, Vol.24, No.2 (1990)
Ward, Alan, 'History and Historians before the Waitangi Tribunal: Some Reflections on the Ngai Tahu Claim', *New Zealand Journal of History*, Vol.24, No.2 (1990)
Winiata, Whatarangi, 'The Treaty of Waitangi and Resource Management', *Public Sector*, Vol.11, No.4 (1988)

Unpublished papers and theses

Bennion, Tom, 'Lands under the sea – foreshore and seabed', February 2004
Conferenz [Auckland], The 3rd Annual Maori Legal Forum: Papers presented on 24, 25 June 2004, Wellington

Hayward, Janine, 'The Treaty Challenge: Local Government and Maori', A Scoping Report, Crown Forestry Rental Trust, Wellington, 2002

Love, R. Ngatata, 'Policies of Frustration: The Growth of Maori Politics – the Ratana-Labour Era', PhD thesis, Victoria University of Wellington, 1977

Loveridge, D. M., 'The Origins of the Native Lands Acts and Native Land Court', A Report for the Crown Law Office, Wellington, October 2000

— 'The Taranaki Maori Claims Settlement Act, 1944', Crown Law Office, Wellington, 25 August 1990

McRae, J., 'Participation: Native Committees (1883) and Papatupu Block Committees (1900) in Tai Tokerau', MA thesis, University of Auckland, 1981

Orange, Claudia, 'A Kind of Equality: Labour and the Maori People 1935–1949', MA thesis, University of Auckland, 1977

— 'The Treaty of Waitangi: A Study of its Making, Interpretation and Role in New Zealand History', PhD thesis, University of Auckland, 1984

Palmer, Matthew, 'Constitutional Issues', Treaty of Waitangi seminar, New Zealand Law Society, Wellington, 2002

Tomas, N., and Kerensa Johnston, 'Ask that Taniwha: Who Owns the Foreshore and Seabed of Aotearoa?', www.library.auckland.ac.nz/subjects/law/pdfs/Taniwha-o-te-Foreshore.pdf

Turner, Phillip, 'The Politics of Neutrality: The Catholic Mission and the Maori, 1838–1870', MA thesis, University of Auckland, 1986

Wainwright, Carrie, 'The Legal Status of the Treaty, the Maori Fisheries Case, the Waitangi Tribunal and Settlements', Treaty of Waitangi seminar, New Zealand Law Society, Wellington, 2002

Websites

Crown Forestry Rental Trust: www.cfrt.org.nz
New Zealand Government: www.beehive.govt.nz
Office of Treaty Settlements: www.ots.govt.nz
Parliamentary Commissioner for the Environment: www.pce.govt.nz
Waitangi Tribunal: www.waitangi-tribunal.govt.nz

Index

Page numbers in italics indicate illustrations.

Aboriginal Australians, Maori knowledge of, 36
Aborigines Protection Society, 100, 102
ACT New Zealand, 238
Adamski, Priscilla, Adam and Peter, 234, *234*
Agriculture and Fisheries, Ministry of, 169, 170
Ahipara, 84
Ahu Moana Report, 273
Akaroa, 12, 18
Alexandra (Pirongia), 71
Alliance Party, 231. *See also* coalition governments
Aoraki/Mt Cook, 226
Aotea District Maori Land Court, 128
Aotearoa Fisheries Ltd, 174
Aotearoa Maori Arts Festival, 200
apologies, Crown: to Te Uri-o-Hau, 186; to Tainui, 222; to Ngai Tahu, 226, 243; as part of settlement package, 254
aquaculture, 272, 273, 278
Arahura purchase, 224, 226
Armstrong, David, *187*
Auckland: settlement, 49, *49*; reliance on Maori trade, 49, 58; capital moved to, 53, 127, 182; military road to Waikato, 68–69, *68*; Maori Community Centre, Fanshawe Street, 134; 1990 commemorations, 199, 200; One Tree Hill protest, 231; attitudes to claims affecting, 263
Auckland City Council, 181

Baker, William, 127
Ballance, John, 90, 230
Barker, A.C., 75
Bassett, Michael, 190
Bastion Point (Takaparawha), 97, 146, *152, 153*, 181, 182
Bay of Islands, 4, 7, 8, 11, 13, 16, 18, 21, 27, 29, 34, 37, 44, 48, 53, 89
Bay of Plenty, 40, 41, 131; land confiscations in, 72, 73, 122, 123, 262

Bay of Plenty Regional Council, 268
Beattie, David, 155, *158*
Bellingshausen, F., 6
Bennett, Bishop Manuhuia, *178*
Bennett, Frederick, 122, *122*
biculturalism, 147, 149, 161, 193
Bill of Rights, 155, 157
Birch, Bill, *205*
Bledisloe, Lord, 125
Bolger, Jim (James), *205*, 208, 218, 222, *222*, 229, 232, 242
Bolger, Joan, *205*
Bourke, Richard, 13, 16
Boyd, Mary, *178, 179*
Bracken, Thomas, 126
Brash, Don (Donald), 271, 276, 277
Bridge, Cyprian, 57
Brierley Investments Ltd, 213
British Crown: Maori relationship with, 8–13, 19, 43–44, 45, 48, 54–59, 64, 75–77, 100–3; plans for colonisation, 16–18; and questions of sovereignty, 18–21, 24, 76–77, 125; and Treaty, 24, 26, 34, 37, 39, 120; and King movement, 61, 64, 67; responsibility transferred to New Zealand government, 77
British Resident: appointment of, 13; powerlessness of position, 13, 16
Browne, Harriet, *63*
Browne, Thomas Gore, 58, *63*, 64, 66, 67
Buck, Peter Henry (Te Rangihiroa), 114, 116, *116*
Bunbury, Thomas, 37, 39, 40, 42, 43
Busby, James: British Resident, *12*, 13, 16; and Declaration of Independence, 13, 16; 1837 report, 16; and Treaty, 24, 31, 34; residence gifted to New Zealand, 125
Butler, Judge, *92*
businesses, Maori, *see* Maori economic development

Cambridge, 71
Canada, 141
Canterbury, 60, 91, 120
Carr, Mate, *264*
Carroll, James, 83, *92*, 116
Carter Holt Harvey, 212, 213
centennial 1940, 126–30, *129*
CFRT, *see* Crown Forestry Rental Trust
Christianity: Maori conversion to, 7, 10, 11, 26, 30, 34, 64; union of two races to be achieved through, 125; churches reappraise role of Treaty, 149. *See also* Church Missionary Society; missionaries; Wesleyan Missionary Society
Church Missionary Society, 4, 7, 11, 24, 32. *See also* missionaries
claims, Treaty: and establishment of Waitangi Tribunal, 144–46, 150–55; historical, 144–45, 155, 157–58, 159–60, 163, 184, 205, 217, 218, 242, 247, 251, 255, 264; on environmental issues, 150–51, 153–54; research into, 158, 159–60, 169, 226, 256, 258, 260–61; radio frequencies, broadcasting assets and radio spectrum, 182; types of, 217, 218; and conservation estate, 219–20; and natural resources, 220; Crown acceptance of prima facie Treaty breach, 242; direct negotiation of, with Crown, 242, 254, 256, 257; negotiation process, 253–58; funding of, 258, 260–62; public debate on, 262–64. *See also* fisheries claims; land claims; settlements; Waitangi Tribunal
claims and settlement process (flow chart), 256–57
Clark, Helen, 186, *241, 245, 246*
Clarke, George, 48
Clarke, George (junior), 52, 86
Clendon, James, 18
Clevedon, 112

'closing the gaps' policy, 246
Cloudy Bay, 39
CMS, *see* Church Missionary Society
Coal Mines Amendment Act 1903, 88
Coalcorp, 167, 196–97, 223
coalition governments: National-New Zealand First (1996–9), 242; Labour-Alliance (1999–2002), 246–48, 269; Labour-Progressive (2002–), 271
coastal space, types of, 274
Coates, Gordon, 199
Colenso, William, 26, *26*, 28, 29, 31, 32, 34, 85
Colonial Office: policy towards New Zealand, 16–18, 18–19, 48, 49, 75; and Treaty, 24, 34, 39, 41; and application of Treaty, 54, 56–58, 80; and King Tawhiao's deputation to Queen, 102; Hirini Taiwhanga's deputation, 101–2
Commission on Middle Island Native Claims, 91
Commonwealth Games, 14th, 200
Confederation of United Tribes: background to, 13; formed, 16; negotiation with chiefs of, 24; recognised by Treaty, 98
confiscation, *see* land confiscation
Conservation, Department of, 121, 227, 253, 255
Conservation Act 1987, 161
conservation estate, 219–20
Constitution Acts *see* New Zealand Constitution Acts, 1846 and 1852
Cooke, Robin, 165, *165*
Cook Strait, *19*, 38
Cook's discovery: impact of, 4, 5, 6; as basis of British sovereignty, 39; commemoration of, 200
Cooper, George, 24
Cooper, Whina, 135, 146, 149, *149*
Coromandel Peninsula, 44, 81
Counties Amendment Act 1961, 137
Court of Appeal, 164–66, 167, 184, 185, 195–96, 197, 216, 266, 270, 272, 274
covenant concept: applied to Treaty, 37, 44, 63, 65, 77, 96, 148; Kohimarama Covenant 1860, 66–67
criminal justice, 195, 210
Crofts, Charles, *224, 225*
Crombie, John Nicol, 65
Crown Forest Assets Act 1989, 185–87, 210, 258
Crown Forestry Rental Trust, 187, 248, 258, 260, 261, 263
Crown Law Office, 159, 168, 185, 253, 254
Crown proposals for settlement, *see* 'fiscal cap'

Crown Task Force on Waitangi Issues, 198–99
Cullen, Michael, 235

Dargaville, 212
Darling, Ralph, 11, 13
Davis, Peter, *246*
Dawson, Martin, *183*
de Thierry, Baron Charles, 16
Declaration of Independence 1835, 13–16, 18, 34, 43, 53; Maori text, *14*; English text, *15*
decolonisation, 141
Delamere, John, 242
Delamere, Monita, *178*
Department of ... *see under* name e.g., Conservation, Department of
Dewes, Koro, 138
Dog Tax Registration Act 1880, 92, 100
Doorbar, David, 155, *155*
Durie, Edward Taihakurei, 150, *178, 238*
Durie, Mason, 220

East Coast, 11, 35, 40, 110, 114, 117, 130, 131, 134
East Coast war, 70
economic development, *see* Maori economic development
education, Maori, 77, 111–12, 113, 134, 135–36, 137, 138, 208, 271, 277; Treaty rights in, 193–94, 277
Education Act 1989, 193
eel fisheries, 86, 90, 91, 96, *171*
Electoral Act 1993, 240
Elias, Sian, *183*
Elizabeth affair, 12–13
Elizabeth II, Queen, 200, *222, 222*
Ellesmere, Lake, 91
Elliott, George, 127
Environment, Ministry for the, 193
Environment Act 1986, 161
environmental claims, 150–51, 153–54
Ereonora, 38

Featherston, Isaac, 76
Fedarb, James, 37, 40; bill of 1 July 1840, *41*
Federated Mountain Clubs, 219
Federation of Maori Authorities, 185, 235
Fenton, Judge, 88
58th Regiment, *54*
'fiscal cap', 217, 218, 222, 228, 229–32, 242, 247, 249, 254
Fish Protection Act 1877, 88
fisheries: in Treaty, 66, 68, 96, 169, 172; Maori rights to, 66, 68, 80, 85–89, *86*, 94, *94*, 96, 121, 122, 169–75, 215, 216; eels, 86, 90, 91, 96, *171*; toheroa-gathering, 87, 114, *114*;

protests over Maori rights to, 89–91; quota management system, 169–72, 175, 211–12, 213, 215, 216; individual transferable quotas, 170–74; Law Commission report on, 169, 170; Te Weehi case, 172; taiapure, 214, 216; mataitai reserves, 216; and public works, 236. *See also* Maori Fisheries Commission; Treaty of Waitangi Fisheries Commission
fisheries claims: Rotorua lakes, 120–21, 169; Lake Taupo, 121, 169; Waikato River, 122; environmental issues, 150–51, 153–54; Muriwhenua, 163–64, 169, 170, 171–72, 173, 248; Ngai Tahu, 169, 170, 212, 248; Sealord deal, 211–16, 219, 262
Fisheries Act 1983, 88, 170, 171, 172, 175, 215
Fisheries Act 1996, 216
Fisheries Amendment Act 1986, 169, 170
FitzRoy, Robert, 49, 56
flags: Aotearoa, *72;* Maori, *229;* New Zealand, 137; Union Jack, 28, 100, 125, 137, *137;* United Tribes of New Zealand, 13, 16, *17*, 18, 38, 125, 137
flagstaff: Kororareka, brought down by Heke, 53–54; re-erection, 102; Waitangi, 125, 136, 137, *137*
flax mill, Clevedon, 112, *112*
flora and fauna claim (WAI 262), 263
Foley, Jane, 72, *72*
food-gathering, Maori rights to, 86, 87, 171, 224. *See also* fisheries
Foreshore and Seabed Bill, 275, 277, 278
foreshore and seabed rights, 87–89, 90, 91, 220; discussion at Waitangi meeting 1881, 100; Rotorua lakes, 120–21, 169; petitions relating to, 122; Court of Appeal decision, 270, 272–75. *See also* lake bed rights; river bed rights
Forestry Corporation, 185
forests: in Treaty, 66, 68; Maori rights to, 66, 68; exotic, Maori role in developing, 113, *113*, 188; Crown Forest Assets Act 1989, 185–87; Kaipara claims, 186, 187; Ngai Tahu claim, 225, 226; and funding for claims, 258, 260. *See also* Crown Forestry Rental Trust
Forsyth, Lake, *171*
France, 18, 29, 30, 64
franchise, Maori, 50, 58, 76–77, 190, 238–39. *See also* representation, Maori
Fraser, Peter, 132, *134*
Freeman, James, 24

INDEX   337

Galway, Lord, 128, *129*
Gardiner, Wira, 169, 230
General Assembly, 58, 59, 72, 75, 76–77, 107
George IV, King, 10, 44
George V, King, 102
gifted land, 149, 219
Gipps, George, 21
Gisborne, 119, 200
Goldfields Act Amendment Act 1868, 88
government departments, 160, 161–62, 198, 203, 205, 208, 227, 265, 266, 269. *See also* specific departments
Graham, Doug (Douglas), 209–10, 212, 217, 218, 219, 221, *222*, *224*, 227, 230, 231, 232, 233, 235, 242
greenstone (pounamu), 224, 226
Greig, Justice, 172
Grey, Earl, 55
Grey, George, 48, 49, 50, 55, 56, 57, 59, *59*, 60, 68, 69
Greymouth, 233, 234
gum-digging, *111*

Hadfield, Octavius, 84
Hakiro, 29
Hamilton, 71
Hamiora, Cilla, *231*
Hamu, Ana, 38
Harawira, Titewai, *159*
Harbours Act 1878 (revised 1950), 88
Harris, Edwin, 52
Hauraki claim, 250
Hauraki Gulf iwi, 36, 37, 212
Hawke's Bay, 42
health, Maori, 111–12, 113, 115, 133, *133*, 208, 210, 267, *267*, 271, 277
Health Research Council, Maori Health Committee, 210
Heaphy, Charles, 19, 86
Heke, Hone, *27*, 30, 53–54, 57
Henare, Denese, 172
Henare, James, *158*
Henare, Tau, 242
Herald, HMS, 21, 24, 27, 28, 34, 37
Herangi, Te Kirihaehae Te Puea, 110, 122, *122*
Hercus, Ann, *160*, 161
Heremaia, Hoani, *208*
Heremaia, Pat, *265*
Heremaia, Steve, *264*
Hight, Makere, *211*
hikoi: 1975, 145, *145*, 146, *146*, *147*, *148*, *149*; 1984, 155, 158, *159*; 2004, 275, *275*, 277
Hingston, Ken, 272
Hipi, Tiemi, 120
Hirangi marae, 220

Hoani Waititi marae, 218
Hobbs, John, *37*
Hobson, William: and British sovereignty (pre-1840), *12*, 18–19, 21; 1837 report, 16; and Treaty, 14, 28, 30, 31–37, 38, 39, 41–42, 45, 50, 125; Patuone presents with mere, 27; proclamation of British sovereignty 1840, 39; Normanby's instructions to, 19, 48; as Governor, 21, 48, 49; arrival commemorated, 107
Hocken, Thomas, 127
Hodgson, Peter, *215*
Hokianga, 16, 34, 36–37, 117
Holyoake, Keith, 147
Hongi Hika, 10, *10*, 44
Hopa, Ngapare, *179*
Hopuhopu military camp, 221
Horeke, *32*
Horomia, Parekura, 235, *245*, *246*
housing, Maori, 128, 132, *132*, 134, 137, 138, 208, 209, 209, 271
Human Rights Commission, 263–64
Hunn Report, 137–38
Hura, Maata Te Reo, 189

Ika Whenua Report, *see* Te Ika Whenua Report
Immigration and Public Works Act 1870, 83
Imperial troops, 54, 69, 70–71, 75–77
Indemnity Act 1865, 73
indigenous peoples: impact of British colonisation on, 17–18, 36, 64; rights to self-determination, 141, 269
intellectual property claim, *see* flora and fauna claim
ITQ, *see* fisheries, individual transferable quotas
iwi locations, *see* Maori tribal locations
Iwi Transition Agency, 188, 189, 208

Jackson, Keith, 240
Jackson, Moana, 195, *277*, 277
Jervois, William, *101*
Jones, Shane, *215*
Jury, Te Whatahoro, 92
Justice, Department of, 159, 184, 188
Justice, Ministry of, 248

Ka Awatea, 208
Kaingaroa district, 113
Kaipara claims, 186, 187
Kaipara district, 81, 87, 227
Kaitaia, 38, 128
Kaituna Report, 151, 153–54
Kapiti, 11, 12, 38
Karaka, Mita, 103

Karaka Bay, *36*
Kauhanganui, 103, 104. *See also* King movement; Parliaments, Maori
Kauwaeranga judgement, 88
kawanatanga, 26, 38, 39, 48, 154, 195, 268
Kawhia, 11, 39, 101, 234
Kawiti, 29, 33, *53*, 54
Kawiti, Maihi Paraone, 102, *102*
Keepa, Tuhiakia, *260*
Kelsey, Jane, 153
Kemp purchase, 120
Kendall, Thomas, *10*
Kerena, Sally Mana Te Noki, *154*
Kihikihi, 71
King, Philip, 8–9
King Country, 95, 101, 110
King movement: formation of, 61; government views on, 64, 67, 68, 69, 74, 98; Maori views on, 66, 67, 101; parliament of, 103, 104; Te Puea Herangi rebuilds, 122; Koroki's attendance at Waitangi gathering, 125; and Waikato-Tainui claim, 221, 222, 223
Kingi, Kia, *230*
Kingi, Wiremu, *see* Te Rangitake, Wiremu Kingi
Kirk, Norman, *140*
Kneebone, John, *179*, *250*
kohanga reo, *193*, 194
Kohimarama Conference 1860, 64–67, 94, 95, 96
Koopu, Areta, *186*
Koroki Te Rata Mahuta Tawhiao Potatau Te Wherowhero, 125
Kororareka (Russell), *9*, 21, *29*, 30, 34, 53–54
Kotahitanga movement: founding of, 94; meetings, 94, 95–100; parliaments, 104–7, *104*, *105*, 111; revival in 1960s, 148, 158
kupapa (government Maori troops), 70, 71, 72
kura kaupapa, 194

Labour governments: (1935–49), 118, 119, 124, 128, (1957–60), 132, 133–36; (1972–75), 138; (1984–90), 156–57, 160, 161–63, 178–79, 185, 188, 190, 195–96, 198–99, 204–5, 211. *See also* coalition governments
Labour Party: and Ratana, 123–24, 138, 144, 241; and Maori, 155; and 'fiscal envelope' concept, 231, 238; and National's policy on Treaty grievances, 238
lake bed rights, 88–89, 120–21, 169, 220

land: sales before 1840, 7–8, 16, 21, 30, 36, 44, 50–52; and New Zealand Company, 17, 18, 51–52; Colonial Office policy, 19, 21, 80; resistance to selling, 36, 50–53, 60–61; and mana, 44, 104; sales after 1840, 48, 50–53, 56, 58, 60–63, 83–84, 110–11, 114, 116–17; 'surplus lands', 51, 133, 227, 236, 255; reserves, 60–61, 81, 83, 110, 224, 233–35; Waitara purchase, 61–63, 64, 67, 80, 236; grants to British troops, 71; customary title to, 80–81, 83, 87, 88, 100, 110, 120, 208; individualisation of title to, 82–83, 104, 117, 221; Maori ownership in 1892, 83–84; compulsory acquisition of, 92, 110–11, 116, 137, 151, 235–38; Rees-Carroll commission, 83, 110; leasing of, 110, 114, 116; Stout-Ngata Commission report, 115; Maori ownership in 1920, 116–17, 120; gifted by Maori, 149, 219; Maori land, 1860–1939 (maps, Appendix Four), 318–19. See also Native Lands Acts; Native Land Court

land, and Treaty: Crown pre-emption, 24, 26, 38, 50, 56, 82, 110; guarantee given to Maori, 29, 37, 39, 51, 55, 56, 64, 68; legislation dealing with, 81–83, 84, 110, 112–14, 115–17, 144–46, 157–61, 166–69, 185–87; opinion of Prendergast, 85; Hoani Te Heuheu cases, 128; and State-Owned Enterprises Act 1986, 162–66, 185, 210, 266; Treaty of Waitangi (State Enterprises) Act 1988, 166–67, 185, 196–97; Maori land, 1860–1939 (maps, Appendix Four), 318–19

land banks, 227, 255

land claims: pre-1840 land sale investigations, 50–52; Ngai Tahu, 61, 167–68, 128, 133, 205, 219, 223–26, 242, 243, 249; settlement by Labour government 1940s, 133; Muriwhenua, 163–64, 259; Orakei, 179–80, 181, 182–83; Waiheke Island, 180–81; Waikato-Tainui, 211, 220–23, 233, 242, 249; Te Roroa, 227–28; Taranaki, 236, 237. See also petitions and deputations

Land Claims Commission, 51

land confiscations, 60, 69, 72–74, 82, 98, 100, 101, 110, 130, 220–21, 236, 237, 254; map of confiscated lands, 1864–67, 74; Sim Commission on, 122–23, 128, 221; and surplus land, 227; Ngati Awa Raupatu Report,

262; Foreshore and Seabed Bill likened to, 275; Maori land, 1860–1939 (maps, Appendix Four), 318–19

land development schemes, 119–20, 134; Hokianga, 117; Waikato district, 122; housing associated with, 132

land march, 1975, 145, 145, 146, 146, 147, 148, 149

Landcorp, 163, 166

Lange, David, 156, 195

Langsbury, Kuao, 225

Langstone, Frank, 128

Laracy, Eugenie, 183

Latimer, Graham, 149, 172, 184, 212

law, British, application to Maori, 48, 50, 56, 58, 67, 77; Maketu case, 48. See also Treaty of Waitangi, in law

Law Commission, 169; Report on Fisheries, 170

Legal Services Act 1991, 261

Legal Services Agency, 261

Lethbridge, Jacqui, 251

Liberal government, 110, 111–14

Lindauer, Gottfried, 38, 59

local government: reforms, 190, 192; and private land, 228; and return of reserves to tribal custody, 255; and Treaty principles, 266–68; and foreshore and seabed rights, 274

Local Government Act 2002, 268

Local Government Amendment (No.2) Act 1989, 192

Local Government Amendment (No.3) Act 1988, 192

Love, Morrie, 249, 251

Mackay, James, 89

Mahupuku, Hamuera Tamahau, 92

Mahuta, Robert, 169, 212, 221, 223, 223

Mair, Ken, 232

Maketu, 48

mana: of the land, 44, 104; of government, 67–68; Treaty guarantee of, 67–68, 95, 202; over fisheries, 90, 96; loss of, 93; of the Treaty, 106, 157; of elders, 149; redressing, 184, 210

Mana magazine, 277

mana Maori motuhake, 132, 157, 210, 220

Mana Motuhake Party, 146

Manaia, 263

Manatu Maori (Ministry of Maori Affairs), 188, 198, 208. See also Te Puni Kokiri

Mangahoe Inlet, Otago, 90

Mangakino, 91

Mangatawhiri River, 69, 69

Mangatu block, 110

Mangungu, 32, 34

Maniapoto, Rewi Manga, 69, 95

Manukau Harbour, 39, 42, 89

Manukau Report, 151, 153, 154, 165, 235

Manutuke marae, 267

Maori Affairs, Department of, 116, 132, 137–38, 144; devolution of functions of, 187–89

Maori Affairs, Ministry of, 188, 198, 208

Maori Affairs Act 1953, 137

Maori Affairs Amendment Act 1967, 137

Maori Affairs Select Committee, 2002–2003, 258

Maori Battalion, 109, 110, 119, 128, 131

Maori Community Centre, Auckland, 134

Maori Congress, 189, 220, 240

Maori Council, see New Zealand Maori Council

Maori Council of Churches, 155, 156, 204

Maori Councils Act 1900, 111–12, 113

Maori customs (ritenga), 32, 56, 102

Maori Development, Ministry of, 208, 217, 229–30, 253

Maori economic development: trade in 1840s and 1850s, 49, 53, 58; land development schemes, 117, 119–20, 122, 134; commercial fisheries, 172, 173–74, 276; Ka Awatea report on, 208; Sealord deal, 211–16, 219, 262; and Hoani Waititi marae, 218; and Waipareira Trust, 218, 219, 269; Tainui, 223; Ngai Tahu, 226, 276; aquaculture and marine farming, 273, 278; Treaty settlements develop sound bases for, 276

Maori Fisheries Act 1989, 174, 211

Maori Fisheries Bill, 215

Maori Fisheries Commission, 174, 175, 211, 212. See also Treaty of Waitangi Fisheries Commission/Te Ohu Kaimoana

Maori land, 1860–1939 (maps), 317–18

Maori Land Act 1993, 272

Maori Land Court, 144, 158, 188, 272, 275. See also Native Land Court

Maori Land Settlement Act 1905, 113–14

Maori Lands Administration Act 1900, 112–13

Maori language, 10, 44, 161, 184, 193. See also Treaty of Waitangi, translations

Maori Language Act 1987, 161

Maori Language Board, 161, 182, 183

Maori Language Broadcasting Funding Agency, 161

INDEX   339

Maori Language Commission, 161, 184
Maori Messenger (Te Karere Maori), 56, 67
Maori Organisation of Human Rights, 148
Maori Perspective Committee, 268
Maori population trends, 1874–2001 (table), 81
Maori Reserved Land Act 1955, 233, 234
Maori Reserved Land Amendment Act 1997, 235
Maori Reserved Land Amendment Act 1998, 235
Maori Social and Economic Advancement Act 1945, 132
Maori tribal locations (maps), *20*, (Appendix Three), *317*
Maori Trustee, 137, 249
Maori Trustee Act 1953, 137
Maori War Effort Organisation, 130
Maori Women's Welfare League, 135, *135*, 138, 240
maps: map of New Zealand (Sydney Parkinson), *5*; Maori tribal locations, *c.*1870, *20*; location of Treaty signings, *40*; confiscated land, 1864–67, *74*; Orakei block of Ngati Whatua, *181*; claimants' boundaries in Taranaki, *237*; Muriwhenua: principal hapu and marae, *259*; iwi locations, 2001 (Appendix Three), *317*; Maori land, 1860–1939 (Appendix Four), *318–19*
Maraetai, 37
Marlborough, 53
Marlborough Sounds, 272
Marsden, Samuel, 9–12, 13
Marshall, Russell, 161
Martin, Mary, 62, *62*
Martin, William, *62*, 63
Massey, William, 107, 116
Matamata, 61
Mathew, Felton, 28
Mathew, Sarah, 29
Mawhete, Rangiputangitahi, 123
McKinnon, Don (Donald), *213*, 228
McLean, Donald, 50, 60, 64, 66, 67, 76, *79*, 93
McRobie, Alan, 240
Mete Kingi, *see* Te Rangi Paetahi, Mete Kingi
Mete Kingi, Takarangi, *92*
Milroy, Te Wharehuia, *250*
Ministry of ... *see under* name e.g., Maori Affairs, Ministry of
Mission Bay, Auckland, 64, *65*
missionaries, 4, 7–8, 13, 24, 27, 28, 30; role in Treaty negotiations, 37–38, 41, 45. *See also* names of individual missionaries

mixed-member proportional representation (MMP), 239–40, 242, 269, 271
Mohaka-ki-Ahuriri claim, 250
Mohaka River Report, 267
Moka, 30
Morgan, Paul, 235
Morris, Joanne, *179*
Motueka, 234
Motunui-Waitara Report, 150, 153, 154, 169
Moutoa Gardens, occupation of, *230*, 231, *231*, *232*
Mt Cook, 226
Muldoon, Robert, 151
multiculturalism, 147
Murihiku Seafood Processing Plant, Bluff, *276*
Muriwhenua, map of principal hapu and current marae, *259*
Muriwhenua claims: fisheries, 163–64, 167, 169, 170, 171–72, 173, 205, 248; land, 163–64, 259
Muriwhenua Fishing Report, 173
Muriwhenua Land Report, 259
'musket wars', 6
Myers Commission, 133

Napier Harbour, 232
national anthem, 126
National governments: (1960–72), 136, 137–38, (1975–84), 145, 150; (1990–96), 205, 208–11, 217–20, 228, 238. *See also* coalition governments
National Party, 204, 271, 277
Native Affairs, Department of, 128, 132, 134. *See also* Maori Affairs, Department of
Native Committees Act 1883, 100
Native Department, 77, 120, 127. *See also* Native Affairs, Department of
Native Land Act 1909, 115–17
Native Land Court, 80–82, 83–84, 87, 88, 95, 100, 101, 110, 111, 112, 116, 132, 182, 242. *See also* Maori Land Court
Native Land Court Act 1894, 110
Native Land Purchase Department, 82
Native Land Purchase Ordinance 1846, 81
Native Lands Act 1862, 80–82
Native Lands Act 1865, 82, 117
Native Land Act 1873, 82–83
Native Land Administration Act 1886, 104
Native Reserves Act 1882, 233
native school system, 77
Native Townships Act 1895, 110

Native Townships Act 1910, 110
Native Trustee, 117, 233
natural resources, and claims, 220
Nelson, 270
Nene, Tamati Waka, 25, *26*, 30, 48, 54, 64
New Plymouth, *52*, 58, 99
New South Wales, 4, 8–10, 11, 12–13, 27; New Zealand a dependency of, 21, 48
New Zealand Constitution Act 1846, 49–50
New Zealand Constitution Act 1852, 58, 102, 190
New Zealand Company, 17–18, 19, 38, 56, 86, 233; ships, *19*
New Zealand Day Act 1973, 138, 144
New Zealand First Party, 231, 240, 242
New Zealand Founders' Society, 138
New Zealand Maori Council: petition to establish, 104; and Labour promises, 123; established 1962, 132; submissions to government, 138; 1987 Court of Appeal case, 164–66, 184, 266; radio frequencies and broadcasting claims, 182, 183; and forest assets, 185; and Maori electoral option, 240
New Zealand Planning Council, 203
New Zealand Settlements Act 1863, 72, 73
New Zealand wars, 68–72, 98; East Coast war, 70; northern war, 54, *57*, 65; Taranaki wars, 61, 62, 65, 67, 69, 70; Waikato war, 68–69, 70, 71; British withdrawal, 71, 75–77; end to, 80
Nga Kaiwhakapumau i te Reo Inc., 161, 182, 183
Nga Puhi, 12, 45, 65, 94, 99–102, 125
Nga Tamatoa, 148
Ngai Tahu, 12, 43, 163, 172, 273; petition 1909, 120; claim, 61, 128, 133, 167–68, 205, 219, 223–26, 242, 243, 249; fisheries claim, 212, 225, 248; ancillary claims, 225, 232, 235
Ngai Tahu Claims Settlement Act 1998, 225, 226
Ngai Tahu Maori Trust Board, 223
Ngai Tahu (Pounamu Vesting) Act 1997, 226
Ngai Tahu Ancillary Claims Report, 235
Ngai Tahu Report, 224, 225
Ngai Tahu Sea Fisheries Report, 212, 248
Ngai Tahu Seafood, 276
Ngai Te Rangi, 73, 87, 90
Ngapora, Tamati, 59
Ngaruawahia, 122, 157, 221

Ngata, Apirana Turupa, 110, 114, 115, 116, 119, 128, 130, *131*
Ngata, Henare, 138, 141
Ngatai, Hori, 87, *87*, 90
Ngatai, Tom, *265*
Ngatata, Wiremu Tako, 52, *53*, 93
Ngati Apa, 272
Ngati Awa Raupatu Report, 262
Ngati Haua, 73
Ngati Hinewaka, 214
Ngati Kahungunu, 273, 277
Ngati Kuri, 277
Ngati Mahanga, 43
Ngati Maniapoto, 73, 95
Ngati Maru, 88
Ngati Paoa, 72, 180–81
Ngati Paoa Development Trust Board, 181
Ngati Porou, 277
Ngati Raukawa, 6, 67
Ngati Ruanui, 70, 207, 264, 265
Ngati Toa, 6, 12, 84
Ngati Tuwharetoa, 42, 121, 128, 163, 189, 220
Ngati Whatua, 42, 45, 87, 94, 95, 97, 98, 99, 152, 153, 180, 181, 182, 268, 273; map of Orakei block, *181*
Ngati Whatua of Orakei Trust Board, 182
Ngatokimatawhaorua, *129*, 200, *278–79*
Ngatuere, Kingi, 92
Nias, Joseph, 28
1990 Commission, 199–200
Normanby, Lord, 19
northern war, 54, *57*, 65
Northland, 114, 125, 131, 133, 174

O'Carroll, Chris, *155*
O'Carroll, Jim, *155*
Office of Treaty Settlements, 226–27, 248, 253, 254–55, 258, 261–62, 263
Ohaeawai, *57*
Okeroa, Mahara, *246*
Oliver, W. H., 180, 182
Omana, Tiaki, 124
'one people' principle, 34, 44, 58, 64, 75, 99, 125, 128, 137, 148, 204
One Tree Hill protest, 231
Onoke, Lake, 89, *89*, 90–91, *90*
Onuku marae, Banks Peninsula, *243*, 246
Orakei Act 1991, 181, 182
Orakei Action Committee, 182
Orakei claim, 179–80, 181, 182–83; map of Orakei block, *181*
Orakei marae, 97. *See also* Bastion Point
Orakei meetings 1879–1881, 96–99; 1888, 106
Orakei Report, 180, 181, 182–83

O'Regan, Tipene, 163, 172, 212, *213*, 225
Orr, Gordon, *178*
Otago, 60, 91, 120
Otaki, 58
Otorohanga, 110
OTS, *see* Office of Treaty Settlements

Pacific Islands, immigration from, 147
Pai Marire movement, 70
Paihia, 11, 14, 28
Paikea, Paraire Karaka, *124*, 130
Paikea, Tapihana (Dobson) Paraire, *134*
Pakaitore, occupation of, *230*, 231, *231*, *232*
Pakirikiri, *104*, *105*
Palliser Bay, South Wairarapa, *214*
Palmer, Geoffrey, 156, *156*, 157, 161–62, 178–79, 185, 195, 197, 202
Panakareao, Nopera, 38, 128
Paora, Hori Tiro, 103
Papawai, Greytown, 92, *92*, *106*
Parakaia, 67
Paraone, Pita, 228
Parata, Tame, 91
Parata, Wiremu Te Kakakura, 84–85, *85*
Parihaka, 98, *98*, 99, 110, 123, 236, *244–46*
Parkinson, Sydney, 3; map of New Zealand, *5*
Parliament, New Zealand, 58, 59, 72, 75, 76–77, 107. *See also* representation, Maori
parliaments, Maori, 98, 100, 101, 102, 104–7, 111, 220. *See also* Kauhanganui; Kohimarama Conference; Kotahitanga movement; runanga
partnership relationship, 132, 144, 165, 188, 189, 190–91, 196, 228, 266, 268, 269, 279
Patuone, Eruera Maihi, *27*, 30
Pearce, Neil, *211*
Penfold, Merimeri, 277, *277*
Peters, Winston, 204, *205*, 208, 242
petitions and deputations: northern chiefs 1831, 11; about *Elizabeth* affair 1830, 12–13; Te Wherowhero 1847, 55; Te Waharoa 1866, 60; Matiaha Tiramorehu, 61; Hirini Taiwhanga 1882, 100–2; King Tawhiao 1884, 100–1, 102; Te Rata Mahuta Potatau Te Wherowhero, 102–3, *103*; Tahupotiki Wiremu Ratana, 103; in 1897, 111; Maori MPs send copy of Treaty to Britain, 120; Tiemi Hipi and Ngai Tahu, 120; Te Puea Herangi and Waikato, 122; Ratana, 123; Eruera Tirikatene, 135

Petroleum Act 1937, 128
Pipiriki, *96*
Pipitea, 52
Piripi, Eruha, 92
Pirongia, 71
Pomare II, 33
Pomare, Eru, *211*
Pomare, Maui Wiremu Piti Naera, 110, 114, 116, *116*, 119, 123
Pompallier, Bishop, 31, 32, 34
population, European: before 1840, 4
population, Maori, 1820–1853, 6, 12; 1870s, 80; trends, 1874–2001, 81; far north, 111; 1951, 135
Porirua, *8*
Potatau I, *see* Te Wherowhero Potatau
Port Nicholson, 18, 38, 53. *See also* Wellington
Pouakani Report, 267
pounamu, 224, 226
Poutu Forest, 186
poverty, *see* socio-economic disparities, Maori
Poverty Bay, 70
Prebble, Richard, 238
Prendergast, James, 85, *85*
principles of the Treaty, *see* Treaty of Waitangi, principles
prisoners, Maori, 195, 210, *210*
Privy Council, 128, 183, 197
Project Waitangi, 203
property portfolio information, 255
protection mechanism and land banks, 227
Protectorate of Aborigines, 48, 50, 86
protests, Maori: increase, 1870s and 1880s, 80; over fishing rights, 89–91; over Bastion Point land loss, 97, 146; background to, 101, 103, 125–26; over land purchases in 1890s, 110–11; on Waitangi Day, 136, 147, 148, 149–50, 155, 194, 201–3, *202*, *203*, 228–29, *229*, 247, 271, *271*, 276; 1950s & 1960s, 136–38; over South African rugby contacts, 136, 139, *139*; Pakeha support of, 141; 1975 land march, 145, *145*, 146; *146*, *147*, *148*, *149*; at Raglan, 146, 151, *151*; 1984 hikoi, 155, 158, *159*; impact of, 155; occupation of Pakaitore, *230*, 231, *231*, *232*; at One Tree Hill, 231; at Manaia, *263*; over foreshore and seabed rights, 271, 275, *275*, 277
protests, Pakeha: over foreshore and seabed rights, 270, 271
Puao-Te-Ata-Tu: Report of the Ministerial Committee on a Maori Perspective for the Department of Social Welfare, 161

INDEX **341**

public attitudes to Treaty issues, 179, 196, 198, 204, 228, 229, 231, 262–64, 270, 271, 272, 274, 276–78

Public Trustee, 233

public works: land taken for, 92, 110, 116, 151, 235–38; and fisheries, 236

Public Works Lands Act 1864, 92

Public Works Act 1876, 92

Public Works Act 1981, 236, 238

Queen Charlotte Sound, *3*

Queen's chain, 274

QMS, *see* fisheries, quota management system

Radiocommunications Act 1989, 182

Raglan, 43, 146, 151, *151*

Ramsden, Irihapeti, *211*

Rangahaua Whanui Project, 226, 249, 255

rangatiratanga: Treaty wording, 26, 39, 44; definitions of, 26, 39, 44, 208; Treaty guarantee of, 48, 59, 98, 169, 172, 175, 195; denial of, 137; balance between Crown sovereignty and, 48, 195, 202. *See also* tino rangatiratanga

Rangihau, John, *160*, 161

Rangihoua, 7, 11

Rangitikei district, *93*

Rata, Matiu, *143*, 144, 146, *168*, 172, 212

Ratana, Haami Tokouru, 123

Ratana, Tahupotiki Wiremu, 103, 123, 124, *124*

Ratana movement, 123, 124, 189

Ratana Party, 123–24, 138, 144

raupatu, *see* land confiscations

Razor Back Hill, *68*

Rees, W. L., 83

Rees-Carroll Commission, 83, 110

Reeves, Paul, *159*, 161, *246*

Reform government, 116–17

representation, Maori, 50, 75, 76–77, 99, 238–40, 242, 269, 271; in local government, 190, 192, 268. *See also* franchise, Maori

Rere-o-maki, 38

research into claims, 158, 159–60, 169, 226, 256, 261; funding for, 258, 260–61

reserved lands, 60, 81, 83, 233–35; Ngai Tahu, 60–61, 224; West Coast Settlement Reserves, 110, 233, 234

resource management, Maori participation in, 192–93, 267–68

Resource Management Act 1991, 192–93, 266–68, 274

Resource Management Amendment Act 2003, 268

Rewa, 29, 48

Richmond, J. C., *59*

Rickard, Eva, 151, *151*, *159*

river bed rights, 88, 220

RMA, *see* Resource Management Act 1991

Rolleston, William, 100

Rotoiti, Lake, *121*

Rotorua, Lake, 153, 169

Rotorua district, 113; title to lake beds, 120–21, 169

Rowling, Bill, 145

Royal Commission on Social Policy, 203

Royal Commission on the Electoral System, 239

Rua Kenana Hepetipa, 110

Ruamahanga River Board, 91

Ruapuke Island, 43

rugby tours, 136, 139

runanga, 93–94, 98, 100, 188

Runanga Iwi Act 1990, 188–89; repealed, 208

Russell, *see* Kororareka

Russell, G. F., 32

Ryan, Erihana, *179*

Sealord deal, 211–16, 219, 262

Seddon, Richard, *106*

Selwyn, Bishop George Augustus, *62*

sesquicentennial commemorations, 198–203

settlements: and Treasury, 183–84, 217; Maori attitudes to, 210; National government proposals for, 217–20; 'fiscal cap' on, 217, 218, 222, 228, 229–32, 242, 247, 249, 254; Auditor-General's report on, 233; principles for, 216, 247, 249; as at 31 March 2004, 252; process of, 253–58; public debate on, 262–64. *See also* individual claims

Sharples, Pita, 218, *218*

Shipley, Jenny (Jennifer), 242, *243*

Shortland, Edward, 86

Shortland, Willoughby, 36, 37

Shortland Beach Act 1869, 88

Sim Commission, 122–23, 128, 221

Social Welfare, Department of, 160, 161; Community Funding Agency, 269

socio-economic disparities, Maori, 111, 112, 136, 209, *209*, 266, 271, 277; 1st Labour government policies, 118, 128, 132, 133; National government policies, 138, 208, 238; effect of 4th Labour government policies, 156, 162–63, 203, 208; 'closing the gaps' policy, 246

SOE, *see* state-owned enterprises

Solomon, Mark, 225

South Africa, rugby contacts with, 136, 139

sovereignty, Crown: background to, 18–21, 24; Treaty wording, 24, 26, 38, 154, 268; explanation of, 1840, 28–29, 37, 41, 196; Maori reactions to explanations of, 30, 31, 36, 38, 42, 43, 66; proclamations of, 34, 38–39, 40, 45; challenges to, 53–54, 56, 61, 67–68; Pakeha desire to assert, 61, 62, 76–77; balance between tino rangatiratanga and, 157, 268–71; and 1987 Court of Appeal Lands case, 166; and fisheries, 169

sovereignty, Maori: 'collective', 13; cession of, 18–19, 24, 37, 39, 66, 67–68, 76–77, 220, 268; Treaty wording, 24, 26, 38, 44, 268; in Treaty, 125, 154; government's understanding of, 131, 196; Maori call for Pakeha acknowledgement of, 148

Spain, William, 52, *52*

state-owned enterprises: State-Owned Enterprises Act 1986, 162–66, 185, 210; and Muriwhenua claim, 163–64; 1987 Court of Appeal Lands case, 164–66, 184, 195–96, 266; Treaty of Waitangi (State Enterprises) Act 1988, 166–67, 185, 196–97; and surplus land, 227; land passed into private ownership, 228

State Services Commission, 203, 264

Stewart Island, 37, 39, 83

Stokes, Evelyn, *179*, *250*

Stout, Robert, 115

Stout-Ngata Commission, 115

Sunderland, Heni, *253*

Suppression of Rebellion Act 1863, 74

Sutton, Jim (James), 273

Swainson, William, 49, 87

Symonds, W. C., 37, 41

Syngas, 151

tables: Maori population trends, 1874–2001, 81; payments for unemployment relief, 118; Treaty settlements or agreements, 252

Tai Tokerau (Northland), 157, 174

taiapure, 214, 216

Taiaroa, Hori Kerei, 89–90

Taiaroa, Te Matenga, 64

Tainui, 166, 167, 172, 196–97, 221. *See also* Waikato-Tainui claim

Tainui Maori Trust Board, 167

Taiwhanga, Hirini Rawiri, 101, 102, *102*

Taiwhanga, Rawiri, 30

Takaparawha, *see* Bastion Point

Tamaki River, *36*, 37

342 AN ILLUSTRATED HISTORY OF THE TREATY OF WAITANGI

Tamihana, Wiremu, *see* Te Waharoa, Wiremu Tamihana Tarapipipi

Tamihere, John, 218, *218*

Tangaroa, Nico, *232*

tangata maori, 4

tangata tiriti, 228

tangata whenua, 148, 192, 228

Taonui, Aperahama, 100

Taraia Ngakuti Te Tumuhuia, 42

Taranaki district, 11, 44, 61, 61–63, 263; land confiscations in, 72, 73, 74, 98, 122, 123, 236, *237*; West Coast Settlement Reserves, 110, 233, 234

Taranaki iwi, 98, 128; map of boundaries, *237*

Taranaki Maori Trust Board, 133

Taranaki Report, 236, 237

Taranaki wars, 61, 62, 65, 67, 69, 70

Tareha, 30

Taumarunui, 110

Taupo, Lake, 121, 169

Taupo district, 113

Tauranga, 41, 42, 43, 69, 74, 87, 90, 122, 123

Tauroa, Hiwi, *158*

Tawhai, Mohi, 36

Tawhiao, Tukaroto Matutaera Potatau Te Wherowhero, 66, *66*, 67, 95, 100, 101, 104

Taylor, Aila, 154

Taylor, Mac, *174*

Taylor, Richard, 32, 36

Te Arawa, 42, 72, 121, 262

Te Arawa Trust Board, 121

Te Aro, *51*, 52

Te Atairangikaahu, 189, 222, *222*

Te Ati Awa, 53, 61, 65, 84, 93, 150, 151, 154

Te Atiawa Iwi Authority, 155

Te Ati Haunui-a-Paparangi, 232

Te Awa-i-taia, Wiremu Nera, *43*

Te Hapuku, 42

Te Heuheu, Georgina, 271, 276

Te Heuheu Tukino II, Mananui, 42, *42*

Te Heuheu Tukino III, Iwikau, 42, *42*

Te Heuheu Tukino VI, Hoani, 128

Te Heuheu Tukino VII, Hepi Hoani, 163, 189, *189*, 220, 232

Te Ika Whenua Report, 267

Te Kanawa, Kiri, 200

Te Karere, see Maori Messenger

Te Kawau, Apihai, 42

Te Kawerau a Maki, 268

Te Kemara, 30

Te Kirikaramu, Heni, 72, *72*

Te Kooti Arikirangi, 70

Te Maari, Piripi, 90–91

Te Maiharanui, 12

Te Mangai Paho, 161

Te Maunga Railways Land Report, 235

Te Moanapapaku, Pauline Hinepoto (Tuutu), *189*

Te Ohu Kaimoana, 212, 215. *See also* Maori Fisheries Commission

Te Pahi, 8–9, *11*

Te Paki o Matariki, 104

Te Puea, *see* Herangi, Te Kirihaehae Te Puea

Te Puni Kokiri, 208, 217, 229–30, 253

Te Rangi Paetahi, Mete Kingi, 75, *75*, 76, *76*

Te Rangi-taka-i-waho, Hoani, 92

Te Rangihaeata, *53*

Te Rangihiroa, *see* Buck, Peter Henry

Te Rangitake, Wiremu Kingi, 44, 61, 62

Te Rarawa, 146

Te Rata Mahuta Potatau Te Wherowhero, 102–3, *103*, 110

Te Rau-o-te-rangi, Kahe, 38

Te Rauparaha, *11*, 12

Te Rauparaha, Tamehana, 61, 66, *66*

te reo Maori, 10, 44, 161, 184, 193. *See also* Treaty of Waitangi, translations

Te Roroa Report, and private land, 227–28

Te Runanga o Ngai Tahu, 225

Te Taonui, Makoare, 36

Te Taumata Runanga, 268

Te Taura Whiri i te Reo Maori, 161, 184

Te Tii marae, *29*, 99–100, 107, 125, *127*, 149, 200, *202*, 228–29

Te Tiriti o Waitangi meeting house, 100, 107, *107*

Te Ture Whenua Maori Act 1993, 272

Te Uri-o-Hau, 186, 187

Te Waharoa, Tupu Atanatiu Taingakawa, *103*

Te Waharoa, Wiremu Tamihana Tarapipipi, 60, *60*, 61, 67, 68, 73

Te Weehi, Tom, 172

Te Weehi case, 172

Te Whaiti, Dick, *214*

Te Whaiti, Haami, *214*

Te Whakatohea, 260

Te Whanau o Waipareira Report, 269

Te Whanau o Waipareira Trust, 218, 219, 268, 269

Te Whanganui-a-Orutu Report, 232

Te Wherowhero, Potatau, 41–42, 55, 61, 67

Te Whiti-o-Rongomai III, Erueti, 98, 99, 101

Te Whiwhi, Henare Matene, 61, 66

Teira, 61–62

Thames foreshore, *86*, 88, 89

Thoms whaling station, *8*

tino rangatiratanga: definitions of, 157, 268–69; Treaty guarantee of, 184, 187–88, 190, 220, 240, 242; balance between Crown sovereignty and, 154, 157, 166, 194, 268–71; position of Maori leaders on, 195. *See also* rangatiratanga

Tiramorehu, Matiaha, 61

Tirarau, 33

Tirikatene, Eruera, 123, *124*, 129

Titford, Allan, 228

Titokowaru, Riwha, 70, 99

Tizard, Catherine, 228, *246*

toheroa-gathering, 87, 114, *114*

Tohu Kakahi, 98, 99

Topeora, Rangi, 38, *38*

Town and Country Planning Act 1953, 137, 145

TOWPU, *see* Treaty of Waitangi Policy Unit

TPK, *see* Te Puni Kokiri

trade: in early New Zealand, 4, 5, 7–8, 9, 11–12, 36, 45; Maori involvement in 1840s and 1850s, 49, 53, 58

Treasury, 162, 183–84, 217, 230, 253

Treaty House, 125–26, *126, 127*, 200, 228, 229

Treaty of Waitangi: Colonial Office considers, 18–19; preparations for, 24; Hobson's role in, 14, 24, 28, 30, 31–37, 38, 39, 41–42, 45, 50, 125; Busby's role in, 24, 31, 34; women involved in, 28, 37, 38, 39; missionaries' role in, 37–38, 41, 45; unifying role for Maori, 80, 95–96, 104; 50th anniversary 1890, 107; centennial 1940, 126–30, *129*; sesquicentennial 1990, 198–203. *See also* claims, Treaty

Treaty of Waitangi, articles: first, 24, 26, 39, 44, 45, 64, 66, 195, 220, 268; second, 24, 26, 39, 44, 45, 59, 64, 66, 67, 81, 88, 161, 169, 170, 186, 195, 220, 268; third, 24, 39, 64, 66, 240; 'fourth', 32; in texts (Appendix One), 280–82

Treaty of Waitangi, issues debated (after signing): 1840s, 54–58, 59; triggered by protests and Waitangi Tribunal reports, 155, 262; at hui in 1980s, 157; at hui in 1995, 229–32; public debate on claims and settlements, 262–64; at hui in 2003, 273–75. *See also* Kohimarama Conference; Kotahitanga movement; parliaments, Maori; petitions and deputations; runanga

Treaty of Waitangi, documents: copy signed at Waikato Heads and Manukau Harbour, 23; original Treaty signed at Waitangi, 31, 32; Treaty in

Maori, *33*, 39, 41; copy signed by East Coast Maori, *35*; 'certified', 39; restored, at Waitangi during centennial celebrations, 127–28; Treaty signatories, 283–316

Treaty of Waitangi, explanations of: in negotiations, 28–29, 32, 33–34, 37–38; Maori reactions to, 30, 31, 36, 38, 41–43, 65; no discussion of differences between English and Maori texts, 41; by Henry Williams, 57; by William Martin, 63; at Kohimarama Conference, 64–67, 95; by Apirana Ngata, 131; Labour government's principles, 196; public education, 203–4

Treaty of Waitangi, in government departments, 160, 161–62, 198, 203, 205, 208, 265

Treaty of Waitangi, in law: Wi Parata case, 84–85; failure to protect Maori interests, 91–94, 95–96, 101; Maori call for recognition of, 110, 123, 124, 135, 138, 141, 149; appended to 1975 Act, 144; 1986 Cabinet directive, 162; 1987 Court of Appeal case, 164–67, 185, 195–96; principles in legislation, 265–68. *See also* claims, Treaty; land, and Treaty; petitions and deputations

Treaty of Waitangi, negotiations and signing: Waitangi, 5 Feb., 27–31; Waitangi, 6 Feb., 31–34; Hokianga, 34, 36–37; Waitemata-Hauraki area, 36, 37; other signings, 37–38; location of signings, *40*; no unanimous Maori agreement, 41–43; reasons for signing, 43–45; re-enactment of signing 1990, 200; Treaty signatories (Appendix Two), 283–316

Treaty of Waitangi, principles, 161, 162, 185, 195–96, 266–68; protection, 24, 28, 32, 39, 67, 82, 95, 196; partnership, 132, 144, 165, 188, 189, 190–91, 196, 228, 266, 268, 269, 279; determined and discussed by Waitangi Tribunal, 144, 153–54, 195, 196; and 1987 Court of Appeal case, 165–66, 185, 195–96; and local government, 190–91; in Resource Management Act, 192, 266–68

Treaty of Waitangi, printing of: by Colenso 1840, 33; in newspapers, 56; in *Maori Messenger*, 56; by Henry Williams, 57; 1945, 135

Treaty of Waitangi, ratification of: at Kohimarama 1860, 67; by Maori, 95; on the basis of Maori understanding, 106; Maori call for, 149

Treaty of Waitangi, translation of: 1840, 24, 26, 28; differences in meaning between Maori and English texts, 39, 41, 66, 141, 144, 153–54; 1865, 127, 266; Maori text added to Waitangi Day Act 1976, 138; in Appendix One, 280–82

Treaty of Waitangi Act 1975, 144–46, 153, 248, 256

Treaty of Waitangi Amendment Act 1985, 157–61, 167

Treaty of Waitangi Amendment Act 1988, 168–69

Treaty of Waitangi Amendment Act 1993, 228

Treaty of Waitangi (Fisheries Claims) Settlement Act, 215, 217

Treaty of Waitangi Fisheries Commission, 212, 215. *See also* Maori Fisheries Commission

Treaty of Waitangi Negotiations portfolio, 209, 226, 246–47, 248, 254

Treaty of Waitangi Policy Unit, 185, 195, 198, 226

Treaty of Waitangi (State Enterprises) Act 1988, 166–67, 185, 196, 197

Treaty settlements or agreements (table), 252

Treaty signings (map), *40*

tribal locations, *see* Maori tribal locations

Tuhaere, Paora, *42*, 66, *66*, 95, 106

Tuhawaiki, Hone, *43*

Tupaea, Hori Kingi, 42

Turanga Health, 267

Turangawaewae marae, 122, 157

Turangi, 220, 232–33

Turia, Tariana, 218, 277

Tutengaehe, Hohua, *211*

Tuwharetoa ki Kawerau claim, 262

unemployment, Maori, 128, 163, 188, 208, 209, 246; relief payments (table), 118

United Nations, 141

United States, 18, 141

urban Maori, 134, 136, 218, 268; and Sealord deal, 216

urban marae, 134, 136, 218

Urewera district, 110, 111

Vercoe, Bishop Whakahuihui, *159*, 201

Victoria, Queen, 28, 29, 38, 42, 43, 45, 55, 57, 77, 100, 101, 102, 111, 200

wahi tapu, *191*, 192

Waiapu Valley, 130

Waiheke Island Report, 180–81

Waikato (chief), 10, *10*, 44

Waikato (district), 11, 39, 58, 62; land confiscations in, 60, 69, 72, 73, 74, 103, 122, 123, 130, 220–21; military road from Auckland, 68–69; military townships in, 71

Waikato (iwi), 41, 45, 55, 67, 73, 100, 101, 102–3, 122, 128, 130, 131, 133. *See also* Tainui

Waikato Raupatu Claims Settlement Act 1995, 221, 222, 223

Waikato River, 69, 122, 223

Waikato-Tainui claim, 211, 220–23, 233, 242, 249

Waikato war, 68–69, 70, 71

Waikerepuru, Huirangi, 161, 184, *184*, 245

Waimate North, 34, 37

Waipareira Trust, 218, 219, 268, 269

Waipatu, Hawke's Bay, 106

Waipoua forest, 227

Wairarapa, 42, 56, 60, 214; lakes dispute, 90–91, *93*

Wairau affair, 53, 54

Wairewa, Lake, *171*

Wairoa, 80

Waitakere City Council, 268

Waitaki, 91

Waitangi, 13, 16; Treaty negotiations at, 27–34, 99–100; 1880s meetings at, 99–100, 104, 106; Kotahitanga parliament at, 106; national memorial at, 125–26, 136; whare runanga built at, 125, 131, *131*; centennial function at, 127–28, 129, *129*; 1985 hui, 157. *See also* Te Tii marae; Treaty House

Waitangi Action Committee, 148

Waitangi Day, 136, 138, 140, *140*, 155, 157, 174, 279; as a forum for protest, 136, 147, 148, 149–50, 155, 158, 159, 201–3, *202*, *203*, 228–29, *229*, *247*, 271, *271*, 276; 1990 commemorations, 200–3, *201*

Waitangi Day Act 1960, 136

Waitangi Day Act 1976, 138

Waitangi National Trust Board, 125, *126*, 136

Waitangi Tribunal, 133, 144–46, 156, 157–61, 178–79; and Treaty principles, 144, 153–54, 195, 196; reports of, 150–55, 173, 179–83, 210, 227–28, 232–33, 248, 253, 254, 262, 267; research of, 158, 159–60, 169, 226, 260–61; binding powers of, 166–67; 1988 expansion of, 167–69; and forest land claims, 185, 186; Crown's position with regard to, 198; Rangahaua Whanui Project, 226, 249, 255; review, 248–50; district inquiry system, 249–50, 251–52;

new approach, 250–53; negotiation process, 253–58; website, 263; future of, 264–65; timeline (Appendix Five), 320–24. *See also* claims, Treaty; settlements; and specific claims and reports

Waitara Borough Council, 151

Waitara purchase, 61–63, 64, 67, 80, 236

Waitemata Harbour, 36, 37

Waitotara, 73

Wakefield, Edward Gibbon, 17

Wakefield, William, 52

Walker, Mere, *260*

Walker, Ranginui, 204, *204*

Wallace, Augusta, *186, 250*

Wanganui, 76, 86, 124. *See also* Whanganui River

Wanganui District Council, 232

Ward, Alan, 87, 88, 110, 226, 248

warfare: Maori intertribal, 6, 11, 12–13, 16, 45. *See also* Imperial troops; 'musket wars'; New Zealand wars;

World War I; World War II

Weld, Frederick, 68

Wellington: settlement, 49, *51*, 58, 107; land sales, 51–52; 1988 Waitangi Day protest, 194; anniversary of settler arrivals, 199; reserved land in, 233, 234; attitudes to claims affecting, 263. *See also* Port Nicholson

Weraroa Pa, 73

Wesleyan Missionary Society, 4, 26, 34

West Coast Settlement Reserves, 110, 233, 234

Westrupp, Captain, 70

Wetere, Koro, 161, 162

Whai, 30

Whaingaroa (Raglan), 43, 146, 151, *151*

Whakaka, Wiremu Hutana, 92

Whakatane, 262

Whanganui River, 86, *94*, 96, 230, 267

Whanganui River Report, 267

Whangara, 273

whaling, 4, *8*, 18

Whangaroa, 4

Wharehoka, Netta, *154*

Wi Koka, 72

William IV, King, 11, 16

Williams, Edward, 24

Williams, Henry, 11, 24, 26, *26*, 28, 30, 32, 33, 37, 38, 40, 44, 50, 57

Williams, Joe, 238, *251*

Williams, William, 24, 35

Williamson, Justice, 172

Wilson, Margaret, 246–47, *248, 264*

Winiata, Whatarangi, 212

WMS, *see* Wesleyan Missionary Society

World War I, 110; returned Maori servicemen, 120, *129*; conscription, 130

World War II, 128, 130–32, 134, 136, 151

Wright, Willie, *187*

Young, Venn, *151*

Young Maori Party, 114–15